THE LIFE OF
FATHER JOHN GERARD.

ROEHAMPTON:

PRINTED BY JAMES STANLEY.

THE LIFE OF

FATHER JOHN GERARD,

OF THE SOCIETY OF JESUS.

BY

JOHN MORRIS,

OF THE SAME SOCIETY.

THIRD EDITION, REWRITTEN AND ENLARGED.

LONDON: BURNS AND OATES.

1881.

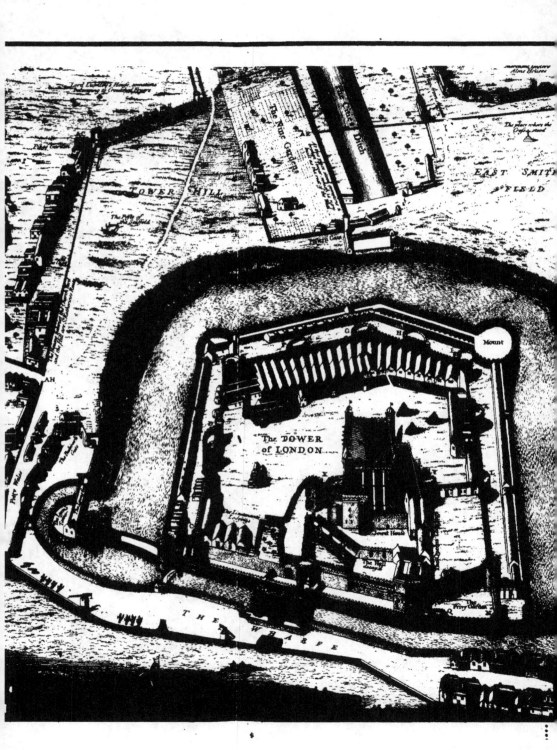

A TRUE AND EXACT DRAUGHT OF THE TOWER LIBERTIES, SURVEYED IN THE YEAR 1597 BY GULIELMUS HAIWARD AND J. GASCOYNE.

BOUNDARIES OF THE LIBERTIES.

AB. The House at the Water Gate called the Ram's Head.
AC. The Place where the Mud Wall was, called Pike's Garden.
AD. The City Wall at the N.E. of the Nine Gardens.
AE. The Place where the Broken Tower was.
AF. Hog Lane End.
AG. The House called the Stone corner House.
AH. The End of Tower Street.
AI. The Stairs without the East End of the Tower.

THE SEVERAL TOWERS.

A. The Middle Tower.
B. The Tower at the Gate.
C. The Bell Tower.
D. Beauchamp Tower.
E. Develin Tower.
F. Flint Tower.
G. Bowyar Tower.
H. Brick Tower.
I. Martin Tower.
K. Constable Tower.
L. Broad Arrow Tower.
M. SALT TOWER.
N. Well Tower.
O. The Tower leading to the Iron Gate.
P. The Tower above the Iron Gate.
Q. THE CRADLE TOWER.
R. . The Lanthorn Tower.
S. The Hall Tower.
T. The Bloody Tower.
V. St. Thomas's Tower.
W. Cæsar's or White Tower.
X. Cole Harbour.
Y. Wardrobe Tower.

PREFACE.

"A JESUIT in disguise" is an idea sufficiently familiar to the English mind. It is less current now than heretofore, and the reason of this is not far to seek. "Jesuits"—and in the term the popular notion included members of all Religious Orders, all ecclesiastics, and not a few laymen—Jesuits are now allowed to show themselves openly, and people who see them and know where they live and what churches they serve, have ceased to frighten themselves with the fear lest any stranger might be a Jesuit in disguise with sinister intentions. The traditional bugbear was foolish and exaggerated, but it had its foundation in facts perverted. Where there was little love, there was little chance of kind or even just interpretations; but the fact was plain enough that Catholic priests and religious resorted to disguises of every kind. The foolishness of the English tradition lay in this, that it attributed to them a love for underhand dealing and a preference for concealments and subterfuges, while the very simple truth was that they came in disguise because they were not allowed to come openly. The following narrative will serve to show why Jesuits came into England and lived there in disguise, and how they did it, in the days when to appear openly would have cost them their lives. In it will be found a minute and detailed description of what befell priests when they were caught, and what manner of life they were obliged to lead in order that they might not be caught. The Life of Father John Gerard will show not only how a Jesuit went about England in disguise, but why.

At Stonyhurst College there are two manuscripts, one in the handwriting of Father Gerard, the other a copy from the original. The former, which is in English, is the History of the Gunpowder Plot, written by Father Gerard in the latter part of the year 1606. The latter, which is in Latin, is a narrative of his missionary life in England, compiled by Father Gerard in 1609 for the information of his superiors.

The History of the Gunpowder Plot was published for the first time in 1871 under the title *The Condition of Catholics under James I.* (London: Longman, Green and Co.). A life of Father John Gerard was prefixed to the work, in which considerable use was made of the autobiography; but, with the view of keeping the life within reasonable compass that it might not exceed the dimensions of an introduction, much was necessarily omitted that Father Gerard had included in his narrative, as well as much of the collateral information from other sources that would have made it more complete. A second edition in 1872 contained the correction of some errors. A third edition is now called for, and it has seemed desirable to separate the life of Father Gerard from his history of the

Powder Plot, in order that it might be possible to give to the life the expansion and completeness which its interest justifies. In this third edition it is accordingly rewritten. Copious additions have been made to the extracts as well from the autobiography as from documents preserved among the State Papers in the Public Record Office. For the translation of the autobiography we are indebted to the pen of the Reverend Father Kingdon S.J. Portions of it were first published in the *Month;* and these, rendered into French by the Reverend Father Forbes, appeared also in the *Etudes Théologiques* at Paris, and have since been reprinted separately. A German translation, taken from the first edition of this work, was published at Cologne in 1875.

To the Reverend Dr. Jessopp the amplest acknowledgements and sincerest thanks are due for the note with which the third Chapter is enriched; and for the readiness with which he has allowed his store of information respecting the Norfolk recusants to be drawn upon, even while his own work on the Walpoles had the first claim on his every leisure moment. That work [1] has since appeared, and a second edition of it was immediately called for. It is a perfect storehouse of facts, and a remarkable monument of untiring personal research into the original documents on which Elizabethan History must rest.

[1] *One Generation of a Norfolk House*, by Augustus Jessopp, D.D. Second Edition. London: Burns and Oates, 1879.

It is a piece of singular good fortune that we should have a view of the Tower of London, taken in the very year in which Father Gerard made his escape from that redoubtable stronghold, and from the point of view most favourable for the illustration of that escape. The loan of the print from which the frontispiece is taken is due to the kindness of Mr. C. Knight Watson, Secretary of the Society of Antiquaries. In 1742 an illuminated drawing by Hayward and Gascoyne of the Tower of London in 1597 was lent to that Society. A coloured copy of the drawing is in their collection, and from this the engraving now reproduced was taken and published by the Society in its *Vetusta Monumenta*, vol. i. plate 63. An excellent copy on a smaller scale, engraved in 1821, was published in the quarto edition of Bayly's *History of the Tower*. It has been considered better to choose for reproduction the older print, rather than the more recent engraving, as well on account of its superior excellence, as from the fact that it is more ancient. In like manner the old print of Louvain by Juste Lipse has been preferred to the version of it given by M. Van Even in his *Louvain Monumental*, though the latter is certainly more artistic. The older prints are more in keeping with the old documents, and may themselves be included among the original sources of history. The old print of Liége fortunately combines antiquity with artistic beauty: and it is but adding words of well-merited commendation to say that the manner of reproduction of all these prints by the Woodbury process leaves nothing to be desired.

The Editor's warm thanks are due to many kind friends for much valuable help, and amongst them it is a pleasure to him to name Fathers Stanton and Knox of the London Oratory, who have given him access to the Archives of the See of Westminster, of which they are the custodians. The sketch of the arms and motto of the Gerard family, which marks the outside of the volume, the Editor owes to the ready and very friendly pencil of Mr. C. A. Buckler, Surrey Herald Extraordinary.

J. M.

Manresa House, Roehampton,
January 6, 1881.

CONTENTS.

———

Contents.

THE LIFE OF FATHER JOHN GERARD.

CHAPTER I.

BIRTH AND PARENTAGE.

1564—1577.

JOHN GERARD was the second son of Sir Thomas Gerard,[1] of Bryn in Lancashire, knight, and of Elizabeth, daughter and coheiress of Sir John Port, of Etwall in Derbyshire, knight. When Father John Gerard had occasion, in his Narrative of the Powder Plot, to speak of his elder brother Thomas, who received knighthood from James I. on his accession, he says:[2] "That was to him no advancement whose ancestors had been so for sixteen or seventeen descents together." This Sir Thomas was made a baronet at the first creation of that dignity in 1611, and from him the present Lord Gerard of Bryn, the first baron and thirteenth baronet, is lineally descended.

John Gerard came of knightly families on his mother's side also, and their names show that they were of the races that are well known to have been faithful to the Catholic Church. His maternal great-grandfather[3] was John Port, Esq., who married Jane, the daughter of John Fitzherbert of Etwall in Derbyshire, widow of John Pole of

---

[1] "William Gerard, son of William who died at Etonhall in 26 Edward III. [1352], by his marriage with Joan, daughter and heiress of Sir Peter Bryn de Brynhill, convertible into Sir Peter Brynhill de Bryn, became possessed of Bryn, Ashton, and other estates, which have remained in the Gerards of Bryn ever since." Baines, *History of Lancashire*, 1836, vol. iii. p. 637.

[2] *The Condition of Catholics under James I.* London, 1872, p. 27.

[3] Wotton's *Baronetage*, 1741.

B

Radburn in the same county; whilst his grandmother, Lady Port, was Elizabeth, daughter of Sir Thomas Gifford of Chillington in Staffordshire, and Dorothy his wife, daughter and coheiress of Sir John Montgomery. Elizabeth, the mother of John Gerard, was the eldest of the three daughters and coheiresses of Sir John Port, and at her father's death in 1557, Etwall became her property and marriage portion. Sir John's second daughter, Dorothy, took Dale Abbey in Derbyshire to her husband George Hastings, fourth Earl of Huntingdon; and Margaret, the third daughter, by her marriage conveyed Cubley in the same county to Sir Thomas Stanhope, grandfather of the first Earl of Chesterfield.

Father Gerard had three sisters, Mary, wife of John Denison; Dorothy, wife of Edmund Peckham; and Martha, wife of John [*or* Michael] Jenison. Documents still existing show us that one of them at least was a zealous Catholic, or, as the phrase ran, "a great recusant" during the persecution. There is a report in the British Museum,[1] dated June 16, 1595, from Edward Cokayne, evidently a Derbyshire magistrate, of assistance given by him to a well known pursuivant William Newall, in searches in that county. The following paragraph relates to Father Gerard's third sister. "The third house that we searched according to his direction was the house of one Mr. Jenison, that married one of my Lady Gerard's daughters, she being a great recusant, and not her husband; howsoever, it is reported that there is great resort of strangers, but what they be we cannot learn, neither at this time did we find any there, but pictures in the chambers according to their profession. Only one West, that was a messenger between the seminaries, was fled six weeks before we came, and whither he is gone as yet we cannot learn." The magistrate had not seen the report of a spy, dated in the previous February, which doubtless was what procured for Mr. Jeni-

---

[1] *Harl. MSS.* 6998, f. 197.

son the honour of a visit from a Queen messenger. It has
survived among the State Papers,[1] and it contains the
following information respecting the house of Father
Gerard's brother-in-law. "*Item*, at Mr. Genyson's house
at Rowllsley, near Bakewell in the Peak, there is John
Redford *alias* Tanfield, a seminary priest, who hath
authority from the Pope to hallow all kind of church stuff,
beads, and such like; and there his library is to be found,
for he studieth there; and there also sojourn Mr. Lenton
and his wife, notable recusants." It is plain that if John
Jenison was not "a great recusant," as well as his wife,
he would have been one if he had dared, and that he was
what our fathers called "a schismatic," whose heart was
with the old religion while he conformed exteriorly with
the new. There were four sons and two daughters in
this family, one of whom became a priest, and another
son, if not two, entered the Society. In the next generation
Michael Jenison, who also became a priest, claims four
Jesuit Fathers as his paternal uncles. Amongst these he
reckons our Father John Gerard, who was his great uncle.[2]

. John Gerard was born on the 4th of October, 1564,[3]
and his probable birthplace was New Bryn, the second of
the four seats which the family has inhabited within the
township of Ashton and parish of Winwick, in West Derby
Hundred in Lancashire.[4] The house was so called to
distinguish it from Old Bryn, near Bryn wood, which was
abandoned five centuries ago. The historian of the county
of Lancaster quotes from "Mr. Barrett in his manuscript
collections" the following account of all that remained
a century ago of Father Gerard's home. "Bryn Hall is
an ancient seat of the Gerards, and has been a good house,

---

[1] State Papers in the Public Record Office, *Domestic, Elizabeth*, vol. ccli.
n. 14. See note at the end of this chapter.

[2] *Diary of the English College, Rome*, edited by Henry Foley, S.J.,
pp. 334, 375.

[3] Stonyhurst MSS., Father Nathaniel Southwell's *Catalogus primorum
patrum*, p. 32.

[4] Baines, *History of Lancashire*, vol. iii. p. 639.

but it is now almost in ruins, the venerable ivy revelling without control on its mouldering walls. Within is a spacious courtyard, the approach to which is by means of a bridge over the moat which surrounds this fabric. The gatehouse is secured by very strong and large doors. Within the court is what has been a rich porch, the entrance into a spacious room called the hall, on the chimney-piece of which are the arms of England in the reign of James I. Across one side of the hall runs a railed gallery, on which persons might stand to see any entertainment below. This gallery is supported by double pillars in the front of pilasters, and forming arches betwixt each other, under which persons may pass from one room to another. On these carved pillars and arches is abundance of rich carved work, but rotten with age and moisture. Most part of the wainscot has been carried to Garswood Hall, the present seat[1] of Sir Thomas Gerard, in 1771."

If born in this baronial house when it was at its best, John Gerard did not live there long enough to become familiar with its grandeur. From the first sentences of his autobiography we learn that when he was a child, his father lived at Etwall as long as Queen Elizabeth allowed him to live in a house of his own at all. "I was born," he says, "of Catholic parents, who never concealed their profession, for which they suffered many inflictions from our heretic rulers ; so much so that, when a child of five years of age, I was forced, together with my brother who was also a child, to dwell among heretics under the roof of a stranger, for that my father, with two other gentlemen, had been cast into the Tower of London, for having conspired to restore the Scottish Queen to liberty and to her kingdom.

[1] "Garswood [was] taken down at the beginning of the present century, [and the family removed to] the New Hall, built by the Launders about the year 1692, and purchased by the Gerards forty years ago." Baines wrote in 1836.

She was at that time confined in the county of Derby, at two miles distance from our house. Three years afterwards my father, having obtained his release by the payment of a large sum, brought us home, free however from any taint of heresy, as he had maintained a Catholic tutor over us."

Sir Thomas Gerard's two friends were Sir Thomas Stanley and Francis Rolston, and they were committed to the Tower in July, 1571.[1] When this occurred, John Gerard was therefore nearly seven years old. In the examination of the Bishop of Ross in the October following their committal, the only mention made of these three Catholic gentlemen in connection with the imprisoned Queen relates simply to their religion. " He saith the Queen of Scots told this examinate that she had understanding from Sir Thomas Stanley, Sir Thomas Gerard and Rolston that they were reconciled to the Pope according to the late Bull, and that so were many other in Lancashire and the North parts."[2]

Father Gerard is wrong in placing " in the county of Derby" the house in which Mary Queen of Scots was then confined. Tutbury is in Staffordshire, but close to the borders of Derbyshire, and Etwall in that county, Sir Thomas Gerard's house, was not far off. Mary's first imprisonment at Tutbury, of which Father Gerard is speaking, was early in 1569 when he was not five years old. The captive Queen was confined there on that occasion less than three months, as she was brought from Bolton under the charge of the Earl of Shrewsbury and Sir Francis Knollys in February, and was transferred to Wingfield towards the end of April. When in January, 158⅔, Mary was taken back to Tutbury, she caught sight of Sir Thomas Gerard's house on the way. She must have

[1] Burghley's *Notes*, in Murdin's *Collection of State Papers*, London, 1759, p. 771.
[2] *Ibid.* p. 35.

known perfectly well that it was the house of a friend who
had suffered greatly for her sake, and Sir Amias Poulet,
her keeper, must have known that she knew it.   There
is therefore something amusing in the *naïveté* with which
she proposed her removal to that house, and with which
Sir Amias relates her proposal.   "'I remember,' quoth
she, 'as I came hitherwards from Derby, I saw a fair
house not far from hence which was said to belong to a
knight called Gerard, and as I hear he lieth not in it.'   I
said I thought this house was too little for her use.   She
prayed me to cause it to be seen, which I promised to do."
This occurs in a letter[1] to Sir Francis Walsingham, dated
August 18, 1585 : and, further on in the same letter,
speaking of another interview with his royal prisoner,
Poulet says, " This Queen, having thus uttered her griefs
and complaints with many words, asked me if I had sought
to inform myself of the houses which she mentioned unto
me. . . . Touching Sir Thomas Gerard's house, I told
her that I had caused it to be viewed, and did find that the
house is newly builded, and standeth as yet in two parts,
and that the hall and kitchen are yet wanting which
should tie those two parts together, besides many other
imperfections."

The name of Sir Thomas Gerard and the Catholic
character of the neighbourhood of Tutbury and Etwall
were well known to Queen Mary's gaolers.   Sir Ralph
Sadler wrote[2] to Walsingham in the previous February,
" Surely, sir, this is a perilous country, for both men and
women of all degrees are almost all Papists.   I need not
tell you what an obstinate Papist Langford is, and Sir
Thomas Gerard is ill as he, which both do lurk here in
their houses, the furthest not past four miles from this
castle.   Neither of them both, their wives nor families

---

[1] *The Letter-Books of Sir Amias Poulet*, p. 76.
[2] *State Papers of Sir R.Sadler*, edited by Arthur Clifford, Esq. Edinburgh,
1809, vol. ii. p. 525.

come to the church, nor yet have our common prayers
or service said in their houses, but do nourish certain
massing priests which do haunt their houses, where it is
thought they have masses secretly, but so closely and
cunningly used as it will be hard to take them with the
manner. These surely be dangerous persons, if they had
power according to their will, and therefore would be looked
unto. I would to God there were no more in this country,
where I hear of very few good. It seemeth that the bishop
of the diocese is not so diligent and careful of his charge
as he ought to be, and therefore would be quickened and
admonished from her Majesty to look better to his flock,
so as they may be induced to come to the church according
to the law, or else that they feel the smart of the same."

There was no need that the bishop of the diocese
should be "quickened" to make Sir Thomas Gerard "feel
the smart" of the law for not going to the Protestant
church, for he was not permitted long to *lurk* as Sir
Ralph Sadler called it, in his own house. On the 23rd of
August, 1586, he was again committed[1] to the Tower of
London on a charge of high treason.

That Sir Thomas Gerard was faithful to his religion at
the beginning of his imprisonment in the Tower, is testified
by the following extract from a State Paper[2] dated March 1,
158⅞. "Sir Thomas Jarrat [Gerard] his keeper, a very
honest man of the lieutenant's, reported that divers of the
lieutenant's men who had keeping of prisoners in the Tower,
were by persuasion and otherwise fallen from our profession
unto Popery. And he affirmed that Sir Thomas Jarrat had
sundry times persuaded him to convert to their profession."

[1] P.R.O., *Domestic, Elizabeth*, vol. ccxv. n. 19. "Return of prisoners in
the Tower," endorsed in Lord Burghley's hand, "2 Julii, 1588" [an error for
August]. "April 1, 1585. *Imprimis*, the Earl of Arundel, prisoner three
years four months. Feb. 14, 1586. Mr. Secretary Davison, prisoner one year
six months. August 23, 1586. Sir Thomas Gerard, knight, prisoner one year
eleven months ; indicted of treason." At the end of the list are the names of
five priests "committed for religion."
[2] P.R.O., *Domestic, Elizabeth*, vol. ccix. n. 3.

But unhappily for his fair fame, Sir Thomas seems to have had the weakness to appear as a witness against his noble and saintly fellow-prisoner, Philip Howard, Earl of Arundel. In the contemporary life of the Earl, published by the late Duke of Norfolk, it is said :[1] "At the Earl's arraignment both Sir Thomas Gerard and Mr. Bennet[2] were brought in person to give witness against him ; the one that he required a Mass of the Holy Ghost to be said for the success of the Spaniards ; the other, that the prayer of twenty-four hours was directed to the same end." Of these two witnesses the writer of the life further says : "Mr. Bennet, the priest, one of those who had accused him, fell not long after into a grievous disease, whereof he also died miserably, with great remorse and grief for what he had done. And Sir Thomas Gerard, who was the other, never prospered after that time, but sold and wasted a great part of his estate, lived a lewd licentious life, fell from the profession of the Catholic faith, and so continued till about a year before his death." That death occurred in September, 1601.

His fall from the Catholic faith was evidently gradual, for in the year 1590, in "A view of the state of the County Palatine of Lancaster both for religion and civil government,"[3] we have a list of "Knights and Esquires not in the

---

[1] *The Lives of Philip Howard, Earl of Arundel, and of Anne Dacres, his wife.* Edited from the original MSS. by the Duke of Norfolk, E.M. London, 1857, pp. 94, 124.

[2] In a list headed "Prisoners removed out of the Tower to other prisons," we have Sir Thomas Gerard, Bennet, Ithell, &c., together in the Counter in Wood Street. P.R.O., *Domestic, Elizabeth,* vol. ccxvii. n. 27. And in a later paper called "The names of sundry persons that have been examined by Mr. Vice-Chamberlain and Mr. Secretary concerning the disorders of the Tower, how they stand charged and where they remain," we have "Counter in Wood Street :—Sir Thomas Gerard, William Bennet, priest, have performed their duties in their confessions very willingly ; John Snowden, first discoverer of all the disorders of the Tower. At liberty upon bonds :—Ralph Cooke, servant to Sir Thomas Gerard, brought the keys into the Tower, confessed very willingly his fault, and hath divers times given advertisement of priests." *Ibid.* vol. cclxv. n. 135.

[3] P.R.O., *Domestic, Elizabeth,* vol. ccxxxv. n. 4.

Commission of the Peace," who were "all of them, though in some degree of conformity, yet in general note of evil affection in religion, no communicants, and the wives of most of them recusants."[1] In this list there appear the names of "Sir Thomas Gerard of the Bryn in Winwick parish, knight," and "Thomas Gerard of Highleycare in Winwick parish, son and heir to Sir Thomas Gerard, knight." To the name of Sir Thomas there is appended the remark, "He hath made show of conformity in our country."

But it is too plain that the author of the life of the Earl of Arundel is right in saying that it was not a mere "show of conformity," but for a time at least a fall from the Catholic faith, for in the life[2] of Father Edmund Arrowsmith the martyr we read that "Mr. Nicholas Gerard, Father Arrowsmith's grandfather by the mother's side, being a constant professor of the Catholic faith, was by order of Sir Thomas Gerard, his own brother, forcibly carried to the Protestant Church."

This is a miserable story to have to tell of the father of John Gerard, and it must have been a sad grief to him all through his missionary life that while helping others he could not help his own father. The condemnation of the Earl of Arundel was in April, 1589, when Father Gerard had been in England as a priest about four or five months, so that his father's fall must soon have reached his ears. And that father had stood out so bravely and had borne so much for his faith. It is said that the estate of Gerard's

---

[1] In the same list there is "Thomas Gerard of Garswood in Winwick parish, soundly affected in religion," that is to say a thorough Protestant. Others of the family were more constant to their faith. "Cicely Gerard, wife of Thomas Gerard of Highlecar, son and heir to Sir Thomas Gerard, knight, of Winwick parish" and "Anne Gerard of Highlecar, widow, in Winwick parish," are both "recusants and thereof indicted." And in October, 1592, there is good testimony of Father Gerard's elder brother. "Mr. Thomas Gerard of High Carre hath had a notorious recusant to his schoolmaster, Roger Dickson by name, for this three years at the least, and another as I take it for many years before." Information of a priest, probably Thomas Bell; P.R.O., *Domestic, Elizabeth*, vol. ccxliii. n. 52.

[2] Challoner's *Missionary Priests.* Derby Edit. vol. ii. p. 130.

Bromley was the price that Elizabeth had imposed on him
for his liberation from the Tower on the occasion of his
first imprisonment, and this estate was transferred to his
kinsman, Sir Gilbert Gerard, Master of the Rolls, whose
eldest son took his title from it when raised to the peerage.
A little before he was imprisoned in the Tower for the
second time Sir Thomas was summoned before the said
favoured kinsman to compound for his recusancy by the
"free offer" of a yearly sum to be paid to the Queen, "to
be freed from the penalty of the statute." As it gives an
excellent idea of the exactions to which wealthy Catholics
were continually subjected in those days, we subjoin Sir
Thomas' "offer." The original in the Public Record Office[1]
is signed by himself.

"14° die Martii 1585[6]. Sir Thomas Gerard saith
that he is greatly in debt by reason of his troubles and
suretyship, and payeth large interest for the same, and
hath sold much of his lands and departed with a large
portion of the rest unto his sons, and hath two daughters
to bestow, so that he is not able to offer any great sums
unto her Highness in this behalf. Yet nevertheless he most
humbly submitteth himself unto her Majesty's pleasure,
offering his person to serve her Highness in any place of
the world. And if he shall not be admitted thereto, then
he offereth with very good will 30*l.* a year, which is the
fourth part of his small portion remaining now left to
maintain himself, his poor wife and children.

"THO. GERARD."

The name of "Dame Elizabeth Gerard" heads a list
of thirty-three "Recusants sometime resident about London
and in Middlesex, but now dispersed into other countries."
And there is another satisfactory mention of Father
Gerard's mother in the State Papers.[2] "Lady Gerard of

[1] P.R.O., *Domestic, Elizabeth*, vol. clxxxvii. n. 48, viii.
[2] *Ibid.*, vol. ccxlv. n. 138.

Etwall " was one of those who were present at a mass that was said at Mr. Langford's by a priest named Robert Gray, which priest was afterwards guilty of the incredible meanness of giving information against her to the Government. The Mr. Langford at whose house the mass was said, was of course Lady Gerard's neighbour in Derbyshire, whom Sir Ralph Sadler stigmatised as "an obstinate Papist."

With regard to the mention of property transferred by Sir Thomas Gerard to his sons, it may be interesting to quote from the information of a spy,[1] given just ten years later, the following details. "*Item*, John Gerard, the Jesuit, hath certain houses in Lancashire, called Brockehouse Row, near Ashton ; he hath made leases, and one tenant hath not paid all his fine : old John Southworth, dwelling thereabouts, is his bailiff, who can show how all the land and title standeth."

————

NOTE TO CHAPTER I.

THE paper,[2] from which two extracts have now been made, is so curious a specimen of *espionage* that, although it contains no further reference to Father Gerard, it deserves insertion in full as a note. For a copy of it we are indebted to the kindness of J. G. Leeming, Esq., a diligent investigator of the State Papers of the reign of Elizabeth.

" 3° Febr. anno 37° Reg. Elizabeth [159$\frac{4}{8}$].

" At Little Ogle, four miles distant from Rowell in Northamptonshire, lieth Mr. Bentley, who hath a priest in his house continually, and commonly a seminary priest, whom his wife calleth her chicken.

" The said Bentley had an old man named Green, a carpenter and mason, who maketh all the little beads that be in little boxes :

[1] See the note to this chapter.
[2] P.R.O., *Domestic, Elizabeth*, vol. ccli. n. 14.

he made a secret place in Mr. Bentley's house at Lea, with a door of freestone, that no man could ever judge there were any such place ; and he maketh all the secret places in recusants' houses in that country. He dwelleth on Mr. Zacheverell's land at Marley, five miles distant from Derby.

"*Item*, Launcelot Blackeborne, a seminary priest, was at Mr. Pallmer's at Kegworth in Leicestershire the 29th of January last, and that house is never without a priest, whether Mr. Pallmer be at home or abroad.

"*Item*, Mr. Williamson dwelleth at Sawley, two miles from Mr. Pallmer's, and there kept a priest called John Redford *alias* Tanfield, until a certain time that Mrs. Williamson having a little dog which barked and made a great noise at mass time, the said Tanfield spurned him down the stairs with his foot and killed him, for which cause she fell out with the priest, and that house is seldom without another. [*In marg.* Mr. Williamson is fled beyond sea, and was a chief man with the Earl of Shrewsbury.]

"*Item*, at Mr. Merrye's house in Burton Park, who married Mr. Pallmer's sister, lieth one Nicholas Wade *alias* Icke, a seminary priest, and he is also often at Mr. Pallmer's.

"*Item*, at one Bakewell's house at Awkemonton [Alkmanton] a mile from Mr. Merrye's, there is great resort of priests.

"*Item*, at Mr. Whitall's house near Ashbourne, four miles from Awkemonton, lieth one Robert Showell, a seminary priest, with a bald head, having one leg bigger than the other : and at the buttery door they go up a pair of stairs straight to the chamber where they say mass.

"*Item*, at one Rawlins' house at Rawson, three miles from thence, before the parlour door there is a spence ¹ where priests and church stuff are to be found. There are many recusants in that town, and they resort all thither to mass.

"*Item*, at Mrs. Ffolgeambe's house at Throwley, commonly called Meverell's house, there is one priest or other to be found.

"*Item*, at Mr. Genyson's house at Rowllsley, near Bakewell in the Peak, there is John Redford *alias* Tanfield, a seminary priest, who hath authority from the Pope to hallow all kind of church

¹ *Spence*, a cupboard, properly, the buttery. Nares' *Glossary*.

stuff, beads, and such like ; and there his library is to be found, for he studieth there ; and there also sojourn Mr. Lenton and his wife notable recusants.

"*Item*, at Mr. Powdrell's house, called West Hallam, four miles beyond Derby, lieth one Richard Showell, an old priest, and sayeth mass there continually.

"*Item*, John Gerard, the Jesuit, hath certain lands in Lancashire, called Brockehouse Row, near Ashton ; he hath made leases, and one tenant hath not paid all his fine ; old John Southworth, dwelling thereabouts, is his bailiff, who can show how all the land and title standeth.

"The said Redford *alias* Tanfield is a fine handsome man, having no hair on his face. And in some of those houses are also these priests, viz., Ruxby *alias* Pickering, a tall man with gray hairs cut near and round ; William Moorecocke, a little man with a clubbed foot ; Mr. Blackman, a big, lean-faced man, yellow-haired ; Launcelot Blackeborne, a black man, cut near, with some gray hairs, and snaffleth in his speech ; Nicholas Icke *alias* Wade, yellow-haired ; and many others. The priests use to cut all the hair off their upper lip, or else all that is nearest the lips, with a few hairs left above."

CHAPTER II.

LIFE BEFORE ORDINATION.

1577—1588.

"AT the age of fifteen," the autobiography resumes, "I was sent to Exeter College, Oxford, where my tutor was a certain Mr. Leutner,[1] a good and learned man, and a Catholic in mind and heart. There however I did not stay more than a twelvemonth, as at Easter the heretics sought to force us to attend their worship, and to partake of their counterfeit sacrament. I returned then with my brother to my father's house, whither Mr. Leutner himself soon followed us, being resolved to live as a Catholic in very deed, and not merely in desire. While there, he superintended our Latin studies for the next two years, but afterwards going to Belgium, he lived and died there most holily. As for Greek, we were at the same time placed under the tuition of a good and pious priest, William Sutton by name, to whom this occupation served as an occasion for dwelling in our house unmolested. He afterwards entered the Society, and was drowned on the coast of Spain, whither Superiors had called him.

"At the age of nineteen I passed over to France, by permission, with the object of learning the French tongue, and resided for three years at Rheims. While there, though yet a lad, and far from being solidly grounded in my humanities, I applied myself to the study of Sacred Scripture, consulting the commentators for the sense of the more difficult passages, and writing down with my

[1] Probably Edmund Lewckener, who appears in the College books as one of the new fellows on Sir W. Petre's foundation in 1566.

own hand the explanations given publicly to the theological students. Being my own master, I did not, as I
ought to have done, lay a sufficiently solid foundation.
My own taste guided my choice of authors, and I sedu-
lously read the works of St. Bernard and St. Bonaventure,
and such other spiritual writers. About this time I made,
by God's providence, the acquaintance of a saintly young
man who had been admitted into the Society at Rome,
but having for reasons of health been sent out for a time,
was then living at Rheims. He gave me the details of
his past life; he told me (may the Lord reward him)
how he had been educated in the household of God;
he taught me how good and wholesome it was for a man
to have borne the yoke from his youth. He taught me
the method of mental prayer; for which exercise we were
wont to meet together at stated hours, as we were not
living in the College, but in different lodgings in the
town. It was there that, when about twenty years of
age, I heard the call of God's infinite mercy and loving-
kindness inviting me from the crooked ways of the world
to the straight path, to the perfect following of Christ in
His holy Society.

"After my three years' residence at Rheims, I went
to Clermont College, at Paris, to see more closely the
manner of the Society's life, and to be more solidly
grounded in humanities and philosophy. I had not been
there one year when I fell dangerously ill. After my
recovery, I accompanied Father Thomas Derbyshire to
Rouen, in order to see Father Persons, who had arrived
thither from England, and was staying incognito in that
city, to superintend the publication of his *Christian
Directory*, a most useful and happy work, which in my
opinion has converted to God more souls than it contains
pages. The heretics themselves have known how to
appreciate it, as appears from a recent edition thereof
published by one of their ministers who sought to claim

the glory of so important a work.[1] To Father Persons, then, did I communicate my vocation, and my desire of joining the Society. But as I was not yet strong, nor fit to continue my studies, and moreover, as I had some property to dispose of, and arrangements to make in England, he advised me to return thither, so as to recruit my health by breathing my native air, and at the same time to free myself from every obstacle which might prevent or delay me in my pursuit of perfection and the religious life. I accordingly went home, and after settling my affairs, set out on my return in about a year; this time, however, without having asked for a licence, for I had no hope of obtaining it, as I did not venture to communicate my plans to my parents."

It is not easy to reconcile the dates at this period of Father Gerard's life, and the only conclusion seems to be that at the time when this was written, when the author was about forty-five, he had forgotten the duration or succession of the various stages of his education. He could not have been nineteen when he went to France, and have lived, as he says, three years at Rheims, one at Paris, and about a year in England before setting out for France again, for he was most certainly a prisoner in the Marshalsea before he had half finished his nine-teenth year. His stay at Rheims and Paris was not after his release from the Marshalsea, for he was more than a full year in that prison, to which he was committed in March, 158¾, and after his discharge in October, 1585, his recognizances were renewed every three months for another year before he left England for Rome, where he arrived in August, 1586. Besides, he was certainly in London on the 20th of April, 1586, as we shall shortly see.

[1] *A Book of Christian Exercises appertaining to Resolution.* By R: P. Perused by Edmund Bunney, who dates his preface "at Bolton Percie, in the ancientie or liberties of York, the 9th of July, 1584," and inscribes it to Edwin Sandes, Archbishop of York. This Bunney was Subdean and Pre-bendary of York. An edition at Oxford and one in London appeared simul-taneously in 1585.

The most probable solution seems to be that the three years at Rheims, if the time was so long, were spent there before he went to Oxford, when as he tells us he was fifteen. The Douay Diary has an entry[1] "that on the 29th of August, 1577, there came from England Mr. Paschall,[2] a gentleman, and one Aldridge a merchant, and at the same time came Mr. Gerard, son of Sir Thomas Gerard, knight." In August or September, 1577, John Gerard was not yet thirteen. At that time the College was not at Rheims, but at Douay; but as he probably accompanied the students who on the 27th of March, 1578, reached Rheims with Dr. Webb on the transfer of the College, it was only natural that he should speak of his time as spent at Rheims.

Supposing John Gerard's year at Oxford to have followed and not to have preceded his residence at Rheims,—and he says that while at Rheims he was "yet a lad"—he must have gone to Clermont College, Paris, after a very short "two years" spent in Latin and Greek at home under Mr. Leutner and William Sutton. After some months there, followed by an illness and convalescence, he went to Rouen with Father Derbyshire to see Father Persons. Now Father Persons edited the first edition of his *Christian Directory* when at Rouen, late in the year 1581, and the second in the winter of 1584.[3] On the latter occasion Gerard was in prison, so that his visit to Rouen was in the autumn or winter of the year 1581, when he was seventeen; and this is borne out

[1] "1577, Aug. 29 die advenerunt ex Anglia Mr. Paschallus vir nobilis et quidam Aldrigius mercator: eodem etiam tempore adventavit Mr. Gerrardus, D. Tho. Gerrardi Equitis Aurati filius." *Second Douay Diary*, p. 128, edited by the Fathers of the London Oratory, 1878.

[2] Probably John Paschall, of Much Baddow in Essex, scholar of Ralph Sherwin the martyr, who entered the English College at Rome at its opening in 1579, returned to England with Fathers Persons and Campion, and afterwards fell from the faith "of frailty and upon fear of torments that were threatened unto him." *Troubles of our Catholic Forefathers*, Second Series, p. 294.

[3] *Troubles*, Second Series, pp. 15, 36.

C

by his saying that it was on Father Persons' arrival from England.   This is all that can be done[1] towards clearing up the dates of Father Gerard's life before he was committed to the Marshalsea, but the date of that event is determined with the greatest exactness by " A note of the recusants remaining in the Marshalsea "[2] in 1584, in which he appears among the "temporal gentlemen," thus—"John Gerrard sent in by Mr. Weekes the 5th of March, 1583[4]."   The latest date given in the list is but two days after this.

Father Gerard thus describes how he come to be sent to the Marshalsea prison.   Having told us that he tried to cross the sea without a licence, he continues in the following terms.   " I embarked then with some other Catholics, and after having been kept five days at sea by contrary winds, we were forced to put in at the port of Dover.   On arriving thither, we were all seized by the Custom-house officers, and forwarded to London in custody. My companions were imprisoned, on a warrant of the Queen's Privy Council. For my own part, though I declared myself a Catholic, and refused to attend their worship, I escaped imprisonment at that time, as there were some of the Council that were friendly to my family, and had procured me the licence to travel abroad on the former occasion. They entertained, it would seem, some hopes of perverting me in the course of time, so I was sent to my maternal uncle's,[3] a Protestant, to be kept in his custody, and if possible, to be perverted.   He, after three months, sought to obtain my full liberty by praying or paying;[4] but being asked whether I had 'gone to church,' as they

---

[1] See Note A at the end of the chapter.

[2] The whole list is given in a note at the end of this chapter.

[3] As his mother had no brothers, his "maternal uncle" must be the husband of one of her sisters—either George Hastings, afterwards Earl of Huntingdon, who was not a bigot like his brother Henry, "the tyrant of the north," or else Sir Thomas Stanhope.

[4] *Prece vel pretio.* MS.

call it, he was obliged to acknowledge that he could never bring me to do so.

"Thereupon the Council sent me with a letter to the pseudo-bishop of London,[1] who, having read it, asked whether I would allow him to confer with me on religious matters. I replied, that as I doubted of nothing, I had rather decline. 'You must in that case,' answered the superintendent, 'remain here in custody.' I replied that in this I was obliged to acquiesce, through force and the command of the Government. He treated me with kindness, with a view perhaps of thus drawing me over. But he ordered his chaplain's bed to be brought into my chamber. At first I repeatedly declared my determination not to enter into any dispute with this man on matters of faith, as to which my mind was settled, nor to receive religious instruction from him; but as he ceased not pouring out abuse and blasphemy against the saints in Heaven, and against our Holy Mother the Church, I was forced to defend the truth, and then almost the whole night was spent in disputing. I soon discovered that in him at least God's truth had no very formidable adversary. After two days, as they saw my case was hopeless, they sent me back to the Council with letters of recommendation forsooth, for the so-called bishop told me that he had greatly striven in my favour, and that he had great hopes of my being set at large. It was, however, a Uriah's letter that I carried, for no sooner had the Council read it, than they ordered me to be imprisoned until I had learnt to be a loyal subject. For they hold him a bad subject who will not subject himself to their heresies and their sacrilegious worship.[2]

"Being committed to the Marshalsea prison, I found there numbers of Catholics and many priests awaiting judgment of death with the greatest joy." There were

---

[1] John Elmer was Bishop of London from 1577 to 1594.
[2] *Habebant enim pro non subdito, qui nolebat subdi erroribus.* MS.

forty-seven Catholics in the prison, of whom seventeen
were priests, and amongst them were William Hartley,
Stephen Rowsham, and John Adams, future martyrs on
the scaffold, Thomas Crowther, who died in prison, and
William Bishop, the first Vicar Apostolic. "In this school
of Christ," Father Gerard says, "I was detained from
the beginning ·of one Lent to the end of the following, not
without abundant consolation of mind and good opportunity for study. We were twice during this interval
dragged before the courts, not to be tried for our lives,
but to be fined according to the law against recusants.
I was condemned to pay 2,000 florins [200*l.*].[1]

"Once on my return from the Court which was in
the country, some six miles out of London, I got leave
to go and visit some friends, having pledged my word
to return to the Marshalsea that night. I went then to
visit a prisoner detained in that horrible dungeon called
Bridewell, as I had heard that he was sick. His story
deserves notice. He had formerly lived in Father Campion's service, and on account of some words he had let
fall in praise of Father Campion, he was arrested and
detained a long time in the Marshalsea. On my arrival
there I saw him laden with heavy fetters on his legs,
besides which he wore a very rough hair-shirt. He was
most lowly and meek, and full of charity. I happened
one day to see a turnkey strike him repeatedly without
the servant of God uttering a single word. He was at
length taken with three others to the filthy Bridewell·
One of their number died of starvation a few days after
their transfer. When I visited this poor man he was lying
ill, being worn out with want of food, and labour on the
tread-wheel. It was a shocking sight. He was reduced
to skin and bone, and covered with lice that swarmed

---

[1] In a letter dated October 3, 1614 (Stonyhurst MSS., *Angl. A.* vol. iv.
n. 24), Father Gerard says that "7 florins of Liége make but 6 of Brabant,
12*s.* English." So we may turn his florins into pounds by taking off the last
cypher.

upon him like ants on a mole-hill; so that I never remember to have seen the like.

"At times our cells were visited, and a strict search made for church stuff, Agnus Dei, and relics. Once we were betrayed by a false brother, who had feigned to be a Catholic, and disclosed our hidden stores to the authorities. On this occasion were seized quantities of Catholic books and sacred objects, enough to fill a cart. In my cell were found nearly all the requisites for saying mass; for my next door neighbour was a good priest, and we discovered a secret way of opening the door between us, so that we had mass very early every morning. We afterwards repaired our losses, nor could the malice of the devil again deprive us of so great a consolation in our bonds."

Not long before John Gerard's imprisonment the following report[1] by the Keeper was made to Lord Burghley, of masses said in the prison of the Marshalsea.

"Found at mass the 24th of August [1582], in the Marshalsea, as followeth. In Mr. Shelley's chamber, Thomas Hartley, priest, said mass, Richard Shelley, William Carew, gent., William Tooker, John Taylor, Mr. Shelley's man, Joan Watts, a stranger (of Oxfordshire), Mrs. Loe. In Mr. Perpoint's chamber, himself, Richard Norris in saying of mass, John Jacob. In Denton's chamber, himself priest, John Harris, his clerk. Their superstitious stuff, their abominable relics, and vile books, I have taken away ready to be showed. My humble request is to have the priests removed from me, and the rest to be examined and punished, as shall best seem good to your honours."

A little later the Bishop of London wrote a letter[2] to Lord Burghley to the same purport, and in it the name of Hartley the martyr recurs.

[1] P.R.O., *Domestic, Elizabeth*, vol. clv. n. 27.
[2] British Museum, *Lansdowne MSS.* 38, n. 87.

" Right honourable and my singular good Lord,—Your
lordship shall understand that I have not been unmindful
of that search which your lordship required to be made in
our Registry and in the prisons about London for the
space of the first eight or nine years of her Majesty's reign.
For the truth is I have done in both what I can, and can
find nothing to the purpose ; for in the Registry, Johnes,
who had the whole doing therein, being dead, nothing
certain can be heard, and the gaolers being oft changed,
have nothing for those years certain. But this I find among
them, and specially in the Marshalsea, that those wretched
priests, which by her Majesty's lenity live there, as it were
in a college of caitiffs, do commonly say mass within the
prison, and entice the youth of London unto them to my
great grief, and as far as I can learn do daily reconcile
them. I have been so bold [as] to shut up one Hartley,
and to lay irons upon him, till I hear from your lordship
what course herein we shall take hereafter. But the Commission being renewed, I doubt not but my Lord of Canterbury will look to those dangerous persons on that side.
And so I take my leave of your good lordship, praying
God to defend you with the shield of His providence in
these malicious and dangerous days. At Fulham, this 5th
of December, 1583. Your good lordship's most assuredly
in Christ,

" JOHN LOND."

Perhaps the "false brother" Father Gerard speaks of
was Thomas Dodwell, and he may not have known who it
was. At all events a spy of this name gave information,[1]
which he called "Of the secrets in the Marshalsea." "One
Tedder, a seminary priest, sent a letter[2] to Rome within

---

[1] P.R.O., *Domestic, Elizabeth*, vol. clxviii. n. 35.

[2] In all probability this very letter is still in existence, for in the Archives
of the Cardinal Archbishop of Westminster, as the Reverend Father Knox of
the Oratory has been so good as to inform us, there is a letter from William
Tedder in prison in London to Father Agazzari, Rector of the English College

four or five days past. There is there four seminary priests
in one chamber and close prisoners, viz., Fenn, Fowler,
Conyers, and Hartley; and yet notwithstanding the often
searching, they have such privy places to hide their massing trumpery that hardly it can be found, that they have
to themselves often mass, and now because Sir George
Carey [or Carew, Knight Marshal] and his servants have
often taken from them their silver chalices, they have provided chalices of tin. . . . They hide their books in such
secret places that when any search is [made] they can find
nothing. They help many to go over beyond the sea.
Mr. More, now prisoner in the Marshalsea, hath four sons
in Rheims, whereof one he sent within this eight weeks.
. . . There is in the Marshalsea certain persons whom
they call Dividents, because they divide that equally
amongst the priests which is sent. They know from whom
this exhibition cometh, and who are the chiefest relievers
of priests. The names of such are Perpoint, now prisoner
in the Tower, Webster and Graye." Another hand has
added, " Instead of Perpoint is Becket."

"In the course of the following year," Father Gerard
continues, and he is speaking of 1585, " my liberty was
obtained by the importunities of my friends, who however were bound as sureties, to the extent of a heavy
sum of money, for my remaining in the kingdom. I was,
moreover, to present myself at the prison at the three
months' end." We are not without record of these bonds.
The sum was 200*l.*, a very considerable sum, be it remembered, in those days. The entry[1] runs thus: " 31 Octob.
1585. John Gerrard of Brinne, in the county of Lincoln
[*sic*], gentleman, bound in 200*l.* to return to the Marshalsea,

at Rome, dated April 20, 1583. This Tedder read his recantation at St. Paul's
Cross, December 1, 1588, a week before Anthony Tyrrell. He is called
Cedder in Bishop Challoner's catalogue of priests banished in 1585. *Missionary
Priests.* Derby Edit. vol. i. p. 190.

[1] P.R.O., *Domestic, Elizabeth,* vol. cc. n. 59; vol. ccv. n. 13. Another
entry dated December 7, 1585, is in *Domestic, Elizabeth,* vol. cxx. n. 59.

prisoner, within three months." "And these sureties," he
adds, "had to be renewed three or four times before I was
able to resume my project. At length the long wished for
opportunity presented itself. A very dear friend of mine
offered himself as bail to meet whatever demand might be
made, if I was discovered to be missing after the appointed
time. After my departure he forfeited, not indeed his
money, but his life; for he was one of the most conspicuous
of those fourteen gentlemen[1] who suffered in connection
with the captive Queen of Scots, and whose execution, as
events soon showed, was but a prelude to taking off the
Queen herself." Babington, to whose plot Father Gerard
here alludes, was executed with his associates on the
20th and 21st of September, 1586, and Mary Queen of Scots
on the 8th of February following. John Gerard had been in
Rome about six weeks when his surety was put to death.

"Being at length free, I went to Paris," is all that
he says of his departure from England; but the man
who "conveyed" him over gave information of it afterwards to Elizabeth's ministers, and thus we know the
names of those who crossed the Channel with him. The
man was Thomas Dodwell, who has already described to
us the interior of the Marshalsea; and he now says:[2]
"Raindall, searcher of Gravesend, receiveth money of pas-
sengers, suffering them to pass without searching. I myself
escaped twice in this manner, having the first time in
my company Bagshawe, who is now a seminary priest,
Morrice,[3] sometime of her Majesty's Chapel but now of

---

[1] The fourteen gentlemen were Anthony Babington, John Ballard, priest,
J. Savage, R. Barnwell, Chidiock Tichborne, Charles Tylney, and E. Abington,
hanged September 20; and T. Salisbury, Henry Dunne, Edward Jones,
J. Traverse, J. Charnock, R. Gage, and Jerome Bellamy, hanged on the
following day.

[2] P.R.O., *Domestic, Elizabeth*, vol. clxviii. n. 35.

[3] "Anthony Harrison sworn the —— of October in Mr. Morrice' room,
who fled beyond the seas anno 25° [1583] from Windsor." *The Old
Cheque-book, or Book of Remembrance of the Chapel Royal from* 1561 *to*
1744. Edited for the Camden Society by Edward F. Rimbault, LL.D.
1872, p. 4.

the Pope's, Owen who is now in Rome; the second time, Hunt, who is now in the Marshalsea, Sir Thomas Gerrat's second son, Knight, Broughton, Afeild, Pansefoot, son and heir of Mr. Pansefoot of Gloucestershire, and the aforesaid Afeild[1] hath conveyed him over within this month."

"Being at length free," says Father Gerard, "I went to Paris; and finding Father William Holt, who had just arrived from Scotland, ready to start for Rome with the Provincial of France, I joined myself to their company." Before leaving England he was present, as he tells us later, at the martyrdom of William Thomson *alias* Blackburn, who suffered at Tyburn for his priesthood on the 20th of April, 1586. The date of his arrival in Rome is marked in the "Pilgrims' Register" of the English College, which records[2] that "Mr. John Gerard of Derbyshire was received in the hospital on the 5th of August [1586] and remained eight days," which was the length of time that pilgrims were received gratuitously who were not poor. He was soon missed in England, for in the British Museum[3] we have the Ecclesiastical Commissioners' lists of "Recusants sent for," "Gentlemen not yet sent for," and "Persons to be sought after." Under this last heading, dated August 9, 1586, we have "The son of Sir Thomas Gerard." "Sir Thomas Gerard of Etwall, knight," is in the list of "Gentlemen not yet sent for."

Father William Holt, with whom John Gerard travelled to Rome, was installed Rector of the English College in that city on the 24th of October, 1586, and in that

---

[1] If Dodwell is here speaking of Gerard's crossing in 1586, the Afeild here mentioned cannot be Thomas Alfield, the martyr, as he was executed at Tyburn for selling Catholic books on the 6th of July, 1585.

[2] "D. Joannes Gerardus Darbiensis receptus est in hospitali 5° Augusti et mansit 8 diebus." Archives of the English College, Rome, *Pilgrims' Register.* Stonyhurst MSS., Father Grene's *Miscell. de Coll. Angl.* p. 19.

[3] *Harl. MSS.* 360, f. 8.

month Gerard entered the College as a convictor.[1]   He
became an alumnus[2] of the College, or as it was then
always called, "an alumnus of his Holiness Pope Sixtus V.,"
on the 5th of April following, taking the College oath in
its earliest form,[3] and in the course of the year 1587 he
received the tonsure and minor orders, the subdeaconship
in August, and the deaconship on the 16th of November.
The date of his ordination to the priesthood is not given,
but it was probably the Christmas Ember-tide of 1587.
Father Gerard's theological course of studies was deplor-
ably short, but happily the evil effects of haste were not
afterwards seen in him, as they undoubtedly were sometimes seen in those whose preparation for the difficult
duties of a priest on the English Mission was hurried
and curtailed.

His own account of his College life is this : "At Rome
I was advised to pursue my studies in the English College,
and to take priest's orders before I entered the Society. I
followed this advice, despite my ardent desire of entering
religion, which I communicated to Father Persons, and to
Father Holt, the then Rector of the English College.
But as the Roman climate was not suited to my constitution, and I had an extreme desire of going to England,
it seemed good to the Fathers to put me at the beginning

---

[1] "Joannes Gerardus Anglus dioecesis Lichfeldiensis annum agens 23ᵐ.,
aptus ad theologiam positivam, receptus fuit in hoc Anglorum Collegium inter
alumnos SSmi.D.N.Sixti V. a P. Gulielmo Holto hujus Collegii rectore
de mandato Illmi. Hippolyti Cardis. Aldobrandini Viceprotectoris sub die
5° Aprilis anno Dni. 1587, cum fuisset antea Convictor per septem menses.
Anno Dni. 1587, mense ———— accepit ordines minores, et mense Augusto
subdiaconatum, et diaconatum 9° mense die 16." *Liber Annal. Coll. Anglor.
de Urbe.*

[2] "Ego prædictus Joannes Gerardus juro me fore semper paratum, jubente
Summo Pontifice vel alio quovis hujus Collegii legitimo Superiore, vitam
ecclesiasticam agere, sacros etiam ordines suscipere, ac præterea in Angliam
ad juvandas animas proficisci, et hoc tactis sacris Scripturis juramento con-
firmo. In ædibus Collegii Anglicani de Urbe die supradicto [5 Apr. 1587].
Ita est, JOANNES GERARDUS." Beneath is written, "Est ex Societate et
operarius in Anglia." *Lib. Annal. Coll. Anglorum de Urbe.*

[3] Stonyhurst MSS., Fr. N. Southwell's *Catalogus primorum Patrum,* p. 32.

of the year to casuistry and controversies ; I went therefore through a complete course of positive theology. Towards its close, when the Spanish Armada was nearing the coasts of England, Cardinal Allen thought fit to send me to England for various matters connected with Catholic interests, but as I still wanted several months of the lawful age for taking priest's orders, a Papal dispensation was obtained. I was most unwilling to depart unless I was first admitted into the Society, so Father Persons, out of his singular charity towards me, obtained my admission to the novitiate, which I was to finish in England. There were at that time in the English College some others who had the like vocation, and we used to strive to conform ourselves as much as possible to the novices at St. Andrew's, serving in the kitchen and visiting hospitals. On the feast of the Assumption of the most Blessed Virgin Mary, in the year of our Lord 1588, our Very Reverend Father General Aquaviva received Father Edward Oldcorne of blessed memory and my unworthy self into the Society of Jesus, and gave us his blessing for the English Mission."

But even in Rome he was not out of sight of Elizabeth's ministers, whose spy system made them lynx-eyed. In "A note of such as are known to be beyond the seas, and of their friends in England as near as is known,"[1] in 1588, he is named as "John Garret, a priest in Rome, son to Sir Thomas Garret." Christopher Buxton[2] the martyr, writing[3] to Father Holt from Paris, June 9, 1587, mentions him, giving his name a similar form. "Remember me unto good Mr. Fitzharbart, Mr. Garratte, Mr. Harte, John Nelson, and bestly unto my countryman Francis." This spelling of the name, which is very frequent, seems

[1] P.R.O., *Domestic, Elizabeth,* vol. ccxix. n. 77.

[2] He suffered at Canterbury in September or October, 1588, with Robert Wilcox and Edward Campion, priests, and Robert Widmerpool, a layman, the former for being priests, the latter for giving hospitality to priests.

[3] Stonyhurst MSS., *Angl. A.* vol. i. n. 32.

to indicate that it was pronounced like "Garrard" or "Jarrard." So Persons was pronounced and sometimes written "Parsons," and Fitzherbert "Fitzharbart." The same pronunciation of *er* we have not yet lost in the words "Derby" and "clerk."

NOTES TO CHAPTER II.

NOTE A.

The dates of Father Gerard's life at this period.

1577.   August.   Arrived at Douay when nearly 13.

1578.   March 27.   College transferred to Rheims.

1579.   October ?   Went to Oxford at the age of 15.

1580.   At home with M. Leutner and Mr. Sutton.

1581.   In spring ?   Went to Clermont College, Paris.

1581.   In autumn.   Met Father Persons at Rouen.

158¾.   March 5.   Committed to the Marshalsea.

1585.   October 31.   Discharged on recognizances.

1586.   April 20.   Present at William Thomson's martyrdom at Tyburn.

1586.   August 5.   Received in the English Hospital at Rome.

1586.   October.   Received in the English College as convictor.

1587.   April 5.   Received there as alumnus.

1587.   August.   Ordained subdeacon.

1587.   November 16.   Ordained deacon.

1587.   December ?   Ordained priest, aged 23 years and 3 months.

1588.   August 15.   Admitted into the Society.

1588.   September 21.   Reached Rheims.

1588.   September 26.   Left Rheims.

1588.   November ?   Lands in England.

NOTE B.

"A note of the recusants remaining in the Marshalsea.[1]

"Temporal gentlemen:

Robert Beckett [*or* Berkett], sent in the 1st of November	1579
John Gray, sent in the 2nd of January	1577
Walter Blunt, sent in the 18th of July	1580
Theobald Greene, sent in the 30th of October	1578
Richard Shelley, sent in the 13th [*or* 18th] of August	1580
William Phillipps, sent in the 6th of November	1578
Edward Moore, [sent] in the 2nd of August	1581
Richard Webster, sent in the 25th [*or* 30th] of March	1573
Edmond Sexton, sent in the 21st [*or* 16th] of March	1581
Peter Carey [*or* Varty], sent in the 15th of October	1578
Gilbert Wells, sent in the 21st of December	1583
George Brytten, sent in by the Right Honourable my Lord of Hunsdon the 3rd of February	1583
John Knightley, sent in the 16th day of February	1583
John Gerard, sent in by Mr. Weekes the 5th of March	1583
William Manneringe, sent in the 7th of March	1583
Thomas Moore, sent in the 28th of April	1582
Nicholas Woolfe, sent in the 7th of December	1583

"Other temporal men:

Richard Reynolds, sent in the 18th of February	1580
John Jacobb, sent in the 16th of August	1581
John Tucker [*or* Tinker], sent in the 23rd of August	1581 [*or* 82]
John Harvie, sent in the same 23rd of August	1581 [*or* 82]
John Harris, sent in the same 23rd of August	1581 [*or* 82]
Walter Taylor, sent in the 23rd of November	1581 [*or* 82]
John Ridge, sent in the 9th of December	1580
Robert Awden, sent in the 10th of December	1582
Peter Lawson, sent in the 1st of February	1582
Henry Sherwood, sent in the 11th [*or* 6th] of February 1581 [*or* 82]	
Eley Jones, sent in the 7th of November	1583
Bartholomew Temple, sent in the 6th of November	1583
Richard Turner, sent in the 4th of October	1583

[1] P.R.O., *Domestic, Elizabeth*, vol. clxix. n. 26, and vol. clxx. n. 11. The entries in brackets are from the second list.

"Seminary priests :

Christopher Smawle, sent in the 25th of May	1582
John Tibbitt, sent in the 3rd of November	1582
Andrew Fowler, sent in the 3rd of November	1582
Samuel Conyers, sent in the 1st of February	1582
William Teddar, sent in the 10th of December	1582
William Hartlie, sent in the 22rd [*or* 16th] of August	1582
Richard Norris, sent in the 17th of December	1581
William Bishopp, sent in the 11th of February	1581
Thomas Crowder, sent in the 22nd of March	1581
John Chapman, sent in the 1st of November	1583
William Warmington, sent in the 10th of December	1582
George Goodsalf [*or* Goodfuest] and Stephen Rusham, sent from the Tower the 12th of February	1583
Robert Fenn, sent in the 16th of February	1583
Thomas Aliet, sent in by warrant from the Council the 24th of February	1583
John Adams, sent in the 7th of March	1583
John Talk, sent in the 18th of December	1583

"Soma of all are 47.

"Thomas Batman, sent in the 16th of February, 1583, Robert Purton, Sir Thomas Lewrey his man, sent in by the Right Honourable Sir Francis Walsingham the 28th of November, 1583, being examined answer that they are determined to go to the church."

CHAPTER III.

ARRIVAL IN ENGLAND.

1588.

" I STARTED then on my homeward journey, in company
with Father Oldcorne and two other priests who had been
students at the English College.

" On our way through Switzerland, after having passed
a night at Basle, we were curious to see the vestiges of
the ancient faith, which the Lutherans usually allow to
remain, and the Calvinists generally destroy. As we were
going round the church we were joined by a certain person,
who offered to show us all the curiosities of the place. We
were somewhat astonished at this ready civility on the
part of a Lutheran towards Catholic priests (for we travelled
in clerical habit), and, as our new friend spoke French, I
began by inquiring of what country he was. I found out
that he was from Lorraine. On inquiring his reasons for
thus forsaking the land and the faith of his fathers, he
replied that he found the laws of the Catholic Church
too stringent. I asked which laws, as the Catholic Church
imposes none other yoke than that of the Gospel, which
as Christ bears witness, is sweet, and the burden thereof
light. At length I discovered that the unhappy man was
a priest, an apostate, who had taken refuge at Basle, and
lived there with a woman he called his wife, in the very
same house at which we had put up, supporting himself
and her by usury. I dealt very earnestly with him to
leave this path of damnation, and to return to the way
of heaven ; to leave a share of his money to the woman,
and to lend no more at unlawful interest ; but to

his future gains by labour or some lawful traffic. He promised at last to take my advice, and gave me a letter for his bishop, asking for reconciliation. I sent it as I passed through Lorraine, and I hope that the poor man persevered in his good purpose.

"As we passed through Rheims, where there was the English Seminary, and through Paris, we kept the strictest incognito."

The Douay Diary[1] gives us the dates of Father Gerard's arrival at Rheims and his departure thence, together with the names of his fellow-travellers. He reached the College on the 21st and left it on the 26th of September, 1588, and the two secular priests he speaks of, as travelling with himself and Father Oldcorne, were Ralph Buckland and Arthur Stratford. The Diary does not notice that the two Fathers were members of the Society of Jesus. It is not possible that it was not known there, and we may regard it as a sign of the caution of which Father Gerard speaks. But his passing through Paris was not as little known as he thought, and without being aware of it he then fell into the gravest of the perils that beset the poor Catholics of England, the "perils from false brethren."

There is a "Secret Advertisement"[2] to Sir Francis Walsingham, dated "From Paris, the 9th of December, 1588," which says, with great exaggeration in the number, no doubt, "There were thirty priests to come over the 14th of this last month of November, whose names I know not unless those that follow : one Beslye and one Tomson, so called, whose right name in very deed is Garret. There is also one Palmer and one White. There were seven

---

[1] "1588, Sept. 21 die, Roma ad nos venerunt D. Rodolphus Buckland, D. Joannes Gerard. filius D. Thomæ Gerard equitis aurati, D. Arthurus Stratford, D. Edouardus Oldcorn, presbyteri. Die 26 Angliam ituri discesserunt D. Jo. Gerard, D. Rodolphus Buckland, D. Arthurus Stratford, et D. Edouardus Oldcorn. *Second Douay Diary.*

[2] P.R.O., *Domestic, Elizabeth*, vol. ccxix. n. 26.

of these to come over at some place near unto Ewe [Eu], and one at another place, but for a certainty there are thirty either come or ready to come." We thus learn that Father Gerard had already taken the name of Tomson, by which he was chiefly known in the latter portion of his life.

But a far more dangerous traitor than this "secret advertiser" was the infamous Gilbert Gifford, Father Gerard's second cousin. This man, whom Sir Edward Stafford, the English Ambassador at Paris, called "the most notable double treble villain that ever lived," was the chief agent employed to ripen the Babington conspiracy, which was designed in order to bring Mary Queen of Scots to the scaffold. By him Mary's communications with her friends in Paris and London were carried on, and all of them passed through the hands of Sir Francis Walsingham and of Thomas Phelippes, "the decipherer." In the midst of this treachery he was ordained priest. He " purposely was made priest, as he confessed, to play the Secretary's spy."[1] Fearing lest his English employers might imprison or execute him, to silence his tongue, when the Queen of Scots was dead, he went over to Paris; but being there arrested for immorality and shut up in the Bishop's prison, other matters soon appeared against him, and he continued in prison till his death in 1590. The Ambassador on his arrest wrote to Sir Francis Walsingham that he thought "that they will put him to a hard plunge, for they mean to take him upon this point, which indeed letters (as I hear that they have of his, with his own hand written to Phelippes) will make hard against him, that he became a priest by cunning to deceive the world, and that he had, being become a priest with that intent, said mass after."[2]

This miserable man—who wrote to the Archbishop of

[1] Stonyhurst MSS., *Angl. A.* vol. i. n. 70.
[2] *Letter-Books of Sir Amias Poulet*, pp. 257, 380.

D

Paris,¹ as "prestre Anglois bachelier en Théologie, disant
que depuis le 19 du moys Décembre il est constitué
prisonier en vos prisons épiscopales, suppliant en toute
humilité en l'honneur de la Passion de nostre Sauveur et
de la trèsglorieuse Vierge Marie"—found means under the
names of Jacques Colerdin and Francis Hartley, to carry
on a correspondence from his prison with Phelippes and
Walsingham, continuing thus to earn the pension of 100*l.*
a year from Elizabeth's Government, which he had received
as the price of Mary Stuart's blood.² This man, who was a
"false brother" if ever there was one, found means to learn
in his prison the news which he sent to his employers.³
"There be eight priests over from Rome, whereof John
Gerard and Arthur Shefford [Stratford, the Douay Diary
calls him], a priest, and his man, will be in England within
five days."

In all unconsciousness Father Gerard proceeds: "At
length we come to Eu, where a College for English
youths had been established,⁴ which was afterwards abandoned on account of the wars, and another more extensive establishment erected at St. Omers. Our Fathers at
Eu, after conferring with those who had the management
of the College in that town, all strongly opposed our
venturing into England, as circumstances then were,
for the Spanish attempt had exasperated the public
mind against Catholics, and most rigid searches for priests
and domiciliary visits had been set on foot; guards were
posted in every village along the roads and streets; and
the Earl of Leicester, then at the height of his favour,
had sworn not to leave a single Catholic alive at the close
of the year, but this man of blood did not live out half
that time himself, for he was cut off in that very same

¹ P.R.O., *Domestic, Elizabeth*, vol. ccxvii. n. 81.
² *Ibid.*, vol. cxcix. nn. 95, 96.
³ *Ibid.* vol. ccxvii. n. 3. The Calendar gives for its date Oct. 1, 1588.
The postscript of the letter bears the date "8 Septembris."
⁴ *Troubles*, Second Series, p. 28.

year. We were compelled then to stay there for a time,
until fresh instructions were sent us by Father Persons
in the name of Father General. They were to this effect,
that the state of affairs had indeed much changed since
our departure from Rome, but that as it was the Lord's
business that we had to do, he left us free either to wait
the return of greater calm, or to pursue the course we had
entered upon. On receiving this desirable message, we
did not long deliberate, but immediately hired a ship, to
land us in the northern part of England, which seemed
to be less disturbed."

The "desirable message" is described a little more
fully by Father Gerard in his "Narrative of the Powder
Plot," [1] where in his own English he relates this journey
and his own and his companion's landing in England.
" They received answer from Father Persons that the times
were much more periculous than was expected when they
went from Rome, yet sith the cause was God's, and their
will so good to prefer the safety of others' souls before the
safety of their own bodies, they might in the name of
God proceed, if their desire still continued, but that it
was left unto their own election. These letters were
received with great joy, and the two Fathers, within few
days after, got a ship wherein they embarked."

When did they embark? "It was about the end of
October," wrote Father Gerard twenty-one years afterwards,
but it is plain that he has not placed their voyage across
the Channel sufficiently late in the year. We have seen
that they left Rheims on the 26th of September. They
went first to Paris, and then to Eu; and at Eu they
remained long enough to receive an answer to a letter
sent to Rome. The very earliest date that we can assign
for their leaving Eu for England is that given in Walsingham's "Secret Advertisement," already quoted, which
names the 14th of November. When Gilbert Gifford, at

---

[1] *Condition of Catholics*, p. 280.

the beginning of October, said that they would "be in England in five days," he was not of course aware of the delay that would be caused by their writing to Rome from Eu.

Both Gilbert Gifford and the other spy speak of eight priests crossing the Channel. We know of only six—the two Jesuit Fathers, Ralph Buckland, and Arthur Stratford, who had accompanied them from Rome, and the two of whom he now comes to speak. "Two priests from Rheims joined us, as our former companions preferred to take time before they faced the dangers which awaited them on the opposite shores. The ship then set sail with four priests on board, a goodly cargo indeed, had not my unworthiness deprived me of the crown, for all those other three suffered martyrdom for the faith. The two priests were soon taken, and being in a short space made perfect, they fulfilled a long time. Their names were Christopher Bales and George Beesley,[1] but my companion, the blessed Father Oldcorne, spent eighteen years of toil and labour in the Lord's vineyard, and watered it at length with his blood.

"After crossing the Channel, as we were sailing along the English coast on the third day, my companion and I, seeing a convenient spot[2] in which the ship's boat might easily set us on shore, and considering that it were dangerous if we were to land all together, recommended the matter to God and took counsel with our companions.

[1] They both suffered in Fleet Street; Christopher Bales on March 4, 15$\frac{89}{90}$, and George Beesley on July 2, 1591. They were condemned under the statute 27° Elizabeth, for having been made priests beyond the seas and exercising their functions in England. The martyrdom of Christopher Bales and of a layman named Nicholas Horner is related by Father Southwell in a letter dated London, March 8, 15$\frac{89}{90}$. P.R.O., *Domestic, Elizabeth*, vol. ccxxx. n. 104.

[2] A complete examination of all the questions that arise connected with Father Gerard's landing and residence in Norfolk will be found in a note appended to this chapter, kindly drawn up some years ago by the Reverend Dr. Jessopp, now Rector of Scarning, who unites to his accurate local knowledge a singularly wide acquaintance with the recusant families of the county.

We then ordered the ship to anchor off that point until dark ; and in the first watch we were put ashore in the boat and left there, whereupon the ship immediately set sail and departed. We remained there awhile commending ourselves in prayer to God's providence ; then we sought out some path which might lead us further inland, at a greater distance from the sea, before the day should dawn. But the night being dark and cloudy we could not strike out any path that would lead us to the open country, but every way we tried always brought us to some dwelling, as we were made aware by the barking of the dogs. As this happened some two or three times, we began to fear lest we might rouse some of the inhabitants, and be seized as thieves or burglars. We therefore turned into a neighbouring wood, where we proposed to rest during the night. But the rain and the cold (for it was about the end of October [or rather, November]) rendered sleep impossible, nor did we dare to speak aloud to one another as the wood was in the neighbourhood of a house, but we deliberated in whispers whether to set out together for London or to part company, so that if one were taken the other might escape. Having pondered the reasons on both sides, we determined to set forth each by himself, and to take different routes.

"At day-dawn, then, we cast lots who should first leave the wood, and the lot fell on the good Father who was also the first to leave this world for Heaven. We then made an equal division of what money we had, and after embracing and receiving one from the other a blessing, the future martyr went along the sea-shore to a neighbouring town, where he fell in with some sailors who were thinking of going to London. Being prudent and cautious, he strove by cheerfulness to accommodate himself to their humours in indifferent things. But twice or thrice he could not withhold from reproving their coarse and filthy language, though he imperilled himself by so doing, as he afterwards told me. And indeed his zeal in this matter was very great, as is proved by many accounts which I have often heard related.

"One instance may serve for all. Father Oldcorne while in London visited a certain Catholic gentleman who was greatly attached to him. On the window of his room was painted an improper picture of Mars and Venus; and although the house was not the property of his friend, but rented by him, the Father could not endure such an object, so he struck his fist through the pane, and told his host how unbecoming it was to allow such things to remain. Such was this good Father's zeal for God's honour, and his love of truth. Joining himself then to the aforesaid sailors, he knew how to combine the prudence of the serpent with the simplicity of the dove, and behaved himself in such sort that though he did not conceal that the evil he saw in them was displeasing to him, yet evil as they were he won their esteem, and by their means, and the protection they unwittingly afforded, he was enabled to reach London without molestation; for the watchers, who were in almost every town through which he passed, taking him to be one of the party, cared not to annoy those whose appearance and carriage distinguished them so completely from those for whom they were keeping watch.

"When my companion had departed I too set out, but by a different road. I had not gone far before I saw some country folks coming towards me. I went up to them and inquired about a stray falcon, whether they had heard the tinkling of his bells. For I wanted them to think that I had lost a falcon, and was going through the country in search of it, as is usual with those who have sustained such a loss, so that they might not wonder why I was strange to the country, and had to ask my way. They, of course, had neither seen nor heard any such thing of late, and seemed sorry that they could not direct my search. I then went with a disappointed air to examine the neighbouring trees and hedges, as if to look for my bird. Thus I was able, without awakening suspicion, to keep clear of the highway, and to get further and further from the sea shore, by going across country. Whenever I saw any one in a field I went up to him and put the same series of questions about the falcon, concealing thereby my anxiety to keep out of the public roads and villages, where I knew sentinels were posted with power to examine every stranger. I thus managed to expend the best part of that day, walking some eight or ten miles, not in a straight line, but by doubling and returning frequently on my steps. At length, being quite soaked with rain, and exhausted with hunger and fatigue, for I had scarcely been able to take any food or rest on board ship for the tossing of the waves, I turned into a village inn which lay in my road, for those who go to the inns are less liable to be questioned.

"There I refreshed myself well, and found mine host very agreeable, especially as I wanted to buy a pony he had in his stable. I concluded the bargain at a reasonable price, for the owner was not very rich; but I took it as a means of more speedy and safer transit, for foot-passengers are frequently looked upon as vagrants, and even in quiet times are liable to arrest.

"Next morning I mounted my pony and turned towards Norwich, the capital of that county. I had scarce ridden two miles when I fell in with the watchers at the entrance of a village, who bade me halt, and began to ask me who I was and whence I came. I told them that I was the servant of a certain lord who lived in a neighbouring county (with whom I was well acquainted, though he was unknown to them), that my falcon had flown away, and that I had come to this part of the country to recover him if he should have been found. They found no flaw in my story, yet they would not let me go, but said I must

be brought before the constable and the beadle,[1] who were
both in church at the time, at their profane heretical
service. I saw that I could neither fly nor resist, nor could
I prevail with these men, so yielding to necessity I went
with them as far as the churchyard. One of the party
entered the church and brought word that the beadle
wished me to come into the church, and that he would see
me when service was over. I replied that I would wait for
him where I was. 'No, no,' said the messenger, 'you must
go into church.' 'I shall stop here,' I returned, 'I don't
want to lose sight of my horse.' 'What!' said the man,
'you won't dismount to go and hear the Word of God! I
can only warn you that you will make no very favourable
impression ; as to your horse, I myself will engage to get
you a better one, if you are so anxious about him.' 'Go
and tell him,' said I, 'that if he wants me, either he must
come at once or I will wait here.' As soon as my message
was taken to him, the beadle came out with some others
to examine me. I could easily see he was not best
pleased. He began by demanding whence I came. I
answered by naming certain places which I had learnt
were not far off ; to his questions as to my name, condition,
dwelling, and business, I made the same answers as above.
He then asked whether I had any letters with me ; on
which I offered to allow him to search my person. This
he did not do, but said he should be obliged to take me
before the Justice of the Peace.[2] I professed my readiness
to go, should he deem it needful, but that I was in a hurry
to get back to my master after my long absence, so that if
it could be managed I should be better pleased to be
allowed to go on. At first he stood to his resolution, and
I saw nothing for it but to go before the Justice and to be
committed to gaol, as doubtless would have been the case.

---

[1] *Ad subcuratorem pacis, et ad censorem.* MS. The above are conjectural
renderings. These seem to have been only village officials.

[2] *Irenarchâ aut curatore pacis.* MS.

But suddenly looking at me with a calmer countenance, he said, 'You look like an honest man : go on in God's name, I don't want to trouble you any more.'

"Nor did God's providence abandon me in my further journey. As I rode onward towards the town I saw a young man on horseback with a pack riding on before me. I wanted to come up with him, so as to get information about the state of the town, and ask the fittest inn for me to put up at, and he looked like one of whom I could make such inquiries without exciting suspicion ; but his horse being better than mine I could not gain upon him, urge my pony how I would. After following him at a distance for two or three miles, it chanced by God's will that he dropped his pack, and was obliged to dismount in order to pick it up and strap it on. As I came up I found he was an unpolished youth, well fitted for my purpose. From him I acquired information that would have been very useful had any danger befallen, but, as it was, by his means the Lord so guided me that I escaped all danger. For I inquired about a good inn near the city gate, that I might not weary my horse in going from street to street in search of one. He told me there was such an inn on the other side of the city ; but that if I wanted to put up there I must go round the town. Having learnt the way thereto and the sign of the house, I thanked my informant, and left him to pursue his road, which led straight through the town, the same way I should have followed had I not met with such a guide, and in that case I should have run into certain danger, nor would any of those things have befallen which afterwards came to pass for God's greater glory and the salvation of many souls.

"Following, then, the advice of the young man, I went round the skirts of the city to the gate he had described, and as soon as I entered I saw my inn. I had rested me but a little while there when a man who seemed to be an acquaintance of the people of the house came in. After greeting me civilly, he sat down in the chimney corner and dropped some words about some Catholic gentlemen who were kept in gaol there ; and he mentioned one whose relative had been a companion of mine in the Marshalsea some seven years since.[1] I silently noted his words, and when he had gone out I asked who he might be. They answered that he was a very honest fellow in other points, but a Papist. I inquired how they came to know that. They replied that it was a well-known fact, as he had been many years imprisoned in the Castle there (which was but a stone's throw from the place where I was) ; that many Catholic gentlemen were confined there, and that he had been but lately let out. I asked whether he had abandoned the faith in order to be at large. ' No, indeed,' said they, ' nor is he likely to, for he is a most obstinate man. But he has been set free under an engagement to come back to prison when called for. He has some business with a gentleman in the prison, and he comes here pretty often on that account.' I held my tongue, and awaited his return.

"As soon as he came back, and we were alone, I told him that I should wish to speak with him apart : that I had heard that he was a Catholic, and for that reason I trusted him, as I also was a Catholic : that I had come there by a sort of chance, but wanted to get on to London : that it would be a good deed worthy of a Catholic were he to do me the favour of introducing me to some parties who might be going the same road, and who were well known, so that I might be allowed to pass on by favour of their company : that being able to pay my expenses I should be no burden to my companions. He replied that he knew not of any one who was then going to London. I hereon inquired if he could hire a person who would accompany me for a set price. He said he would look out some such one, but that he knew of a gentleman then in the town

[1] Here Father Gerard's memory is inaccurate, for it was less than five years since he was committed to the Marshalsea.

who might be able to forward my business. He went to find him, and soon returning desired me to accompany him. He took me into a shop, as if he were going to make some purchase. The gentleman he had mentioned was there, having appointed the place that he might see me before he made himself known. At length he joined us, and told my companion in a whisper that he believed I was a priest. He led us therefore to the cathedral, and having put me many questions, he at last urged me to say whether or no I was a priest, promising that he would assist me—at that time a most acceptable offer. On my side, I inquired from my previous acquaintance the name and condition of this third party [Edward Yelverton of Grimston [1]]; and on learning it, as I saw God's providence in so ready an assistance, I told him I was a priest of the Society who had come from Rome. He performed his promise, and procured for me a change of clothes, and made me mount a good horse, and took me without delay into the country to the house of a personal friend, leaving one of his servants to bring on my little pony.

"The next day we arrived at his house, where he and his family resided, together with a brother of his [Charles Yelverton] who was a heretic. They had with them a widowed sister [Jane, the widow of Edward Lumner], also a heretic, who kept house for them, so that I was obliged to be careful not to give any ground for them to suspect my calling. The heretic brother at my first coming was very suspicious, seeing me arrive in his Catholic brother's company unknown as I was, and perceiving no reason why the latter should make so much of me. But after a day or so he quite abandoned all mistrust, as I spoke of hunting and falconry with all the details that none but a practised person could command. For many make sad blunders in attempting this, as Father Southwell, who was afterwards my companion in many journeys, was wont to

[1] See Dr. Jessopp's note at the end of the chapter.

complain. He frequently got me to instruct him in the technical terms of sport, and used to complain of his bad memory for such things, for on many occasions when he fell in with Protestant gentlemen he found it necessary to speak of these matters, which are the sole topics of their conversation, save when they talk obscenity, or break out into blasphemies and abuse of the saints or the Catholic faith. In these cases it is of course desirable to turn the conversation to other subjects, and to speak of horses, of hounds, and such like. Thus it often happens that trifling covers truth,[1] as it did with me on this occasion.

"After a short sojourn of a few days I proposed to my newly-found friend, the Catholic brother, my intention of going to London to meet my Superior. He therefore provided me with a horse, and sent a servant along with me, begging me at the same time to obtain leave to return to that county, and to make his house my home, for he assured me that I should bring over many to the faith were I to converse with them publicly as he had seen me do. I pledged myself to lay his offer before Father Garnet, and said that I would willingly return if he should approve of it. So I departed, and arrived in London without accident, having met with no obstacle on the road. I have gone into these particulars to show how God's providence guarded me on my first landing in England; for without knowing a single soul in that county, where until then I had never set foot, as it was far distant from my native place, on the very first day I found a friend who not only saved me from present peril, but afterwards, by introducing me to the principal families in the county, furnished an opportunity for many conversions; and from the acquaintance I then made, and the knowledge the Catholics in those parts had of me in consequence, all that God chose hereafter to do by my weakness took its origin, as will appear by the sequel."

[1] *Ut vanitas veritatem occultet.* MS.

NOTE TO CHAPTER III.

BY THE REVEREND AUGUSTUS JESSOPP, D.D.

I. AT what point on the coast of Norfolk did John Gerard land, and by what road did he reach Norwich?

1. He landed at a part of the coast where a vessel could ride at anchor close to the shore, and where a boat could "conveniently" put a passenger ashore even in the dark. This excludes Yarmouth (which for other reasons could not have been the place of landing), and also excludes any spot on the coast from Blakeney to Lynn. It also excludes Weybourn, where the landing is at all times dangerous, and there only remains the coast between Sherringham and Happisburgh.

2. But any one landing between Sherringham and Bacton would find himself to the north of Aylsham and North Walsham, and travelling on the high road (as it is plain Gerard did), he must needs pass through one or the other of these towns, as it is plain Gerard did *not*. This narrows the part of the coast on which the landing took place to the three or four miles between Happisburgh and Bacton, and I am inclined to place the landing point at or near the latter place. There were dwellings close to the shore, and many of them, so that wherever Gerard turned, he came upon a house, and this would certainly hold good of Bacton; added to which is the consideration that close to this place stood the Priory of Bromholme, with its church, two hundred feet long then, and still (though now in ruins) a landmark for vessels at sea.

3. Carefully picking his way, he stopped at a *village* five or six miles from his place of landing. Assuming the landing place to be Bacton, this would bring him to Honing, Dilham, or Stalham, on the way to Norwich. He would have left North Walsham well to his right, and some four miles behind him. At this village he spent the night, and bought his pony.

4. Next morning he proceeds on his way, and after a couple of miles' riding, he comes upon another village, evidently on the road to Norwich. The "constable" and "beadle" are both in the church, and it is fair to infer from this that the place was

of some size and importance, and the church a church of some
pretension. It is probable that this village was the village of
Worsted, a large village, with the remains of the woollen manu-
facturers still languishing there, even in Queen Elizabeth's time,
and a church which is one of the grandest in the county at the
present day.   Here Gerard was detained.

5. Worsted is about thirteen miles from Norwich.   On being
released from the clutches of the beadle, who probably knew
that a justice of the peace was far to seek in this neighbourhood,
Gerard pushed on, and fell in with the man with the pack,
and on his asking advice about an inn, he is told that he must
"make a circuit of the city before he can get at the inn named."
Coming from Bacton through Stalham and Worsted, it is clear
that he must have been on the high road from either Holt or
North Walsham.   It may have been either, and it would have
been prudent after being stopped on the latter road to make
across country to the former.   At any rate, he was making for
one of the northern gates of the city, either the Magdalen or
St. Augustine's gate—probably the latter.   Turning down from
the high ground, now called Upper Hellesdon, he would drop
down to Heigham, and skirting the city, would strike the old
wall, which is still in part standing, and which bounds Chapel
Fields, and leaving St. Giles' gates behind him, would enter the
city by the "Brazen Gates," as they were called, close to the
present militia barracks, and in a couple of hundred yards further
on would find his inn, which was clearly one of those many inns
that even to this day cluster round the Market Hill, and all
"within a stone's throw" of the Castle.   Here he made his
first acquaintance.

II. Who was this acquaintance?

The person in question had been many years in prison;
he was very obstinate; he had been lately let out of the Castle
under an engagement to come back to prison when called for,
and he had business with a gentleman who was detained in
prison.

Now there were six or seven of the recusant gentry of Norfolk
detained in the Castle at Norwich as early as 1580; and, indeed,

one or two of them in 1578. These gentlemen appear to have
had a common room and common table, and to have lived
pretty much as the recusants subsequently lived at Wisbech and
Ely. They were in some danger of getting into great trouble
in 1580, as may be seen in Strype's *Annals*,[1] and their names
then were: (1) Robert Downes, (2) Michael Hare, (3) Roger
Martin, (4) Humphrey Bedingfeld, (5) Edward Sulliard.

Mr. Martin and Mr. Sulliard were Suffolk gentlemen, and
their names disappeared from the lists of Norfolk recusants
shortly after this time, only to appear among the Suffolk men.
Besides these five, there were others who were in the Castle, viz.,
Ferdinando Paris, Robert Gray—(there was a man of this name
in the Marshalsea with Gerard)—Walter Norton, and Robert
Lovell. It is hardly necessary to say that they were all men
of substance, and able to pay their way. At a meeting[2] of the
Privy Council at St. James', on the 25th of August, 1588, order is
taken that a letter be written the Bishop of Norwich to "inform
himself of the behaviour of James Bradshaw, keeper of the gaol
at Norwich, being complained of to have given more liberty to
such [as] are obstinate recusants than is fit," &c. And on the
18th of October again, a letter is to be sent to the Sheriff of
Norfolk, for that their lordships understand that the recusants
that are prisoners in the common gaol within that county do
much harm and infect the county by the liberty which they enjoy
there." Accordingly they are to be delivered to the custody of
Gray, keeper of Wisbech, &c. This order was apparently never
executed, though the names of the gentry are given, viz.: (1)
Walter Norton, (2) *George* Downes, (3) Ferdinando Paris, (4)
Robert Lovell, (5) Humphrey Bedingfeld, (6) Robert Gray. I
say this was not executed, for I find Ferdinando Paris was never
sent to Wisbech at all, and *was* sent to Ely in March $\frac{89}{90}$, and
that all the rest were at Norwich in the Castle as late as the 5th
of April, 1590, and I have strong reason for believing that they
were never sent out of the county at all.

These men occasionally had liberty to go out on business,
giving bail for their reappearance, thus, *e.g.*, "A warrant[3] to the

---

[1] Vol. ii. part ii. p. 634.   [2] Privy Council Book.
[3] Privy Council Book, 7th January, 1587-8.

keeper of Norwich Gaol to take bonds of Walter Norton, gent., remaining prisoner under his custody with two sufficient sureties in the sum of 1,000*l.* to her Majesty's use, with condition to return himself prisoner at the end of one month following into his custody, and thereupon to set him forthwith at liberty." Again, 20th March, 1588–9 : "A letter to the High Sheriff of Norfolk. Whereas Humphrey Bedingfeld, gent., hath been long time a prisoner for recusancy in Norwich Gaol . . . He was required to take order that Bedingfeld might be delivered to the custody of Mr. Rowe, parson of Quidenham, to remain with him," &c. It will be noticed that the last list of names of prisoners in the Castle in October, 1588, instead of *Robert* Downes the name of *George* Downes occurs.[1]

Was the *first* acquaintance Robert Downes ?

III. I have pleased myself with the conjecture that the gentleman alluded to as *in the Castle* was Ferdinando Paris.[2] He had a house at Pudding Norton, in the neighbourhood of the Walpoles, Yelvertons, and others with whom I feel sure Gerard was brought into close relations by and by. *If this were so,* the fact of Ferdinando Paris having some business to transact in connection with his property, might account for a neighbour of his being in Norwich on the day when Gerard arrived there ; that neighbour being come up perhaps to meet Downes on Paris' business.

IV. Who was this neighbour ? That is to say, who was the *second* acquaintance whom Father Gerard made in Norwich, whose house afterwards became his head-quarters in the county ?

1. He lived two days' journey from Norwich.

2. He lived with a brother of his who was a heretic.

3. He had as a housekeeper a widowed sister, also a heretic.

4. And he had a married sister, whose husband was "a man of rank" with "great possessions."

[1] This is certainly a mistake ; *Robert* Downes had indeed a younger brother *George*, but he was dead before this time, and he lived, not in Norfolk, but in Herefordshire.

[2] He was afterwards knighted. I cannot tell when and where, but in some MSS. in Pembroke College, Cambridge, which came from him, he is repeatedly styled Sir Ferdinando Paris.

Now it must be remembered that Father Gerard wrote his account of these events twenty years after their occurrence, and it may well happen, indeed it is almost inevitable, that there must have been some confusion in such matters of detail as *dates* and *family relationships*. With this consideration to serve as a caution against requiring too faithful a record and too minute a correspondence between the assertions made and the facts that may crop up in examining such evidence as we have at hand, I proceed to deal with this further problem. But before doing so I must add another caution. The evidence which Heralds' pedigrees furnish us with are, as a rule, very untrustworthy, and in the matter of *dates* especially are very little to be relied on. Where family alliances are recorded, the dates of marriages, births, and deaths are of very secondary importance : the names of the persons entering into matrimonial contracts are the main thing in the eye of the genealogist.

I believe and feel morally certain that the person indicated by Father Gerard as having afforded him his first asylum in Norfolk was Edward Yelverton of Grimston, and that he had at this time living with him his brother Charles, who was afterwards knighted, and his half-sister Jane, who had become a widow in that very year 1588 by the death of her husband Edward Lumner of Mannington, Esq. He was then himself about thirty years of age, and he was a widower, having lost his first wife shortly after his marriage. His second wife was Nazareth, daughter of Edmund Bedingfeld, Esq. This Edward Yelverton was the son of William Yelverton of Rougham, Esq. He was the eldest son of a second family, the father having married first Anne, daughter of Sir Henry Farmour of Basham, co. Norfolk, and secondly Jane, daughter of Edmund Cockett of Hampton, co. Suffolk. The old man died in 1586, and by his will appears to have done his utmost to provide for his second family as well as for the first, insomuch that a dispute arose on the interpretation of the will, and the matter being brought before the Lords of the Privy Council in 1587, they referred the cause to three arbitrators, who I suppose settled it without letting the litigants go into court. At his father's death in 1586 Edward Yelverton inherited, in virtue of a marriage settlement, a considerable estate

E

in Grimston and the adjoining parishes, extending over about
five thousand acres. The two families numbered at least fifteen
children, and in the pedigrees considerable confusion has arisen,
and many inaccuracies are to be found, some of which I am in
a position to correct.

Of the brothers, one *Christopher* Yelverton was nominated a
Judge of the Queen's Bench on the 2nd February, 1602.

Of the sisters, one whose name was Jane was married to
Edward Lumner of Mannington, and left a widow in 1588.

Another was married to Sir Philip Woodhouse, son and heir
of Sir Roger Woodhouse of Kimberley.

"Two of my father's sisters are still alive," their nephew
Charles Yelverton wrote in 1601,[1] "of whom one, Grisel, is
the wife of Sir Philip Woodhouse, knight; the other, Jane, is
the widow of Robert [Edward] Lumner. Both were Catholics,
but one of them [Lady Woodhouse] on account of her husband's
violence, which often used to break out against her, has lately
relapsed into heresy."

I find in a Recusant Roll of the 34th Elizabeth (1592), among
the names of those from whom fines are due, the following two
consecutive entries :

"*Jane Lumner*, nuper de Kymberley, vidua *cccl.* pro consimili.

"*Nazareth Yelverton*, nuper de Sandringham, uxor Edwardi
Yelverton de eadem generosi, *cccl.* pro consimili."

It may be asked, why should Jane Lumner be described as
of Kimberley? The answer is obvious. Her sister Grisel, being
the wife of Sir Philip Woodhouse, might reasonably have been
expected to be able to afford her some protection, the Wood-
houses being powerful people in Norfolk and serving the office
of High Sheriff for the county again and again.

But who was the "man of high rank" whom one of the
sisters of his host had married? I can hardly doubt that it was
this Sir Philip Woodhouse to whom Gerard alludes: and,
"reading between the lines," I can hardly resist the conviction
that Grisel, and afterward Sir Philip, became his converts, though
as time went on they both "fell back."

Once more: On one occasion one of the ladies alluded to

[1] *Records of the English Province*, by Brother Foley, S.J., vol. i. p. 143.

held anxious converse with Dr. Perne, who was master of Peter-
house, Cambridge, when Edward Yelverton, Philip Woodhouse,
Henry and Edward Walpole were there as undergraduates, and
died April 26, 1589. Dr. Perne was born at East Bilney, the
next parish to Rougham, the ancestral seat of the Yelvertons, and
he had an estate at Pudding Norton in the same neighbourhood.
He must have known the Yelvertons and Walpoles from their
childhood. Add to this that Nazareth, wife of Edward Yelverton,
was a daughter of Edmund Bedingfeld of Oxburgh; that Grimston or Appleton or Sandringham—at which places Edward
Yelverton appears to have lived[1] between 1588 and 1596—are
all within four or five miles of Houghton and Anmer;
that the Walpoles both of Houghton and Anmer were apparently among the first who resorted to Gerard in his new home,
and one of them at least served Father Gerard as a most
faithful and devoted "esquire;" that Henry Walpole, as his
letters show, in 1590 knew all about Gerard's movements in
Norfolk, and was in direct communication with "Ned Yelverton"
at the time; that the Townshends of Rainham, the Cobbs of
Sandringham, the Bastards of Dunham, the Bozouns of Whisson-
sett, the Kerviles of Wiggenhall, and many others of less note
and importance, who figure in the Recusant Rolls, were all within
a ten miles' ride of Grimston—and the *cumulative* evidence of
Edward Yelverton of Grimston having been Gerard's host and
protector in Norfolk, becomes so strong as almost to amount to
a demonstration.

A. JESSOPP.

December 28, 1875.

[1] Recusant Rolls *penes me.*

CHAPTER IV.

RESIDENCE IN NORFOLK.

1588 and 1589.

"On my arrival in London,[1] by the help of certain Catholics I discovered Father Henry Garnet, who was then Superior. Besides him, the only others of our Society then in England were Father Edmund Weston [William Weston, commonly called Father Edmunds], confined at Wisbech (who, had he been at large, would have been Superior), Father Robert Southwell, and we two new-comers.

"My companion, Father Oldcorne, had already arrived, so the Superior was rather anxious on my account, as nothing had been heard of me; but yet for that very reason hopes were entertained of my safety. It was with exceeding joy on both sides that we met at last. I stayed some time with the Fathers, and we held frequent consultations as to our future proceedings. The good Superior gave us excellent instructions as to the method of helping and gaining souls, as did also our dear Father Southwell, who much excelled in that art, being at once prudent, pious, meek, and exceedingly winning. As Christmas [1588] was nigh at hand, it was necessary to separate, both for the consolation of the faithful, and because the dangers are always greater in the great solemnities.

"I returned then to my friend in the county where I was first set ashore. This time the Superior provided me

[1] "Father Oldcorne and he [Father Gerard] met at London according to their appointment, and by good hap found the Superior [Father Garnet] then in London, though his ordinary abode were then [1588] in Warwickshire, almost a hundred miles from London." Father Gerard's Powder Plot, *Condition of Catholics*, p. 282.

with clothes and other necessaries, that I might not be a
burden to my charitable host at the outset. But afterwards, throughout the whole period of my missionary
labours, the fatherly providence of God supplied both for
me and for some others. My dress was of the same
fashion as that of gentlemen of moderate means. The
necessity of this was shown by reason and subsequent
events ; for, from my former position, I was more at ease
in this costume, and could maintain a less embarrassed
bearing than if I had assumed a character to which I was
unaccustomed. Then, too, I had to appear in public, and
meet many Protestant gentlemen, with whom I could not
have held communication with a view to lead them to a
love of the faith and a desire of virtue had I not adopted
this garb. I found it helped me, not only to speak more
freely and with greater authority, but to remain with
greater safety, and for a longer interval of time, in any
place or family to which my host introduced me as his
friend and acquaintance.

"Thus it happened that I remained for six or eight
months [of 1589], with some profit to souls, in the family
of my first friend and host ; during which time he took
me with him to nearly every gentleman's house in the
county. Before the eight months were passed I gained
over and converted many to the Church ; among whom
were my host's brother [Charles], his two sisters [Jane
Lumner and Grisel Woodhouse] and, later on, his brother-
in-law [Sir Philip Woodhouse]. One of these two sisters,
as I have before mentioned, was my friend's housekeeper, and had been all along a notable Calvinist.
Her brother[1] is a judge, who even now is the

---

[1] *In quibus erat unus frater hospitis mei, et sorores duo, et postea maritus
sororis: quarum una erat illa vidua quæ erat in domo ejus ut materfamilias, et
erat sane antea insignis Calvinista. Item soror cujusdam judicis, qui partes
Calvini maxime fere omnium adhuc tuetur.* MS. The translation of the
latter portion of this ran thus as originally published, "I reconciled moreover
the sister of a judge, &c." This was the chief difficulty in Dr Jessopp's way

most firm support of the Calvinist party.[1] This lady, having been brought up in his house, had been strongly imbued with this heresy. A very remarkable thing had happened to her some time previously. Being very anxious as to the state of her soul, she went to a certain doctor of the University of Cambridge, of the name of Perne,[2] who she knew had changed his religion some three or four times under different sovereigns, but yet was in high repute for learning. Going to this Doctor Perne, then, who was an intimate friend of her family, she conjured him to tell her honestly and undisguisedly what was the sound orthodox faith whereby she might attain Heaven. The doctor finding himself thus earnestly appealed to by a woman of discretion and good sense, replied, 'I conjure you never to disclose to another what I am going to say. Since, then, you have pressed me to answer as if I had to give account of your soul, I will tell you that you can, if you please, *live* in the religion now professed by the Queen and her whole kingdom, for so you will live more at ease, and be exempt

in identifying the family of Father Gerard's first host. The words of the narrative may be purposely ambiguous, in order that the mention of Justice Yelverton might not betray the family; but it may well be taken as we have now rendered it. There was a reason why Jane Lumner, the widow, should be called the sister of Sir Christopher, which does not apply to Edward Yelverton or to Grisel Lady Woodhouse, for Jane and Christopher were children of William Yelverton by the first marriage, and Edward and Grisel of the second. *One Generation,* p. 151. The original phrase, *et postea maritus sororis,* shows us that the brother-in-law was not converted within the eight months. No doubt he was Sir Philip Woodhouse, who is described afterwards as *vir magnus et potens.*

[1] The name Yelverton is added in the margin. Sir Christopher Yelverton was at this time Queen's Serjeant, and subsequently Speaker of the House of Commons and Puisne Judge of the King's Bench. He died in 1607, though Gerard, writing at Louvain in 1609, did not know it. His son, Sir Henry Yelverton, Judge of the Court of Common Pleas, condemned Father Edmund Arrowsmith in 1628, and died a few months after. Father Arrowsmith was Father John Gerard's first cousin once removed, the martyr's father, Robert Arrowsmith, having married Margery Gerard, the daughter of Nicholas, John Gerard's uncle.

[2] Dr. Andrew Perne, Master of Peter-house, Cambridge, and second Dean of Ely.

from all the vexations the Catholics have to undergo ; but by no means *die* out of the faith and communion of the Catholic Church if you would save your soul.' Such was the answer of this poor man, but such was not his practice ; for putting off his conversion from day to day, it fell out that, when he least expected, on his return home from dining with the pseudo-Archbishop of Canterbury, he dropped down dead as he was entering his apartment, without the least sign of repentance or of Christian hope of that eternal bliss which he had too easily promised to himself and to others after a life of a contrary tendency. She to whom he gave the above-mentioned advice was more fortunate than he, and though she at first by no means accepted his estimate of the Catholic faith, yet later on, having frequently heard from me that the Catholic faith alone was true and holy, she began to have doubts, and in consequence brought me an heretical work which had served to confirm her in her heresy, and showed me the various arguments it contained. I, on the other hand, pointed out to her the quibbles, the dishonest quotations from Scripture and the Fathers, and the mis-statement of facts which the book contained. And so, by God's grace, from the scorpion itself was drawn the remedy against the scorpion's sting, and she has lived ever since constant in her profession of the Catholic faith, to which she then returned.

"I must not omit mentioning an instance of the wonderful efficacy of the sacraments, as shown in the case of the married sister of my host [Lady Wood-house]. She had married a man of considerable position, and, being favourably inclined to the Church, she had been so well prepared by her brother, that it cost me but little labour to make her a child of the Catholic Church. After her conversion she endured much from her husband when he found that she refused to join in heretical worship, but her patience withstood and over-came all. It happened on one occasion that she was so exhausted after a difficult and dangerous labour, that her life was despaired of. A clever physician was at once brought from Cambridge, who on seeing her said that he could indeed give her medicine, but that he could give no hopes of her recovery, and having prescribed some remedies, he left. I was at that time on a visit to the house, having come, as was my wont, with her brother. The master of the house was glad to see us, although he well knew we were Catholics, and used in fact to confer with me on religious subjects. I had nearly convinced his understanding and judgment, but the will was rooted to the earth, 'for he had great possessions.' But being anxious for his wife, whom he dearly loved, he allowed his brother to persuade him, as there was no longer any hope for her present life, to allow her all freedom to prepare for the one to come. With his permission, then, we promised to bring in an old priest[1] on the following night; for those priests who were ordained before Elizabeth's reign were not exposed to such dangers and penalties as the others.[2]

[1] Anthony Tyrrel in September, 1586, names " Redman, *alias* Redshawe, an aged man, made priest in Queen Mary's time," and " Moore, an old man, priest in King Henry's time," as serving the Catholics in Norfolk. P.R.O., *Domestic, Elizabeth*, vol. cxciii. n. 13.

[2] The Act of the 27th of Elizabeth, under which most of the martyrs were put to death after the year 1584, in which it was passed, applied to those who were ordained after the feast of St. John the Baptist in the first year of the Queen's reign, and thus the Marian priests were exempted from its operation. But they fell under the other penal laws, which were severe enough. It was high treason by the 1st Elizabeth to maintain the power or jurisdiction of any foreign prelate or potentate within these realms, on a third conviction. By the 5th Elizabeth the first conviction brought the penalty of *premunire*, and to refuse the oath of supremacy after such a conviction, or on a second tender of the oath was high treason. By the 13th Elizabeth, suing for or using Bulls from the Bishop of Rome was high treason. By the 23rd Elizabeth withdrawing any from the religion established was high treason, and saying Mass was punished with a fine of 200 marks and imprisonment. James Bell, who suffered at Lancaster, April 20, 1584, was the only one of the priests of Queen Mary's time who was condemned to death in virtue of these statutes, but their names are sometimes found in the prison lists with other priests. Owing to the kindness of Canon Toole we are able to give the following interesting extract from the register of deaths of Manchester Cathedral, formerly the Collegiate Church. " 1581, August 7. Richard Smith, an old pryst. Died in p[ri]son in the Fleete for religion."

We therefore made use of his ministry in order that this
lady might receive all the rites of the Church. Having
made her confession and been anointed, she received the
holy Viaticum ; and, behold, in half an hour's time she so
far recovered as to be wholly out of danger ; the disease
and its cause had vanished, and she had only to recover
her strength. The husband, seeing his wife thus snatched
from the jaws of death, wished to know the reason. We
told him that it was one of the effects of the holy
sacrament of Extreme Unction, that it restored bodily
health when Divine Wisdom saw that it was expedient
for the good of the soul. This was the cause of his
conversion ; for admiring the power and efficacy of the
sacraments of the true Church, he allowed himself to be
persuaded to seek in that Church the health of his own
soul. I, being eager to strike the iron while it was hot,
began without delay to prepare him for confession ; but
not wishing just then that he should know me for a priest,
I said that I would instruct him as I had been instructed
by priests in my time. He prepared himself, and awaited
the priest's arrival. His brother-in-law told him that this
must be at night-time. So, having sent away the servants
who used to attend him to his chamber, he went into the
library, where I left him praying, telling him that I would
return directly with the priest. I went down stairs and
put on my cassock, and returned so changed in appearance
that he, never dreaming of any such thing, was speechless
with amazement. My friend and I showed him that our
conduct was necessary, not so much in order to avoid
danger, but in order to cheat the devil and to snatch
souls from his clutches. He well knew, I said, that I could
in no other way have conversed with him and his equals,
and without conversation it was impossible to bring round
those who were so ill-disposed. The same considerations
served to dispel all anxieties as to the consequences of my
sojourn under his roof. I appealed to his own experience,

and reminded him that though I had been in continual contact with him, he had not once suspected my priestly character. He thus became a Catholic ; and his lady, grateful to God for this two-fold blessing, perseveres still in the faith, and has endured much since that time from the hands of heretics. [1]

"Besides these, I reconciled to the Church during the period of my appearance in public more than twenty fathers and mothers of families, equal, and some even superior, in station to the above mentioned. For prudence' sake I omit their names. As for poor persons and servants, I received a great many, the exact number I do not re-member. It was my good fortune, moreover, to confirm many weak and pusillanimous souls. I also received numbers of general confessions. Many, too, received at that time the inspiration to a more perfect life, among whom I may mention the present Father Edward Walpole, [2] professed of three vows, who was then living a good and pious life, and had to endure much for conscience' sake, and not from strangers only, 'for his enemies were those of his own household.' He was heir to a large estate, but his father was a Calvinist, and the rest of his family were also heretics. His father at his death disinherited him, and divided the estate between his younger brother and his mother, who was to hold one-half during her life-time, so that his only share was a yearly revenue of four hundred florins [40*l.*], on which he was then living. His father's house was less a home than a prison. He lived there without

---

[1] It is clear that Father Gerard knew, when he wrote this, that Sir Philip Woodhouse had relapsed ; but he did not know that Lady Woodhouse also, "on account of the madness of her husband, which very frequently broke out against her, had lately fallen from the Church." So her nephew Charles Yelverton stated when admitted into the English College at Rome in 1601. *One Generation of a Norfolk House*, p. 209. *Records of the English Province*, vol. i. p. 142.

[2] All that is known about the Walpoles, and among them about Edward and his cousin Michael, will be found, admirably told by Dr. Jessopp, in his *One Generation of a Norfolk House.*

seeing or speaking to any one save at meals ; the rest of
the day he spent in his room, and he diligently read the
Fathers and Doctors, as he had already studied humanities
and philosophy at Cambridge. At that time he began to
visit me, and to frequent the sacraments. He thus obtained
that vocation which he followed a year after, when he went
to Rome and entered the Society. He persuaded his
cousin, Michael Walpole, who is now professed of the four
vows, to accompany him. At this period of my story the
latter was my assistant, and used to go with me as my
confidential servant to the houses of those gentlemen with
whom it was necessary for me to maintain such a position.
The two cousins are now zealous labourers in the Lord's
vineyard, and by their great abilities have made up for
what my neglect or mediocrity has marred or left undone.

"After some six or seven months I received a visit
from a Catholic gentleman of another county, a relative
of one of my spiritual children, who was very desirous to
make acquaintance with a Jesuit. He was a devout young
man, and heir to a pretty considerable estate, one half of
which came into his possession by his brother's death, the
other portion being held for life by his mother, who was a
good Catholic widow lady. Her son lived with her, and
they kept a priest in the house. He had then sold a
portion of the estate, and devoted the proceeds to pious
uses, for he was fervent and full of charity. After the
lapse of a few days, as I saw his aspirations to a higher
life and his desires of perfection wax stronger, I told him
that there were certain spiritual exercises, by means of
which a well-disposed person could discover a short road
to perfection, and be best prepared to make choice of a
state of life. He most earnestly begged to be allowed to
make them. I acceded to his request, and he made great
spiritual profit thereby, not only in that he made the best
choice, which was that he would enter the Society of
Jesus as soon as possible, but also because he made the

best and most proper arrangements to carry his purpose into execution, and to preserve meanwhile his present fervour. After his retreat, he expressed the greatest wish that I should come and live with him, and I had no rest until I proposed to submit the matter for my Superior's approval. For mine own part, I could not but reflect that my present public mode of life, though in the beginning it had its advantages, could not be long continued, because the more people I knew, and the more I was known to, the less became my safety, and the greater my distractions. Hence it was not without acknowledging God's special providence that I heard him make me this invitation. So, after having consulted with my Superior, and obtained his permission to accept the offer, I bade adieu to my old friends, and stationed a priest where they might conveniently have recourse to his ministry. He still remains there, to the great profit of souls, though in the endurance of many perils."

From an enemy we learn who Father Gerard's second host was, and the name of the place where he lived from the autumn of 1589 to that of 1591. William Watson, the priest who was executed for a plot against James I. soon after his accession, had occupied himself in attacking the Jesuits, for which he begged their pardon on the scaffold. He wrote against them a book that it was not penal to publish in England — "A Decacordon of ten Quodlibetical Questions concerning Religion and State," which was "newly imprinted in 1602." His attack on Father Gerard fortunately enables us to identify several of the persons who are not mentioned by name in the autobiography. This is the case here. "First, Father John Gerard was the man that caused Henry Drury to enter into this exercise [that is to say, to make a retreat, as Father Gerard has told us], and thereby got him to sell the manor of Losell in Suffolk and other lands to the value of 3,500*l.*, and got all the money himself, the said

Drury having chosen to be a lay-brother. Afterwards he sent him to Antwerp to have his novitiate by the Provincial there, by name Oliverius Manareus (for at that time Father Garnet had not his full authority to admit any), where after twelve or fourteen days he died, not without suspicion of some indirect dealing. Father Holt the Jesuit ascribed it unto the alteration of his diet, saying that he might have lived well enough if he had remained at home and not have come thither."[1]

We have come across a note[2] elsewhere of the use to which the proceeds of the sale of Losell were put. "The money raised by the sale of the estate of Mr. Drury, when he entered the Society, was divided amongst the clergymen in prison or otherwise in want, and among other poor Catholics labouring under persecution." In May 1587, before Father Gerard's arrival in England, "Henry Drury of Lawshull [Losell] in Suffolk, prisoner in the Marshalsea," is mentioned[3] amongst "Common receivers, harbourers and maintainers of Jesuits and Seminary priests."

[1] *Decacordon*, p. 89. This passage, with the exception of the last sentence, is quoted in *The Anatomie of Popish Tyrannie*, by Thomas Bell, the apostate priest, which was published in London in 1603 with a dedication to Tobie [Matthew, then] Bishop of Durham. This is not the only instance in which Bell quotes Watson imperfectly.

[2] *A Modest Defence of the Clergy and Religious*, 1714, p. 11.

P.R.O., *Domestic, Elizabeth*, vol. cci. n. 53.

CHAPTER V.

RESIDENCE IN SUFFOLK.

1589 to 1591.

"IN my new abode I was able to live much more quietly and more to my taste, in as much as nearly all the members of the household were Catholics; and thus it was easier for me to conform to the manner of life of the Society, both as regards dress and arrangement of my time; and moreover I had leisure to pursue my studies.

"In this house I found some matters which needed change or improvement. Among other things, the altar furniture was not only antique but antiquated, and by no means calculated to excite devotion, but rather to extinguish it. But I saw that I must be cautious, lest the chaplain, who had been some time in the house, should take offence at these changes being introduced by me, especially as he could not but notice that the master of the house followed my advice in all things. But, by God's help, all went off admirably. As for the things that required immediate attention, I took care to get the master of the house himself to propose and carry them through. Then also I showed some church ornaments that had been given to me, the beauty of which quite captivated the good widow, and made her set about making as good for herself. But this was not all: the good priest hearing the master of the house extol the Spiritual Exercises, wished to try them himself for once. He went through them with great profit, and frequently declared that until he had made them he knew not what was the duty of a priest. He conceived moreover a great attachment to me, as I afterwards experienced by his alms and the

charity he showed me when I was imprisoned; he ever
consulted me in his doubts and difficulties; he gained
thrice as many souls as before to God and His Church,
and was more esteemed of all. When an Archpriest was
at length elected, he was appointed one of his assistants,[1]
and remains so still.

"While in this residence (and I was there all but two
years) I gave much time to my studies. At times I
made missionary excursions, and not only did I reconcile
many, but I confirmed some Catholic families in the faith,
and placed two priests in stations where they might be
useful to souls. I also received many general confessions;
among others that of a widow lady of high rank, who for
the rest of her days applied herself to good works, and
gave an annual sum of one thousand florins [100*l.*] to the
Society; another widow gave seven hundred [70*l.*]"

Watson names as "gentlewomen, whom Gerard draweth
to his Exercise," " the Lady Lovel, Mistress Haywood and
Mistress Wiseman now prisoner," and he adds, "By drawing Mistress Fortescue, the widow of Master Edmund
Fortescue, into his Exercise, he got of her a farm worth
50*l.* a year and paid her no rent." If Edmund Fortescue's
widow is probably the second here mentioned by Father
Gerard, Lady Lovel was almost certainly the first. She
was Mary Roper, daughter of John, first Lord Teynham,
the widow of Sir Robert Lovel, and in 1619 she founded
the monastery of the English Teresian nuns at Antwerp.[2]
Mrs. Elizabeth Vaux, with whom Father Gerard afterwards
resided, was her sister.

[1] "The names of the six first assistants to the Archpriest were these:
1. Dr. John Baven, 2. Dr. Henry Henshaw, 3. Mr. Nicholas Tirwitt, 4. Mr.
Henry Shaw, 5. Mr. George Birket, 6. Mr. James Standish." Dr. John
Southcote's MS. *Note Book*, in the possession of the Bishop of Southwark.
Anthony Tyrrel, just three years before this, reported that the priest at Henry
Drury's, was "Hance, *alias* Draiton, brother to Hance that suffered," that is
in all probability, William the brother of Everard Hanse, who was martyred
at Tyburn July 31, 1581. P.R.O., *Domestic, Elizabeth*, vol. cxciii. n. 13.

[2] *An English Carmelite:* Life of Catharine Burton, by Father Thomas
Hunter, S.J. London, 1876, p. 6. *Troubles*, First Series, p. 255.

Here it may be well to arrest the narrative for a moment, in order to anticipate a criticism that may be made on this and similar passages of Gerard's auto-biography. Nothing could be easier than to say, in the spirit of the writers of the " Decacordon" and of the "Anatomie of Popish Tyrannie," that Father Gerard's object was money, and that he records his success osten-tatiously— a hundred pounds here, seventy pounds there. But it must be remembered that we have before us in the autobiography we are printing, a private and con-fidential report, written for his Superiors, who wished to understand exactly how the difficult and secret work of the English mission was carried on. This is why Father Gerard shows where the money came from.

That those should have given freely of their substance, who held their lives cheap in comparison with the work of restoring the Catholic faith that they themselves tena-ciously and fervently retained, is not surprising. " Is not the life more than the meat, and the body more than the raiment ? " The life of every one who harboured a priest was forfeited to the law. It was but natural that those who sheltered the priest should forward his work. Those who gave him hospitality at the risk of being hanged for it, are not likely to have begrudged him clothes to wear and horses to ride, that he might go where he was needed and mix in society without suspicion. When it was only as a gentleman that the priest could do the work that he had come to do, those that longed to see it done, took care that he went forth to it appointed as a gentleman.

The cost must have been enormous which in those days the wealthy Catholics had to meet, especially of those expenses that were defrayed by a systematic organization like the Society. In a few lines further on Father Gerard says that Father Garnet was obliged to have two or three houses always ready where his subjects might be

sure to find him; and no wonder, for at a moment's
notice the pursuivants might be upon him and he would
require immediate shelter. A large sum might be expended
upon a house and all its hiding places prepared, and
suddenly it might have to be abandoned, owing to some
act of treachery to which the Catholics were continually
exposed. Then there was provision to be made of
"Church stuff" and Catholic books. Books were necessarily dear,[1] for they were printed on the Continent, and
were seized wholesale. Church vestments and altar furniture are costly things, and they had to be constantly
replaced, for sometimes they were swept away in searches
a cartload at a time. The maintenance of the confessors
in prison, who had to pay largely to their gaolers for
exemption from the squalid miseries of the common prison,
was a constant and very heavy charge to be defrayed,
as in the days of the Roman persecutions, by their brethren
in the faith. And the supply of future clergy had to
be looked to, and promising boys were sent over to
the seminaries to be trained for the priesthood, always
at great expense. The missionaries were in duty bound
to urge on the faithful to be liberal in their almsgiving,
and to give something more than their superfluities. They
spoke to willing ears, and nothing could have been nobler
than the way in which the wealthy Catholics showed that
they held their goods, as well as their lives, for the service
of God. Watson and Bell and similar spirits delighted to
attribute this generous devotion to "the Exercise," as if
the Exercises of St. Ignatius contained what they called
"cozenage." Father Gerard would not have denied the power

---

[1] Gee says, thirty years later, that the Douay Old Testament "sold
for 40*s*., which at an ordinary price might be afforded for 10;" the Rheims
New Testament in 4to "sold for 16 or 20*s*. which might be afforded for a
noble [6*s*. 8*d*.] or less;" the same in 16mo "sold for 12*s*. which might well
be afforded for 4;" St. Augustine's Confessions, translated by Toby Matthew,
"sold for 16*s*. being but a little book in 8vo and might be afforded for 2*s*. 6*d*."
The Pseudo-Scripturist by Father Norris, S.J., "a book of some 12 sheets of
paper and sold for 5*s*." *Foot out of the Snare*, by John Gee, 1624.

F

of the Exercises to induce the resolution to. "make friends
of the mammon of iniquity;" but this, as all who have
followed the Exercises of St. Ignatius know by experience,
is only because the eternal truths assert themselves with
unparalleled force in the meditations of the Exercises. On
the subject of almsgiving St. Ignatius proposes three
rules,[1] and they are characteristically sober—"Do as you
would advise a stranger to do for the greater glory of
God : Observe the form and measure in your alms that
you would wish you had observed when you come to die :
Take that rule which at the Day of Judgment you would
wish you had taken." All the "cozenage" is in these
simple rules, and in the conclusion drawn by St. Ignatius
that "in every state of life, due proportion kept, he is
better and safer who the most restrains himself and
diminishes his expenditure on himself and the state
of his household, and most nearly approaches to our
High Priest, Example and Rule, Christ our Lord."
In other countries at this time wealthy Catholics were
founding and endowing Colleges, as they had founded and
endowed monasteries in former generations ; it was but
natural that in England those who were touched by the
sense of the eternal truths should give freely of their
wealth to promote the missionary work on which the
salvation of so many souls and the future of the country
manifestly depended.

Father Gerard therefore continues in the same strain,
but he speaks of nobler sacrifices than money. "At the
same time I gave the Spiritual Exercises to some with
considerable benefit. First I had two gentlemen who
were related to each other ; they both resolved to enter
the Society, and after they had settled their affairs, they
went to France, where, having finished their studies, one
of them, Father Thomas Everett, was admitted [into the
Society], and is now a zealous labourer in the English

---

[1] *Exercit. Spirit.* Regulæ pro distribuendis eleemosynis.

Mission ; the second took priest's orders, but being rather pusillanimous wished first to return to England, and ill came of it."

Father Thomas Everett, more usually called Everard, entered the Society at Tournay on the 4th of June, 1593, having been ordained priest in the September of the previous year. After forty years of religious life he died in the odour of sanctity at the age of seventy-three. He was several times imprisoned, and more than once sent into exile. Towards the end of his autobiography Father Gerard narrates two anecdotes of this Father's missionary life.[1]

Father Everard's relative is not named by Father Gerard, and the language of the original respecting him seems studiously obscure ; but by Watson's help he is easily identified. "Two other," he says, "had the Exercise given them at that time by Father Gerard, viz., Master Anthony Rowse, of whom he got above 1,000*l.*, and Master Thomas Everard, of whom he had many good books and other things." Father Gerard's obscurity of language is owing to the fact that Anthony Rowse abandoned the Catholic religion, and became a spy and betrayer of his brethren. He was the cause of the apprehension of the martyr Father Thomas Garnet, S.J., in 1607. It is instructive to observe that in his case, as in that of several other apostates, he had much to suffer before he fell. He was in Newgate[2] in February, 159⅞, and he was banished in 1606.[3] A neighbour in Suffolk, "Mr. Michael Hare, gave land which was sold for 300*l.*, with obligation of paying the rent of it to Mr. Rowse in case of his repentance. The rent was twenty marks a year, which Rowse enjoyed for many years. After his death it was given for the use of some of the Society helping the poor

---

[1] The documents relating to Father Thomas Everard will be found collected in Brother Foley's *Records of the English Province*, vol. ii. p. 399.

[2] *Troubles*, Second Series, p. 272, note.

[3] Challoner's *Missionary Priests*, vol. ii. p. 29.

Catholics in Suffolk or Norfolk."[1] This act of charity enables us to know that the poor man repented and persevered for many years. His mother, "widow Rowse," is named by Tyrrell with the best Catholic families of the eastern counties, among whom we find Michael Hare of Brustyard Everatt, the Drurys of Losell, the Rookwoods of Coldham Hall, Lady Lovel, and others with whom Father Gerard was in communication.[2]

We now come to the first mention of a family whose name will often recur in these pages. The Wisemans of Braddocks, in the parish of Wimbish in Essex, the elder branch of an ancient stock, are closely associated with the

---

[1] *Records of the English Province*, vol. ii. p. 483.

[2] *Troubles*, Second Series, p. 365. The name appears in the following instructive list of "Sums paid by Recusants" from Michaelmas to March 10, 1594-5. P.R.O., *Domestic, Elizabeth*, vol. ccli. n. 53.

"NORFOLK.	Edmund Townsend	...	...	28s.
	Robert Lovel	...	...	16l. 13s. 4d.
	Edward Yelverton	...	...	100s.
	Humphrey Bedingfeld	...	...	50s.
	George Willoughby	...	...	10l.
	John Yaxley	...	10l.	
	Humphrey Bedingfeld	...	...	18l. 2s. 7d.
	Eliza Bedingfeld	...	...	6l. 13s. 4d.
	Robert Gray	...	...	59l. 4. 9d.
	Id. ...	...	...	4l.
	Walter Norton, dec.	...	...	18l. 6s. 8d.
	Robert Downes	...	...	49l. 10s. 4d.
	Henry Karvile	...	...	36l. 13s. 5d.
	Ferdinando Paris	...	...	120l.
"SUFFOLK.	John Bedingfeld	...	...	7l. 13s. 4d.
	Michael Hare	...	...	140l.
	Henry Everard	...	...	16l. 19s. 8d.
	William Mannock	...	...	11l. 8s. 4d.
	Eva Yaxley	...	...	10l. 11s. 8d.
	Robert Jetter	...	...	19l. 18s. 1d.
	Roger Martin	...	...	38l. 11s. 1d.
	John and William Daniell	...	...	15l.
	Robert Rookwood	...	...	51l. 7s. 3d.
	Robert Gray	...	...	11l. 8s. 10d.
	Edward Rookwood	...	...	120l.
	Eliza Drury	...	...	100s.
	Henry Hulbert	...	...	26s. 8d.
	Edward Suliard	...	...	140l.
	Anne Rowse	...	...	30l.

life of Father John Gerard for a very considerable time. In the autumn of 1591, to which period we have now arrived, the family consisted of the mother, Jane, widow of Thomas Wiseman, whose maiden name was Vaughan ; William, the eldest son, and his wife Jane, the daughter of Sir Edmund Huddlestone ; three other sons, Thomas, John, and Robert ; and four daughters, Anne and Barbara, then at Rouen among the English Nuns of Sion, and Jane or Mary and Bridget, who were still at home.

Father Gerard first speaks of the two younger sons Thomas and John. Of John we know nothing more than Father Gerard tells, but Thomas is mentioned several times in the State Papers. In 1586 he went with his elder brother on a pilgrimage to St. Winifred's Well, and thus passing through Chester fell into the hands of a great persecutor of Catholics, William Chadderton, the Protestant bishop. Edmund Garnull, Mayor of Chester, writing[1] to Sir Francis Walsingham, September 5, 1586, about some pirates that were hindering ships from leaving Chester and Liverpool for Ireland, adds, " I have likewise thought it my duty to signify unto your honour that two gentlemen naming themselves Wiseman, being brethren, and born in Essex and coming thence (as they affirmed), were brought before me and the Lord Bishop of this diocese the last week, who alleged to have none other occasion to travel into these parts than occasioned to Hallywell [Holywell] to seek for ease of some infirmity wherewith they was detained ; and therefore, and in that we suspected their conformity in matters of religion, we sent them both to the Earl of Derby, whereof I have thought it my duty to advertise your honour."

A little later on in the year the two brothers appear in London in a " List of Bonds."[2] " November 17, 1586. Thomas Wiseman of Winsbyshe in the county of Essex,

[1] P.R.O., *Domestic, Elizabeth,* vol. cxciii. n. 14.
[2] *Ibid.* vol. cc. n. 59 ; vol. ccv. n. 13.

gentleman, bound in the sum of 50*l*. with a surety, to be
at any time forthcoming within three days' warning being
given at Richard Wiseman's house in St. Laurence's,
Poultry, in London. November 17, 1586. William Wiseman, of the same town and county, bound as abovesaid
to be forthcoming within three days' warning."

Leaving William Wiseman for a short time, we turn
to Father Gerard's account of the two younger brothers
Thomas and John. "I also gave a retreat to two fine
young men who were brothers, who both came to
the resolution of entering the Society. One of them
[Thomas Wiseman] had gone through his course of
humanities and philosophy at Cambridge, and had
been a law-student in London for nine years, and being
very clever and indefatigable in his application to study,
he made such progress that I have known competent
judges to rank an opinion of his as high as that of any
of the most celebrated lawyers, whether of past or present
times. He was so prudent and grave in his bearing, that
Father Southwell said to me, at a time when the young
man himself had never dreamt of changing his state, that
if he had a vocation to our body none would be so fit
for government as he. By the advice, then, of my host
[Henry Drury of Losell], who was an intimate friend of
theirs, they placed themselves under my direction and
went into retreat. The younger brother [John] met with no
obstacle whatever ; but the elder during the first week
was in a state of complete dryness. He afterwards found
out the reason thereof, and removed it. I had counselled
him to adopt certain regulations for the treatment of his
body, which were comparatively unimportant, and, as he
objected on the score of health, I yielded ; but afterwards
deeming this reluctance of his, though in a slight matter,
a hindrance to God's grace, one day as I visited him to
exhort and console him under his desolation, he threw
himself at my feet, and, begging pardon, refused to rise

until in token of full forgiveness I would allow him to
kiss my feet. After that he was ever overflowing with
consolation, and a light arose in his heart which showed
him so clearly the way wherein he should walk, that there
was no room left for doubt. Hence, though he had much
to do both with his own affairs and the business of others
before he could leave England, and had determined to
sell his estate, so as to preclude all desire of returning,
with such wonderful rapidity did he settle it all, that
within five or six weeks he had started with his brother
for Rome. Before his departure, among other alms-deeds,
he gave to the Society from eleven thousand to twelve
thousand florins [1,100*l.* to 1,200*l.*].

"This was a mark of God's special care for the Society
at the period it began to increase in England ; for shortly
after the capture of Father Southwell [June 30, 1592], who
was wont to reside in London, Father Garnet was obliged
to take up his abode in that city that he might the more
easily communicate with all our people, who were widely
scattered, and might himself be in a more central position,
and more easy of general access. But this entailed great
expense, for as the persecution was more violent there
than elsewhere, it was necessary that he should have two
or three houses always ready for his use, and therefore ·
kept up at his own expense. But at that time we had
few friends whose hands were open to supply our general
wants. Father Southwell, while he was with us, had
indeed a great benefactress [Anne, Countess of Arundel],
by whose liberality he maintained himself and other
priests, and kept a private house wherein he usually
received the Superior when the latter came to London.
It was here that I first saw them both ; and here also
he kept a private printing press, whence issued his incom-
parable works. But after we had lost Father Southwell,
the Society would have been reduced to great straits if God
had not called those two persons of whom I have spoken

to our assistance, to wit, the young law-student I have just mentioned [Thomas Wiseman], and my host [Henry Drury], who bestowed nearly one half of his goods upon our Society.

"The two brothers, on their arrival in Rome, went to the novitiate of St. Andrew's [on the Quirinal] without delay ; they completed their training under the names of Starkie and Standish, which they assumed as a remembrance of me, for under these I passed in the first and second county where I took up my residence. The younger of the two died holily (as I heard) at St. Andrew's ; the elder, while pursuing his studies in the Roman College, being perhaps somewhat indiscreet in his fervour, fell into consumption, and coming some time after to Belgium, died at St. Omers, to the great regret but no less to the edification of all who knew him.

"Besides these, I gave the Spiritual Exercises to some others ; who drew thence fruits of conversion and amendment of life. Two of their number were among the leading Catholics of the county ; one of them got as far as the last day but one of the second week without any spiritual motion, but at that time the south wind, so to speak, blew over his garden, and elicited such copious showers of tears, that for three or four days he could not refrain from weeping ; even when his affairs forced him to go out for a time, he could scarce speak to any one but in a broken voice with sobs ; and he followed me about weeping, like a child one year old, so that the chaplain, whom I have mentioned above, was wont thereafter to call him 'the weeper,' and to write about him— 'John the weeper wants this or that,' or—'makes you a present of so and so.' This gentleman abounded henceforth in good works, and died most happily.

"About the same time, I persuaded another of the Walpole family, Christopher[1] by name, to leave Cambridge.

---

[1] Christopher Walpole entered the English College at Rome, Feb. 22, 1592, and was admitted into the Society Sept. 27 in the same year. He died at Valladolid in 1606. *One Generation of a Norfolk House*, p. 298.

I supplied him with a provision for the journey, and sent him to Rome ; where, having completed his studies, he entered the Society and was made a priest. He was sent into Spain, and died there, to the great sorrow of all, and the great disadvantage of his country."

The date of these retreats and vocations is shown us by the following extract from a letter[1] of Father Henry Walpole, the martyr, from Brussels, to Father Holt at the English College at Rome, dated August 22, 1591. "I send you herewith two blanks [letters, apparently blank paper] from Mr. J. Gerard, the one for yourself, the other for Mr. Per[sons], that is Peckam. You must put them in fear of the fire to make them speak [that is, being written in orange juice, you must heat them in order to read them]. I suppose he hath written in commendation of them who desire to be 222 [Jesuit[2]], and came directed over to the purpose. Two be very virtuous gentlemen [Thomas and John Wiseman], and one of them a singular benefactor. They expect means to live (if it may be made over) of themselves. The third [Christopher Walpole] is my brother, who hath spent two years in your Seminary, able to begin his course. I hope he will do as well as the others. I wish them with you, if not to the great charge of the College."

The spies kept their eyes on Thomas Wiseman, but of John his brother they seem to have known nothing. Thus in a "Note of such as are known to be beyond the seas and of their friends in England, as near as is known,"[3] we have : "Thomas Wiseman, son of Mrs. Jane Wiseman of Wimbish in Essex. Thomas is a Jesuit at Rome, and two of her daughters that are nuns, and two more of her

[1] Stonyhurst MSS., *Anglia A.* vol. i. n. 58, edited by Dr. Jessopp in the *Letters of Henry Walpole.*

[2] In Father Baldwin's cypher "229" was "Jesuit." The letter will be found later.

[3] P.R.O., *Domestic, Elizabeth*, vol. ccxix. n. 77 ; incorrectly dated 1588 in the Calendar.

daughters that went over lately, and [had] Father Edmund's [William Weston's] blessing before they went."

Thomas, "who had been a law-student in London for nine years," had been a zealous Catholic for some time before he made his retreat under Father Gerard, so that a priest on his landing in England would be sure of a welcome from him. James Young, a priest, whose *aliases* were George Dingley and Thomas Christopher, stated[1] when examined by Lord Keeper Puckering on the 27th of August, 1592, that "this examinate at his first coming to London after his landing came to Thomas Wiseman's lodging at Garnet's Rents in Lincoln's Inn Field, being not sent to him by any man, but hearing one Ireland an Englishman at Civyll [Seville] give the said Roberts a token to go to the said Wiseman by, viz., that when Ireland went last from him they brake a cake between them; and by this token this examinate went to Wiseman, who received him and gave this examinate his diet and lodging for two or three nights in his lodgings at Garnet's Rents, during which time no persons repaired to him there, nor did he say any mass there then. But from thence this examinate departed to my Lady Throckmorton to her house (as he thinketh called Ripton) near Stebnethe [Stepney] within three or four days of his coming to London first as aforesaid, and there made her acquainted that he was a priest, as the said Wiseman had before let her understand, and then tarried with her about a month, being kept there very secret in a chamber, having his diet brought by one Jane her maid and by no other body; and this examinate, in a chamber in the house at the end of a gallery, did often say mass to my Lady Throckmorton and her maid, and my lady helped to say mass [that is, served mass], and the said lady at this examinate's departure gave him twenty marks, and sent him to Mr. Mompesson, a gentleman living at Clerkenwell, under pretence to be

[1] P.R.O., *Domestic, Elizabeth*, vol. ccxlii. n. 122.

tabled [boarded] there, and to make way for marriage with a young gentlewoman there called Temperance Davys; and the examinate stayed there till Christmas after, during which time he said mass to Mrs. Mompesson every Sunday, and one other named Patenson,[1] being a priest and since executed, said mass to the rest of the household, at whose masses Mr. Mompesson would stand behind the door to hear the masses and not to be seen of his servants, as though the master had not known Patenson to be a priest. And there repaired to this examinate while he was there one James Jackson of the Bishopric of Durham, and one Ffayrbek of Durham, and no more; and they well knew that this examinate was a priest, and persuaded this examinate to go down into the north and there to exercise his function, rather than here, being a dangerous place; and being a search made at that house, this examinate escaped out [of] a back door, and went to Mr. Wiseman to Garnet's Rents and told him what had happened, and tarried with him that night; who sent him to Coles a schoolmaster at the upper end of Holborn, where he this examinate stayed till Easter week last was passed; to whom during that time repaired one Mr. Stampe (as he thinks of Derbyshire). And this examinate did often in that time say mass to the said Coles and his wife, and to the said Mr. Stampe, and one Mrs. Mary Felton, dwelling at Hyegate [Highgate]. And this examinate further saith that he said mass often to Mr. Wiseman in his chamber upon the Sundays, none being present but his servant called William Smythe, a little man; and yet he remembereth that Mrs. Mary Best, dwelling in Fetter-lane, came twice to mass to Mr. Wiseman's house, and heard mass, the said Mr. Wiseman, whom she called cousin, being present. And he saith that Mr. Wiseman about Christmas last delivered to this examinate keys of his lodging to come in at all times at his pleasure, and the same keys being

---

[1] William Patenson was martyred at Tyburn, Jan. 22, 159½.

found about this examinate when he was apprehended, he
sent Mr. Wiseman word thereof, wishing him to alter the
locks presently, that it might not be known to what locks
those keys served. He saith that one Mush a priest met
this examinate in Gray's Inn Fields and told this examinate that they should both dine at Mr. Wiseman's that
day, but this examinate was apprehended before he could
come to Mr. Wiseman's. And the said Mush and one
Bell [1] also a priest (who goeth as Mush's man) are gone
down into Yorkshire, and thinketh he will remain there
about York, but at whose houses he never heard him tell ;
but Mush said to him that he had been much thereabouts,
and that the gentlemen were much fallen off, but that the
gentlewomen stood steadfastly to it.

"This examinate, being asked what Jesuit or priests he
knoweth, saith he knoweth all that have come from Rome
these seven years, as, namely, one Oldcorne, Cowper,
Garret [Gerard], Southwell, Holtby, and divers others
which this examinate knoweth if he see them and will
endeavour himself to call their names to his remembrance.
The said Cowper was with this examinate at Clerkenwell
at Mr. Mompesson's, that he resorteth much about the
Tower hill, but to what place he knoweth not.

"He saith that the Smythe, whom he named in his
letter to Mary Best to help him to his apparel, and to
let his friends know his want, was William Smythe, Mr.
Wiseman's man, and the young gentleman that should see
it conveyed without danger, so mentioned in his letter, he
meant to be the same Mr. Wiseman. And for Jones, that
should be his bail, with Sergeant Lloyd, whom Jones also
procured, this examinate had no acquaintance with either
of them, but that by means of another prisoner in the

---

[1] John Mush was the author of Mrs. Clitherow's life, and probably also of
the "Yorkshire Recusant's Relation," *Troubles*, Third Series, pp. 85, 360.
Thomas Bell became a spy. *Ibid*, p. 300. See the Queen's letter from
Hampton Court to the Earl of Derby, Oct. 30, 1592. Lord Derby's report
says : "Bell's repair to his lordship and conversation being generally known,
bred suspicion." P.R.O., *Domestic, Elizabeth*, vol. ccxliii. nn. 51, 71.

Counter, Jones was content for twenty marks to procure him bail."

In a letter[1] written on the day of this examination, Young says : " Remembering a token which I heard Father Persons speak of to one of them who came like galley slaves [this was the way in which some of the party of students to which Young belonged left Seville], I enquired for one Thomas Wiseman about the Inns of Court, with whom at last I met." And further on : " Cole being called into trouble *a little before Easter last*, I was again forced to repair to Wiseman, with whom yet I could not continue because he was to ride out of the city. Then I lay at an inn, at the White Swan at Holborn bridge, where I remained till my apprehension and bringing before Mr. Young at the beginning of Easter term last, and ever since have been prisoner in the Poultry."

It would seem from this that Thomas Wiseman did not go straight to Rome after seeing Father Walpole in Brussels in August, 1591, but returned to London perhaps to settle his money matters. In 1592 Easter day was March 26th, and by the 26th of May Thomas Wiseman and his brother John were at Rome safe in the Novitiate at St. Andrew's on the Quirinal. From a record[2] of them among the Stonyhurst manuscripts, we learn not only that Thomas took the surname of Starkey, and John that of Standish, out of affection to Father Gerard, but that they changed their Christian names also, Thomas calling himself William, after their elder brother, and John changing his name to that of their remaining brother Robert. They were respectively twenty-four and twenty-one years old when they thus entered the Society, and the record adds that Thomas died at St. Omers in 1596 and John in the Novitiate in 1592.

[1] P.R.O., *Domestic, Elizabeth,* vol. ccxlii. n. 121.

[2] " Admissi Romæ in domo probationis S. Andreæ.

" 1592, Gulielmus Starcheius alias Wiseman, 26 Maii, æt. 24, ex Anglia. Obiit Audomari 1596.

" —— Robertus Standish alias Wiseman, 26 Maii, æt. 21, ex Anglia. Obiit in Novitiatu 1592."

CHAPTER VI.

THE WISEMANS OF BRADDOCKS.

"THE elder of the above-mentioned brothers [1] [Thomas
Wiseman], before he left England, succeeded in persuading
his eldest brother [William], over whom he had great
influence, to make a trial of the Spiritual Exercises. This
gentleman was indeed a Catholic, but without the least
care for Christian perfection. He had lately come to his
estate, on the death of his father, and had made himself a
large deer-park in it. There he lived like a king, in ease
and independence, surrounded by his children, to whom,
as well as to his wife, he was tenderly attached. As he
kept clear of priests from the seminaries he lived unmolested, feeling nothing of the burden and heat of the
day, for the persecutors troubled chiefly those who harboured the Seminarists, not caring to inquire after those
who kept the old priests, that is, those who had taken
orders before the reign of Elizabeth. So now-a-days a
great difference is made between seculars and the priests
of the Society, the persecution being much fiercer against
ours and our friends, as may be seen from what occurs
when those who afford us comfort and shelter are discovered. The cause of this I take to be that seeing our
numbers increase, and seeing that some of the other priests
have opposed themselves to us, the authorities try to crush
first the most uncompromising party, and to deter our
friends by terrible examples from sheltering and supporting

[1] Dr. Oliver, in his *Collectanea* (under the name Walpole Edward),
mistakenly understands this to refer to the Walpole brothers, and speaks of
the gentleman here mentioned as the eldest brother of the Walpoles. This is
proved to be an error by the context.

us. But the Israelites increased, despite the rage of Pharao who sought their lives.

"This good gentleman, then, who lived in calm and safety in his house and possessions, and evaded so cautiously the wiles of the persecutor, perceived not and dreaded not enough the wiles of Satan; yet he did not escape the toils of God's grace, but came to them willingly, and once taken wished not to be free. On the third day of the Exercises, after having well pondered the purpose of God in creating him and all other things, feeling the stirring of the waters, he went down into the pool and was healed. He succeeded admirably in each meditation, as the resolutions he made and the lights vouchsafed to him proved. He left nothing within or without which he did not strive to rectify and order unto God's greater glory; he resolved no longer to enjoy, but only to use all created things, and that sparingly; to govern his household as a charge committed unto him by God, and to get two other priests, one of whom he insisted should be a Jesuit, to whom he would commit the direction of himself and of all belonging to him. He further purposed to spend his leisure hours in pious reading, or in the translation of spiritual books. For he was learned and able, and did afterwards publish many such translations, among others the Life of our Blessed Father, *The Dialogues* of St. Gregory the Great, Father Jerome Platus' work on the *Advantages of the Religious State,* and others of the same kind. He set himself very useful rules of conversation, not only for his personal direction, but in order to brotherly correction and the encouragement of virtue in his neighbours.

"Such were his resolutions; such too was his subsequent practice. From the first he expected an obstacle, which he could not but foresee. His servants were heretics for the most part, and he could not hope that his wife would second his plans. Again, he had as chaplain one of the old priests, and these were not often wont to agree with younger men, especially with those of the Society, whom they looked upon as troublesome reformers. He could not then but be anxious. But having, through God's goodness, conceived a firm and practical resolution, he determined to dismiss his servants in a kindly and open-handed way, and to take good Catholics in their stead; to prevail over the opposition of his lady and the chaplain if possible by reason and affection, but should these fail, to show that he was master of the family, and to make use of the authority given him by God.

"This being settled, he began to urge me with all earnestness to come and take up my abode with him, alleging reasons that I could not fairly meet. Moreover, at that time my host [Henry Drury], for whose sake especially I had come to my present abode, was preparing to depart, for Father Garnet had settled that he should come and live with him in London until he could be sent abroad, and the good priest I found there was well able to administer to the spiritual wants of this gentleman's mother. Another advantage of this proposed change was that it brought me nearer to London, and placed me in a family where I could do much more good than in my present abode after the departure of my host. I submitted all these considerations to the judgment of my Superior, with whom I was going to leave my hospitable friend [Henry Drury] after I had introduced him. As Father Garnet approved my availing myself of this new opportunity which God's providence had offered me, I accepted the invitation, and after a couple of months I went to my new dwelling [early in the year 159½], having taken care, in order to escape odium and jealousy, to get my host to inaugurate his improvements, so far as could be done, before my arrival, so that he, and not I might appear to be the prime mover.

"We procured then a staff of good and faithful

domestics, whom I had formerly known in other places, and whose characters I had proved. Nor did I find it so difficult as we had feared, to bring the lady of the house [Jane, daughter of Sir Edmund Huddlestone], and the old priest to consent to the changes. Far from opposing, they furthered my views; the wife especially outshone all the household in her zeal for the decoration of the altar, and the charity she showed to my wants. This lady was of a rather quick temper, and had great difficulty in observing the rules of patience with her servants and others, yet I never let any such fault pass without either private or (if the nature of the case required it) public notice and reproof. This I never omitted during the whole of my stay with this family, but this notwithstanding, she not only bore with me cheerfully, and tried to subdue her temper, but ever showed me fresh marks of attachment and respect, as will appear in the sequel.

"As to the chaplain, when he saw that after my arrival he and all that belonged to him were placed on a better footing, he not only became friendly, but both by word and deed repeatedly showed his satisfaction at my coming. For the increase of piety and devotion in the household had wrought a corresponding increase of reverence for him, and he gained many other advantages which he had not had before; and though all things were arranged in the house in accordance with my advice, yet he found that his own influence had increased rather than otherwise.

"In this house there was living my host's mother [Jane Wiseman] a most excellent widow lady, happy in her children, but still happier in her private virtues. She had four sons and daughters. These latter without exception devoted their virginity to God. Two [Anne and Barbara Wiseman] had already joined the holy order of St. Bridget before my arrival, and one of these [Barbara] is even at this day Abbess in Lisbon. I sent

G

the two others [Jane or Mary and Bridget] to Flanders, where they still serve God in the order of St. Augustine [at Louvain]. Her sons were all pious young men; two [Thomas and John] died in the Society, as was related above; a third [Robert] chose the army, and was lately slain in a battle with the heretics in Belgium,—he fell fighting when many around him had surrendered; the fourth [William] was the master of that house, who, to his mother's great joy, had given himself up to every good work. Such was this good widow's fervour, that she deemed herself to have attained the summit of her desires in this world.

"At my first entrance into this house, she desired her son to bring me up to her chamber; as I came in she fell at my feet, and besought me to allow her to kiss them, saying I was the first of the Society she had seen; as I refused, she kissed the ground on which I stood, and arose filled with a holy joy, which still abides in her: and now, living apart from her son, she maintains with her two priests of our Society, having in the meantime endured a great many tribulations, which shall be related hereafter."

The chaplain at Braddocks was probably Richard Jackson, of whom, some years earlier, Anthony Tyrrell[1] gave information. "Jackson, priest in Queen Mary's time, [resorts to] Michael Hare of Brusiard at Acton." This was in 1586. In a paper endorsed "Massmongers" in the Public Record Office[2] are given two forms of indictment, dated Jan. 12, 159⅔, by which time Father Gerard had made Braddocks his head-quarters for a twelve-month. The first is against Richard Jackson of Wimbish in the county of Essex, clerk, for having said mass at Wimbish on the 25th of August, 34° Eliz. [1592], and against William Wiseman of Wimbish, esquire, Jane Wise-

---

[1] P.R.O., *Domestic, Elizabeth,* vol. cxciii. n. 13.
[2] *Ibid.,* vol. ccxliv. n. 7.

man his wife, John Ruffoote of Wimbish, yeoman, Jane Wiseman, widow, Bridget and Jane Wiseman, spinster, daughters of Widow Wiseman, and Edward Harrington of Wimbish, yeoman, for hearing the mass. The other is against Richard Jackson for saying mass there on the 8th of September, and against Jane Wiseman, widow, Bridget and Jane her daughters, Thomas Hytchecock of Wimbish, yeoman, and Edward Harrington for hearing it.

The seizure of the old chaplain, and many other particulars respecting the Wisemans, are reported to Lord Keeper Puckering by Justice Young in the following letter,[1] the date of which we learn from the foregoing indictments. The search it relates was probably made during one of Father Gerard's missionary journies, or he would have made some mention of it.

"It may please your Honour to be advertised that I have here signified unto your Honour such matters and occurrents as are lately come to my knowledge meet for your lordship to be acquainted withal, and because your Honour required to be informed of Mr. William Wiseman's house in Essex I first begin therewith.

"First, there was found in the said house three horsemen's armour and seven other armours, two muskets and two cullivers, bow and arrows, a jack and a shirt of mail, with all things complete to the said armours, which were in a vault behind a door very well and finely kept. Mr. Nicholls a Justice of Peace was there with the pursuivants and took notice of the said armour.

"Also they found in a secret place between two walls in the said house an old priest named Thomas Jackson [the indictments call him Richard] who hath been beyond sea, and there was also found all the furniture belonging to mass, and the said priest useth ordinarily to say mass there, as is confessed.

[1] P.R.O., *Domestic, Elizabeth,* vol. ccxliii. n. 95.

"*Item*, most of the servants in the house are recusants, although at their coming thither they were otherwise ; and Mr. Wiseman's two daughters Mrs. Jane and Mrs. Bridget, and two gentlewomen who would not declare their names.

"There were found also in the said house divers letters written from Wisbech, the contents whereof are here briefly set down as followeth.

"1. *Imprimis*, a letter written by Mr. Thomas Metham,[1] priest, to Mrs. Wiseman, dated 25 Jun., giving her thanks for her great benevolence bestowed upon the company at Wisbech. The sum of money he could not set down for that it came into the hands of Blewett the priest.

"2. She sent to Metham a handkerchief and a book.

"3. Father Edmonds'[2] letter of thanks to Mrs. Wiseman for her gift.

"4. Another letter to her from him with thanks for a jewel. These letters without date.

"5. A letter from Thomas Metham, priest, to Mrs. Wiseman, giving her thanks for her great benevolence, and having no date.

"6. A like letter from him, dated 13° *Martii*, 1591.

"7. A letter sent by Dollman the priest to Mrs. Wiseman, dated 28° *die Junii*, advertising her of her son Thomas and her son John their healths, and of his going to Wisbech, and that he was sorry her daughter Jane had no warning whereby she might have wrote an epistle in Latin to the priests at Wisbech, that they might have understood her zeal.

"8. A letter sent by Father Edmonds to Mrs. Wiseman without date, mentioning a great jewel which she had given him, touching her sepulchre.

"9. A letter from John Wharton to Mrs. Wiseman, giving her thanks for her charitable entertaining of priests.

---

[1] This is Father Thomas Metham, of the Society of Jesus, who is reckoned among the martyrs as he died in prison. *Troubles*, Second Series, p. 246.

[2] Father William Weston took the name of Edmonds out of affection for Father Edmund Campion. *Ibid.* p. 6.

"10. A letter sent by Mrs. Wiseman to the priests at Wisbech, thanking them for her great cheer, and being sorry that she came not to them on pilgrimage on her bare foot.

"11. A letter from Mr. Metham sent to Mrs. Bridget and Mrs. Jane, daughters to Mrs. Wiseman.

"12. Another letter from Mr. Metham to Mrs. Wiseman, giving her thanks for her liberality.

"13. A letter from Father Edmonds to Mrs. Wiseman with like thanks for her great liberality and benevolence towards him.

"14. Another letter to her from the said Edmonds, giving thanks for her token, desiring to give Mr. Thomas thanks for his tokens.

"15. Another letter to her from the said Father Edmonds, giving her thanks for the great gifts which he had seen, reviewed, and reviewed, and esteemeth to be of an inestimable value.

"16. A letter from Dollman, the priest, to Mrs. Wiseman, willing her to be careful of her health for the comfort of God's Church in these dismal days, and for the encouraging of her said daughters to papistry.

"17. Another letter from Dollman to the same effect, wherein he signifieth that he will carry her letters to the Reverend Fathers that they might joy and pray together for her and hers, with thanks for her benevolence.

"18. Another letter from Dollman to Mrs. Wiseman, giving her thanks for her great liberality.

"19. A letter from one unknown, for that his name is cut out, to Mrs. Wiseman that he is ready to entertain her daughters Bridget and Jane, although he live not in that security he was wont to do; neither is the company together as it was but scattered into divers places and some not to return before St. Andrew's day, yet he is not alone (as he saith). Dated 24 *Octobris*, 1591.

"20. A letter written to Mrs. Wiseman of the great and joyful accepture of her token, being her own invention and workmanship, by the Reverend Fathers at Wisbech, and that they were held in admiration of the workmanship: that Mr. Metham and Father Edmonds would buy as much satin as would make a vestment for the accomplishment of a suit for principal feasts.

"21. A letter from Mr. Thomas Wiseman to his mother, wherewith he sendeth two bonds of 50*l.* a piece to be received of Mr. Moore of the Temple, which (if he die) he giveth to those to whom she shall pay it: which bonds are made in his Uncle Richard's name, and the letter is without date.

"Edward Harrington, servant to Mr. William Wiseman, confesseth that he hath dwelt with him seven years, and since that time hath not been at church. He saith that on Friday the 9th day of September, 1592, Mr. Jackson said mass in Mr. Wiseman's house, and that John Ruffote, Mr. Wiseman's man, helped him to mass; whereat was present old Mrs. Wiseman and her two daughters Bridget and Jane, Elizabeth and Margaret maidservants, the butler and this examinate.

"Also he saith that on Sunday was three weeks the said Jackson said mass, whereat was present Mr. William Wiseman and his wife and two of his men that are now ridden with him, and all the company before named; and Ruffote helped the priest to mass.

"May it please your Honour to be advertised that whereas we have a commission to enquire of recusants and to make certificate of them quarterly, that the Commissioners cannot be had or brought together to set down and agree upon their certificate and to signify their proceedings, unless there may be severe strait letters from your Honours to require them very earnestly to execute the commission.

"RYC. YOUNG."

Of some of the members of the Wiseman family just mentioned by Father Gerard, whose names occur in Young's letter, there is not a little to be said. To the two sons Thomas and John, who became Jesuits, we need not return ; and of Robert, who died in the army in Belgium, we have only this further mention that he was caught at a mass in his mother's house on New Year's day or thereabouts, 159¾, and on the 14th of April following Justice Young wrote[1] of him, " Robert Wiseman, her other son, is also an obstinate recusant and will by no means take the oath. He is prisoner in the Clink." To the eldest son we soon return.

The names of the two eldest daughters, Anne and Barbara, appear in 1580 among the signatures of the thirty Nuns of Sion, then at Rouen, in a petition to the Catholics of England,[2] praying them not to allow "the only Religious Convent remaining of our country" to perish for want of support. The Convent reached Lisbon in 1594 and in 1863 returned to England and settled at Spetisbury near Blandford. It is the only Religious house in England that can trace an unbroken descent from a foundation made before the Reformation. Sion House was founded by Henry V. in 1413.

The remaining sisters Jane and Bridget became Canonesses of St. Augustine in the Flemish Convent of St. Ursula in the " Half-street" at Louvain, which Convent is the mother house of the existing English Convents of the Order at Newton Abbot and at Bruges. The Convent now at Newton Abbot in Devonshire was originally founded at Louvain, under the title of St. Monica's, and from the interesting Chronicles of that house we learn much of the history of the families to which the Nuns belonged. Jane, or as they there called her, Mary Wiseman,[3] was Subprioress of St. Ursula's, and Bridget her

[1] P.R.O., *Domestic, Elizabeth*, vol. ccxlviii. n. 68.   [2] *Ibid.* vol. cxlvi. n. 114.
[3] *Troubles*, First Series, p. 48.

sister Infirmarian, when on the 9th of November, 1609, they left their first Religious home, to help to found a colony of the Order that should be entirely English. Mary Wiseman was professed at St. Ursula's on the 8th of May, and Bridget on the 5th of June, 1595. Mary Wiseman, whom the Flemish Nuns would have elected their Prioress, if at the time of their election she had had the canonical age of forty years, was elected the first Prioress of St. Monica's, and she governed that house for twenty-four years. The Chronicles of her Convent give the following charming account of her father and mother.

"Our Reverend Mother Mary Wiseman was of very holy parentage. Her father lived and died a constant confessor of Catholic religion,[1] named Thomas Wiseman, of Braddocks in Essex, an Esquire of ancient family, who suffered much for his conscience, his house being a receptacle for priests and religious men.

"He brought up his children, not only very virtuously, but also to learning of the Latin tongue, as well the daughters as the sons, himself being their master. Besides that, in his house was order kept resembling a monastery. At the meals for half an hour was something read, unless strangers were there of higher degree than himself; otherwise this worthy custom was not omitted. Himself lived for the most part a reclused life, by reason that being troubled with the gout, he resided above in his chamber, giving himself to prayer and holy lecture: as also every Friday he would make an exhortation to his children in Latin, thereby to exercise them in that language, as also to give good instruction.

---

[1] It would appear that the father Thomas Wiseman temporarily yielded to the storm, for in 1570 he is named in "A note of such as have been dealt withal by my lords this progress for refusing to come to Church." Brit. Mus. *Cotton. MSS.*, Titus B iii. n. 61.

"Essex. Mr. West of Depeden ⎫
         Mr. Henry of Bradbury ⎬ All these come to the Church."
         Mr. Thomas Wiseman ⎭

"By which worthy education they profited so much that, having four daughters, the two eldest came over seas, and became Nuns of St. Bridget's Order, and have both governed the Monastery at Lisbon in Portugal, being chosen at several times by mutual interchange Abbesses (for their order is to change at some years); and at this present 1631 the one·is Abbess and the other Prioress. The two younger daughters came to St. Ursula's, to St. Augustine's Order, leaving the kind cherishings of most loving parents, to embrace the strictness of poverty and want, whereof we have spoken.¹ Such was their fervour to God's service even in tender age, following the example of their most virtuous parents.

"For to speak now of their worthy mother, whose life hath partly been set down by some that knew her well. Her name before her marriage was Jane Vacham [Vaughan], her father being of ancient house in Wales, but her mother was a Tewder [Tudor] of the blood royal. She, being left a ward by her parents' death, passed many troubles and molestations to avoid marriage by those who had her in keeping. For having no mind to marry by reason that she was drawn through God's instinct to delight in spiritual things, her uncle by the mother's side, Mr. Guinneth,² who was a priest and had been curate of a parish church in London in Catholic time, took especial care of her, although he could not assist her in all so well as he desired, being long time kept in prison when heresy

¹ *Troubles*, First Series, p. 35.
² "Gwyneth" in Welsh means "North Wales," which name he must have taken instead of Tudor. John Gwyneth was Rector of St. Peter Cheap, London, from Sept. 19, 1543, when he was presented by Thomas Lord Audeley, to Nov. 19, 1556, when he resigned. Newcourt's *Repertorium Ecclesiasticum Parochiale Londinense*, London, 1708, vol. i. p. 522. He had been previously presented by Henry VIII. to St. Beuno's Church at Clynnog Vaur in Caernarvonshire, in 1538, but he seems to have been dispossessed in 1542 on the ground that the presentation belonged to the see of Bangor. Browne Willis' *Survey of Bangor* (London, 1721), p. 260. Anthony a Wood says that he took the degree of Doctor of Music at Oxford in 1531, and published several Catholic books in London in 1554 and 1557. *Athen. Oxon.*

came in, but at length getting freedom, he was desirous to match this his niece worthily and as should be best for her soul's good. Wherefore, one day he met with Mr. Wiseman, a young gentleman of the Inns of Court, and liked him so well that, upon the proposition of one in the company, he became content to marry his niece with him and brought him unto her, persuading her, if she could like him, to take him for her husband.

"But she was ever very backward in that matter, in so much that having no less than thirty suitors, some whereof had seven years sought her good will, yet she could not settle her love upon any. But now it was God's will that she should yield herein unto her uncle, and so was married to Mr. Wiseman, who brought her home to his house in Essex, where she found both father and mother-in-law and a house full of brothers and sisters, among whom she passed some difficulties, not having things always according to her mind. But all happened to make her virtue more refined, for she ever carried herself both loving and dutiful to her husband, who loved her dearly, as also to his kindred, and assisted them all she could, living in the state of marriage irreprehensible, and bringing up her children in all virtue.

"After her husband's decease, exercising the works of a holy widow, it pleased our Lord to rank her among the troops [not only] of constant Confessors, but also as we may say of valiant Martyrs, and of the most famous women that England afforded in these our miserable times of heresy; for she was ever most fervent and zealous, and so devout in prayer, that she was once heard to say by her daughter, our Reverend Mother, 'It seems,' said she, 'that if I were tied to a stake and burnt alive for God I should not feel it, so great is the love to Him which I feel in my soul at this time.'

"Wherefore Almighty God, to make her love for Him indeed apparent, permitted that Topcliffe, the cruel persecutor, did vehemently set against her. And at length, only for proving that she had relieved a Catholic priest,[1] giving him a French crown, [Topcliffe] brought her before the bar to be condemned to death for felony. But she constantly refused to be condemned by the Jury, saying that she would not have twelve men accessory to her innocent death; for she knew [that] although they could not by right find her guilty, yet they could be made to do it when her enemies pleased. Hereupon they told her that she was by the law to be pressed to death if she would not be tried by the Jury; but she stood firm in her resolution, being well content to undergo so grievous a martyrdom for the love of Christ. Yea, when they declared unto her the manner of that death in the hardest terms, as the custom is at their condemnation, the worthy woman, hearing that she must be laid with her arms across when the weights were to be put upon her, exulted with joy and said, 'Now blessed be God that I shall die with my arms across, as my Lord Jesus;' and after this, when her sons lamented with sorrow, she rejoiced and cheered them up. There was at the same time a Catholic gentleman, named Mr. Barnes,[2] brought also before the Bench to be arraigned with her, who being a man, yet had not such courage as she to be pressed to death, but was content to be tried by the Jury, who were made to find him guilty as she knew well enough, although by right they could not do it, and so he was condemned to hanging for felony.

"But neither he nor she died at that time, for Almighty God, accepting of this courageous matron's fervour to martyrdom, would not let her depart so soon out of this life, that she might have a longer time of suffering for Him, as also do more good for His honour. [He] therefore

[1] Father John Jones *alias* Buckley, O.S.F., who was martyred at St. Thomas Waterings in Southwark, July 12, 1598.

[2] See his narrative in Tierney's *Dodd*, vol. iii. App. n. xxxvii., printed from Stonyhurst MSS., *Angl. A.* vol. ii. n. 41. Challoner miscalls him Barnet.

ordained that Queen Elizabeth, who then bore the sceptre in England, hearing of her condemnation,[1] stayed the execution, for by bribes her son got one to speak a good word unto the Queen in his mother's behalf; who, when she understood how for so small a matter she should have been put to death, rebuked the Justices of cruelty, and said she should not die.

"Notwithstanding both she and Mr. Barnes remained in prison so long as the Queen lived; in which time Topcliffe ceased not often to molest her with divers vexations, in so much that she was made for a good space to lie with a witch in the same room, who was put in prison for her wicked deeds. And it was a strange thing to see that many resorting to the same witch there in prison, to know things of her by art magic, she never had the power to exercise her necromancy in the room where Mrs. Wiseman was, but was forced to go away into another place.

"One thing also we will not omit, which was a miraculous thing. Upon a time her friend Topcliffe passed under her window, being mounted on a goodly horse, going to the Queen; and Mrs. Wiseman espying him, thought it would not be amiss to wash him a little with holy water. Therefore [she] took some which she had by her and flung it upon him and his horse as he came under her window. It was a wonderful thing to see: no sooner had the holy water touched the horse but presently it seems he could not endure his rider, for the horse began so to kick and fling that he never ceased till his master Topcliffe was flung to the ground; who looked up to the window and raged against Mrs. Wiseman, calling her an old witch who with her charms had made his horse to lay him on the ground; but she with good reason laughed to see that holy water had given him so fine a fall.

---

[1] This was in July 1598. The circumstances of this condemnation are related by Father Gerard a few chapters further on.

"After Queen Elizabeth's death this valiant woman lived some years out of prison, but wanted not good occasions to exercise patience by one that was allied to her, a most perverse fantastical woman who used her very ill; so that both in prison and out of prison she wanted not crosses to make her the more renowned by a long martyrdom in all, as I find written of her. She exulted in mind and abounded with spiritual comfort, out of the loyal and fervent love which she bore to God; until in the year 1610, when her merits were accumulated unto a greater measure for eternal glory, she fell into a most painful and grievous sickness; where amidst her great pains she would rejoice and give Almighty God thanks that He pleased to accept of those her sufferings in place of greater which she had desired to pass for His sake. And coming to her happy death, the last words which she said to the priest were *Pater, gaudeo in Deo* ['Father, I rejoice in God'], and so rested in our Lord.

"These were the parents of our first Prioress, who had also four sons. Two died priests[1] of the Society of Jesus, the other died a good Catholic, and the eldest, Sir William Wiseman, is yet living, a man more of heaven than of this world."

This was written in 1631, in the lifetime of Mary Wiseman, the Prioress of St. Monica's, and her death two years later is thus recorded in the Chronicles of her Convent. "In the year 1633, upon the 8th day of July, died most blessedly our worthy Mother Prioress, after many years of continual weakness and sometimes great pain, especially the last year of her life, being scarce able to go out of her chamber. She was a woman of a great spirit and a great courage, resembling her mother Mrs. Wiseman, of whom we have made large mention. She had her Latin tongue perfect, and hath left us many homilies and sermons of the holy Fathers translated into

---

[1] They were not priests.

English, which she did with great facility whilst some small respite of health permitted her : for she was sickly almost all the time of her government, which was a great cross to us all. Nevertheless such was her wisdom and prudence that she guided us with great peace and tranquillity, which peace she left established in the Cloister after her death."

In the reign of James I. William Wiseman of Braddocks was knighted. This however was no great sign of royal favour in days when the heads of families of wealth and position were obliged to " take out their knighthood," that they might be obliged to pay the fees. Sir William and his wife Jane had one son, John, and two daughters, Dorothea and Winifred. The records of St. Mary's Abbey, East Bergholt, say that Winifred Wiseman entered the Novitiate of the Benedictinesses at Brussels on the 22nd of March, 1602, and was professed August 6, 1603, and died in 1647, *æt.* 63, being called in Religion "Dame Agatha." And as to Dorothea, the Chronicle of St. Monica's, now at St. Augustine's Priory, Newton Abbot, from which we have largely drawn, relates that "Mrs. Brooksby, a young widow, our Reverend Mother's niece, daughter to Sir William Wiseman, her brother, came here to Louvain to see her friends in 1610." John the son, who married Mary, daughter of Sir Rowland Rydgeley, had two daughters, Lucy and Elizabeth, and an only son, Aurelius Piercy Wiseman, who was killed in a duel in London in 1680. The following inscription on his grave in Wimbish Church is given by Wright.[1] " Here rest the sad remains of Aurelius Piercy Wiseman, of Broad Oak, in this parish, Esq., the last of the name of that place, and head and chief of that right worshipful and ancient family, who was unfortunately killed in the flower of his age, December 11, 1680."

Three baronetcies were conferred on various branches of

[1] *History of Essex*, vol. ii. p. 134.

the family, Sir William Wiseman of Canfield (1628), Sir
Richard Wiseman of Thundersley (1628), and Sir William
Wiseman, Knight, of Riverhall (1660).   The two last mentioned are extinct.   The Wisemans of Braddocks were the
eldest branch of the descendants of John Wiseman, Esq.,
who purchased the estate in Northend about 1430, and
was the first of the family who lived in Essex.   The late
Cardinal Nicholas Wiseman, Archbishop of Westminster,
was of the same stock, being descended from a younger
son of one of the junior branches of the family, who was
made Protestant Bishop of Meath.   The children of the
bishop settled in Ireland, and his descendants were
Catholics.

CHAPTER VII.

WORK IN ESSEX.

1592.

BRADDOCKS or Broadoaks—its very name indicates that it was an old English country place—is a house that still stands in the fields two miles from Wimbish Church in Essex. A century ago[1] there were some remains of the moat that surrounded it in the days when Father Gerard made it the head quarters of his missionary life. He continues his autobiography thus.

"When the house had been thus settled, I found time both for study and for missionary excursions. I took care that all in the house should approach the Sacraments frequently, which none before, save the good widow, used to do oftener than four times a year. Now they came every week. On feast days, and often on Sundays, I preached in the chapel; moreover I showed those who had leisure the way to meditate by themselves, and taught all how to examine their conscience. I also brought in the custom of reading pious books, which we did even at meals, when there were no strangers there; for at that time we priests sat with the rest, even with our gowns on. I had a cassock besides and a biretta, but the Superior would not have us use these except in the chapel.

"In my excursions I almost always gained some to God. There is however a great difference to be observed between these counties where I then was, and other parts

[1] "It [Braddocks] seems to have been formerly moated round, and two sides of the moat remain at present." Morant, *History of Essex*, London, 1768, vol. ii. p. 559.

common people are Catholics, and almost all lean towards the Catholic faith, it is easy to bring many into the bosom of the Church, and to have many hearers together at a sermon. I myself have seen in Lancashire two hundred together present at mass and sermon ; and as these easily come in, so also they easily scatter when the storm of persecution draws near, and come back again when the alarm has blown over. On the contrary, in those parts where I was now staying there were very few Catholics, but these were of the higher classes ; scarcely any of the common people, for they cannot live in peace, surrounded as they are by most violent heretics. The way of managing in such places, is first to gain the gentry, then the servants : for Catholic masters cannot do without Catholic servants.

"About this time I gained to God and the Church my hostess' brother, the only son of a certain knight. I ever after found him a most faithful friend in all circumstances. He afterwards took to wife a cousin of the most illustrious Spanish Duke of Feria. This pious pair are so attached to our priests, that now in these terrible times they always keep one in their house, and often two or three."

His "hostess' brother" was Henry, son of Sir Edmund Huddlestone[1] of Sawston in Cambridgeshire, who married Dorothy, daughter of Robert, first Lord Dormer, by his wife Elizabeth Browne, daughter of Anthony, first Viscount Montague. The "cousinship" with the Duke of Feria is by affinity and half-blood. Jane, daughter of Sir William Dormer, by his first wife Mary Sidney, married Don Gomez Suarez, Count of Feria ; and Dorothy's father, Robert Lord Dormer, was a son of Sir William by his second wife, Dorothy Catesby.[2]

[1] "While the house at Sawston was erecting, Sir Edmund resided on his estates in Essex, and served the office of Sheriff for that county in 20, 21 [1578-9] and 30 Elizabeth" [1588]. Burke's *Landed Gentry*, 1850, vol. i. p. 602.

[2] Burke's *Peerage*.

H

Henry Huddlestone was one of those who suffered by the Gunpowder Plot. He was arrested in Warwickshire,[1] and examined November 8, 1605, when he is called Henry Hurlestone[2] of Paswick, Essex. Mrs. Vaux wrote to Sir Richard Varney, Sheriff of Warwickshire, that Mrs. Huddlestone, who was with her, begged that her husband might go up to London with the Lord Lieutenant.[3] Winter in his evidence exculpated him.[4] He was in the Marshalsea, where his wife asked access to him.[5] In another examination, December 6, 1605, he says that he met Father Gerard, *alias* Brooke, at Mrs. Vaux's house.[6] He took the news to Harrowden where Father Gerard was.[7] On the 5th of February, 1607, the King wrote to Salisbury concerning the grant to Sir John Leigh of the forfeiture of Huddlestone in Essex, a recusant.[8]

Father Gerard's next paragraph refers to the Rookwoods of Coldham in Suffolk. The "heir to a goodly estate, who was put to death on a charge of treason," was Ambrose Rookwood, who was executed for the Gunpowder Plot. "The devotion and resolute mind of this gentleman was very well known to many," Father Gerard says of him in his "Narrative of the Gunpowder Plot,"[9] "and he was very much pitied, as he had been much beloved." The secular priest his brother was living in 1624, and is called by Gee "Townsend *alias* Ruckwood." Watson in the "Decachordon" mentions "Dorothy Ruckwood, Mr. Richard Ruckwood's daughter of Suffolk, who had a great portion given unto her by the Lady Elizabeth Drury her grandmother." Dorothy Rookwood was, it would seem,

---

[1] P.R.O., *Gunpowder Plot Book*, n. 75.
[2] *Ibid. Domestic, James I.*, vol. xvi. n. 31.
[3] *Ibid.* n. 227.
[4] *Ibid.* n. 146.
[5] *Ibid.* vol. xvii. n. 14.
[6] *Ibid.* vol. xix. n. 43.
[7] *Ibid.* n. 13.
[8] *Ibid.* vol. xxvi. n. 44.
[9] *Condition of Catholics*, p. 221.

about two years in Belgium before she entered Religion, for she was professed at the Flemish Augustinian Convent of St. Ursula at Louvain, with Bridget Wiseman and Margaret Garnet, Father Henry Garnet's sister, on the 5th of June, 1595. She died " about the time the Dutch Mother was elected" in 1607, "very sweetly as she had lived, for she was a mild virtuous soul, sweet and affable in her conversation, and beloved of all her sisters." She did not therefore live long enough to be one of those sent out to found the English Convent of St. Monica's in 1609.

" It was in this same year [probably Father Gerard is speaking of 1592, the year in which St. Omers College was founded] that I sent into Belgium the daughter and three sons of a Catholic gentleman. The sister became a nun in the Order of St. Austin at Louvain, where she gave such edification both in life and death that she was the talk of all : nay, they still speak of her with wonder, and stick not to call her a saint. In fact how great her esteem and love was of religious life may be known from this, that she was ever most thankful for that little help in her vocation which she got from me. She had praised me so much beyond my due in that convent, that when I came to Louvain, numbers flocked to me. Nay, one of the Belgian Sisters, who had been especially dear to her while she was alive, had learnt the English language on purpose to make her confession to me, and others were trying to do the same. That this happened by the providence of God, I gather from the fact that it proved the salvation of some who otherwise would not have placed such trust in me. Her three brothers were among the first students of the Seminary of St. Omers. One, after finishing his studies well, died holily in Spain ; the second, who was heir to a goodly estate, was put to death by the heretics on a charge of treason ; the third is still living and toiling in England, a learned and good priest, and a friend of our Fathers.

"Of my host's two sisters I have spoken before; but these I did not send till afterwards. I had previously persuaded their mother, the good widow [Jane Wiseman], to go to her own house and maintain there a priest whom I recommended, in order that so noble a soul and one so ready for all good deeds, might be a profit not only to herself but to many, as in fact she became. Her house was a retreat and no small protection both to ours and to other priests. She used moreover so to abound with joy when I or others came to her house, that sometimes she could not refrain from clapping her hands or some like sign of gladness; she was indeed 'a true widow,' given to all manner of good works, and especially occupied with zeal for souls.

"Indeed, besides others of less standing whom she brought me to be reconciled, she had nearly won over a certain great lady, a neighbour of hers. Though this lady was the wife of the richest[1] lord in the whole county, and sister to the Earl of Essex (then most powerful with the Queen), and was wholly given to vanities, nevertheless she brought her so far as to be quite willing to speak with a priest, if only he could come to her without being known. This the good widow told me. I consequently went to her house openly, and addressed her as though I had something to tell her from a certain great lady her kins-woman, for so it had been agreed. I dined openly with her and all the gentry in the house, and spent three hours at least in private talk with her. I first satisfied her in all the doubts which she laid before me about faith; next I set myself to stir up her will, and before my departure I so wrought upon her, that she asked for instructions how to prepare herself for confession, and fixed a day for making it. Nay, she afterwards wrote to me earnestly protesting that she desired nothing in the world so much

[1] Lady Penelope Devereux, daughter of Walter first Earl of Essex, wife of Robert third Lord Rich, afterwards Earl of Warwick.

as to open to me the inmost recesses of her heart. But the judgments of God are a deep abyss, and it is a dreadful thing to expose oneself to the occasions of sin. Now there was a baron[1] in London who had loved her long and deeply; to him she disclosed her purpose by letter, perchance to bid him farewell; but she roused a sleeping adder. For he hastened to her, and began to dissuade her in every kind of way; and being himself a heretic and not wanting in learning, he cunningly coaxed her to get him an answer to certain doubts of his from the same guide that she herself followed; saying that if he was satisfied in this, he too would become a Catholic. He implored her to take no step in the meantime, if she did not wish for his death. So he filled two sheets of paper about the Pope, the worship of saints, and the like. She sent them with a letter of her own, begging me to be so good as to answer them, for it would be a great gain if such a soul could be won over. He did not however write from a wish to learn, but rather with the treacherous design of delaying her conversion. For he got an answer, a full one I think, to which he made no reply. But meanwhile he endeavoured to get her to London, and succeeded in making her first postpone, and afterwards altogether neglect her resolution. By all this however he was unwittingly bringing on his own ruin: for later on, returning from Ireland laden with glory, on account of his successful administration, and his victory over the Spanish forces that had landed there (on which occasion he brought over the Earl of Tyrone, who had been the most powerful opponent of heresy in that country, and most sturdy champion of the ancient faith), he was created earl by his present Majesty; and though conqueror of others, he conquered not himself, but was kept a helpless captive by his

[1] Charles Blount, eighth Baron Mountjoy, who in 1603 was created Earl of Devonshire. He was married December 26, 1605, to Lady Rich, after her divorce and in the lifetime of her husband. The Earl of Devonshire died in a few months after this marriage, April 3, 1606.

love of this lady. This madness of his brought him to
commit such extravagancies that he became quite notorious, and was publicly disgraced. Unable to endure this
dishonour, and yet unwilling to renounce the cause of it,
he died of grief, invoking, alas, not God, but this goddess,
'his angel,' as he called her, and leaving her heiress of all
his property. Such was his miserable end, dying in bad
repute of all men. The lady, though now very rich, often
afterwards began to think of her former resolution, and
often spoke of me to a certain Catholic maid of honour
that she had about her. This latter coming into Belgium
about three years back to become a nun, related this to
me, and begged me to write to her and fan the yet
unquenched spark into a flame. But when I was setting
about the letter, I heard that she had been carried off by a
fever, not however before she had been reconciled to the
Church by one of ours. I have set this forth at some
length, that the providence of God with regard to her
whose conversion was hindered, and His judgment upon
him who was the cause of the hindrance, may more clearly
appear."

CHAPTER VIII.

EXCURSIONS.

"I USED also to make other missionary excursions at this time to more distant counties towards the north. On the way I had to pass through my native place, and through the midst of my kindred and acquaintance; but I could not do much good there, though there were many who professed themselves great friends of mine. I experienced in fact most fully the truth of that saying of Truth Himself, that no prophet is received in his own country; so that I felt little wish at any time to linger among them. It happened once that I went to lodge on one of these journeys with a Catholic kinsman.[1] I found him in hunter's trim, ready to start for a grand hunt, for which many of his friends had met together. He asked me to go with him and try to gain over a certain gentleman who had married a cousin of his and mine. I answered that some other occasion would be more fit. He disagreed with me however, maintaining that unless I took this chance of going with him, I should not be able to get near the person in question. I went accordingly, and during the hunt joined company with him for whose soul I myself was on the hunt. The hounds being at fault from time to time, and ceasing to give tongue, while we were awaiting the renewal of this hunter's music, I took the opportunity of following my own chase, and gave tongue myself in good earnest. Thus, beginning to speak of the great pains that we took over chasing a poor animal, I brought the conversation to

[1] William Wiseman, Richard Fulwood, and Ralph Willis, whose names soon reappear in the story, were with Father Gerard at Lady Gerard's house before Michaelmas, 1592. P.R.O., *Domestic, Elizabeth*, vol. ccxlviii. n. 103.

the necessity of seeking an everlasting kingdom, and the proper method of gaining it, to wit by employing all manner of care and industry; as the devil on his part never sleeps, but hunts after our souls as hounds after their prey.   We said but little on disputed points of faith, for he was rather a schismatic than a heretic, but to move his will to act required a longer talk.   This work was continued that day and the day after; and on the fourth day he was spiritually born and made a Catholic. He still remains one, and often supports priests at home and sends them to other people.

"On an occasion of this kind there happened a very wonderful thing.   He went once to visit a friend of his who was sick in bed.   As he knew him to be an upright man, and one rather under a delusion than in wilful error, he began to instruct him in the faith, and press him at the same time to look to his soul, as his illness was dangerous. He at last prevailed with him, and was himself prevailed upon by the sick man to send for a priest to hear his confession.   Accordingly, after instructing the invalid how to stir up in himself meanwhile sorrow for his sins and make ready his confession, the other went away.   Not happening to have a priest at home at the time, he had some difficulty in finding one.   In the meantime the sick man died, but evidently with a great desire of confession; for he repeatedly asked whether that friend of his was coming who had promised to bring a physician with him, under which name priests often visit the sick.   What followed seemed to show that his desires had stood him in good stead.   Every night after his death there appeared to his wife in her chamber a sort of light flickering through the air and sometimes entering within the curtains.   She was frightened, and ordered her maids to bring their beds into the room and stay with her; they however saw nothing, their mistress alone saw the appearance every night and was troubled at it.   At last she sent for that

Catholic friend of her husband, disclosed to him the whole cause of her fear, and asked him to consult some learned man. He asked a priest's advice, who answered that very probably this light meant that she should come to the light of faith. He returned with the answer, and won her over. The widow, on becoming a Catholic, had mass said in the same room for a long time, but still the same light appeared every night. This increased her trouble, so that the priest consulted other priests, and brought back an answer to the widow, that probably her husband's soul was on the way to Heaven, by reason of his true conversion of heart and contrition accompanied with a desire of the sacrament, but still he stood in need of prayers to free him from his debts to God's justice. He bade her therefore have mass said for him thirty days, according to the old custom of the country. She took the advice, and herself communicated several times for the same intention. The night after the last mass had been celebrated in the room, she saw three lights instead of one as before. Two of them seemed to hold and support the third between them. All three entered within the bed-curtains, and after staying there a little while, mounted up towards Heaven through the top of the bed, leaving the lady in great consolation. She saw nothing of the sort again; from which all gathered that the soul had then been freed from its pains, and carried by the angels to Heaven. This took place in the county of Stafford.

"My journeys northwards were undertaken for the purpose of visiting, and strengthening in the faith, certain persons who there afforded no small aid to the common cause. Among them were two sisters of high nobility, daughters of an earl of very old family who had laid down his life for the Catholic faith.[1] They lived together, and

[1] Thomas Percy, Earl of Northumberland, who was beheaded at York in 1572, had four daughters: Elizabeth, wife of Richard Woodroff; Lucy, wife of Sir Edward Stanley; Jane, wife of Lord Henry Seymour; and Mary, the second Abbess of the English Benedictine Convent at Brussels.

manifested a great desire to have me not merely visit them sometimes, but rather stay altogether with them. Though this could not be, they gave themselves up entirely to my direction, that I might lead them to God. The elder [Lady Elizabeth Woodroff], who had a family, became a pillar of support to that portion of our afflicted Church. She kept two priests with her at home, and received all who came to her with great charity. There are numbers of priests in that part of the country, and many Catholics, mostly of the poorer sort. Indeed I was hardly ever there without our counting before my departure six or seven priests together in her house. Thus she gave great help to religion in the whole district during her abode there, which lasted till I was seized and thrown into prison ; whereupon she was constrained by her husband to change her abode and go to London, a proceeding which did neither of them any good, and deprived the poor Catholics of many advantages. Her sister [Lady Mary Percy] was chosen by God for Himself. ˙ I found her unmarried, humble, and modest. Gradually she was fitted for something higher. She learnt the practice of meditation ; and profited so well thereby, that the world soon grew vile in her eyes, and Heaven seemed the only thing worthy of her love. I afterwards sent her to Father Holt in Belgium. He wrote to me on one occasion about her in these terms : ' Never has there come into these parts a country-women of ours that has given such good example, or done such honour to our nation.' She had the chief hand in the foundation of the present convent of English Benedictine Nuns at Brussels,[1] where she still lives, and has arrived to a great pitch of virtue and self-denial. She yearns for a more retired life, and has often proposed to her director to allow her to live as a recluse, but gives in to his reasons to the contrary.

---

[1] This venerable community was transferred, in 1794, to Winchester, and in 1857 to East Bergholt in Suffolk. This was the first English Convent founded after the Reformation, and the first to come to England at the French Revolution.

" At first I used to carry with me on these journeys my altar furniture, which was meagre but decent, and so contrived that it could be easily carried, along with several other necessary articles, by him who acted as my servant. In this way I used to say mass in the morning in every place where I lodged, not however before I had looked into every corner around, that there might be no one peeping in through the chinks. I brought my own things mainly on account of certain Catholics my entertainers not having yet what was necessary for the Holy Sacrifice. But after some years this cause was removed; for in nearly every place that I came to they had got ready the sacred vestments beforehand. Moreover I had so many friends to visit on the way, and these at such distances from one another, that it was hardly every necessary for me to lodge at an inn on a journey of one hundred and fifty miles ; and at last I hardly slept at an inn once in two years."

CHAPTER IX.

A VISIT TO FATHER GARNET.

1591.

"I USED to visit my Superior several times a year, when I wished to consult him on matters of importance. Not only I, but all of us used to resort to him twice a year to give our half-yearly account of conscience and renew the offerings of our vows to our Lord Jesus. I always remarked that the others drew great profit from this holy custom of our Society. As for myself, to speak my mind frankly, I never found anything do me more good, or stir up my courage more to fulfil all the duties which belong to our Institute, and are required of the workmen who till the Lord's vineyard in that country. Besides experiencing great spiritual joy from the renewal itself, I found my interior strength recruited, and a new zeal kindled within me afterwards in consequence ; so that if I have not done any good, it must have come from my carelessness and thanklessness, and not from any fault of the Society, which afforded me such means and helps to perfection—means peculiar to itself and not shared by any other religious order.

"On one occasion we were all met together in the Superior's house while he yet resided in the country, and were employed in the renovation of spirit. We had had several conferences, and the Superior had given each of us some advice in private, when the question was started what we should do if the priest-hunters suddenly came upon us, seeing that there were so many of us, and there were nothing like enough hiding-places for all. We numbered then, I think, nine or ten of ours, besides other priests our friends, and some Catholics who were forced to seek concealment. The blessed Father Garnet[1] answered, 'True, we ought not all to meet together now that our number is daily increasing : however, as we are here assembled for the greater glory of God, I will be answerable for all till the renovation is over, but beyond that I will not promise.' Accordingly, on the very day of the renovation, though he had been quite unconcerned before, he earnestly warned every one to look to himself, and not to tarry without necessity, adding, 'I do not guarantee your safety any longer.' Some, hearing this, mounted their horses after dinner and rode off. Five of ours and two secular priests stayed behind.

" Next morning, about five o'clock, when Father Southwell was beginning mass, and the others and myself were at meditation, I heard a bustle at the house door. Directly after I heard cries and oaths poured forth against the servant for refusing admittance. The fact was that four priest-hunters, or pursuivants as they are called, with drawn swords, were trying to break down the door and force an entrance. The faithful servant withstood them, otherwise we should have been all made prisoners. But by this time Father Southwell had heard the uproar, and, guessing what it meant, had at once taken off his vestments and stripped the altar ; while we strove to seek out everything belonging to us, so that there might be nothing found to betray the lurking of a priest. We did not even wish to leave boots and swords lying about, which would serve to show there had been many guests, though none of them appeared. Hence many of us were anxious about our beds, which were still warm, and only covered according to custom previous to being made.

---

[1] When this was written, the strict laws of Urban VIII. had not yet been made, which forbid the introduction of any public religious veneration except by the authority of the Holy See.

Some therefore went and turned their beds over, so that the colder part might deceive any body who put his hand in to feel. Thus while the enemy was shouting and bawling outside, and our servants were keeping the door, saying that the mistress of the house, a widow, had not yet got up, but that she was coming directly and would give them an answer, we profited by the delay to stow away ourselves and all our baggage in a cleverly-contrived hiding-place.

"At last these leopards were let in. They raged about the house, looking everywhere, and prying into the darkest corners with candles. They took four hours over the business, but failed in their search,[1] and only brought out the forbearance of the Catholics in suffering, and their own spite and obstinacy in seeking. At last they took themselves off, after getting paid, forsooth, for their trouble. So pitiful is the lot of the Catholics, that those who come with a warrant to annoy them in this or in other way, have to be paid for so doing by the suffering party instead of by the authorities who send them, as though it were not enough to endure wrong, but they must also pay for their endurance of it. When they were gone, and were now some way off, so that there was no fear of their returning, as they sometimes do, a lady came and summoned out of the den not one but many Daniels. The hiding-place was under ground, covered with water at the bottom, so that I was standing with my feet in water all the time. We had there Fathers Garnet, Southwell, and Oldcorne (three future martyrs), Father Stanny and myself, two secular priests, and two or three lay gentlemen. Having thus escaped that day's danger, Father Southwell and I set off the next day together, as we had come : Father Oldcorne stayed, his dwelling or residence being not far off."

Father Oldcorne's residence was Henlip House near

---

[1] Defecerunt scrutantes scrutinio.—*MS.* Psalm lxiii. 7.

Worcester, the seat of the Abingtons, where he and Father Garnet were discovered and captured, at the time of the Gunpowder Plot, after a search of eight days. To Father Oldcorne we return in the next chapter: our present duty is to illustrate the account of the search in Father Garnet's house that Father Gerard has just given us.

The house was that in which Mrs. Brooksby and Anne Vaux lived in Warwickshire, and the date was October the 15th to the 18th, 1591. As to the house, Father Gerard has already told us that Father Garnet did not come to live in London or its neighbourhood till Father Southwell was imprisoned in July 1592. The county in which he previously resided is indicated by Father Gerard in his "Narrative of the Powder Plot,"[1] where he says that "Father Oldcorne and he [Father Gerard himself] met at London according to their appointment, and by good hap found the Superior [Father Garnet] then in London, though his ordinary abode were then [1588] in Warwickshire, almost a hundred miles from London."

This house was confusedly indicated to Government in "the confession of George Snape," which is signed by Justice Young.[2] "Moreover I have heard for a truth, and I do verily persuade myself that it is so indeed, that in Warwickshire dwelleth one of the Lord Vaux his daughters, whose husband's name I marked not, and yet I think I have heard him named. She is not far distant from one Mrs. Brooks, a recusant, if I be not deceived. This Mrs. Vaux entertaineth commonly a priest or two in her house, and is resorted to by divers others, so that sometimes there are to be found in the house at one time five or six priests together. They have very safe and close places of convenience in the house for them to lurk in, as it should seem, for Mr. Hodgkins hath been there

---

[1] *Condition of Catholics*, p. 282.

[2] P.R.O., *Domestic, Elizabeth*, vol. ccxxix. n. 78; dated in the Calendar 1589.

divers times and searched the house, when there hath been three or four together, and yet could find none of them. When I heard the report of this, if I had thought so much of the matter as I have done sithence, I would have informed myself more in particular of the situation and state of the house, but I took no great heed at that time to the reporter's words."

The ladies were Anne Vaux and Eleanor, widow of Edward Brooksby, daughters of William third Lord Vaux by his first wife Elizabeth, daughter of John Beaumont of Gracedieu in Leicestershire, Esq. Their half-brother George Vaux left a widow with whom Father Gerard lived at a later period of his missionary life, and when he describes her position in life he says that it was in the house of her husband's sisters, " one unmarried, the other a widow," that Father Garnet lived so long.

The very meeting and search at Father Garnet's residence in Warwickshire described by Father Gerard he has himself given some account of in a letter to Father Claud Aquaviva the General of the Society, which has been already printed.[1] It would however be well to place the descriptive portion of it in juxtaposition with Father Gerard's Narrative. Father Christopher Grene, from whose transcript[2] it is translated, introduces this part of the letter with the words, " He then tells how they met on St. Luke's day, 1591, for the renewal of vows, and were freed from imminent peril."

"That solemn meeting of ours was fixed for the three days that precede the Feast of St. Luke [October 18] . . . The house we had chosen for the purpose of our assembly was that which we had almost always employed on former occasions. It was the house of two sisters, one a widow, and the other a virgin, both of them illustrious for good-

---

[1] *Troubles*, First Series, p. 149.
[2] Stonyhurst MSS., Father Grene's *Collectan. P.,* f. 556.

ness and holiness, whom in my own mind I often compare
to the two women who received our Lord. . . .

"Of a sudden there arrives a Queen's messenger. . . .
Rosaries, chalices, sacred vestments, all other signs of
piety are, with the men, thrown into a cavern; the mistress of the house is hidden away in another hiding-place.
. . . On this occasion, as often enough on others when
the pursuivant came, the younger sister, the unmarried
one, passed herself off for the mistress of the house. . . To
all the other discomforts this is to be added, that in cases
like this it is necessary to contend with men who are hard
to satisfy. This the young lady always did with such
skill and prudence as to be able to control their pertinacity
and talkativeness. She was remarkable at all times for
her virginal modesty and shamefacedness, but in the cause
of God and the defence of His servants the *virgo* became
virago. She is almost always ill, but we have seen her
when so weakened as to be scarce able to utter three
words without pain, on the arrival of the pursuivants
become so strong as to spend three or four hours in contest
with them. When she has no priest in the house she feels
afraid; but the simple presence of a priest so animates
her that then she makes sure that no devil has any power
over her house. This was proved to be true in this cruel
search in particular. . . . For, quite miraculously, one pursuivant who took into his hand a silver pyx which was
used for carrying the Blessed Sacrament from place to
place, straightway put it down again, as if he had never
seen it. Before the eyes of another lay a precious dalmatic
folded up. He unfolded everything else, but that he did
not touch. I should never stop if I were to write down
all the edifying things that have happened in this or other
searches."

The martyr-poet Father Southwell refers in one of his
letters to the pleasure these meetings gave him. The
occasion related by him was some little time before that

I

on which this search was made, as his letter is dated March 8, 15$\frac{89}{90}$. The letter is translated by Bishop Challoner from the Spanish of Yepez; in the following extract some alterations are made in accordance with the original Latin.[1] "We have all together with the greatest joy renewed our vows, according to our custom, spending some days in mutual exhortations and conferences. *Aperuimus ora et attraximus spiritum.*[2] It seemed to me that I saw the cradle of the Catholic religion which is now being born in England, the seeds of which we now sow in tears that others may come and bear the sheaves in gladness. We have sung the canticles of the Lord in a strange land, and in this desert we have sucked honey from the rock and oil from the hardest stone. But *extrema gaudii luctus occupat*, the end of these our joys was in sorrow. Sudden fears dispersed us, but in the end we escaped with much danger but little hurt. I and another of ours, seeking to avoid Scylla, had like to have fallen on Charybdis, but by the mercy of God we passed betwixt them both without being shipwrecked, and are now sailing in a safe harbour."[3]

Another Father who is named by Father Gerard as present at this meeting in October 1591, and as shut up in the same hiding-place with himself, is Father Thomas Stanny. In November 1609, that is, about the time when Father Gerard wrote his autobiography, this Father wrote a "Relation about Martyrs" which is not now known to exist, but of which a few fragments are preserved for us by Father Christopher Grene.[4] He thus mentions Father Garnet, and the search at the renewal of vows in 1591. "He being sent into England, and shortly after Father

---

[1] P.R.O., *Domestic, Elizabeth*, vol. ccxxx. n. 104.

[2] Psalm cxviii. 131.

[3] Father Southwell has written this as an introduction to two different letters bearing the same date, one of which refers to the other, in which he has described the martyrdom of Bales and Horner.

[4] Stonyhurst MSS., Father Grene's *Collectan. P.*, f. 581.

Weston the Superior happening to be taken . . . blessed Father Henry Garnet succeeded him, and for the space of almost twenty years performed that office with great charity and edification . . . and with great increase of the Catholic faith and benefit of our Society, for at his first coming into England he there found only one Father of our Society, but at his glorious martyrdom he left behind him above forty of our Society. . . .

"Amongst other virtues, he had special devotion unto the Blessed Sacrament, in so much that he very seldom omitted to say mass for any troubles or travels. It was his custom always during the whole Octave of Corpus Christi to reserve the most Blessed Sacrament upon the altar with great ornaments, reverence, devotion and processions.[1] And when some said unto him, 'Your Reverence should do very well to be more wary in these dangerous times,' . . . he made them this most confident answer, 'God, without doubt, will both defend and protect Himself and us likewise, if we firmly trust and rely on Him.' . . .

"He had likewise a very great care that those that were not professed should, according to our rules, diligently twice a year renew their vows, which for some twelve or fourteen years he caused us to observe very exactly; although that, by reason of searching and such like troubles, divers were much against our meeting: yet his trust and confidence in God was so great that by no means he would omit it . . . but always said, 'By the grace of God I will take charge of you all until you have made your renovation, but afterwards provide for yourselves.' For which cause most of us did depart the same day, because that divers times it fell out that the very next day, when the greatest part were gone, the pursuivants came to search the house; as twice I myself had trial thereof, when the next morning seven of us were driven

[1] See *Troubles*, Second Series, p. 144.

to hide ourselves in secret caves under ground. At our meeting were made divers sermons, one by our Superior himself, the rest by others of our Society."   ·

Against such men a powerful Government was engaged in a war of extermination, and false brethren were found to betray them.   In the following year James Young *alias* George Dingley, *alias* Thomas Christopher, the poor priest with whom we have already made acquaintance, made the following offer[1] to Lord Keeper Puckering. "This term time divers priests will be in London, and as I think Garnet the Jesuit will also be here, or some other of the chief of them, with whom I should haply meet abroad and covertly give your honour to understand of them, that therein also your lordship may have experience of my sincere meaning and desire to requite in some sort her Majesty's most princely favour and your honour's bounty towards me. Thus wearied with irksome imprisonment, yet content with your lordship's determination, I commend your lordship to the safe tuition of Almighty God. From my prison this 30th October, 1592."

[1] P.R.O., *Domestic, Elizabeth*, vol. ccxliii. n. 50.

CHAPTER X.

FATHER OLDCORNE.

"SINCE I have mentioned Father Oldcorne's residence, I will set forth in short how he came to take up his abode there. When he first arrived in England he stayed some time with the Superior, as he had no place of his own to go to. At a little distance from his Superior's residence in the country, there was a fine house belonging to a Catholic gentleman, a prisoner in the Tower of London for the Faith."

This was Thomas Abington, whose wife was Lord Mounteagle's sister, and he was in the Tower in 1588 on the pretext of the Babington Plot. "The house," Father Gerard says in the "Narrative of the Powder Plot,"[1] "was called Henlip, two miles distant from the city of Worcester, and so large and fair a house that it might be seen over great part of the country; and indeed it was so fair and commodious a house that it had often caused the owner of it much trouble, being an eyesore unto some Puritans of great wealth that were neighbours within some miles, and nothing so well seated; who therefore procured often warrants to search that house in hope to find some priest there, for which the house and whole estate of the gentleman might be forfeited to the king, and so begged by them that were the causers and actors of such apprehension. But this being often essayed was never permitted by God until" the time when Fathers Garnet and Oldcorne were taken there, soon after the Gunpowder Plot. Dorothy was the name of Thomas Abington's sister, of whose conversion[2] by

[1] *Condition of Catholics*, p. 149.   [2] *Ibid.* p. 283.

Father Oldcorne Father Gerard next speaks. "He had a sister, a heretic, who had been bought up at the Queen's court. There she had drank so deep of the poison of heresy, that no physician could be found to cure her, though many had tried. She readily spoke with them all about religion, but she did so all for the sake of argument, and not for the sake of learning. Thus no profit was made of an excellent Catholic's house, of which she had the charge while her brother was away. The house was one which surpassed all in the county for beauty, pleasant situation, and the many advantages it offered to Catholics.

"After many attempts had been made on the lady without effect, Father Garnet wished Father Oldcorne to go and try his hand for once. He went, and found her very obstinate ; he plied her with arguments from Scripture, reason, and authority, but all in vain. The woman's obstinacy however did not foil the man's perseverance. He turned to God, and strove to cast out the dumb devil by prayer and fasting. She, seeing the Father eating nothing for the first and second day, began to wonder at his way of going on. Led on notwithstanding by obstinacy or curiosity, she said to herself, 'Perhaps he is not a man but an angel ; so I will see whether he subsists on angels' food ; and if he does not, he shall not convert me.'

"Accordingly the good Father kept up his fast for four days without tasting anything. By this steadfastness he discomfited the devil, and the woman was cured from that hour. He had truly obtained for her ears to hear, for from being very obstinate and headstrong, she became henceforth very obedient and humble. Indeed it seems likely that the reason why other priests could not win her to God, was because the Divine Providence had destined her for this Father, and designed not only her, but nearly the whole county to be brought over in consequence. He lived for sixteen years together in this residence and by his fruitful labours in this and the neighbouring counties, he won many to the faith, strengthened the wavering, and restored the fallen, besides stationing priests in divers places." Or, as Father Gerard expresses it elsewhere, "In which time of his abode in those parts it is not easy to be believed how many obstinate heretics he converted, how many weak Catholics he confirmed, how many scholars he sent over to the Seminaries and religious women to monasteries, how many houses he brought to that degree of devotion that he might and did settle priests in them."

"This it was that made several apply to him what St. Jerome writes of St. John, that 'he founded and governed all the domestic churches in those parts;' and in good sooth all looked up to him as their father. Such was his prudence, that he fully satisfied all; such his diligence and endurance of toil, that he never failed any one in the hour of need; and his alms supplied the wants of many poor Catholics. In fact his house might have been one of our residences in a Catholic country, such was the number of Catholics flocking there to the Sacraments, to hear his sermons, and to take advice in their doubts. His helpmate was Father Thomas Lister,[1] a man of distinguished learning.

"While thus serving others, Father Oldcorne treated his own body with great harshness. Not satisfied with the labours I have set forth, and his 'care for all the churches' in those parts, which really in great measure seemed to depend on him for everything, he had many ways of macerating his flesh. He applied hard to study while at home. Of his fasts I have already spoken. He

---

[1] As this Father was imprisoned at Middleburg in Lent 1598, his work with Father Oldcorne must by that time have ended, and about the end of Elizabeth's reign he was stationed "with Mr. Cotton of Warblington in Hampshire." *Troubles*, First Series, pp. 166, 191.

made use of the hair-shirt, and still more of the discipline, with great fervour. By all this put together, while he thought only of chastising his enemy and bringing it under subjection, he nearly made himself an unprofitable servant. First he broke a blood-vessel, which caused him to vomit blood in quantities. He managed to get over this, but almost every year he fell into such a weakness that his strength could hardly be restored. From this infirmity there came a cancer in his mouth, which increased to such a degree as to be incurable. The doctors said, as he told me afterwards, that some bones which seemed decayed would have to be taken out. The good Father fearing thereby to be hindered from preaching, in which he was gifted with a marvellous talent, resolved first to go on a pilgrimage to St. Winifred's Well, a famous place and a sort of standing miracle.

"St. Winifred was a holy maiden in North Wales, comely of face, and comelier still for her faith and love of chastity. A son of one of the Welsh chieftains loved her and sought her hand. She rejected him, as well on account of his being a heathen, as because she had already vowed her virginity to God at the hands of the bishop of the place, and was unwilling to yield it to man. The enraged chieftain's love turned into fury, and he cut off the maiden's head with a stroke of his sword. As this happened on the slope of a hill, the head rolled down to the bottom, where instantly burst forth a powerful spring of water. Ever since, the glen, which before got its name from its dryness,[1] has had in it a copious stream of water, which takes its rise at that spring and flows on to the sea. Such a volume of water gushes out of the spring every minute, that it suffices to turn a mill at fifty paces distance. There are very large stones in the

---

[1] " Beunonus igitur cum Teuyth patrocinio suum fixit tugurium in convalle quæ Britonum lingua *Sechnant* appellabatur." From the Life of St. Winifred in Cott. MSS. Claud. A. 5, published in the *Lives of the Cambro-British Saints*, Llandovery, 1843, p. 199.

well, all red, as if covered with fresh blood. The people
of the place are very loth to allow pieces to be cut off.
Such pieces are also red, and the place of the cut changes
from white to red in time. In the stream are also found
many stones either covered or sprinkled with blood. The
Catholics gather these, and treasure them up as objects
of devotion, as they do the sweet-smelling moss that sticks
to the stones.[1] The water in it is very cold; but drinking
it or bathing in it out of devotion has never done any one
any harm. I myself have taken several draughts together
fasting without hurt. On the feast of St. Winifred (the
3rd of November), the water rises a foot higher than
usual. It turns red on that day, and on the morrow is
clearer than before. I visited it once on that day to
witness the change, and found the water troubled and of
a reddish hue, whereas it is generally so clear that you
can see a pin at the bottom. It was winter, and freezing
so hard at the time, that, though the ice had been broken
the night before by the people crossing the stream, I
had hard work to ford it on horseback the first thing
next morning. Notwithstanding this severe frost, I went
into the well, as all pilgrims do, and lay down and prayed
there for a quarter of an hour. On coming out my shirt
was of course dripping wet, but I did not change. I put
on my clothes over it, and took no harm whatever.

"These are wonderful facts, but in addition to them
very signal miracles are often wrought there. A heretic
visitor seeing the Catholics bathe out of devotion, said
scoffingly, 'What makes these fellows bathe in this water?
—I'll wash my boots in it.' He jumped in as he was with
his boots on, and sword in hand. No sooner had he done
so than he felt the supernatural power of the water, which
before he had refused to believe. He was at once palsied

[1] The red lichen and the moss are both odoriferous. Of the former Pennant
says that "the stone to which it adheres easily betrays itself by the colour
being as if smeared with blood, and, if rubbed, yields a smell like violets."

and lost the use of his limbs, and his sword could hardly be got out of his hand. For several years he was drawn about in a little cart, a cripple, to punish his own unbelief and to strengthen the belief of others. I myself have spoken to several persons who saw the lame man, and heard the story vouched for both by the man himself and by all who knew him. I learnt from them that the cripple afterwards repented, and recovered his soundness in the same well where he had lost it. There are many other stories of the same sort.

"Such was the place where the blessed Father Old-corne determined to go, but St. Winifred was beforehand with him. He chanced on his way to reach the house of two maiden sisters, poor indeed in their way of life, but rich in the fear of God. They lived together in His service, keeping a priest in their house, whom they supported and honoured as a father. This good priest had a stone taken out of the stream that flows from the well, sprinkled with blood as I described before. He used to place it on the altar with the other relics. When Father Oldcorne saw it, he took it and kissed it with great reverence. Then going apart he fell on his knees and began to lick the stone, praying inwardly as he held part of it in his mouth. In half an hour all pain was gone, and the disease was cured. He travelled on to the well, however, rather to return thanks than to ask any further favour. There he recovered also from the weakness of body which was thought to have brought on the cancer, and returned home as strong and hale as he had been for many a year. These are the words in which Father Oldcorne himself told me the story. The priest also, in whose abode he found the stone, lately vouched for the facts when I met him at St. Omers. He gave me an account of other marvels that happened at the death of Father Oldcorne, of which hereafter. So much then for Father Oldcorne, I return now to my own poor self."

CHAPTER XI.

RELICS.

"DURING my stay in this third residence, I gave the
Spiritual Exercises to several persons. Among them were
two gentlemen, who still stand to the good purposes they
then made. They are our staunchest friends in the districts
where they live. One of them, Mr. John Lee, lately
defended philosophy at Rome: he is always ready to
entertain ours and furnish them with money. The other
has shown himself worthy of trust in many matters of
moment. After five or six years each of them made
another retreat with the most consoling result.

"I sent also some young men abroad to study, with
the view of entering on a more perfect state. One died at
Douay, after great advancement in his studies, and with a
wide-spread reputation for holiness. He had been a com-
rade of the blessed martyr Father Francis Page, S.J. They
were both in an office in London. It was through his
means that the blessed Father was first brought to me,
to his no small profit, as I shall show hereafter. Some
are now Fathers of the Society; for instance, Father
Silvester and Father Clare, now living I think at the
Seminary of Valladolid. Others of my sending are now
serving God in divers places and divers conditions: among
whom is Father John Bolt. Great talent for music had
won him the warmest love of a very powerful man. He
spurned this love, however, and all worldly hopes with
it, to attach himself to me; and lent his ear to the
counsels of Christ in the Spiritual Exercises."

Father Thomas Silvester was Minister of the College of

Valladolid when Father Weston was Rector.[1] Father John Clare must not be confounded with Sir John Warner who took the name of Clare.

Father John Bolt was not a Jesuit, but died a secular priest in 1640, having been chaplain and organist to St. Monica's Convent for twenty-eight years.[2] He was arrested in March 159¾, with William Wiseman, in a house hired by Father Gerard in Golding-lane, and those then taken were called by Father Garnet "our friends and chiefest instruments." We have his examinations on that occasion, and they will be given when we come to that stormy period in Father Gerard's life. Before that however our autobiographer had an interval of comparative calm, and he has time to think of holy relics.

"At this time I had given me some very fine relics, which my friends set for me very richly. Among them was an entire thorn of the holy Crown of our Lord, which the Queen of Scots had brought with her from France (where the whole Crown is kept), and had given to the Earl of Northumberland, who was afterwards martyred. He always used to carry it in a golden cross about his neck as long as he lived, and at his death made it over to his daughter, who gave it to me. It was enclosed in a golden case set with pearls: it is now in the hands of my Superior, along with three other cases made of silver with glass in front. Two of them are old relics, rescued from the pillage of a monastery. They came to me from a source that I could trust. The third contains the forefinger of the martyr, Father Robert Sutton, brother of him whom I mentioned in the first chapter. By a wonderful providence of God, this finger, along with the thumb, was kept from decay, though the whole arm had been set up to be eaten by the birds of heaven. It was taken away

---

[1] *Troubles*, Second Series, p. 282.
[2] *Troubles*, First Series, p. 297, where the name is in the first instance misprinted "Best."

secretly by the Catholics after it had been there a year, and was found quite bare. The only parts that were covered with skin and flesh were the thumb and finger, which had been anointed at his ordination with the holy oil, and made still more holy by the touch of the Blessed Sacrament. So his brother, another pious priest, kept the thumb himself and gave the finger to me."

The relics mentioned thus far by Father Gerard were, he tells us, in the hands of his Superior: those that he afterwards describes were left in the care of various private persons "in trust for the Society." The latter, as far as is known, have all perished ; but the account of the former is of great interest to us, as these relics have come down safe to our times, and are all at Stonyhurst.

The two "old relics, rescued from the pillage of a monastery," are there. They have labels in a fourteenth century handwriting, but they are not easily decipherable, and probably Father Gerard could not read them, as he gives no names to the relics.

The thumb of Robert Sutton, priest and martyr— Father Gerard is wrong in calling it the forefinger—is there also, in a small gilt upright cylindrical reliquary. With it there is enclosed a paper in Father Gerard's handwriting,[1] giving the same account of the relic that he has given above.

There were two martyrs of the name of Robert Sutton.[2] One was a layman, a schoolmaster, who was put to death at Clerkenwell, October 5, 1588.[3] The other, whose relic this is, suffered at Stafford,[4] according

[1] " Pollex Dni. Roberti Suttoni Sacerdotis, qui Staffordiæ vinctus, nocte ante passionem in carcere magna luce circumfusus orare visus est. Partes autem corporis, postquam volatilibus cœli per annum expositæ fuissent, a Catholicis sublatæ, hoc pollice et indice intactis, cæteris ad ossa usque consumptis, inventæ sunt."

[2] Dr. Oliver has confounded the two ; he says that Robert Sutton was " formerly Rector of Lutterworth," but he quotes no authority for so saying.

[3] Challoner, *Missionary Priests*, vol. i. p. 245.

[4] *Ibid.* vol. i. p. 206.

to some on the 27th of July, according to others on the 3rd of March, 1587. The brother, who gave this relic to Father Gerard, was Abraham Sutton, who was ordained with Robert at Douay February 23, 157⅞. They were sent together upon the English mission on the 19th of March, when they had been just a year at the College, and having both been imprisoned, they were banished together in 1585. Abraham, who was at one time tutor to two of the young Fitzherberts,[1] was again banished in 1606. The martyr had two other brothers, William and John, both Jesuits, of whom the elder was Father Gerard's tutor.

The relic of the Crown of Thorns has a curious history. The relics previously mentioned were brought from Liége to Stonyhurst on the transfer of the College in the year 1794, and the thumb of Robert Sutton is mentioned in a letter from Father William Strickland to Father Marmaduke Stone, dated April 7, 1806. The relic of the Crown of Thorns was never at Liége. It was taken to St. Omers about the middle of the seventeenth century, probably in December 1665, as the permission for it to be exposed for public veneration was given by the Bishop of St. Omers on the 8th of January, 1666. This permission was countersigned, after the arrival of the relic in England, by the Vicar Apostolic of the Western District, Charles Walmesley, O.S.B., Bishop of Rama, on the 11th of December, 1790, at which time the relic belonged to Mr. Weld of Lulworth, and by the Vicar Apostolic of the Northern District, William Gibson, Bishop of Acanthos, on the 4th of November, 1803, when the relic had been given to Stonyhurst College.

Father Charles Plowden, in his account of the suppression of the English College at Bruges, to which city the College that had existed for two centuries at St. Omers had been transferred a few years before, says that "some

[1] P.R.O., *Domestic, Elizabeth*, vol. ccxxxv. n. 88.

young gentlemen of the College chanced to get into their
possession the beautiful and precious reliquary of the Holy
Thorn which Queen Mary of Scotland brought away with
her from the Royal Chapel of Holyrood House; and
knowing that other valuable deposits were in the Carthusian Convent, one of them in his journey to England
left the Holy Thorn there, as in a place of security,
consigned to the hands of Father Norris. Father Mann,
Prior of the Carthusians, leaving them, voluntarily surrendered the treasures he had received to the Government,
taking Father Norris with him to Bruges for that purpose.
The Holy Thorn fell into the hands of a scrivener named
Van de Steine, who sold it in 1781 to Mr. Thomas Weld
for seven guineas, the value of the gold, and under promise
to restore it if redemanded by the Government of Maria
Teresa. In 1803 Mr. Weld gave it to the Reverend
Marmaduke Stone for Stonyhurst."

This account of the purchase by Mr. Weld is perfectly
accurate, but the rest of the story as told by Father
Plowden is imperfect and incorrect.[1] The facts are these.
On the suppression of the Society, not unnaturally, the
English boys at the *Grand Collége* at Bruges became very
unruly and unmanageable on the loss of their masters, and
the Government, which had desired to preserve the College
for the benefit of the city of Bruges, was obliged to send
them away. Some went to Liége and others to their own
homes. Among the boys there was the Hon. Hugh
Edward Henry Clifford, afterwards the sixth Lord Clifford,
then a boy of seventeen. The property of the Jesuits had
been seized, and the cupboards were sealed by the Commissaries of Maria Teresa. Mr. Clifford, knowing how the
relic of the Holy Thorn was prized by the Jesuit Fathers,
broke open the cupboard in which it was, and gave it to a

[1] The writer's best thanks are due to W. H. James Weale, Esq., of
Bruges, for the reference to the Abbé Mann's letter and for information
respecting the relic at Ghent.

scholastic of the name of Jameson, who was then starting for England in charge of the two sons of Sir James Haggerstone, Bart. Their way lay through Nieuport, where existed the last remains of the famous Carthusian house of Sheen, which had kept up its continuity in the Low Countries all through the times of the persecution in England, to perish in the French Revolution. Father Augustus Mann, better known afterwards as the Abbé Mann, was then Prior, and on learning from Mr. Jameson that he had this treasure with him, he induced him, by fear of excommunication for stealing a relic and by threats of the indignation of Maria Teresa's Government, to leave the relic at Nieuport. The Prior then sent it to the Bishop of Bruges, with a letter dated the 16th of October, 1773 ; but when it reached the Bishop, the Commissaries had left Bruges, and the reliquary was handed over to their notary, Van de Steine, who kept it, and ultimately sold it, as Father Plowden says, to Mr. Weld of Lulworth.

The reliquary is very light and graceful, of the renaissance period, made in gold with little enamels inlaid. Under the foot is the following inscription : " + Hæc spina de Corona Doi. sancta, fuit primo Mariæ Reg. Scot. Mart., ab ea data Comiti Northumb. Mart., qui in morte misit illam filiæ suæ Elizᵗ, quæ dedit Soc., hancq. I. Wis. ornavit auro." "My friends set it for me very richly," says Father Gerard. Who can doubt that the "I. Wis." of the inscription is "Jane Wiseman ? "

Father Gerard speaks only of one reliquary, and that one in which the relic is "set with pearls." Several spiral strings of pearls surround the relic at Stonyhurst. But there is another reliquary in existence the very counterpart of it, of exactly the same form and materials, with precisely the same inscription under its foot, containing also a little relic of one of the Holy Thorns. It is clear that, though he has not recorded it, Father Gerard divided into two parts the relic which he received from Lady Elizabeth Woodroff, and Jane Wiseman had two reliquaries made by the same artist. The second differs from the first only in having no strings of pearls. At the time that the first was taken to St. Omers, the second was taken to the English Jesuit Novitiate at Watten by Father John Clerk, the Provincial, who, at the request of Father Martin Grene the Rector, wrote an authentication dated the 17th of January 1666, which was approved by the Bishop of St. Omers on the 5th of February. The inscription, being under the foot, was never read by Father Clerk, who could only attest that it had been kept in the Provincial's room in London, and always venerated by his predecessors as a true relic of the Crown of Thorns. On the expulsion of the Society from France a few years before the suppression, the College of St. Omers became the *Grand Collége* at Bruges, and the school at Watten the *Petit Collége* in the same city ; but though the relics and archives of St. Omers were taken to Bruges, those of Watten were deposited in the Tertianship at Ghent, and there they were seized at the time of the suppression. By some means the Watten relics passed into the possession of Maximilian Macharius de Meulenaere, Dean of the Chapter of St. Bavon and Vicar General of Ghent, who kept them for some years, obtaining for the Holy Thorn the approbation of the Bishop of Ghent, Govardus Gerardus van Eersel on the 23rd of March 1774. Besides the relic of the Holy Thorn, the Dean had the magnificent relic which bears the inscription "A peece of the stump of the crosse of o. Savio.," which was once in the Tower of London with the crown jewels of James I. The Holy Cross the Dean ultimately gave to the Bishop of Ghent, and it is now preserved in the Treasury of the Cathedral of St. Bavon. The Holy Thorn he gave to the confraternity of the Holy Cross in the Church of St. Michael at Ghent on the 24th of April 1808, and in the sacristy of that Church it now is.

We may now let Father Gerard finish what he has

J

to say about the relics that came into his possession, and then we accompany him into scenes of danger.

"I had given me about the same time a silver head of St. Thomas of Canterbury; also his mitre set with precious stones. The head, though neither large nor costly, is very precious from having in it a piece of the skull of the same Saint, which we think was the piece that was cut off when he was so wickedly slain. It is of the breadth of two gold crowns. The silver head was old and had lost some stones, so the gentleman, in whose house I was, had it repaired and better ornamented. On this account, the Superior afterwards let him keep it in his private chapel in trust for the Society.

"In like manner another Catholic gentleman in that county has by the same permission a large piece of the arm of St. Vita, virgin, daughter of a king in the west of England. Many churches in England are dedicated in her honour under the name of Whitchurch. This relic reached me by God's will in this manner. The parson of the place where the whole or great part of her body used to be kept in olden times with due honour, began to be troubled in his rest, insomuch that he could not sleep. The annoyance had lasted for some time, when one day the thought struck him that his troubles came from his not paying proper respect to these bones which he had in his keeping, and that he ought to give them to the Catholics, the rightful owners. He did so, and his rest was never again broken. A good priest told me this story, and gave me a large bone, which a pious Catholic is keeping at present for the Society.

"There was also given me some beautiful altar furniture, which I used to the great comfort and increase of devotion as well of the Catholics of the house as of visitors."

NOTE TO CHAPTER XI.

It may be as well to place on record here the documents relating to the history of these relics. And first we give the paper preserved at Stonyhurst with the Holy Thorn.

Sacratissima spina (ex Corona quæ venerando Christi Domini Salvatoris capiti imposita et impressa fuit) quam nitidissimo vitro inclusam in theca aurea servant Patres Angli Societatis Jesu in Seminario Audomarensi, fuit Mariæ Stuartæ Serenissimæ Reginæ Scotiæ, quæ in Anglia pro fide et justitia martyrium subiit. Hæc eamdem legavit Henrico Percy, Northumbriæ Comiti, qui Catholicam fidem sanguine pariter consignavit. Hic Comes reliquit illam filiæ suæ, lectissimæ feminæ Elizabethæ, quæ deinde eam donavit Patribus Societatis Jesu, a quibus multos annos religiosissime servabatur, et quantum in hæretica gente periculosis temporibus licuit, fidelium venerationi proposita fuit: nuper vero, quo tutiore loco sit, neque debito cultu ac veneratione diutius fraudetur, ex Anglia transmissa et apud R. P. Rectorem Seminarii Audomarensis deposita est. In una basi sive pede thecæ qua includitur, quæ puro constat auro, hæc verba insculpta leguntur: *Hæc spina de Corona Domini sancta, fuit primo Mariæ Reginæ Scotiæ martyris, et ab ea data Comiti Northumbriæ martyri, qui in morte misit illam filiæ suæ Elizabethæ, quæ dedit Societati; hancque J. Wis. ornavit auro.*

Illmus. ac Revmus. Dnus. Epus. Audomarensis permittit præfatam Sacratissimam Spinam exponi publicæ hominum venerationi. Datum Audomari, Januarii 8, 1666.

De mandato, J. DE LA RAMONERIJ, *Secret.*

Eamdem Sacratissimam Spinam exponi publicæ venerationi permisi. Die 11 Decem. 1790.

CAROLUS EPUS. RAMATEN, V^{cus} *Aplicus.*

Eamdem Sacratissimam Spinam exponi publicæ venerationi permisi. Die 4 Nov. 1803.

GULIELMUS EPUS. ACANTHENSIS, *Vic. Apus.*

2. Prior Mann's letter to Mgr. Caimo, Bishop of Bruges, is copied from the original in the *Archives de l'Etat* at Bruges, in the *Palais de Justice, Collection spéciale*, n. 10, f. 96.

Nieuport, le 16 Oct. 1773.

Monseigneur,

Etant absent de chez nous une partie de la journée d'au hier, dans cet intervalle il est passé par chez nous le nommé Jameson, cidevant maître de classe au Grand Collége des Jésuites Anglois à Bruges, passant en Angleterre avec les deux fils du Chevalier Baronet Haggerston. Il a découvert qu'il avait avec lui *un petit Reliquaire d'or emaillé et orné d'environ une 50ᵉ de fines perles orientales, dans lequel est enchassée une Epine de la Couronne de Notre Seigneur, le tout dans un étui noir et près de 6 pouces de hauteur.* L'on dit que ce Reliquaire ait appartenu autrefois à Marie Reine d'Ecosse. Jameson disoit que ce Reliquaire a été pris par un jeune seigneur étudiant dans ce Collége, et fils ainé du milord Clifford, une des plus illustres familles d'Angleterre ; que ce Reliquaire est enregistré sur l'inventaire des biens de ce Collége, et que M. Clifford, pour l'avoir, a ouvert ou forcé l'armoir ou endroit ou il étoit enserré. On a tellement preché ce M. Jameson sur ce vol sacrilège, et que ce cas étoit à encourir l'excommunication et l'indignation du Gouvernement contre tous ceux qui y avoit part, que ce Reliquaire est resté chez nous, dans l'intention d'en donner part, et de le remettre à ceux qu'il appartient.

Comme ce cas me paroit grief, et peut avoir des suites facheuses pour un jeune Seigneur et famille illustre, et que nous avons lieu de croire qu'il est tellement sçu entre les autres étudiants qu'il ne peut pas longtems rester secret, je l'ai crû de mon devoir de donner immédiatement connoissance du tout à Votre Grandeur, le laissant à votre sagesse d'agir la dedans, et à en prevenir les suites, par les moyens les plus convenables. Je serois bienaise cependant de voir ce jeune seigneur et son frere cadet partir de ce païs, d'ou milord Clifford ne manquera point de les rappeler aussitôt que les nouvelles de ce qui vient de passer dernièrement à l'égard des membres de l'éteinte Société lui parviendront.

Je prie Votre Grandeur de vouloir bien examiner la lettre que j'ensers pour M. le Conseiller Van Volden, Commissaire de ce Collége sur l'affaire en question, et de la lui faire parvenir, ou de la supprimer comme vous jugerez convenable. Je ne cherche que de remplir mon devoir, et satisfaire à ma conscience dans ces affaires critiques. . . . J'ai l'honneur d'être, avec le plus profond respect, dévouement et soumission,

Monseigneur, de Votre Grandeur

Le très humble et très obeiss.t serviteur,

AUG. MANN.

Endorsed, La relique mentionée en cette lettre a été remise aux commissaires de Sa Maj.té.

3. Father Clerk's attestation that accompanies the relic which is now in the Sacristy of the Parish Church of St. Michael in Ghent is as follows.

Joannes Le Clerque, Provinciæ Anglicanæ Societatis Jesu Præpositus Provincialis.

Cum P. Martinus Grenus, Rector Domus Probationis Wattenis a me petiit ut testimonium darem de quadam Spina Coronæ Christi Domini quæ jam est Watenis, hisce testatum facio me prædictam sacram Spinam quæ crystallo in crucis forma facto inclusa est et circumdatur corona spinea ex auro facta et viridi colori obducta, habetque inferius pedem aureum, ac superius nomen IHS factum ex auro variis coloribus picto, hisce inquam testatum facio me prædictam sacram Spinam in prædicta theca inclusam, in Provincialis cubiculo Londini servavisse, et a prædecessoribus accepisse. Testor insuper me bona fide credere dictam Spinam veram esse unam ex Spinis Coronæ Domini, ac ut talem a prædecessoribus meis servatam et in honore habitam fuisse. Denique testatum facio me prædictam sacram Spinam, cum sua theca aurea misisse Watenas ut ibi cum majore reverentia tutiusque servaretur, donec mihi vel successoribus meis placuerit eamdem repetere. In quorum fidem has manu mea subscriptas, ac officii mei sigillo munitas dedi. Watenis 17 Januarii 1666.

L ✠ S JOANNES LE CLERQUE.

Illmus. ac Rmus. Dnus. Epus. Audomarensis præmemoratam sacram Spinam Coronæ Christi Domini permittit exponi publicæ hominum venerationi.   Datum Audomari quinta Februarii 1666.

De mandato, J. DE LA RAMONERIJ, *Secret.*

Govardus Gerardus van Eersel Epus. Gandavensis permittit has reliquias exponi fidelium devotioni.   Gandavi 23 Martii 1774.

De mandato, M. M. DE MEULENAERE, *Secret.*

CHAPTER XII.

THE SEARCH AT NORTHEND.

1593.

WE now come to a period in Father Gerard's life in which his relations with the Government were too close to be pleasant. To us this is an advantage, for, thanks to the free access to the State Papers now given to historical students, we are able to follow his narrative in the Government documents, and thus we can supply names and dates that he suppressed, and in some cases even we are admitted to secrets that were mysteries to him.

Hence, when Father Gerard says that he had persuaded Mrs. Wiseman, or "the Widow Wiseman," as it seems more natural to call her, "to go to her own house and there maintain a priest whom he recommended," we are able to say that the name of the priest was Brewster, and that her house was at Northend in the parish of Great Waltham—an estate which had been in the possession of the family since the time of Henry VI. We learn that the search of this house when the priest escaped took place on the 26th of December 1593, but that the widow was not then arrested as Father Gerard thought. We learn that the treacherous servant was called John Frank, and that his was "a white house in Lincoln's Inn Fields;" that the house which Father Gerard says "had been lately hired in London for my own and my friend's purposes" was a house then lately built "in the upper end of Golding-lane;" that William Wiseman and others were arrested in it on the 15th of March 159¾; that the house in which Father Gerard was taken was called Middleton's, and that his capture was before the 12th of May 1594. And lastly, there is a strong probability that the pursuivants were put on Father Gerard's track by an unhappy priest of the Tichborne family, of whom Father Gerard had no suspicion. All these points we shall see in detail in due time.

Father Gerard thus passes from his accounts of relics and vestments to searches and imprisonments.

"But there is a time for gathering stones together, and a time for scattering them. The time had now come for trying the servants of God, my hosts, and myself along with them. And that they might be more like in their suffering to their Lord for Whom they suffered, God allowed them to be betrayed by their own servant whom they loved. He was not a Catholic, nor a servant of the house, but had once been in the service of the second brother [Thomas Wiseman], who when he crossed the sea recommended him to his mother and brother. He lived in London, but often used to visit them, and knew nearly everything that happened in either of their houses. I had no reason for suspecting one whom all trusted. Still I never let him see me acting as a priest, or dressed in such a way as to give him grounds to say that I was one. However, as he acknowledged afterwards, he guessed what I was from seeing his master treat me with such respect; for he nearly always set me two or three miles on my journeys. Often too my host would bear me company to London, where we used at that time to lodge in this servant's house. I had not yet found by experience, that the safest plan was to have a lodging of my own. Such were the facts which, as the traitor afterwards stated, gave rise to his suspicions. Feeling sure that he could get more than three hundred pieces of silver from the sale of his master, he went to the magistrates and bargained to betray him. They, it seems, sent him for a while to spy out who were priests, and how many there were of them haunting the houses of the widow and her son."

This servant, John Frank, whom Thomas Wiseman

had recommended to his mother and brother, and who thus repaid their kindness, was examined by Justice Young on the 12th of May, 1594, after Father Gerard's apprehension. In the copious extracts from his deposition that we are about to give, it will be remarked that he says that Mr. William Wiseman and Father Gerard were at his house together at the Midsummer of 1593. Father Gerard has just told us that he used to go there till he got a lodging of his own.

Frank's house is named in one of Father Henry Walpole's examinations in the Tower at the very time when Frank had begun to give information. It is dated[1] May 3, 1594. "He had one direction for England, and had also a note containing some business to be done in England for his kinsman Edward Walpole the priest, who then was at Tournay in Artois. This examinate was also thereby directed to a house in Lincoln's Inn Fields, but he utterly denieth to disclose the name of the owner of the said house or of the gentleman to whom he was directed that lodged in the same house, and yet he knoweth the said house and the name of the said gentleman, but refuseth for conscience' sake (as he saith) to reveal the same. Being further examined whether it were the house of one Frank, a white house in Lincoln's Inn Fields, he answereth he will neither deny it nor affirm it. Being asked again of the gentleman that lodged in the said house in Lincoln's Inn Fields to whom he was directed, which gentleman was of acquaintance as well with this examinate as with the said Edward Walpole, he refuseth to disclose his name, and yet he confesseth he knoweth the gentleman and doth well remember his name. He saith that the name of one Spiller[2] was not set down in any of the said directions given to this examinate.

[1] P.R.O., *Domestic, Elizabeth*, vol. ccxlviii. n. 91.
[2] Mr. Robert Spiller is mentioned in her Life (p. 240) as steward to Anne Countess of Arundel.

And being told that a house called Braddox in Essex was set down in one of his directions, he saith he will neither affirm nor deny the same. Being told that the name of Mrs. White was contained in his direction for England, he utterly denieth it."

The result of Frank's information was that "the widow's house was first searched. The priest that usually dwelt there was then at home, but escaped for that time by taking refuge in a hiding-place. As for the pious widow, they forced her to go to London, there to appear before the judges who tried cases concerning Catholics. At her appearance she answered with the greatest courage, more like a free woman than a grievously persecuted prisoner. She was thrown into gaol." From Frank's deposition [1] we learn that the search was made on the 26th of December, 1593. "The said examinate saith that one Brewster, a priest, being a tall man with a white flaxen beard, was at old Mrs. Wiseman's house at Northend from Michaelmas until Christmas last, and was in the house when the pursuivants were there on Wednesday the 26th of December last, hid in a privy place in a chimney in a chamber. And William Suffield, Mr. William Wiseman's man, came thither for him on Thursday in the Christmas week, at five of the clock in the night, and carried him to Mr. William Wiseman's house at Braddocks, as this examinate heard. And afterwards Suffield came again and rode with old Mrs. Wiseman to the Lord Rich's." The seat of Lord Rich was at Lee Priory, not far from Northend. The widow therefore was not arrested on this occasion.

"*Item*, he saith that between Midsummer and Michaelmas last, Scudamore the priest was there by the name of John Wiseman and stayed there one night, and he told

[1] P.R.O., *Domestic, Elizabeth*, vol. cxlviii. n. 103. By a singular error a duplicate of this paper has been calendared under the date of April 1606, *Domestic, James I.*, vol. xx. n. 52 *.

this examinate that he was a priest, and that he had
reconciled John Jeppes, Mrs. Wiseman's man, about the
first of September.

"*Item*, he saith that one Rooke Chapman, a priest born
in Samford, came thither and stayed there but one night
a fortnight before Christmas last.

"*Item*, he saith that Mr. Gerard, *alias* Tanfield, *alias*
Staunton, the priest Jesuit, was at Mr. William Wiseman's
house at Braddocks all the Christmas last, and Richard
Fulwood was his man attending on him, and was two
years coming and going thither, and was also with Mr.
Wiseman in Lancashire a little before Michaelmas was
twelve months, as Ralph Willis, who then attended on
Master Gerard, told this examinate, and were at the Lady
Gerard's house, she being at home.

"*Item*, he saith that he hath seen Mr. Gerard dine and
sup ordinarily with Mr. Wiseman at his own table in his
house at Braddocks about twelve months past, and that
at Midsummer was twelve months they were both together
in this examinate's house, and Mr. Ormes, the tailor of
Fleet-street was there with him, and did take measure of
Mr. Gerard by the name of Mr. Tanfield, to make him
garments. . . .

"*Item*, he saith that the said Willis told this examinate
since his imprisonment that John Jeppes could do all the
hurt that was to be done in revealing of matters, and that
the said Jeppes did let Staunton [Father Gerard] and the
said Willis through his grounds from Mr. Wiseman's house
at Braddocks. . . .

"*Item*, he saith that about three weeks before Michaelmas last or thereabouts, this examinate was sent by old
Mrs. Wiseman to Mr. Gerard, from Northend to London
with Scudamore *alias* John Wiseman the priest, and a boy
named Richard Cranishe of the age of 16 years, son of
Robert Cranishe, and afterwards Mrs. Jane Wiseman and
Mrs. Bridget Wiseman, sisters to Mr. William Wiseman

came up also ; and William Savage, tailor, servant to old
Mrs. Wiseman, and Richard Fulwood, Mr. Gerard's man,
attended on them, and John Jeppes came up at the same
time ; all of which persons, saving Jeppes, lay at this
examinate's house a week. And then Scudamore, the two
gentlewomen, Cranish, Savage and this examinate, embarked themselves at Gravesend in one Motte his bark,
and went over to Middleburg, and there lay at one Charles
his house about a fortnight, and then went to Antwerp,
and this examinate returned back again ; but whether
Mr. William Wiseman did know of their going over or no
he cannot tell.

"*Item*, he saith that Burrowes the priest told this
examinate in Lent last that he was at Mr. William
Wiseman's house at Braddocks and rode upon a gelding
that Mr. William Wiseman bought of Edward Hamond,
and wore Mr. Wiseman's cloak. And the said Burrowes
did also tell this examinate that Mr. Wiseman said to him
at his coming from him that it was very dangerous for him
to come to this examinate's house, because of the watches
and often searches made there. And the said Burrowes
told this examinate also that Jeppes, meeting him riding
by the way, did know the horse upon which he rode, and
challenged him to be Mr. Wiseman's.

"*Item*, he saith that the said Burrowes did enquire of
this examinate where he might meet with William Suffield,
Mr. William Wiseman's man, being then in London, and
as Burrowes went down to Fleet-lane, he met with the
said Suffield, and this examinate found them both together
in a house in Fleet-lane half an hour after."

These are the portions of Frank's depositions that bear
on the time of the Christmas search at Northend. Immediately after the search Justice Young made his report[1]
to Sir John Puckering, the Lord Keeper. " Right honourable, my hearty duty remembered. This is to advertise

---

[1] P.R.O., *Domestic, Elizabeth*, vol. cxlvii. n. 3 ; dated Jan. 2, 159$\frac{3}{4}$.

your honour that the bearers hereof, Mr. Worsley and Mr. Newall," pursuivants who were Topcliffe's chief aiders in the searches made in the houses of Catholics, "hath been in Essex at Mrs. Wiseman's house, being a widow, and there they found a mass a preparing, but the priest escaped, but they brought from thence Robert Wiseman her son, and William Clarke a lawyer, and Henry Cranedge [Cranishe] a physician, and Robert Foxe, who doth acknowledge themselves all to be recusants, and do deny to take an oath to answer truly to such matters as shall touch the Queen's Majesty and the State, whereupon I have committed them close prisoners, one from another. Also they found in the said house one Nicholas Norffooke, Samuel Savage, and one Daniell, servants unto the said Mrs. Wiseman ; and one Mrs. Anne Wiseman a widow, and Mary Wiseman her daughter, and Elizabeth Cranedge, and Alice Jenings wife of Richard Jenings, and Mary Wiseman daughter to Mr. George Wiseman of Upminster and [he] is in commission of the Peace : and all these in the said house are all recusants. Wherefore if it may stand with your lordship's good liking, I think it were well that they were all sent for hither to be examined ; for that the said Mrs. Jane Wiseman her house is the only house of resort for all these wicked persons. She was at Wisbech with the Seminaries and Jesuits there, and she did repent that she had not gone barefooted thither, and she is a great reliever of them, and she made a rich vestment and sent it them, as your lordship doth remember, as I think, when you and my Lord of Buckhurst sent to Wisbech to search, for that I had letters which did decypher all her doings."

To the widow Jane Wiseman Father Gerard now turns, and thinking by an error of memory when he wrote that she was arrested in the search at her house at Christmas 1593, he enters into detail respecting her conduct during her subsequent imprisonment, and shows how she was a martyr in will, though not in deed. "As for the pious widow," he says, and it was true before long, "they forced her to go to London, there to appear before the judges who tried cases concerning Catholics. At her appearance she answered with the greatest courage, more like a free woman than a grievously persecuted prisoner. She was thrown into gaol, where she so united piety with patience, as to do her own work like a menial, cook her food with her own hands, and wash the dishes. Her aim in this was to find her way by humiliations to true humility of heart, and also to save expense so as to be able to support more Catholics. During her imprisonment she always used to send me one half of her yearly income, to wit six hundred florins [60*l.*] ; with the other half, besides many other good works, she maintained a priest, to bring her Holy Communion at stated times, and assist her fellow-prisoners. She spent all her time either in prayer or in working with her hands, making altar furniture which she sent to divers persons. The holy woman persevered in these good works, till in two[1] years' time God called her to higher things.

"It was His will that the heretics should come to know that she received visits from a priest. If I remember well, the priest was Father Jones, a Franciscan Recollect, afterwards martyred. They resolved therefore to use the law against the widow. She was brought up, and the

---

[1] How long Jane Wiseman was in prison is not clear, but it must have been more than two years, as John Jones, O.S.F., *alias* Godfrey Morris, *alias* Buckley, was martyred at St. Thomas Waterings on the 12th of July 1598. Three days after his martyrdom Father Garnet wrote an account of it (Stonyhurst MSS., Father Grene's *Collectan. P.,* vol. ii. n. 40), of a portion of which the following is a translation. "After labouring with no little fruit for nearly three years in the Lord's Vineyard, he lived for about two years in prison, of which one was less strict custody, and that in a way that was very wonderful on account of the almost incredible concourse of Catholics. This was a fruitful year for him, though spent in a barren field, and he might for a still longer time have borne himself bravely in God's husbandry, if in God's Providence that Topcliffe who is so well known to the whole world, had not either become greedy of the goods of two Catholics or envious of their constancy. Some traitor let Topcliffe know that for some time before his appre-

usual false witnesses appeared, to accuse her of being privy to the maintenance of priests, contrary to the law of the land. The judges at once empanelled a jury, to pronounce her guilty or not guilty. The godly woman seeing that the consciences of the jury would be stained with her blood, if she let them give their verdict in the case, made up her mind to hold her peace and answer nought to the judges' demand whether she was guilty or not guilty. At the same time she knew well the provision of the law, that men or women who refused to plead in a matter of life and death should have far more keen and dreadful torments than convicted felons. They are laid on their backs upon a sharp stone ; then a heavy weight is put upon their breasts, which crushes the sufferer to death. Till the time of which I treat we had only had two female martyrs, not counting the Queen of Scots. One named Clitherow,[1] at York, chose the same sort of martyrdom as the widow, and for the same reason, namely, to spare the consciences of the jury, who she was sure would find her guilty as usual to please the judges, even though conscious of the injustice they were doing. The godly widow of whom I am speaking, resolved to follow this holy martyr's example. She had made up her mind to take the same course and bear the same punishment. So for her silence she was sentenced to be crushed to death.

hension this Reverend Father had for motives of piety visited two persons who were then in the same prison, Mr. Robert Barret [Barnes], and Mrs. Jane Wiseman, a most excellent woman who had two sons in the Society ; that he had stayed two days with them, had celebrated masses before them, and had received money from them. Topcliffe then on this pretext, in the beginning of July, put them on their trial, accusing them of a capital offence for helping a priest with money. They were both condemned, and Mrs. Wiseman, who refused to be judged by the twelve jurymen lest they should be guilty of her blood and ignorant men should on her account incur eternal damnation, was condemned to the extremely cruel death of being crushed by heavy weights placed on her breast. At this sentence with a cheerful and steady countenance she said in Latin, what she had always had every moment on her lips, *Deo gratias.* It is the common opinion that both will be spared.'
   [1] *Troubles*, Third Series, p. 431.

She went from the court rejoicing that she had been held worthy to quit life in this manner for the name of Jesus. However, on account of her rank, and the good name which she had, the Queen's councillors would not let such barbarity be practised in London. So they transferred her after her condemnation to a more loathsome prison, and kept her there. They wanted at the same time to seize her income for the Queen. Now if she had been dead, this income would not have gone to the Queen, but to the widow's son, my host. The godly woman therefore lived in this prison, reft of her goods but not of her life, of which she most desired to be reft. She pined in a narrow and filthy cell till the accession of King James, when, as is usual at the crowning of a new king, she received a pardon, and returned home ; where she now serves the servants of God, and has two of ours with her in the house. So much then for the good widow ; to return to ourselves."

CHAPTER XIII.

THE SEARCH AT GOLDING-LANE.

1594.

FAILING to apprehend Father Gerard or any other priest at Mrs. Wiseman's house at Northend, the next proceeding of the persecutors was to try what could be found at the house taken in Golding-lane. Father Garnet, in a letter[1] to Father Persons at Rome, dated the 6th of September, 1594, and therefore long enough after the event to contain some account of Father Gerard's subsequent apprehension and imprisonment, thus describes this search. "The Friday night before Passion Sunday [March 15] was such a hurly-burly in London as never was seen in man's memory; no, not when Wyatt was at the gates. A general search in all London, the Justices and chief citizens going in person; all unknown persons taken and put in churches till the next day. No Catholics found but one poor tailor's house at Golding-lane end, which was esteemed such booty as never was got since this Queen's days. The tailor and divers others there taken lie yet in prison, and some of them have been tortured. That mischance touched us near; they were our friends and chiefest instruments. That very night had been there *Long John with the little beard*, once your pupil [in the margin is written *John Gerard*] if I had not more importunately stayed him than ever before. But soon after he was apprehended, being betrayed we know not how; he will be stout I doubt not. He hath been very close, but now is removed from the Counter to the Clink, where he may

[1] Stonyhurst MSS., Father Grene's *Collectan. P.* vol. ii. p. 550.

K

in time do much good. He was glad of Mr. Homulus [1] his company, but he had been taken from him and carried to Newgate, whence he hopeth to redeem him again."

Before listening to Father Gerard's account of the search at Golding-lane, we will make the persecutors give theirs. And first, the magistrates employed by the Lord Keeper of the Great Seal made the following report,[2] dated March 16, 159¾. "We have made search according to your Honour's direction. We find four persons greatly to be suspected, *videlicet* in a house lately builded in the upper end of Golding-lane. They were very loth to permit us to come into the said house : it seemed they sought all means to have escaped. When we came into the house, he which opened the door said his name was Wallis, and that by occupation he was a tailor. One other we found lay hidden under stairs behind a door. His name he said was likewise Wallis. We found two other in an upper chamber in one bed, the one having his clothes upon. They said they were brethren, and their names were Fulwood. They said they had been serving-men, but upon divers questions demanded, they seemed to vary. So likewise did the two Wallisses, for not any one of them could tell an even tale. One of the said Wallisses said he loved a mass, and that he had heard mass, as well in Queen Mary's time as in her Majesty's time. Being demanded whether he were a Seminary or Jesuit, answered, 'O Lord, no! I am not learned. I would to God I were worthy to carry their shoes,' and such like words, &c. He said to some of the officers he was glad that we had made a search in that house this night, for now should he suffer some persecution for his religion. It seemed they were all masterless

[1] Mr. "Homulus" is Ralph Emerson, the lay-brother, of whom Father Campion wrote to the General, *Homulus meus et ego,* "My little man and I.' It was of the greatest consequence that no names to strike the eye should appear in letters, in case they were intercepted.

[2] P.R.O., *Domestic, Elizabeth,* vol. ccxlviii. n. 31.

men : but one of the Wallisses said he was servant to the master of that house, and that his master was in the country, but he said he knew not his master. There was very great store of new apparel, as hose, doublets, in great quantity, which Wallis said he had made, but knew not the owners of any one parcel of the same. We found some letters, which being well perused we think will discover much. We found beads of certain stone or amber, and pictures in paper. We committed these four to several prisons : and think we shall deliver the rest of our travail better by speech to your Honour.

"Your Honour's humble at command,

"RO. WATSON.   EDW. VAUGHAN."

Endorsed—" Mr. Vaughan and Mr. Watson. The two Fullwoods in the Counters. The Wallis in Newgate and Finsbury prison."

The capture of William Wiseman is not mentioned in the State Papers, but we learn the manner of it from Father Gerard. After his being taken, Justice Young sent on the 14th of April to Lord Keeper Puckering[1] "the names of them that were found in Mr. Wiseman's house: John Fulwood, Richard Fulwood, Richard Wallis, William Wallis, William Suffield, Ralph Williamson, John Stratforde. These men are all recusants, and will not take an oath to the Queen's Majesty, nor to answer to anything. One Thomas was apprehended when his master was taken, and he fled away with his master's best gelding and a handful of gold that his master gave him. All these were servants to Mr. William Wiseman, who is a continual receiver of all Seminary priests, and went to Wisbech to visit the priests and Jesuits there, and since his imprisonment there was a Seminary priest in his house which escaped away from the Justices and pursuivants, and left his apparel behind him." This was, as we shall see, Father Gerard himself, and later on he was made to try on the clothes

[1] P.R.O., *Domestic, Elizabeth*, vol. ccxlviii. n. 68, I.

thus found, and "they were just a fit." All this was to prove Mr. Wiseman guilty of harbouring him, "which," Father Gerard says, "they were never able to do." Justice Young adds, "Mrs. Jane Wiseman, his mother, hath been also a great receiver and harbourer of Seminary priests, and went to Wisbech with her two daughters, where (as she saith) she was absolved and blessed by Father Edmonds the Jesuit, and since that time her daughters are sent beyond seas to be professed nuns, as other two her daughters were before, and she hath a son named Thomas who is a Jesuit in Rome or in Spain.

"Robert Wiseman, her other son, is also an obstinate recusant and will by no means take an oath. He is prisoner in the Clink. Mrs. Jenings, her kinswoman, sojourned in her house and is a perverse recusant.

"Henry Cranishe, William Clerke, Robert Foxe, three recusants did sojourn in her house and were apprehended.

"Anne Wiseman, widow, Mary Wiseman, spinster, Elizabeth Cranishe, wife of Robert Cranishe, Elizabeth Crowe *alias* Lowe, all these perverse recusants and were abiding with Mrs. Wiseman and taken in her house.

"Mr. Wiseman and his mother had many more servants, both men and maids, all which were recusants, and none of them would come to church, to the great offence and scandal of all her Majesty's good subjects in that country." As this was written after the subsequent search at Braddocks, which was on the 1st of April, Young has included all the prisoners taken on both occasions. At Goldinglane Father Gerard tells us, in accordance with the magistrates' report, "three Catholics and one schismatic" were taken, of whom the latter was the tailor, the ostensible owner of the house.

Father Gerard tells his story thus. "The hidden traitor [John Frank], wholly unknown to his master, was watching his chance of giving us up without betraying his own treachery. At first he settled to have me seized in a

house [in Golding-lane], which had been lately hired in
London to answer my own and my friend's purposes.
From his master's employing him in many affairs, he could
not help knowing the place which his master had hired
for my use. Consequently he promised the magistrates
to tell them when I was coming, so that they might
surround the house during the night with their officers
and cut off my escape. The plan would have succeeded,
had not God brought it to pass otherwise through an act
of obedience.

"My Superior [Father Garnet] had lately come to live
four or five miles from London.[1] I had gone to see him,
and had been with him a day or two, when, having
business in London, I wrote to those who kept the house
to expect me on such a night, and bring in certain friends
whom I wanted to see. The traitor, who was now often
seen in the house, which belonged ostensibly to his master,
learnt the time, and got the priest-hunters to come there
at midnight with their band.

"Just before mounting my horse to depart, I went to
take leave of my Superior. He would have me stay that
night. I told him my business, and my wish to keep my
appointment with my friends; but the blessed Father
would not allow it, though as he said afterwards, he knew
no reason, nor was it his wont to act in this manner.
Without doubt he was guided by the Holy Ghost; for
early next morning we heard that some Papists had been
seized in that house, and the story ran that a priest was
among them. The fact was that my servant, Richard
Fulwood, was caught trying to hide himself in a dark
place, there being as yet no regular hiding-places, though

---

[1] Three years later, that is in March 1597, Father Garnet was living near
Uxbridge, 12 or 13 miles from London in a house called Morecroftes. He
had at the same time a house in' Spitalfields. *Troubles*, First Series, pp. 177,
179. Later on he lived at White Webbs in Enfield Chase, called "Dr.
Hewick's house." P.R.O., *Gunpowder Plot Book*, n. 70.

I meant to make some. As he cut a good figure, and neither the traitor nor any one else that knew him was there, he was taken for a priest. Three Catholics and one schismatic were seized and thrown into prison. The latter was a Catholic at heart, but did not refuse to go to the heretics' churches. As he was a trusty man, I employed him as keeper of the house, to manage any business in the neighbourhood. At their examination they all showed themselves steadfast and true, and answered nothing that could give the enemy any inkling that the house belonged to me instead of to my host. It was well that it was so; for things would have gone harder with the latter had it been otherwise. The magistrates sent him a special summons, in the hope that my arrest would enable them to make out a stronger case against him. As soon as he arrived in London, he went straight to the house, never dreaming what had happened there, in order to treat with me as to the reason of his summons, and how he was to answer it. So he came and knocked at the door. It was opened to him at once; but, poor sheep of Christ, he fell into the clutches of wolves, instead of the arms of his shepherd and friend. For the house had been broken into the night before, and there were some ministers of Satan still lingering there, to watch for any Catholics that might come, before all got scent of the danger. Out came these men then; the good gentleman found himself ensnared, and was led prisoner to the magistrates. 'How many priests do you keep in your house?' 'Who are they?' were the questions poured in upon him on all sides. He made answer that harbouring priests was a thing punishable with death, and so he had taken good care not to run such a risk. On their still pressing him, he said that he was ready to meet any accusation that could be brought against him on this head. However they would not hint anything about me, because though disappointed this time, they still hoped to catch me later, as the traitor was as yet unsuspected.

"My host had on hand a translation of a work of Father Jerome Platus, 'On the happiness of a Religious State.' He had just finished the second part, and brought it with him to see me about it. When he was seized, these papers were seized too. Being asked what they were, he said it was a book of devotion. Now the heretics are wont to pry into any writings that they find, because they are afraid of anything being published against themselves and their false doctrine. Not having time to go on with the whole case, they were very earnest about his being answerable for those papers. He said that there was nothing contained in them against the State or against sound teaching; and offered on the spot to prove the righteousness and holiness of everything that was there set down. In so doing, as he told me afterwards, he felt great comfort at having to answer for so good a book. He was thrown into prison, and kept in such close confinement that only one of his servants was allowed to go near him, and that was the traitor. Knowing that his master had no inkling of his bad faith, they hoped by his means to find out my retreat and seize my person much sooner than they could otherwise have done."

The following is William Wiseman's examination,[1] in which will be found the defence of Father Jerome Platus, which Father Gerard so accurately remembered and embodied in his narrative.

"The examination of William Wiseman of Wimbish in the county of Essex, gentleman, taken the 19th day of March in the six and thirtieth year of her Majesty's reign [159¾].

"He saith that he had the murrey [mulberry coloured] beads (showed unto him upon his examination) of a gentlewoman and friend of his, and that he will not tell her

[1] P.R.O., *Domestic, Elizabeth,* vol. ccxlviii. n. 36.

name for that she is a Catholic, as he termeth her; and
saith that he hath had these beads about a year and a
quarter, and received the same at Wimbish aforesaid at
his house there called Broadoaks; and saith now, upon
better advertisement, that his sister Bridget Wiseman,
now being beyond sea, did get the same beads and string
the same for him this examinate, but where she had them
he cannot tell.   Being demanded whether he know a book
(showed to him upon his examination) called *Breviarium
Romanum,* he denieth that he knoweth the book or whose
it is.   He supposeth that a letter showed unto him upon
his examination, beginning *Dear son, this day,* &c. &c.,
and ending with *Commendations to all my friends* is his
mother's own handwriting, and sent unto him this examinate to his house aforesaid to-morrow shall be a sevennight.

"And saith that a friend of his hath hired the house
in Golding-lane where he was apprehended, but denieth
to tell his name for charity' sake; but saith that his friend
hired it of Mr. Tute dwelling in the next house unto it,
and saith that he hired it this last term.   And saith that
his friend did hire the said house for him this examinate
and his mother, and saith that he was never at the house
before but came to the said house by such description as
his friend made to him of it, and that this examinate
came thither on Saturday at night to lie there, and his
man (whose name *he will not tell* [1] is Richard Fulwood)
provided him by his commandment and appointment a
bed and furniture belonging to the same in the same
house, and knoweth not whether the bedding was in the
house before he this examinate hired the said house or no,
but thinketh some of the bedding that now is there was
in the house before.

---

[1] In the original the words "is Richard Fulwood" are interlined, and "he
will not tell" underlined or erased.

"He saith that the said Richard Fulwood hath served him about Shrovetide last was two years.[1]

"And saith that since he this examinate was confined, he hath used John Fulwood, brother to the said Richard Fulwood, in travelling about his business.

"And saith that his servant Thomas Barker, after he was apprehended and under arrest, was sent by this examinate to his inn, to return to him again, as he saith; and further saith that before the said Thomas Barker went out of the constable's custody, he this examinate laid two angels[2] in the headborough's hand and to take them to his own use if his servant did not return again. He thinketh he is gone to this examinate's house, and denieth that he gave any message to the said Thomas Barker, save only that he should signify to his housekeeper where he this examinate was; and saith that Thomas Barker hath dwelt with him above a year past, and was commended to him by a friend of his being a Catholic, and refuseth to tell his name; and saith that both his said servants have been recusants ever since they dwelt with him.

"And confesseth that a book entitled *Hieronymi Plati*[3] *de Societate Jesu de bono statu religionis* is his own, and that he caused the same to be bought at Cawood's shop in Paul's Churchyard, and saith that the book containeth nothing but true doctrine, and that he translated it through with his own hand—which was found and yet remaineth—the book; and that his servant Richard Fulwood bought the same, and [that he] hath had it or the like by the space of these two years and more; and saith that certain of his friends [being learned *erased*]

---

[1] This may serve to help to fix the date of Father Gerard's going to live at Braddocks. "Shrovetide last was two years" will have been the days preceding Ash Wednesday, Feb. 8, 159½.

[2] The angel was worth 10s.

[3] In the Calendar of State Papers the name is misread *prælati*.

coming to him this examinate, he this examinate commended the said book to them to be a good book, and
delivered the same book to them to be seen and read of ;
and saith within the said two years he this examinate
bought divers of the said book, and hath sent of the same
to some of the examinate's friends, as namely to the
priests at Wisbech, that is to say, Father Edmonds and
to no other by name but to him, but generally to the
priests, which is about a year past ; and that the said
Father Edmonds returned thanks [in] answer to the
examinate that he liked the book very well ; and this
book he sent and received answer by his said servant
Thomas Barker, who was born in Norwich ; and saith
that this examinate hath read over the first and half the
second of the said book unto the 12th chapter, and that
he dare to take upon him to defend so much to be sound
and true ; and saith that this examinate was with Father
Edmonds at Wisbech about Michaelmas last was twelvemonths [1591], and there saw and spake with him both
privately and in company.

                                        "W. WISEMAN.

    " Examined by Edw. Coke, Will. Danyell, Edw. Vaughan,
R. Watson, Ryc. Young."

NOTE TO CHAPTER XIII.

THE examinations of the other persons taken at Golding-lane are thrown into a note, as in the text they would check the progress of the narrative.

"20*mo. Martii*, 1593. John Bolt, of the City of Exeter, of the age of thirty years or thereabout, examined the day and year abovesaid, saith as followeth :

"The said John Bolt saith he serveth not any nor hath done this half year or more, and did lastly serve Sir John Petre, and was discharged out of his service about Midsummer last past : and went then first after into Warwickshire to Mr. Verney his house to teach Mr. Bassett's children to sing and play on the virginalls : and sithence for the most part with one Mr. Morgan Robins, a gentleman that hath a lodging in Finsbury fields, where sometime he lay when the said Mr. Morgan lodged there. And being demanded what was the cause of his repair to the house in the upper end of Golding-lane, saith that the cause of his last repair thither was to fetch a pair of stockings he had left there. And the first time of his coming thither was but about the end of Hilary term last past, and sithence four or five several times he hath been there. And now at his coming to the house, [he] came from out of Essex from one Mr. Wiseman his house, called Braddocks, where he had been all that week, and came to William Wallis.

"And saith that one book bound in parchment, beginning with a piece of Scripture, viz., *There is no other Name under Heaven*, &c., &c., is his book and of his writing. And also one little book written, called *St. Peter's Complaint* is his, but of whose writing he knoweth not, but borrowed it of Mr. Wiseman. Being showed one paper book which was read to him, after he had seen the same, saith that the same little paper book which was found in his cloak-bag, containing about a dozen leaves of paper containing matter of Campion, whereof two written and the other six unwritten is his, and that he wrote the same with his own hand and copied it forth out of one other written book he borrowed of one Harry Souche servant to Mr. Morgan, who he thinketh went away from the said Mr. Morgan about three years sithence and hath heard he is beyond the sea. And that he hath had the same book these five or six years, but did not deliver any copies thereof to anybody.

"JOHN BOLT.

"Edw. Vaghan
Maltus Ayard
John Cornwall
Edward Caterward."

"The examination of John Bolt, late of Thorndon in the County of Essex, yeoman, taken the 21st day of March, 1593.

"He confesseth that certain leaves containing divers and many verses beginning *Why do I use my paper, pen, and ink ?* &c., &c., and ending thus *To Jesu's Name which such a man did raise ?* is all of his own handwriting; and that he wrote the same about five years past in London, out of a paper which one Henry Souche, servant to Mr. Morgan, delivered him at Mr. Morgan's house in Finsbury field; and that he hath read the same sithence about five or six times.

"And saith that about the end of the last term, he resorted to the said house in Golding-lane from Mr. Wiseman's house called Braddocks, and since that time he hath resorted to the said house about five or six times; and thinketh that the said house is Mr. Wiseman's; and knoweth both his men Richard and William Wallis, who keep the said house.

"JOHN BOLT."

"21*mo. Martii.* The said Bolt being further examined upon his oath saith that he hath not been at church by the space of these two years, neither received at any time these seven years.

"Being demanded who did reconcile him from the Church of England to the Romish Church, desireth to be pardoned, for he will not answer thereto, albeit his oath taken, and also charged as a Catholic.

"Being also further demanded if the Pope or King of Spain should invade the land and bring in any foreign power to the end to plant the Romish religion, whether then he would take part with the said Pope or King of Spain, or with her Majesty, being her Highness' natural subject born, and defend this religion here planted and established—to this he will not answer.

"JOHN BOLT.

"Ryc. Young
  Edw. Vaghan."[1]

This is Mr. John Bolt of whose talent for music Father Gerard has already spoken and of whom the Chronicler of St. Monica's Convent at Louvain gives so interesting an account.[2] He had lived "for two or three years at Court, being in great request for his voice and skill in music," but "having a great desire to become a Catholic, he stole away from the Court and came to live among Catholics, where after some time he was reconciled." "The Queen having heard of his departure, fell out with the Master of Music, and would have flung her pantoufle at his head for looking no better unto him; but he lived secretly in gentlemen's houses, being welcome everywhere for his good parts." The good religious then relates how on his apprehension Topcliffe took him for a priest, "but the wicked fellow was mistaken. Notwithstanding he made him to be kept prisoner and caused also irons to be put on him," but "Our Lord took care of him and made his brother, who is now a Knight, to take his defence in hand. When the cruel Topcliffe sought to bring him torments that he might compel him to confess what he knew of priests and Catholics, then did his friends so work for him that the Lady Rich wrote in his behalf a letter, having known him in the Court; so that at length, after much ado, he got free out of danger." Notwithstanding an offer "to live in the Court at his pleasure without molestation for his conscience," he went over to St. Omers where in due time he was made priest, and going to Louvain in 1613 to be present at Sister Magdalen Throckmorton's profession, he was induced to remain at St. Monica's Convent "to maintain their music to the honour and glory of God," and there he died August 3, 1640.

[1] P.R.O., *Domestic, Elizabeth*, vol. ccxlviii. nn. 37, 38, 39.
[2] *Troubles*, 1st series, p. 297.

It is touching to see the books he carried about with him, for the possession of which he was called in question. The first, which he had written out for himself, "beginning with a piece of Scripture," was it is needless to say that beautiful devotion known among Catholics by the name of the "Jesus Psalter." It is ascribed to one of the Bridgettine monks of Sion House, and as the lists of papers found on recusants in searches show, it was a very favourite devotion with our persecuted ancestors and helped to maintain their fervour in their trials. It is to be regretted that it should now be comparatively forgotten.

St. Peter's Complaint is Father Southwell's poem,[1] and the "matter of Campion" beginning *Why do I use my paper, pen, and ink?* is Father Henry Walpole's, written by him shortly after the conversion which he attributed to the warm blood of Father Campion which fell upon him at his martyrdom.

We have still to give the examinations[2] of the servants who were taken in Golding-lane. We are glad of any information respecting the faithful Richard Fulwood, by whose means, as we shall subsequently see, Father Gerard escaped from the Tower.

"The examination of Richard Fulwood taken the 21st day of March, 1593.

"He saith that he was born at Weston in Warwickshire, and that his father Thomas Fulwood and Alice Fulwood his mother dwelt there; and knows not what his grandfather's name [was]; and that his mother's name was Allen before her marriage; and knoweth that she had a brother called Allen but knoweth not his Christian name and knoweth not whether she had any more brothers or no; but knoweth not where her brother dwelt: and knoweth not whether she had any sisters or no, neither what countrywoman she was, and saith that he hath no sisters and that he hath three brethren, William the eldest dwells with his

---

[1] The poem was published at the end of the contemporary black letter "True report of the martyrdom of Mr. Campian, written by a Catholic priest," and it appeared in the *Month* for January—February, 1872, p. 116. Father Christopher Grene (*Collectan. N.* 1, f. 3; Stonyhurst MSS.) says that of the four poems annexed to the black letter book, Father Walpole was the author of the first two, and he adds from a letter of Father Persons that if Walpole had not fled he would have lost his ears for writing them, as Valenger did.

[2] P.R.O., *Domestic, Elizabeth*, vol. ccxlviii. n. 40.

mother, his second brother Anthony dwells also with his mother, and the third John ; and knoweth not how many brethren or sisters his father had, or whether he had any or no.

"And saith that he never served Mr. Wiseman as his servant, and saith that for this year and more he hath served no man. And the last man that he served was Richard Allen, my old Lord Windsor's steward, and that he served him about half a dozen years ; and before that he served Mr. Foljambe of Derbyshire, Sir James Foljambe's son, and served him twelve years ; and before that served old Mrs. Foljambe of Calburgh in Derbyshire by the space of a year or thereabouts ; and denieth that he was ever in Mr. Wiseman's house at Braddocks, but saith that he hath been with his (examinate's) mother this last year and was maintained by her and that which he had gotten in services, and saith that he was never at the said house in Goldinglane before Wednesday at night the last week, neither knoweth Mr. Wiseman nor his mother, nor ever was at Mr. Wiseman's house at Braddocks ; and saith that he never received the communion in his lifetime ; and knoweth not whether a gentleman or gentlewoman either lay in that house or dined or supped there on Wednesday or Thursday the last week.

"Saith that he came from his mother's house at his last coming to this town, but where he lay or baited by the way he knoweth not, but saith he came to the town on Wednesday was sevennight. He met with William Wallis in the street and hath been acquainted, but knoweth not where or how long, and that the said Wallis desired him (this examinate) home to the said house.

"Richard Fulwood."

"The examination of John Tarboocke taken the day and year aforesaid.

"He saith that one called Little Richard have been divers times within this last year at Mr. Wiseman's house at Braddocks, and that he hath tarried there sometime a week and sometime a night, and sometimes more and sometimes less ; when he waiteth there and carrieth up meat to dinner and supper as other of his master's servants have done ; and did wear such a cloak with sleeves as other of his master's men did ; which cloak he yet weareth : and being now confronted with the said Little Richard, who calleth himself Richard Fulwood, affirmeth to his face all this examinate's confession to be true. And saith that he never heard the said Little Richard called Richard Fulwood.

"Examined by us." [Not signed.]

"The examination of John Fulwood taken the day and year abovesaid.

"He saith that his father's name was Thomas Fulwood and his mother's name is Alice ; and that her name before her marriage was Allen ; and that she had divers brethren Thomas, William, Robert and John, and that she had three sisters but what their names were he knoweth not. And that this examinate was born in Staffordshire, at Weston where his father and mother dwelt ; and saith that he hath five brethren ; and denieth that he hath been at Mr. Wiseman's at Braddocks but in his father's lifetime and never since ; but being confronted by the said John Tarboock, who affirmed that he saw him at Braddocks since Christmas last, confesseth the same to be true ; and that he was called there Lazy John, and was not there called John Fulwood, and saith that about two months ago he was first at the said house in Golding-lane, and meeting with Richard Wallis, the tailor, he carried him to the said house in Golding-lane, but tarried not there and lay at the Ram Inn in Smithfield and from thence went to Mr. Thomas Baskervile in Norfolk and tarried there two or three days, and from thence he went to Staffordshire to his mother's house and tarried three weeks with his brother Richard Fulwood, and then they came away together but parted by the way, and this examinate to Burton the first night, and the second night to Leicester, and the third to Northampton, and from thence to St. Alban's, and so to London.

"JOHN FULWOOD."

"The examination of William Suffield the day and year abovesaid.

"He saith that he hath seen the said John Fulwood at Mr.

Wiseman's house twice within this two years as he thinketh, and that Richard Fulwood was Mr. Wiseman's servant, and served him about a quarter of a year after this examinate came to Mr. Wiseman, and never heard either the said Richard or John called Richard Fulwood or John Fulwood but only Richard and John, and confesseth that he was a weaver by his occupation and used his trade in Norfolk before his coming to Mr. Wiseman's service.

"All these former examinations were taken by us

" Edw. Coke   Edw. Vaughan   Ryc. Topcliffe
  Willm. Danyell   Ryc. Young."[1]

It does not seem probable .that Richard Fulwood was a Jesuit lay-brother, as Dr. Oliver calls him. When Father Gerard describes those who served him, he carefully mentions in the other cases those who entered the Society. When Fulwood landed in Belgium with Father Gerard himself in May 1606 Father Baldwin wrote to Father Persons, "I take it he be Jesuit also," but in July when he had seen him at Brussels he simply calls him Richard Fulwood. When Father Gerard wrote in 1609 he only says of him that "he yet remains in banishment, doing good service to our mission notwithstanding." Dr. Oliver asserts that he "died at Liége in a good old age, September 18, 1641." This however is extremely doubtful, and rests on what is apparently a misprint in the Annual Letters of that year, which call the Richard Fulwood who then died at Liége "a temporal coadjutor." If he had been Father Gerard's Richard Fulwood, his life would not have been passed over without mention; and the *Summaria Defunctorum* and *Florus Anglo-Bavaricus*, the latter a Liége book, both say that Richard Fulwood who died at Liége in 1641 was a scholastic in his second year of Theology.

[1] P.R.O., *Domestic, Elizabeth*, vol. ccxlviii. n. 40.

L

CHAPTER XIV.

SEARCH AT BRADDOCKS.

1594.

"On learning the seizure of our house in London," Father Gerard continues, "and my host's imprisonment, I went to his country house to settle with his wife and friends what was to be done, and put all our effects in safe keeping. As we wanted the altar furniture for the approaching Easter, we sent very little of it to our friends. Of course I could not stay away from my entertainers at so holy a time, especially as they were in sorrow and trouble. In Holy Week the treacherous servant came from London with a letter from his master, wherein the latter set forth all that had befallen him, the questions that had been put to him, and his answers. This letter, though seen, had been let pass for the credit of the bearer, to give him a chance of seeing whether I was in the house at this solemn season. He brought me another letter from my servant, whose capture I spoke of above. When by the traitor's information they knew him to be my servant, hoping to wrest from him the disclosure of his friends and abettors, they kept him in solitary confinement in the loathsome prison of Bridewell. The purport of the letter[1] was how he had denied everything, what threats had been

---

[1] It was of the last importance for the friends of a prisoner to know, if possible, what replies he had really given, not only that they might take measures, if necessary, for their own safety, but also that they might know how far to go in their own answers when summoned. The persecutors were constantly in the habit of publishing all sorts of pretended replies which they said had been given by prisoners in their secret examinations, so that prisoners seized every possible opportunity of communicating the truth to their friends; often, as we shall see, in the most ingenious way.

held out to him, and what his sufferings were in prison. He had, he said, hardly enough black bread to keep him from starving; his abode was a narrow strongly built cell, in which there was no bed, so that he had to sleep sitting on the window-sill without taking off his clothes. There was a little straw in the place, but it was so trodden down and covered with vermin that he could not lie on it. But what was most intolerable to him was their leaving all that came from him in an open vessel in that narrow den, so that he was continually distressed and almost stifled by the smell. Besides all this he was daily awaiting an examination by torture.

"While reading the letter to my hostess in the presence of the traitor, I chanced to say at this last part, 'I wish I could bear some of his tortures so that there might be less for him.' It was these words of mine that let us know later on who was the traitor, and author of all our woes. For when I was taken and questioned, and declared that I was quite unacquainted with the family, those who were examining me forgot their secret, and cried out, 'What lies you tell!—did you not say so and so before such a lady, as you read your servant's letter?' But I still denied it, giving them good reasons however why, even if it had been true, I could and ought to have denied it."[1]

The paragraph in Frank's examination, to which Father Gerard refers, runs thus: "*Item,* he saith that the

[1] It will be noticed both from this passage and many others, that the persecuted Catholics followed that common doctrine of Theologians, maintained also by many Protestant moralists, that an unjust oppressor has no right to exact or expect true answers from his victims, if such true answers would help his unjust designs, except where the question is of the faith of the prisoner. It is quite likely that many will be startled now-a-days at such direct denials, owing to our present freedom from those extreme circumstances in which such denials were made. The English law, with a tenderness then unknown, now protects a man from all efforts to make him criminate himself, and it encourages every one who is on his trial to plead "Not guilty." The persecutors themselves, who showed such indignation at their victims' falsehoods, told lies systematically *in order to ensnare the Catholics;* a thing which no code of morality ever countenanced, whether Catholic or Protestant. This subject will be more fully discussed in the sequel.

said Gerard lay one night at the Lady Mary's in Blackfriars (as he thinketh) a little before Easter last,[1] and
Ralph Willis, his servant, lay that night at this examinate's
house, and that Richard Fulwood, since his imprisonment
in Bridewell at Easter last, wrote a letter and sent it from
Bridewell to the Lady Mary's, and there this examinate
received it and went down with it to Mr. Gerard, who was
at Mr. William Wiseman's house at Braddocks all the
Easter last, and hidden in the house while the pursuivants
were there, which letters aforesaid this examinate did
deliver to Ralph Willis, who carried them immediately to
Mr. Gerard. And this examinate saw the letters in Mr.
Gerard's hands, and heard him read them. Wherein
Fulwood wrote that he expected torture every day, and
Mr. Gerard wished that he might bear some of Fulwood's
punishment."

"Scarcely had I done so," Father Gerard resumes,
"when the searchers broke down the door and forcing
their way in, spread through the house with great
noise and racket. Their first step was to lock up the
mistress of the house in her own room with her two
daughters;[2] and the Catholic servants they kept locked
up in divers places in the same part of the house.
They then took to themselves the whole house, which
was of a good size, and made a thorough search in
every part, not forgetting even to look under the tiles of
the roof. The darkest corners they examined with the
help of candles. Finding nothing whatever, they began to

---

[1] The Lady Mary Percy, of whom mention has been previously made.
She "was a devout Catholic, and had come to London a little before my
imprisonment, to get my help in passing over to Belgium, there to consecrate
herself to God. She was staying at the house of her sister," who had lost the
faith, Jane, the wife of Lord Henry Seymour, with whose Protestant servants
Father Gerard was confronted later on. "I dined with them on the day the
witnesses mentioned. It was Lent; and they told how their mistress ate meat,
while the Lady Mary and I ate nothing but fish" (*infr.* p. 195).

[2] Dorothy and Winifred Wiseman; the youngest of whom was ten years
old.

break down certain places that they suspected. They measured the walls with long rods, so that if they did not tally, they might pierce the part not accounted for. Thus they sounded the walls and all the floors, to find out and break into any hollow places that there might be.

"They spent two days in this work without finding anything. Thinking therefore that I had gone on Easter Sunday, the two magistrates went away on the second day, leaving the pursuivants to take the mistress of the house, and all her Catholic servants of both sexes, to London, to be examined and imprisoned. They meant to leave some who were not Catholics to keep the house, the traitor being one of them. The good lady was pleased at this, for she hoped that he would be the means of freeing me, and rescuing me from death: for she knew that I had made up my mind to suffer and die of starvation between two walls, rather than come forth and save my own life at the expense of others. In fact during those four days that I lay hid, I had nothing to eat but a biscuit or two and a little quince jelly, which my hostess had at hand and gave me as I was going in. She did not look for any more, as she supposed that the search would not last beyond a day. But now that two days were gone, and she was to be carried off on the third with all her trusty servants, she began to be afraid of my dying of sheer hunger. She bethought herself then of the traitor, who she heard was to be left behind. He had made a great fuss and show of eagerness in withstanding the searchers, when they first forced their way in. For all that, she would not have let him know of the hiding-places, had she not been in such straits. Thinking it better however to rescue me from certain death, even at some risk to herself, she charged him, when she was taken away, and every one had gone, to go into a certain room, call me by my wonted name, and tell me that the others had been taken to prison, but that he was left to deliver me. I would then answer, she said, from behind the lath and plaster where I lay concealed.

"The traitor promised to obey faithfully, but he was faithful only to the faithless,[1] for he unfolded the whole matter to the ruffians who had remained behind. No sooner had they heard it, than they called back the magistrates who had departed. These returned early in the morning, and renewed the search. They measured and sounded everywhere, much more carefully than before, especially in the chamber above mentioned, in order to find out some hollow place. But finding nothing whatever during the whole of the third day, they purposed on the morrow to strip off all the wainscot of that room. Meanwhile they set guards in all the rooms about, to watch all night lest I should escape. I heard from my hiding-place the pass-word which the captain of the band gave to his soldiers, and I might have got off by using it, were it not that they would have seen me issuing from my retreat: for there were two on guard in the chapel where I got into my hiding-place, and several also in the large wainscotted room which had been pointed out to them.

"But mark the wonderful providence of God. Here was I in my hiding-place. The way I got into it was by taking up the floor, made of wood and bricks, under the fire-place. The place was so constructed that a fire could not be lit in it without damaging the house ; though we made a point of keeping wood there, as if it were meant for a fire. Well, the men on the night-watch lit a fire in this very grate, and began chatting together close to it. Soon the bricks, which had not bricks but wood underneath them, got loose and nearly fell out of their places, as the wood gave way. On noticing this and probing the place with a stick, they found that the bottom was made of wood ; whereupon they remarked that this was something curious. I thought that they were going there and then to

[1] Fidelis tantum erat infidelibus.—*MS.*

break open the place and enter, but they made up their
minds at last to put off further examination till next day.
Meanwhile, though nothing was further from my thoughts
than any chance of escaping, I besought the Lord
earnestly, that if it were for the glory of His Name, I
might not be taken in that house, and so endanger my
entertainers ; nor in any other house, where others would
share my disaster. My prayer was heard. I was preserved in that house in a wonderful manner ; and when,
a few days after, I was taken, it was without prejudice
to any one, as shall be presently seen.

"Next morning therefore they renewed the search most
carefully, everywhere except in the top chamber which
served as a chapel, and in which the two watchmen had
made a fire over my head and had noticed the strange
make of the grate. God had blotted out of their memory
all remembrance of the thing. Nay, none of the searchers
entered the place the whole day, though it was the one
that was most open to suspicion, and if they had entered,
they would have found me without any search ; rather,
I should say, they would have seen me, for the fire had
burnt a great hole in my hiding-place, and had I not got a
little out of the way, the hot embers would have fallen on
me. The searchers, forgetting or not caring about this
room, busied themselves in ransacking the rooms below, in
one of which I was said to be. In fact they found the
other hiding-place which I thought of going into, as I
mentioned before. It was not far off, so I could hear their
shouts of joy when they first found it. But after joy
comes grief : and so it was with them. The only thing
that they found, was a goodly store of provision laid up.
Hence they may have thought that this was the place
that the mistress of the house meant ; in fact an answer
might have been given from it to the call of a person in
the room mentioned by her.

"They stuck to their purpose however, of stripping off

all the wainscot of the other large room. So they set
a man to work near the ceiling, close to the place where I
was: for the lower part of the walls was covered with
tapestry, not with wainscot. So they stripped off the
wainscot all round, till they came again to the very place
where I lay, and there they lost heart and gave up the
search. My hiding-place was in a thick wall of the
chimney, behind a finely inlaid and carved mantelpiece.
They could not well take the carving down without risk of
breaking it. Broken however it would have been, and
that into a thousand pieces, had they any conception that
I could be concealed behind it. But knowing that there
were two flues, they did not think that there could be
room enough there for a man. Nay, before this, on the
second day of the search they had gone into the room
above, and tried the fireplace through which I had got
into my hole. They then got into the chimney by a
ladder to sound with their hammers. One said to another
in my hearing, 'Might there not be a place here for a
person to get down into the wall of the chimney below, by
lifting up this hearth?' 'No,' answered one of the pursuivants, whose voice I knew, 'you could not get down that
way into the chimney underneath, but there might easily
be an entrance at the back of this chimney.' So saying,
he gave the place a kick. I was afraid that he would hear
the hollow sound of the hole where I was. But God, who
set bounds to the sea, said also to their dogged obstinacy,
'Thus far shalt thou go and no further;' and He spared
His sorely-stricken children, and gave them not up into
their persecutors' hands, nor allowed utter ruin to light
upon them for their great charity towards me.

"Seeing that their toil availed them nought, they
thought that I had escaped somehow, and so they went
away at the end of four days, leaving the mistress and her
servants free. The yet unbetrayed traitor stayed after the
searchers were gone. As soon as the doors of the house

were made fast, the mistress came to call me, another
four-days-buried Lazarus, from what would have been my
tomb had the search continued a little longer. For I was
all wasted and weakened, as well with hunger as with want
of sleep, and with having to sit so long in such a narrow
space. The mistress of the house too had eaten nothing
whatever during the whole time, not only to share my
distress, and to try on herself how long I could live without food, but chiefly to draw down the mercy of God on
me, herself, and her family, by this fasting and prayer.
Indeed her face was so changed when I came out, that she
seemed quite another woman, and I should not have
known her but for her voice and her dress. After coming
out I was seen by the traitor, whose treachery was still
unknown to us. He did nothing then, not even send
after the searchers, as he knew that I meant to be off,
before they could be recalled.

CHAPTER XV.

CAPTURE.

1594.

"As soon as I had taken a little refreshment and rest, I set out and went to a friend's house, where I kept still for a fortnight. Then, knowing that I had left my friends in great distress, I proceeded to London to aid and comfort them. I got a safe lodging with a person of rank."

This was the unfortunate Anne Countess of Arundel, whose husband Philip Howard, Earl of Arundel, was at this time in the tenth year of his imprisonment in the Tower. He died the following year in the same prison, the noblest victim to the jealous and suspicious tyranny of Elizabeth, *non sine veneni suspicione*, as his coffin-plate still testifies. From the Life[1] of the Countess, edited by the late Duke of Norfolk, we learn that during the Earl's imprisonment "she hired a little house at Acton, Middlesex, six miles distant from London."

If the following mention of John Gerard in a spy's information[2] be intended for our John Gerard, it is misdated in the Calendar 1601. "That Church told me that John Garrat lay most commonly at the Countess of Arundel's house, and that Dr. Bagshawe would write to them. That Garrard lieth most commonly at Mrs. Soutler's house in the County of Suffolk, with whom John Bennet is greatly acquainted [*in marg.* and at Mr. Lounde in Clerkenwell]." He adds what is certainly inapplicable to our Father John Gerard, but which may be intended for either Miles Gerard the martyr or Alexander his brother,

[1] P. 308.   [2] P.R.O., *Domestic, Elizabeth*, Addenda, vol. xxxiv. n. 38.

"that John Garrat the Jesuit is a very little man." Father
Gerard seems to have lived but a very short time in the
Countess of Arundel's house.

"A year ago," he says, "it had been Father Southwell's abode, before his seizure and imprisonment in the
Tower of London, where he now was.[1] I wanted, however, to hire a house where I might be safe and unknown,
and be free to treat with my friends; for I could not
manage my business in a house that was not my own,
especially in such a one as I then dwelt in. I had recourse
to a servant of Father Garnet named Little John,[2] an
excellent man and one well able to help me. He it was
that used to make our hiding-places; in fact, he had made
the one to which I owed my safety. Thanks to his
endeavours, I found a house well suited for my purpose.
The next thing was to agree with the landlord about the
rent, a matter which was soon settled. Till the house was
furnished, I hired a room in my landlord's own house.[3]
There I resolved to pass two or three nights in arranging
my affairs, getting letters from my friends in distress, and
writing back letters of comfort in return. Thus it was
that the traitor got sent to the place, which was only
known to a small circle of friends. It was God's will
that my hour should then come.

"One night, when Little John and I had to sleep in
that room, the traitor had to bring a letter that needed
an answer, and left with the answer about ten o'clock.
I had only come in about nine, sorely against the will
of the lady, my entertainer, who was uncommonly earnest
that I should not leave her house that night. Away went
the traitor then, and gave information to the priest-hunters

---

[1] Father Southwell was martyred $\frac{\text{Feb. 21}}{\text{Mar. 3}}$, 159$\frac{4}{5}$.

[2] This holy martyr's true name was Nicholas Owen. Father Gerard
speaks at some length about him further on, and more fully still in his
Narrative of the Powder Plot, p. 182.

[3] We learn from Frank that it was called Middleton's.

both when and where he had left me. They got together a band, and came at midnight to the house, just as I had gone to sleep. Little John and I were both awakened by the noise outside. I guessed what it was, and told John to hide the letter received that night in the ashes where the fire had been. No sooner had he done so and got into bed again, than the noise which we had heard before seemed to travel up to our room. Then some men began knocking at the chamber-door, ready to break it in if it was not opened at once. There was no exit except by the door where our foes were; so I bade John get up and open the door. The room was at once filled with men, armed with swords and staves, and many more stood outside, who were not able to enter. Among the rest stood two pursuivants, one of whom knew me well, so there was no chance of my passing unknown.

"I got up and dressed, as I was bid. All my effects were searched, but without a single thing being found that could do harm to any man. My companion and I were then taken off to prison. By God's grace we did not feel distressed, nor did we show any token of fear. What I was most afraid of, was that they had seen me come out of that lady's house, and had tracked me to the room that I had hired; and so that the noble family that had harboured me would suffer on my account. But this fear was unfounded; for I learnt afterwards that the traitor had simply told them where he had left me, and there it was that they found me."

Of Father Gerard's arrest, Father Garnet said, "Soon after [his escape at Golding-lane] he was apprehended, being betrayed we know not how." Father Garnet wrote this in September, about four months after Father Gerard's apprehension and very soon after his removal from the Counter, where "he hath been very close." It may be that Father Gerard had not yet learned the part that John Frank the servant had had in betraying him, or perhaps

Father Garnet had reason to suspect that some other treacherous agency had been at work, and thus came to say that "we know not how" he was betrayed.

It is quite possible that there was another traitor at work in this matter of whose communications with the Lord Keeper of the Great Seal neither Father Garnet nor Father Gerard knew anything. His machinations we know better than they. Owing to the extreme caution of the man we cannot be quite certain who it was that he was striving to betray, but it seems probable that Father Gerard was his intended victim. From the Fleet prison Benjamin Beard *alias* Tichborne wrote thus to Lord Keeper Puckering on the 28th of February 159¾ to open communications.[1] "Albeit I was unwilling during my imprisonment to undertake any matter concerning these causes, lest missing (as being in prison haply I might) the performance thereof, your lordship might any way conceive hardly of me, having some inkling of two Jesuits lately arrived, and when and where they did frequent, and of their exercise, where if I had been at liberty as I then expected I myself should have been present, the parties being apparelled in silks, wearing shirts of hair underneath, by which only mark I judge them to be Jesuits. Wherefore I am to inform your lordship that if your lordship will stand my honoured friend for my liberty (the hindrance whereof this bearer shall impart unto your lordship), I do here under my hand undertake to perform such service unto her Majesty in the causes aforesaid as any heretofore hath not done better. And my liberty obtained, if I do not before the beginning of the next term deliver some of those persons unto your lordship, I will be content that your Honour shall commit me to perpetual imprisonment without any favour. Craving this further, that in executing hereof such course and plot as I shall set down unto your lordship, that I may not be

---

[1] P.R.O., *Domestic, Elizabeth,* vol. ccxlvii. n. 104.

discovered or suspected of them herein, and none to have knowledge thereof but your lordship and the bearer hereof ; for otherwise it would be a great disgrace to me, for that my mother and all my own kindred are papists and recusants."

This man in another letter speaks of his grandmother Mrs. Tichborne, and elsewhere of his uncle Benjamin Tichborne and his cousin Mrs. Shelley. He was prisoner for debt in the Fleet, and in the hope of obtaining his release by showing the Lord Keeper that he would be a useful spy, he wrote him many letters of information against Catholics, of which no less than fourteen belonging to the year 1594 are preserved amongst the State Papers. One or two of them we proceed to give as apparently they refer to Father Gerard, and besides they are of interest as introducing the name of Tregian, the worthy confessor of the Faith, at a later date than the Narrative[1] of his imprisonment, the latest date mentioned in which was July 20, 1593.

The following letter[2] is addressed to the man who was his go-between with Sir John Puckering, but the letter is endorsed with the names of the persons mentioned in it in Sir John's handwriting, according to his usual fashion. "Mr. Jones,—This day about five of the clock towards night there came hither one Mrs. Stafford. She was Abington's wife, that was executed. In her company came one, without question of exceeding great weight, a Jesuit as by all circumstance I gathered. With him was one Mr. Leonard Farley of Filey bordering on the seaside in Yorkshire. They all being above at Mr. Tregian's, myself then also present, Mr. Wade and Justice Young came into the Fleet even at supper time, to examine the knight Sir Thomas Tresham.[3] Whereupon Mr. Tregian,

---

[1] *Troubles*, First Series, p. 61.
[2] P.R.O., *Domestic, Elizabeth*, vol. ccxlviii. n. 43.
[3] The interrogatories and answers are nn. 44, 45 of this vol. ccxlviii.

having understanding thereof, and for that he thought they came about Mrs. Shelley, being much amazed all of them willed me to go down, lest upon some occasion I should be called for, because the Warden did malice me much about Mrs. Shelley, and had threatened to have me examined about some matter touching her. After which I went presently to my chamber and made a little note, thinking to send for you to dog them to their lodging, but could not by any means get any one to carry it. Neither durst I make the Warden or any acquainted with it, for that at Michaelmas when Mrs. Shelley was first discharged of her close imprisonment, to draw her to live as his ward, [1] he persuaded her by all means possible that I was made an instrument to bring her further in question both of her life and living, and that her liberty was for no other purpose granted her. [He has] bidden Mrs. Tregian and other of the papists beware of me, for that they had letters of my own hand which I should write to Mr. Young while I was in the Counter, to prove that I was such a person. By reason whereof they were jealous of me till they found that the Warden's malice was only for the gain of Mrs. Shelley. And so by good discretion I gained my credit again among them, albeit by that abuse of the Warden many services of greatest moment were hindered, &c. It is not very uneasy [difficult] to learn out where Mrs. Stafford lieth, being a known papist about the town. Upon my life, where her lodging is, there you shall find the party. He was here apparelled in a coat of wrought velvet, and wrought velvet hose [2] and silk grogram cloth, physician wise, and of age

---

[1] *Endorsed* "Mr. Beard about Mrs. Shelley, and the Warden's seeking to make gain of her."

[2] In his examination John Frank saith that the satin doublet and velvet hose which were found in Middleton's house at the apprehension of Mr. Gerard, were Mr. Wiseman's, and the ruffs were Mrs. Wiseman's; and if they had not been taken, the apparel should have been carried by this examinate the next day to Mr. Wiseman in the Counter.

about thirty-six, of brown hair and somewhat well set and of reasonable stature. To-morrow morning I shall hear further of him. Tregian's two men went out with them about seven of the clock this night. Because of my coming away upon Justice Young's coming into the house I know not whether they had mass or not, as likely being scared so they had not. [They came at five in the evening and went away at seven.] But [to] confession I am sure most of them went. Thus late at night I cease, praying you to come to me to-morrow and you shall hear more. Fleet, this 25th of March 1594 [the first day of the year, old style].

"Your poor friend, BENJAMIN BEARD."

"To his assured friend Mr. Morgan Jones at Gray's Inn give these."

Three days later Beard writes[1] to Sir John Puckering "It behoveth me to carry myself even among them lest I mar my harvest before my corn be ripe. This Easter I am most assured, if the house in Chancery-lane called Doctor Good's house, and Payne's house in Fetter-lane be well seen unto, that divers of the seditious parties will be there found, and [I] would (if I had liberty) lose my own life if I roused not two or three of them; for in both those places on Easter day I am assured they will be, or the parties there remaining will repair very early in the morning to such other place as the rest remain in. . . . This day (if a man had but any notes [descriptions] of them) a hundred to one some of the parties might be had at the tavern called 'the Bell' in New Fish-street, for there were they wont to meet and make their Maundy."

By the 29th of April the person Beard had written about was taken, as we learn from his letter of that day. This was about the time of Father Gerard's arrest, the exact date of which we do not know. It may therefore

---

[1] P.R.O., *Domesti·, Elizabeth*, vol. ccxlviii. n. 47.

very possibly have been he who visited the Fleet prison
on the 25th of March, which day that year was Monday
in Holy Week. We know that he was at Blackfriars in
Lent on a visit to Lady Mary Percy and Lady Jane
Seymour "a little before Easter," and he would have had
full time to go to Braddocks for the three last days of
Holy Week. If the "green man" mentioned in the two
following letters[1] as taken is "the fellow that followed
him as his man," it will have been Nicholas Owen or
Little John, who wore a green cloak. Frank in his examination "saith that Nicholas Owen, who was taken in bed
with Mr. Gerard the Jesuit, was at Mr. Wiseman's house
at Christmas was twelvemonths, and called by the name
of Little John and Little Michael, and the cloak that
he wore was Mr. Wiseman's cloak a year past, and was
of sad green cloth with sleeves, caped with tawny velvet
and little gold strips turning on the cape."

"Mr. Jones,—I am still of the opinion that the party
you know of is one of them we look for, and as at
his first coming hither I judged him so by the reverence
done unto him by those here, so am I still by all likelihood and circumstances more and more therein confirmed ;
for were he not for certain a man of weight there would
be good laughing among them at the manner of his taking,
as at one whom they affirmed to be taken lately about
Westminster for a Seminary, and of another lately committed to the Clink for hearing of a mass at Dieppe. If
he be wisely handled, he may without great difficulty be
quickly discovered [that is, torture will soon extort from
him an avowal of who he is]. But howsoever, in any case
handle the matter so as it come not to his own knowledge
that other than Justice Young's *commendam* is upon him,
nor any notice to Justice Young that either by my means
or yours the party is taken, nor any question moved to
him of his being at the Fleet : for though there may

[1] P.R.O., *Domestic, Elizabeth*, vol. ccxlviii. nn. 83, 99.

M

happen to be some notable villainy among them, yet may not these here be suddenly baulked ; though if any matter of importance come to light thereby, they may with good discretion be called to account well enough, saving any their suspicion, whereof we may advise when we see certainly what the party is.

"I did yesternight sup at Tregian's, where in the midst of our supper Phillips, Tregian's man, came in sweating ; whom suddenly Tregian asked 'What news ?' who answered 'Very bad'; whereat Tregian looked won-derful pale and went from the table, and called Phillips with him into his study. It was sure[ly] about the party, for the fellow that followed him as his man was here and went out not two hours before with the same Phillips. If that party were one day wisely dogged, the true harbour of the other might be found out, though in this space they have shifted all matter of moment from thence.

"Having also some speech of the dangerousness of the time, and how narrowly Catholics were sifted, 'Yet for all that,' saith Tregian's wife and Mrs. Warnford who supped there also, 'that infinites run daily into the Church and were reconciled to the Catholic faith.' As also how those good men, making no account of losing their lives, did hazard themselves to save men's souls, affirming that they thought in their conscience that (as dangerous as the time was) yet within the Court there was now daily as many masses said as commonly in any country abroad, and many lately called to forsake the world that have heretofore seemed to be wonderful stiff on the contrary part.

"And asking how it were possible they could be long secure about the Court, it was answered that if I were at liberty and did follow some nobleman, it were an easy matter for me to shroud a priest a long time before he should be taken ; and for example [they] named young Roper who serveth Sir Thomas Heneage ; with which

Roper I saw the party that was here with Mrs. Stafford on Our Lady day in Lent, go through the Palace at Westminster, when I was at the Hall about my own business.

"But among all these speech was now and many more before to the like effect, not any one word passed of the green man, which is the greater presumption that he is the same man we look for, and that for that he was taken after his being here, they are afeard to speak of him or his taking. Therefore be sure that he be well looked into. Justice Young, no doubt, hath skill enough to find him what he is : albeit if Justice Young know that he is taken by my means, he doth malice me so much about my cousin Shelley, he will not stick under his hand [in an underhand way] to tell the papists of it."

This news, which in another letter[1] assumes the more precise shape "that there are three Seminaries that daily frequent the Court where they use their ungodly exercise, maintained and harboured there of gentlemen that are retainers to some noblemen," was duly reported by Jones to the Lord Keeper, who endorsed his letter in the following legal polyglot, *Jones circa prestes pres le court.* The consequence was that Beard was called upon to repeat his story of the supper and the conversation with Mrs. Tregian over and over again. One more of these letters we venture to insert, though it involves some little repetition and adds nothing to our knowledge of Father Gerard, for the sake of the vivid picture it gives of life in prison and of priests riding about in a nobleman's "livery and cognizance, with chains of gold about their necks."

"Right honourable, my most humble duty remembered. I have received this morning early a letter from Mr. Jones whereby I am advertised that your lordship requireth a recital from me of sundry matters as well by me formerly written to your lordship as else by word of mouth spoken to Mr. Jones. First therefore touching the words spoken

---

[1] P.R.O., *Domestic, Elizabeth,* vol. ccxlviii. n. 94.

by Tregian's wife and others touching matters about the
Court, &c. The manner of these speeches were as followeth. About the second night after the green man was
taken, bending my wits all I could to have notice of that
party, I sent for Rhenish wine into the town in a choice
bottle, feigning it to be sent me for excellent good from
a special friend, and bestowed it on her, who desired me
to stay supper; where was one Mrs. Warnford and her
daughter, here prisoners also at that instant. Even as
supper was almost ended, Phillips, Tregian's man, came in
hastily and sweating; whereupon Tregian and Roscarrock
rose and went with Phillips into the study, his wife, myself
and the rest sitting still. After this divers speeches passed,
as how there was one Marcomba (as I remember they
called him so) imprisoned in the Clink for hearing of a
mass at Dieppe; whereunto another of them replied that
that was somewhat like the taking of a gentleman a little
before Easter for a Seminary at Westminster.

"Upon these speeches saith Tregian's wife that notwithstanding the great searches, and hold and keep for
good men, and the rigour used to Catholics, yet did the
number of the Church rather increase than decrease by
it. To which I said that, by her leave, many of late since
the Statute [27º Eliz. 1584] did go to Church and were
fallen. Whereunto she answered that where one was
fallen from the Church, there was ten reconciled unto
it; as likewise how dangerously, without all care of their
lives, good men did venture to save souls. And that
she thought in her conscience that there was more masses
said about the Court than was about London.

"And asking how that can be, 'Think you,' saith she
to me, 'that if I myself did belong to any nobleman
about the Court, that it were not an easy matter for me
to conceal a priest a long time?' saying that there were
many noblemen about the Court that full little knew
how many such persons were about them. But in par-

ticular of any that did harbour these persons there was not anything precisely uttered, though Roper and Inglefield being here the afternoon before, for that Roper was in his chain, I asked whom he served; who said 'Sir Thomas Heneage,—a man,' saith she, 'that is as earnest against Catholics as any other: yet,' saith she, 'he hath some good men about him, as well as others.' Infinite other speeches to this effect which were too long to write.

"Touching Mr. Cornwallis, at his house at Fisher's Folly on Easter Monday there met Knight of Chancery-lane and his wife, and cousin Yates' wife, Tregian's wife and her two elder daughters here and divers at Clerkenwell, as I did formerly advertise your lordship, where one Jones *alias* Norton, and one Butler, priests, said mass. But [I] cannot tell whether Mr. Cornwallis were privy to it or not. Their business done, Tregian's wife came home hither to dinner, and bring [brought] a casing bottle of holy water with her. Her daughter Yates dined at Clerkenwell and came hither after dinner, of whom I understood the whole.

"This Butler was sometime chamberfellow with one Harrington[1] that serveth the Lady Southampton, which maketh me guess that, since I [am] here and he is come over, that he is also still harboured by him. They lay there about eight years since in Southampton House, next chamber to Robert Gage that was executed; and then [he] fled, being nominated to be of Babington's conspiracy.

"I know also one Selby, a northern man, towards [in the service of] my Lord Chamberlain, and little John Shelley that did serve the Lord Montague, who, if they attend on them now, as if they be in town I am sure they do, are likest men to be harbourers of such persons. In the life of my old Lord Montague, that Shelley did

---

[1] This is not William Harrington the priest and martyr, for he was executed on the 18th of February in this year. *Troubles*, 2nd series, p. 105.

carry Fennell and Richards, both priests, up and down
with him in my Lord his livery and cognizance, with
chains of gold about their necks.   This will I justify
with my blood, though I would endure any misery rather
than to scandalize myself wilfully in any occasion, unless
some great profit might redound thereby to the State.
Neither doubt I but, if your lordship please to make trial
of me, but in short space to effect those services as shall
be to the State great benefit, and to your lordship so
acceptable as your lordship shall have no cause to repent
the honour and charitable favour you have done me.
And thus in all humility I cease, praying God evermore
to preserve and bless your lordship.   From the Fleet,
this eighth day of May, 1594.

"Your lordship's everlastingly bounden,

"BENJAMIN BEARD."

To this story and to his offer to betray some of the
priests whom he had led Sir John Puckering to believe
were concealed about the Court, Beard owed his liberty,
and on the 28th of May he dated his letter[1] from Green-
wich, where he must have felt that he had no easy task
before him.   "As for Roper I could not see of him all
day, though I walked the park and town, and will do
again this day, which I am enforced to stay here by
reason that, meeting with one Byrd, brother to Byrd of
the Chapel,[2] I understand that Mrs. Tregian, Mrs. Charnock and Mrs. Sybil Tregian will be here at the Court
at this day, by whose coming peradventure some good
may be done."   Evidently Mrs. Tregian, who was Lord
Stourton's sister, and her daughters were about to appeal
to Elizabeth's mercy in behalf of that faithful confessor
Francis Tregian,[3] who had now been a prisoner seventeen
years.   It is needless to say that their appeal was made

[1] P.R.O., *Domestic, Elizabeth*, vol. ccxlviii. n. 118.
[2] *Troubles*, 2nd series, p. 143.   [3] *Troubles*, 1st series, p. 136.

in vain. When Tregian was banished after eleven other years of imprisonment, Elizabeth was dead. We here leave Benjamin Beard, waiting for the poor ladies who were coming on their hopeless errand, and we pity them all the more for the treachery that lent its aid to the cruelty with which they were persecuted for their faith.

CHAPTER XVI.

THE COUNTER.

1594.

AFTER this long break we must allow Father Gerard to resume his narrative, and we will leave him to tell the story of his life in prison with as little interruption as possible.

"The pursuivant who knew me, kept me in his house two nights; either because those who were to examine me were hindered from doing so on the first day, or (as it struck me afterwards) because they wished first to examine my companion, Little John. I noticed the first night, that the room where I was locked up was not far from the ground; and that it would be easy to let myself down from the window, by tearing up the bed-clothes and making a rope of them. I should have done so that very night, had I not heard some one stirring in the next room. I thought that he was put there to watch me, and so it turned out. However, I meant to carry my plan out the night after, if the watchman went away; but my keeper forestalled me; for to save the expense of a guard, he put irons on my arms, which hindered me both from bringing my hands together and from separating them. Then in truth I was more at ease in mind, though less in body; for the thought of escape vanished, and there came in its place a feeling of joy that I had been vouchsafed this suffering for the sake of Christ, and I thanked the Lord for it as well as I could.

" Next day I was brought before the Commissioners,[1] at the head of whom was one who is now Lord Chancellor of the realm. He had been a Catholic, but went over to the other side, for he loved the things of this world.

" They first asked me my name and calling. I gave them the name I passed by; whereupon one called me by my true name, and said that I was a Jesuit. As I was aware that the pursuivant knew me, I answered that I would be frank and open in everything that belonged to myself, but would say nothing that could affect others. So I told them my name and calling, to wit that, though most unworthy, I was a priest of the Society of Jesus.

"'Who sent you into England?' they asked.

"'The Superiors of the Society.'

"'To what end?'

"'To bring back stray souls to their Creator.'

"'No, no,' said they, 'you were sent for matters of State, and to lure people from the obedience of the Queen to the obedience of the Pope.'

"'As for matters of State,' I replied, 'we are forbidden to have anything to say to them, as they do not belong to our Institute. This prohibition, indeed, extends to all the members of the Society; but on us missioners it is particularly enjoined in a special instruction. As for the obedience due to the Queen and the Pope, each is to be obeyed in that wherein they have jurisdiction; and one obedience does not clash with the other, as England and all Christian realms have hitherto experienced.'

"'How long have you been doing duty as a priest in this country?'

"'About six years.'

---

[1] Honorarios arbitros seu examinatores.—*MS.* Sir Thomas Egerton, afterwards Lord Ellesmere and Viscount Brackley, was Attorney General at this date, 1594, and Lord Chancellor in 1609, when this was written. That this persecutor had been a Catholic is an interesting fact which his biographers have passed over in silence.

"' How and where did you land, and where have you lived since your landing ?'

"' I cannot in conscience answer any of these questions,' I replied, ' especially the last, as it would bring mischief on others ; so I crave pardon for not satisfying your wishes.'

"' Nay,' said they, ' it is just on these heads that we chiefly desire you to satisfy us, and we bid you in the Queen's name to do so.'

"' I honour the Queen,' said I, ' and will obey her and you in all that is lawful, but here you must hold me excused ; for were I to mention any person or place where I have been lodged, the innocent would have to suffer, according to your laws, for the kind service they have done me. Such behaviour on my part would be against all justice and charity, and therefore I never will be guilty of it.'

"' You shall do so by force, if not by good will.'

"' I hope,' I said, ' by the grace of God, it shall not be as you say. I beg you, therefore, to take this my answer, that neither now nor at any other time will I disclose what you demand of me.'

"Thereupon they wrote a warrant for my imprisonment, and gave it to the pursuivants, bidding them take me to prison. As we were leaving, he who is now Chancellor said that I must be kept in close confinement, as in cases of high treason. ' But tell the gaolers,' he added, ' to treat him well on account of his birth.' It seems, however, that the head gaoler gave orders at variance with this humane recommendation, for I was lodged in a garret[1]

[1] Father Gerard was first confined in the Counter, as he tells us later. Father Garnet in one of his letters speaks of the Counter as "a very evil prison and without comfort." There were in London three prisons of this name : the Counter, a part of the parish church of St. Margaret in Southwark ; the Counter in the Poultry, "some four houses west from the parish church of St. Mildred "; and the New Counter in Wood-street, removed from Bread-street in 1555. Stow's *Survey of London*, ed. Thoms, pp. 99, 131.

where there was nothing but a bed, and no room to stand
up straight, except just where the bed was. There was
one window always open, through which foul air entered
and rain fell on to my bed. The room door was so low,
that I had to enter not on my feet, but on my knees, and
even then I was forced to stoop. However, I reckoned
this rather an advantage, inasmuch as it helped to keep
out the stench (certainly no small one) that came from the
privy close to my door, which was used by all the prisoners
in that part of the house. I was often kept awake, or
waked up, by the bad smell.

"In this place I passed two or three days of true
repose. I felt no pain or anxiety of mind, and enjoyed,
by the blessing of God, that peace which the world does
not and cannot give. On the third or fourth day, I was
taken for a second examination to the house of a magistrate called Young. He it was who had the management
of all the searches and persecutions that the Catholics in
the neighbourhood of London had to endure ; and it was
to him that the traitor had given his information. Along
with him was another, who had for many years conducted
the examinations by torture, Topcliffe by name. He was
a man of cruelty, athirst for the blood of the Catholics,
and so crafty and cunning, that all the wily wit of his
companion seemed abashed into silence by his presence ;
in fact, the justice spoke very little during the whole
examination. I found the two of them alone, Young in
a civilian's dress, Topcliffe with a sword by his side and
in a Court dress. He was an old man, grown grey in
wickedness. Young began questioning me as to my place
of abode, and the Catholics that I knew. I answered that
I neither could nor would make disclosures that would
get any one into trouble, for reasons already stated. He
turned then to Topcliffe and said : 'I told you how you
would find him.'

"Topcliffe looked frowningly at me and said : 'Do

you know me ? I am Topcliffe, of whom I doubt not you have often heard.'

"He meant this to frighten me. To heighten the effect, he had laid his sword on the table near his hand, as though he were ready to use it on occasion. But he failed certainly, and caused me not the least alarm ; and whereas I was wont to answer with deference on other occasions, this time I did quite the contrary, because I saw him making a show to scare me. Finding that he could get no other manner of reply from me than what I had given, he took a pen and wrote an artful and malicious form of examination.

"Here,' says he, 'read this paper ; I shall show it to the Privy Council, that they may see what a traitor you are to the realm, and how manifestly guilty.'

"The contents of the paper were as follows : 'The examinate was sent by the Pope and the Jesuit Persons, and coming through Belgium there had interviews with the Jesuit Holt and Sir William Stanley : thence he came into England, on a political errand, to beguile the Queen's subjects, and lure them from their obedience to their Sovereign. If, therefore, he will not disclose the places and persons with whom he has lived, it is presumed that he has done much mischief to the State, &c.'

"On reading this, I saw that I could not meet so many falsehoods with one single denial ; and as I was desirous that he should show my way of answering to the Council, I said that I also wished to answer in writing. Hereat Topcliffe was overjoyed, and cried out, 'Oh ! now you are a reasonable man': but he was disappointed. He had hoped to catch me in my words, or at least to find out my handwriting, so that some of the papers found in the houses of the Catholics might be proved to be mine. I foresaw this, and therefore wrote in a feigned hand as follows : 'I was sent by my Superiors. I never was in Belgium : I have not seen Father Holt since the time that

I left Rome. I have not seen Sir William Stanley since
he left England with the Earl of Leicester. I am forbidden to meddle with matters of State; I never have
done, and never will do so. I have tried to bring back
souls to the knowledge and love of their Creator, and to
make them show obedience to the laws of God and man;
and I hold this last point to be a matter of conscience.
I humbly crave that my refusal to answer anything concerning the persons that I know, may not be set down to
contempt of authority; seeing that God's commandment
forces me to follow this course, and to act otherwise would
be against charity and justice.'

"While I was writing this, the old man waxed wroth.
He shook with passion, and would fain have snatched the
paper from me.

"'If you don't want me to write the truth,' said I, 'I'll
not write at all.'

"'Nay,' quoth he, 'write so and so, and I'll copy out
what you have written.'

"'I shall write what *I* please," I answered, 'and not
what *you* please. Show what I have written to the Council,
for I shall add nothing but my name.'

"This I signed so near the writing, that nothing
could be put in between. The hot-tempered man,
seeing himself disappointed, broke out into threats and
blasphemies.

"'I'll get you put into my power, and hang you in the
air, and show you no mercy; and then I shall see what
God will rescue you out of my hands.'

"From the abundance of his heart he poured forth
these evil words; but by this he raised my hopes, just
the opposite effect to what he wanted.[1] Neither then nor

---

[1] Even the gentle Father Southwell could not but show his estimate of
this reprobate man. We translate the following from Father More's *History
of the English Province,* lib. v. n. 15.—"Though he readily answered the
questions of others, yet if Topcliffe interposed he never deigned him a reply;
and when asked the cause of this, he answered: 'Because I have found by
experience that the man is not open to reason.'"

since have I ever reckoned aught of a blasphemer; and
in sooth I have found by experience, that God increases
the confidence of His servants, when He allows strife to
rise up against them.   I gave, therefore, this short answer:
'You will be able to do nothing without the leave of God,
Who never abandons those that hope in Him.   The will
of God be done.'

"Thereupon Young called the gaoler who had brought
me, to take me back to prison.   As he was leading me
off, Topcliffe addressed him and bade him put irons on
my legs.   Both then fell a-chiding him for having brought
me by himself, fearing perchance lest I should escape from
his hands.

"When I had crept back to my little closet, my legs
were garnished according to order.   The man seemed
grieved that put the fetters on.   For my part, instead
of grief, I felt very much joy, such is God's goodness to
the most unworthy of His creatures.   To pay the man
for the kind turn that he had done me, I gave him some
money for his job; and told him it was no punishment
to suffer in so good a cause."

Father Garnet described this act of faith and courage
in the following terms in a letter[1] to the General of the
Society, which we translate from the Italian.   "This
father has always been very courageous, and when he
was first taken, and the gaoler put very heavy irons on
his legs, he gave him some money.   The following day
the gaoler, thinking that if he took off the irons doubtless
he would give him more, took them off, but got nothing.
After some days he came to put them on again, and
received a reward, and then taking them off did not get
a farthing.   They went on playing thus with one another
several times, but at last the gaoler, seeing that he did
not give him anything for taking off his irons, left him

---

[1] Stonyhurst MSS., *Angl. A.* vol. ii. p. 27; Father Grene's *Collectan. P.*
vol. ii. p. 604.

for a long time in confinement, so that the great toe of
one foot was for almost two years in great danger of
mortification. So your Reverence sees that in these times
the courage of true Christian soldiers is not wanting.
May our Lord give him perseverance, and to those who
follow him the grace to imitate him."

"Here I stayed," said Father Gerard, "upwards of three
months. During the first month I made from memory, as
well as I could, the Spiritual Exercises; giving four and
sometimes five hours a day to meditation. God lavished
His goodness on me throughout, and I had proof that He
opens His bounteous hand to His servants most of all, when
He has closed up the sources of earthly comfort to them.

"While I was quietly lodged in prison, without being
brought out or undergoing any further examination for
many days, they examined and put to the torture Richard
Fulwood, whom the traitor had pointed out as my servant,
and Little John, who had been taken with me. Unable,
either by coaxing or bribery, to draw anything from them
that would compromise others, they had recourse to threats
and then to force: but the force of the Holy Ghost in
them was too great to be overcome by men. They were
both hung up for three hours together, having their arms
fixed into iron rings, and their bodies hanging in the air;
a torture which causes frightful pain and intolerable exten-
sion of the sinews. It was all to no purpose; no disclosure could be wrested from them that was hurtful to
others; no rewards could entice, no threats or punish-
ments force them, to discover where I or any of ours
had been harboured, or to name any of our acquaintance
or abettors.

"Here I ought not to pass over in silence God's great
goodness and mercy to me, the most unworthy of all His
servants. It was shown in this, that there was not a
single traitor, either among those that were then seized
in my house or in the house of the good gentleman,

my entertainer; no, nor even among those that in the other persecutions, which by God's providence afterwards befell me, were imprisoned, tortured, and treated with the utmost cruelty. Not one of them, I say, ever yielded, but all by the grace of God held steadfast through everything. Those whom I used as companions, or the servants I entrusted with commissions to the gentlemen of my acquaintance, as they necessarily knew all my friends, would have been able to do very great mischief, and enrich themselves by ruining others: yet no one of them ever caused any harm either by word or deed, wittingly or unwittingly; nor, as far as I remember, did they ever give any one matter of complaint. On many of them, God, in His goodness, poured the choicest gifts of His Holy Spirit.

"John Lasnet,[1] the first that I had, died in Spain a lay-brother of the Society. The second that I had for some little while was Michael Walpole, who is now a priest of the Society and labouring in England. The third was [Ralph] Willis.[2] He had a vocation, so I sent him to study in the Seminary at Rheims, where he went through his course of philosophy. His behaviour there was orderly, but afterwards at Rome he joined a turbulent party, thus returning evil for good. He was the only one of my helpmates that walked at all awry. He was, however, made priest, and sent into England. There he was seized, and condemned to death for the faith, and answered unflinchingly before the tribunal; but instead of losing his life, he was kept some time in prison; whence he effected his escape, and is still labouring in England.

"After him I had a godly man of the name of John Sutton, the brother of three priests, one of whom was a

---

[1] Dr. Oliver seems to have read "Larnet."

[2] The MS. has "Lillus." The true name is given us in John Frank's examination.

martyr, and another died in the Society. Father Garnet kept him in his house for many years, up to the time of his own arrest.

"The next that I had was Richard Fulwood, of whom I have spoken above. He managed to make his escape, and during my imprisonment was employed by Father Garnet until that Father's happy death. He managed nearly all his master's business with strangers, not without the knowledge of the persecutors, who offered a handsome sum for his capture, and were still more earnest about it after Father Garnet was taken. In fact they gave the poor man no peace until they drove him into banishment, where he yet remains, doing good service to our mission notwithstanding.

"After him I had John Lilly, a man well-known at Rome; he died lately in England, a lay-brother of the Society. Next came two other godly men, whom I did not take to keep, but merely as make-shifts, till I could get a man every way suited to my wants, and endowed with a religious spirit. I found one at length; and when I quitted England, I took him with me, and left him at St. Omers. There he was well grounded in Greek and Latin, and became a great favourite with all the fathers, who sent him into Spain with the highest recommendations. He still remains there, growing always in virtue and learning. Not long ago I had a letter from the Father Prefect of Studies, in which he tells me that he is the best student in his course.

"Such were the mercies of God vouchsafed to me His unworthy servant, in answer to my constant prayers. Many gentlemen entrust themselves and their interest to our servants' good faith no less than to ours; so that there could be no greater let or hindrance to our good work, than any treachery on their part: indeed the defection of such a one would be likely to cause the most frightful ruin among Catholics. For if one servant,

N

and he neither a Catholic nor one of the household, like the traitor of whom I have spoken, made such havoc in his master's family, what mischief could a priest's servant do to the many persons of high rank, that had harboured him and his master! God has hitherto kept me free from the like betrayal.

"To return to my story. They could wrest nothing out of Little John and Fulwood; and none of my host's Catholic servants would make any avowal, or own that he knew me. Seeing that they could bring no witness against him, the heretics gradually lost the hope they had of seizing all his chattels and revenue.

"Sometimes they would bring me up for examination, when they had anything new against me. Once they called me to try on a suit of clothes, which had been found in my host's house, and which the traitor said were mine. I put them on and they were just a fit, for the truth was that they had been made for me; however I would not own them, nor admit them to be mine. Hereupon Young flew into a passion, calling me a headstrong and unreasonable man. He was so barefaced as to add: 'How much more sensible is Southwell, who after long wilfulness is now ready to conform, and wishes to treat with some man of learning.'

"'Nay,' I answered, 'I will never believe that Father Southwell wishes to treat with any one from any wavering in his faith, or to learn what to believe from a heretic; but he might perchance challenge any heretic to dispute with him that dared, as Father Campion did, and as many others would do if you would let them, and appoint proper umpires.'

"Then Young seizing hold of the book and kissing it, cried: 'I swear upon this book that Southwell has offered to treat, with a view of embracing our religion.'

"'I do not believe he ever did so,' said I.

"'What,' said an officer of the court, 'do you not believe his oath?'

"'No,' was my reply, 'I neither can nor will believe him; for I have a better opinion of Father Southwell's firmness than of his truthfulness; since perhaps he thinks that he is allowed to make this statement to beguile me.'

"'No such thing,' said Young: 'but are you ready to conform if he has done so?' To conform in the Protestant sense, means to embrace their deformed religion.

"'Certainly not,' I answered; 'for if I keep myself free from heresy and heretical meetings, it is not because he or any man on earth does the same; but because to act otherwise would be to deny Christ, by denying His faith, which may be done by deed as well as by word. This is what our Lord forbade under pain of a heavier punishment than man can inflict, when He said, "He that shall deny Me before men, him will I deny before My Father Who is in Heaven."'

"To this the heretic answered not a word, save that I was stiff-necked, (a name that was applicable rather to himself,) and bade them take me back to prison.

"Another time I was sent for to be confronted with three witnesses, servants of a certain nobleman named Lord Henry Seymour, son of the Duke of Somerset. They were heretics, and avouched that on a certain day I had dined with their mistress and her sister, whilst they among others waited at table. The two sisters were daughters of the Earl of Northumberland. One of them was a devout Catholic, and had come to London a little before my imprisonment, to get my help in passing over to Belgium, there to consecrate herself to God. She was staying at the house of her sister, the wife of the aforesaid lord. She wanted to bring back this sister to the Catholic faith, which the latter had abandoned after her good father's death. I dined with them on the day the witnesses mentioned.   It was in Lent ; and they told how their mistress ate meat, while the Lady Mary and I ate nothing but fish.   Young flung this charge in my teeth with an air of triumph, as though I could not help acknowledging it, and thereby disclosing some of my acquaintances.   I answered that I did not know the men whom he had brought up.

"'But we know you,' said they, 'to be the same that was at such a place on such a day.'

"'You wrong your mistress,' said I, 'in saying so.   I, however, will not so wrong her.'

"'What a barefaced fellow you are!' exclaimed Young.

"'Doubtless,' I answered, 'were these men's statement true : as for me, I cannot speak positively in the matter, for reasons that I have often alleged : let them look to the truth and justice of what they say.'

"Young then, in a rage, remanded me to prison."

CHAPTER XVII.

THE CLINK.

1594—1597.

"AFTER three months, some of my friends made efforts to have me removed to another more comfortable prison, seeing that nothing could be proved against me except my priesthood ; and this they obtained by means of a handsome bribe to Young. So they went to my prison, which was called the Counter, and took off my fetters. These were rusty when they were first put on ; but by wearing and moving about in them every day, I had rendered them quite bright and shining. My cell was so small, that a man who had his legs free, might take the whole length of it in three steps. I used to shuffle from one end to the other, as well for exercise, as because the people underneath used to sing lewd songs and Geneva psalms ; and I wanted to drown, by the clanking of my chain, a noise that struck still harsher on my ear. My fetters then being removed, and my expenses paid, (which were not great, as I had had little but butter and cheese to season my bread withal,) they brought me before Young, who, making a show of anger, began to chide and upbraid me more than was his wont, and asked me whether I was yet willing to acknowledge where and with whom I had lived ? I answered that I could not do so with a safe conscience, and therefore would not.

" 'Well then,' said he, 'I will put you in closer confinement, where you shall be safer lodged, and have iron bars before your window.'

"'Forthwith he wrote a warrant, and sent me to the prison that is called the Clink.[1] He made all this show, that he might not appear to have taken money for what he did. The fact was, that the prison to which I was now sent was far better than the other, and more comfortable for all prisoners ; but to me it afforded especial comfort, on account of the great number of Catholics whom I found there.

"They could not now hinder me from approaching the sacraments, and being comforted in divers other ways, as I shall afterwards show ; for when I had been there a few months, the place was by God's grace so improved, that as for discharging all the duties of the Society, I should never wish to be at large in England, provided I could always live in the like prison and after the like fashion.[2] So my being shut up in the Clink, seemed like a change from Purgatory to Paradise. Instead of lewd songs and blasphemies, the prayers of some Catholic neighbours in the next room met my ear. They came to my door to cheer me up, and showed me a way by which we could open a freer communication. This was through a hole in the wall, which they had covered with a picture, that it might not be seen. By means of it, they gave me, on the morrow, a letter from my friends ; and at the same time furnished me materials for writing back. I wrote therefore to Father Garnet, and told him the whole truth of what had happened to me, and what manner of replies I had made, as I have set forth above.

[1] This was a prison in Southwark, adjoining the palace of the Bishops of Winchester. In Father More's Latin narrative it appears as *Atrium Wintoniense*. "It was a small place of confinement on the Bankside, called the Clink from being the piison of the 'Clink liberty or manor of Southwark' belonging to the Bishops of Winchester." Brayley, *History of Surrey*, vol. v. p. 348.

[2] Father Garnet writes, November 19, 1594 : "Sir Thomas Wilks goeth into Flanders, as it is thought for peace ; whereupon the arraignment of the three Jesuits, Southwell, Walpole and Gerard is stayed. Gerard is in the Clink, somewhat free ; the other two so close in the Tower that none can hear from them." Stonyhurst MSS. Father Grene's *Collectan. P.* vol. ii. p. 550.

"I also confessed, and received the most holy Body of Christ, through that same hole. But I had not to do this long, for the Catholics contrived to fashion a key that would open my door; and then every morning, before the gaoler got up, they brought me to another part of the prison, where I said mass, and administered the sacraments to the prisoners lodged in that quarter; for all of them had got keys of their cells.

"I had just such neighbours as I would have picked out, had I had my choice. My next door neighbour was our Brother, Ralph Emerson, of whom Father Campion in a letter to Father General makes mention in these terms, 'My little man and I.' He was indeed small in body,[1] but in steadfastness and endurance he was great. He had been already many long years in bonds, ever keeping godly and devout, like a man of the Society: and after my coming to the Clink, he remained six or seven years more. At last he was sent off, with other confessors of Christ, to the castle of Wisbech, where he was attacked with palsy. One half of his body was powerless, so that he could not move about or do the least thing for himself. He lived notwithstanding, to add by his patience fresh jewels to the crown that awaited him. Being driven into banishment with the same company, he came to St. Omers, and died a holy death there, to the great edification of the by-standers. I found this good Brother my next neighbour in the Clink; overhead I had John Lilly, whom God's providence had shut up there for his own good and mine. I had other godly men around me, all true to their faith.

"These having the free run of the prison, any one might visit them without danger. I arranged therefore, that when any of my friends came to the prison, they

---

[1] "He is a very slender, brown little fellow."—Confession of Ralph Miller: P.R.O., *Domestic, Elizabeth*, vol. clxxiii. n. 64. Brother Emerson had in 1594 spent more than three years in the Counter and ten in the Clink. *Troubles*, Second Series, p. 43.

should ask to see one of these; and thus they got to have talk with me without its being noticed. I did not however let them into my room, but spoke to them through the aforesaid hole.

"So I passed some time in great comfort and repose; striving the while to gather fruit of souls, by letter and by word of mouth. My first gaoler was a sour-tempered man, who watched very closely to see that there were no unlawful doings amongst us. This called for great wariness on our part, to avoid discovery: but ere long God summoned him from the wardenship of the prison, and from the prison of his body at the same time.

"His successor was a younger man of a milder turn. What with coaxing, and what with bribes, I got him not to look into our doings too nicely, and not to come when he was not called for, except at certain fixed times, at which he always found me ready to receive him.

"I used the liberty thus granted me for my neighbours' profit. I began to hear many confessions, and reconciled many persons to the Catholic Church. Some of these were heretics, but the greater number were only schismatics, as I could deal more freely with these than with the others. It was only after long acquaintance, and on the recommendation of trusty friends, that I would let any heretics know how little restraint was put upon me. I do not remember above eight or ten converts from heresy, of whom four entered religion. Two joined our Society, and the other two went to other Orders. As for schismatics, I brought back a goodly number of them to the bosom of the Church. Some became religious; and others gave themselves to good works in England during the persecution. Of these last, was Mr. John Rigby, afterwards martyred. His martyrdom was on this wise.

"On one occasion he appeared before the judges, to plead the cause of a Catholic lady [Mrs. Fortescue,

daughter of Sir Edmund Huddlestone and sister of Mrs.
Wiseman]. They, unwilling to grant any boon to a
Catholic family, asked the advocate of what religion he
was himself, that he pleaded so boldly in behalf of another;
was he a priest?

"'No,' he answered.

"'Are you a Papist?'

"'I am a Catholic.'

"'Indeed; how long have you been one?'

"'For such a time.'

"'Who made you a Catholic?'

"Not to implicate me, he gave the name of a priest
who had been martyred shortly before [Father Jones
alias Buckley O.S.F.].

"'So you have been reconciled to the Church of
Rome?'

"Such a reconciliation is high treason by their unjust
laws, and it was of this that they wanted to make him
out guilty. He did not notice the snare. He had been
taught that it was sinful to say that one was not a
Catholic; and thought perchance that it was forbidden
also to throw the burden of proof on the persecutors, as
is the custom of those that are wary. So like a right-
hearted, godly, and courageous man, as he was, he frankly
answered that he had been reconciled. He was at once
handcuffed, and thrown into prison. At his trial he
made another good confession of his faith, declaring that
he gloried in being a Catholic. He received the sentence
of death with joy. Whilst it was being pronounced, and
he standing before the judges the while, of a sudden the
gyves were loosened of themselves, and dropped off his
legs. They were replaced by the gaoler, and if I mistake
not, dropped off a second time. He was led back to
prison, whence, shortly before his martyrdom, he wrote
me a letter full of thanks for having made him a Catholic,
and helped (though little indeed) to place him in those

dispositions, which he hoped would soon meet with their reward from God. He also sent me the purse which he was used to bear about with him : I use it now, in honour of the martyr, to carry my reliquary in.

"As he was being drawn to the place of punishment, he was met by a certain Earl [the Earl of Rutland], in company with other gentlemen. The Earl seeing him dragged on the hurdle, asked what he had been guilty of. The martyr overheard him, and answered : 'Of no offence against the Queen or State. I am to die for the Catholic faith.' The Earl, seeing him to be a stalwart and comely man, said : 'By my troth, thou wast made rather for gallantry than for martyrdom.'

"'As for the matter of gallantry,' the martyr answered, 'I call God to witness, that I die a virgin.' This statement I can myself confirm. The Earl was much struck at what he heard ; and from that time began to look upon Catholics and their religion in a better light, as he has often since given proof. So the holy man went to Heaven, where I doubt not that he pleads before the throne of God for his unworthy father in Christ."

John Rigby was martyred at St. Thomas Waterings on the 21st of June 1600. He was very barbarously executed, and he was sentenced to the death of a traitor for no crime but for having been reconciled to the Catholic Church. His life was frequently offered to him if he would attend the Protestant church. He was a younger son of Nicholas Rigby of Harrock, in the parish of Eccleston in Lancashire.

"During my stay in this prison, I found means to give the Spiritual Exercises. The gaoler did as I wished him to do ; he never came to me without being called, and never went into my neighbours' rooms at all. So we fitted an upper chamber to serve as a chapel, where six or seven made the Exercises, all of whom resolved to follow the counsels of Christ our Lord, and not one of them flinched from his purpose.

"I found means also to provide for a very pressing need. Many priests of my acquaintance, being unable to meet with safe lodgings when they came to London, used to put up at inns till they had settled the business that brought them. Again, as my abode was fixed, and easy to find, the greater part of the priests that were sent from the seminaries abroad had instructions to apply to me, that through me they might be introduced to their Superior, and might receive other assistance at my hands. Not having always places prepared, nor houses of Catholics to which I could send them, I rented a house and garden in a suitable spot, and furnished it, as far as was wanted, by the help of my friends. Thither I used to send those who brought letters of recommendation from our Fathers, and who I was assured led a holy life and seemed well fitted for the mission. I maintained them there, till I had supplied them, through the aid of certain friends, with clothes and necessaries, sometimes even with a residence, or with a horse to go to their friends and kinsmen in the country. I covered all the expenses of this house with the alms that were bestowed on me. I did not receive alms from many persons, still less from all that came to see me; indeed, both out of prison and in prison, I often refused such offers. I was afraid that if I always accepted what was offered, I might scare from me souls that wished to treat with me on the business of their salvation; or receive gifts from those that could either ill afford it, or would afterwards repent of it. I made it a rule therefore, never to take alms except from a small number of persons, whom I knew well. Most of what I got was from those devoted friends, who offered me not only their money but themselves, and looked upon it as a favour when I took their offer.

"I gave charge of this house to a very godly and discreet matron of good birth, whom the Lord honoured with martyrdom.[1] Her maiden name was Heigham, but she bore the name of Line from her deceased husband. Both she and her husband were beloved by God, and had much to suffer for His sake. This lady's father was a Protestant, and when he heard of his daughter's becoming a Catholic, he withheld the dower which he had promised her. He disinherited one of his sons for the same reason. This son, called William Heigham, is now in Spain, a lay-brother of the Society. It is twenty-six years since I knew him [*i.e.* in 1583]. He was then a well-educated gentleman, finely dressed like other high-born Londoners. He supported a priest named Thomson, whom I afterwards saw martyred [at Tyburn on the 20th of April, 1586]. As soon as his father learned that he too had become a Catholic, he went and sold his estate, the rents of which were reckoned at 6,000 florins [600*l.*] yearly, that it might not pass to his son. The son was afterwards arrested for the faith, and he and his priest together, if I mistake not, were thrown into the prison of Bridewell, where vagrants are shut up and put to hard labour under the lash. I paid him a visit there, and found him toiling at the tread-mill, all covered with sweat."

Father Gerard's remembrances are borne out by the records.[2] In a list of "Recusants in the Counter in Wood-street, June 14, 1586," we meet "William Heigham and Roger Line, gentlemen. They were taken without Bishops-gate at mass with Blackborne *alias* Tomson that was hanged. They are in execution for a hundred marks

[1] Anne Line was executed at Tyburn, February 27, 1601, for harbouring a Catholic priest. "She told her confessor, some years before her death, that Mr. Thomson (Blackburn), a former confessor of hers, who ended his days by martyrdom in 1586, had promised her, that if God should make him worthy of that glorious end, he would pray for her, that she might obtain the like happiness." Challoner from Champney's MS. History.

[2] P.R.O., *Domestic, Elizabeth*, vol. cxc. n. 33; vol. cxci. n. 37; vol. cxcv. n. 51.

apiece. They have been divers times examined before Mr. Justice Young." In another list we are told that they were "Line, Heigham, gentlemen under 19 years"; and in a third we learn that "Roger Line [was] committed by Sir Francis Walsingham the 19th of February, 1585[6], and William Heigham [was] committed by his Honour also, the 30th of July 1585."

"On recovering his freedom, he hired himself out as a servant to a gentleman, that had to wife a Catholic lady whom I knew. She intrusted her son to his care : he taught the boy the groundwork of the Latin tongue, besides giving him lessons on the harp, which he himself touched admirably. I went to see him in this situation, and had a long talk with him about his call to his present state.

"Mistress Line, his sister, married a good husband and a staunch Catholic. He had been heir to a fine estate; but his father or uncle (for he was heir to both) sent a message from his death-bed to young Line, then a prisoner for the faith, asking him to conform and go to some heretical church for once, otherwise he would have to give up his inheritance to his younger brother. 'If I must either give up God or the world,' was his courageous answer, 'I prefer to give up the world, for it is good to cleave unto God.' So both his father's and his uncle's estate went to his younger brother. I saw this latter once in his elder brother's room, dressed in silk and other finery, while his brother had on plain and mean clothes. This good man afterwards went into Belgium, where he obtained a pension from the King of Spain, part of which he sent to his wife ; and thus they lived a poor and holy life. His death, which happened in Belgium, left his widow friendless, so that she had to look to Providence for her support. Before my imprisonment, she had been charitably taken by my entertainers into their own house. They furnished her with board and lodging, and I made up the rest.

"She was just the sort of person that I wanted as head of the house that I have spoken of, to manage the money matters, take care of the guests, and meet the inquiries of strangers. She had good store of charity and wariness, and in great patience she possessed her soul. She was nearly always ill from one or other of many divers diseases, which purified her and made her ready for Heaven. She used often to say to me, 'Though I desire above all things to die for Christ, I dare not hope to die by the hand of the executioner; but perhaps the Lord will let me be taken some time in the same house with a priest, and then be thrown into a chill and filthy dungeon, where I shall not be able to last out long in this wretched life.' Her delight was in the Lord, and the Lord granted her the desires of her heart.

"When I was rescued out of prison, she gave up the management of my house; for then so many people knew who she was, that her being in a place was enough to render it unsafe for me. So a room was hired for her in another person's house, where she often used to harbour priests. One day (it was the feast of the Purification of the Blessed Virgin) she let in a great many Catholics to hear mass, a thing which she would never have done in my house. Good soul, she was more careful of me than of herself. Some neighbours noticed the throng, and called the constables. They went upstairs into the room, which they found full of people. The celebrant was Father Francis Page, of the Society of Jesus, who was afterwards martyred.[1] He had pulled off his vestments before the priest-hunters came in; so that they could not readily make out which was the priest. However, from the father's grave and modest look, they thought that he must be their man. Accordingly they laid hold of him, and began questioning him and the others also. No one

---

[1] Father Francis Page S.J. suffered at Tyburn, April 20, 1602, for his priesthood.

would own that there was a priest there; but as the altar
had been found ready for mass, they acknowledged that
they had been waiting for a priest to come. While the
Catholics and their persecutors were wrangling on this
point, Father Francis Page, taking advantage of some
one's opening the door, got away from those that held
him and slipped out, shutting the door behind him. He
then went upstairs to a place that he knew, where Mrs.
Line had had a hiding-place made, and there he ensconced
himself. Search was made for him the whole house over,
to no purpose.

"So they took Mrs. Line and the richer ones of the
party to prison, and let the others go on bail. God
lengthened out the martyr's life beyond her expectation.
It was some months before she was brought to trial, on
a charge of harbouring and supporting priests. To the
question of 'guilty or not guilty,' she made no direct
answer, but cried out in a loud voice, so that all could
hear her, ' My lords, nothing grieves me, but that I could
not receive a thousand more.'[1] She listened to the sentence of death with great show of joy, and thanksgiving
to the Lord God. She was so weak, that she had to be
carried to court in a chair, and sat there during the whole
of the trial. After her return to prison, a little before her
death, she wrote to Father Page, who had escaped. The
letter is in my hands at present. She disposed therein
of the few things that she had, leaving to me a fine large
cross of gold that had belonged to her husband. She
mentioned me thrice in the letter, calling me her father.
She also left some few debts which she begged me to see
paid. Afterwards she bequeathed me her bed by word
of mouth. I wanted to purchase it from the gaolers, who
had plundered everything found in her cell after her death;
but I could only get the coverlet, which I used ever after
during my stay in London, and reckoned it no small safe-
guard.

[1] These words are given in the MS. in English.

"Being arrived at the place of punishment, some preachers wanted to tease her, as usual, with warnings to abandon her errors ; but she cut them short, saying, 'Away ! I have no dealings nor communion with you.' Then kissing the gallows with great joy, she knelt down to pray, and kept on praying till the hangman had done his duty. So she gave up her soul to God, along with the martyr Father Filcock,[1] of the Society of Jesus, who had often been her confessor, and had always been her friend. Her martyrdom, however, happened six or seven years after the time of which I am now speaking.[2] She managed my house for three years, and received therein many holy priests.

"I always had a priest residing in this house, whom I used to send to assist and console my friends, as I was unable to visit them myself. The first[3] I had there was Father Jones, a Franciscan, afterwards martyred, but then newly arrived in England. I was glad to be able to provide for him there, as I hoped thereby to establish a good feeling between his order and ours. He, however, finding a number of friends whom he was desirous of assisting, after thanking me for the hospitality afforded him, in a few months betook himself to his own connections. A little later he was taken, and suffered martyrdom with great constancy.

"After him I received another priest, lately arrived from Spain, and formerly known to me, Robert Drury by name. He was of gentle birth and well educated, and could consequently associate with gentlemen without

[1] Roger Filcock S.J., *alias* Arthur, executed for his priesthood, with Mark Barkworth *alias* Lambert, O.S.B., and Anne Line, at Tyburn, February 27, 1601.

[2] "They have executed three or four poor priests (one [John Pibush, priest] condemned four or five years ago) and Anne Line, a Catholic gentlewoman, only for harbouring priests." Advices sent to Thomas Phelippes, April $\frac{3}{13}$, 1601. P.R.O., *Flanders Corresp.*

[3] John Jones *alias* Buckley suffered at St. Thomas's Watering, July 12, 1598 ; and Robert Drury at Tyburn, February 26, 160$\frac{8}{9}$, for being priests in England.

causing any suspicion. I introduced him, therefore, to my chief friends, and he assisted them well and zealously for two years and more that he tarried in my house. This good priest also God chose to be His witness and martyr. For after my escape from England, two years ago from this present writing, he was taken, found guilty of high treason, and executed accordingly; although they had nothing to bring against him, save only that he was a priest, and refused to take the new-invented oaths. At his martyrdom happened a noteworthy circumstance. When he had arrived at the scaffold, some of the principal officers pressed him to have pity on himself, to conform to the King's laws, to go to the Protestant church, and to save his life.

" 'Well, my masters,' said the martyr, 'can you warrant me that I shall truly be saved from death, if I consent to go to your churches ?'

" 'Aye, verily can we,' they replied, 'and we promise you this in the King's name, that you shall not die.'

" Then the martyr turned him to the people, and said aloud : 'You see now what sort of high treason they find us guilty of. You see that religion is the only cause for which I and other priests are put to death.'

" Hereupon the officers were enraged, and revenged themselves by cutting him down directly he was turned off, and disembowelling him while he was still alive. But they killed his body only, and had nothing more they could do to him.

" In that house of mine, while I was in prison, there lived a while one of our fathers, who was in ill health, Father John Curry.[1] There also he died, and there he

---

[1] Father Curry entered the Society in France in 1583, æt. 34, and though he was sent back to England immediately, he soon returned to France, for in 1587 he had spent three years in the study of theology at Pont-à-Mousson. He left Chideock House for London about Michaelmas 1593. *Troubles,* Second Series, p. 24. His death, occurring while Father Gerard was in prison, will have been between May 1594 and October 1597.

O

lies buried in some secret corner. For those priests who live secretly on the mission, we are obliged also to bury secretly when they die.

"All this while my good host [William Wiseman], who had been taken a little before me, was kept imprisoned; and for the first four months so straitly, that neither his wife nor any of his friends were allowed to have any access to him. After this, however, the persecutors, seeing that they could not produce any proof against him, because none of the Catholic servants would acknowledge anything, and the traitor had never seen me in priest's guise, and was only one witness after all, by degrees relaxed a little of their harshness, and permitted him to be visited and cared for, though they still kept him in strict custody.

"While thus close shut up, he wrote a work by no means contemptible, which he divided into three parts, and called *Three Farewells to the world, or three deaths in different states of soul.*[1] In the first book he described a man of moral life, and virtuous in the opinion of men, but directing himself in all things by his own lights. In the second book he described a good and pious lady, who at first wished to be guided in everything, but subsequently, deceived by the devil, determined in some things to follow her own ideas. In the third book he described the death of a pious and devoted man, who, though living in the world and possessed of riches, yet always sought and followed the counsels of his spiritual father, manifesting himself entirely for the purpose of being directed by him to the greater glory of God.

"It was written, not with ink, but merely with pencil, upon loose scraps of paper, for at that time he was kept so close that he could get no ink. As he finished each of the three parts, he sent it to me, that I might correct anything I might find against sound doctrine. He gave as a reason for writing the work, that he had himself found,

[1] Tres valedictiones mundo datæ a tribus in diverso statu morientibus.—*MS.*

as he thought, so immense a benefit from giving himself thoroughly to the direction of his spiritual guide, and had felt in consequence so undisturbed a peace of mind, even when the malice of the persecutors was daily threatening him with death, that he could not refrain from recommending the same course to others whom he loved. He said, moreover, that he wrote the book, not for the public, but principally for his own family, and secondly for his relations and friends : for that, as he could not communicate with them by word of mouth, he desired to show them in writing the most secure and meritorious way to perfection while living in the world. For he endeavoured to prove that perfection was even more necessary for those who lived in the world than for religious.

"Such were the sentiments of this good man. He nowise regretted that he had during four years given himself up to my direction, though he found himself in consequence exposed to such extreme distresses, and saw his family and fortune made a mark for the persecutors as a result of having harboured me. Nay, it was not only that he bore all these trials patiently, but he really thought it all joy to suffer thus for the good cause. His wife also, though she loved her husband most tenderly, and was of a peculiarly sensitive mind, yet in this juncture bore everything with a singular sweetness and patience. After I was transferred to the Clink, where there was more chance of communicating with me either by word or letter, she took a house in the immediate neighbourhood of my prison, in order that she might consult me constantly, and provide me with everything I needed. In this house she and her husband, who obtained his release after a time by large payments of money, resided, while I remained in that prison. But after my escape from the Tower, they betook themselves back to their country seat, in order that they might have me with them there again."

Though this is not the last mention of the Wisemans

in Father Gerard's life, this is a convenient place for inserting a proof of their steadiness and perseverance in the faith in spite of their persecutions. Sir Arthur Capell wrote[1] to Secretary Cecil from Hadham, August 12, 1599, as follows. "The townsmen of Starford have brought me John Gurgeene, whom they stayed upon suspicion of being a Jesuit priest, with certain superstitious wafers, which I send together with his examination, and a book written by him, containing some Popish prayers and the form of mass. He only confesses that he was a messenger to carry the wafers and some other apparel to Mr. Wiseman's house at Broadoaks in Essex. Mr. Wiseman's house has been long known to be Popish, and his mother now stands condemned for entertaining a priest ; so I send him up to you, not knowing whether there may be any further matter to be got out of him."

"In the meantime," Father Gerard continues, "I was so fully taken up in the prison with business, and with the visits of Catholics, that in the next room, which was Brother Emerson's, there were often six or eight persons at once, waiting their turn to see me. Nay, many of my most intimate and attached friends have oft-times had to wait many hours at a stretch, and even then I have been obliged to ask them to come another time.

"Among other occupations I heard many general confessions. One case was that of a Catholic gentleman of great wealth, who had always lived quietly, cautiously avoiding anything that savoured of danger. At length however, God so willing, he was taken and thrown into the same prison with me, an occurrence which was certainly the very last he looked for. He was all the more perplexed because the persecutors alleged so slight and trivial a cause for his imprisonment. When he spoke to me of this, I replied that all things indeed happened by permis-

[1] P.R.O., *Domestic, Elizabeth*, vol. cclxxii. n. 36.

sion of God, but especially things of this sort : that He
often warned men by such means to 'agree with their
adversary quickly' while time allowed, and that this was •
our Lord's own advice, Who wished to be rather a Father
than a Judge. I advised him then to take the opportunity
of this forced retirement, to enter into himself, and take
account of his soul, how much he owed his Lord ; and
that the rather, as he knew not whether he should ever
after have the like opportunity. This was, I told him,
sent him perhaps as a sort of last summons to hold himself
prepared for death. He yielded to my advice, read the
book called "Memoriale," by Father Louis of Granada,
prepared himself for confession, and made it with great
exactness, much to his own consolation and mine. At this
time he was in strong and perfect health, but a few days
later, being released from prison, he took ill and died
within two months.

"About this time I assisted several persons to turn
their minds from secular things, and by God's grace to
follow the counsels of our Lord. Among these were two
young men, friends, who were writers in a certain office
in London, an occupation which gave them a considerable
income. One was Father Francis Page, afterwards
enrolled in the glorious army of martyrs. His friend, a
man of excellent parts, gave himself to the study of
theology, with the view of becoming a priest and entering
the Society ; but he died during his studies, leaving
behind him a reputation for great virtue and holiness.

"Mr. Francis Page was the son of well-to-do parents,
and being both handsome and very winning in manner,
was beloved by the daughter of his employer, a man of
great wealth. The love was mutual ; indeed it was by the
lady's means that he had become a Catholic ; and they
had engaged with each other to marry when the consent
of their parents might be had. The young lady was herself
a good and devoted soul : she used frequently to

come to me for direction, and at last introduced Mr.
Page to me. He was already a Catholic, but was, as I
have said, looking forward to live in the married state.
There shone in him however so singular a modesty and
candour of mind, and I found him so powerfully drawn to
virtue, that I could not doubt he was intended for higher
things. I began therefore to speak with him of the uncertainty of riches, and of the delusive hopes of happiness
in this world, and put before him the possibility of a more
perfect life. I did this the rather, because I thought it
unlikely that the parents of the young lady would consent
to her marrying below her degree. After this, I gave him
some meditations, and some writings to copy out which
treated of the spiritual life ; and God in His goodness
gradually weaned his mind from the love of transitory
things and fixed it on things eternal. In fact he came to
the determination of giving up both his place in the office
and the thought of marrying ; and, in order that he might
be nearer to me for a time, he came to live as a servant in
the house of the lady my hostess, though such a position
was of course far below that which he was leaving. But
he wished to prepare himself for greater things which he
hoped for, and in this he was much helped by Father
Edward Coffin, who was then residing in my hostess'
family. This same Father often visited me, and consoled
me much. I shall have occasion to speak more of Father
Francis Page hereafter.

"While I remained in this prison, I sent over numbers
of boys and young men to Catholic seminaries abroad.
Some of these are, at this present, priests of the Society,
and engaged on the English Mission : others still remain
in the seminaries, in positions of authority, to assist in
training labourers for the same field. On one occasion I
had sent two boys on their way to St. Omers, and had
given them letters of recommendation, written with lemon-
juice, so that the writing was not visible on the paper.

In the paper itself I wrapped up a few collars, so that it might seem that its only use was to keep the collars clean. The boys were taken, and, on being questioned, confessed that I had sent them. They let out also that I had given them this letter, and had told them, when they came to a certain college of ours, by which they had to pass to reach St. Omers (for they had to pass by Ostend, which is not the usual way, and thus they came to be taken), to bid the fathers steep the paper in water, and they would be able to read what I had written. On this information, then, the paper was steeped by the authorities, and two letters of mine were read, written on the same paper. One was written in Latin to our Belgian Fathers ; this I had consequently signed with my own proper name. The other was addressed to our English fathers at St. Omers. The letters having been thus discovered, I was sent for to be examined.

"Young however was no longer to be my examiner. He had died in his sins, and that most miserably. As he lived, so he died :[1] he lived the devil's confessor, he died the devil's martyr : for not only did he die in the devil's service, but he brought on his death through that very service. He was accustomed to work night and day to increase the distress of the Catholics, and to go forth frequently in inclement weather, at one or two o'clock in the morning, to search their houses. By these labours he fell into a consumption,[2] of which he died. He died more-over overwhelmed with debt, so that it might be clear that he abandoned all things for the devil's service. Notwith-standing all the emoluments of his office, all the plunder he took from the persecuted Catholics, and the large bribes they were constantly giving him to buy off his malicious

---

[1] Qualis vita, finis ita.—*MS.*

[2] Morbum regium.—*MS.* Consumption is a form of scrofula or King's-evil, and seems to be the form most likely to be brought on by the causes here mentioned. In classical Latin, however, *morbus regius* signifies *jaundice*, and this may be the meaning here.

oppression, his debts were said to amount to no less a sum than a hundred thousand florins [10,000*l.*] ; and I have heard even a larger sum mentioned than this. Perhaps he expected the Queen would pay his debts ; but she did nothing of the sort. All she did, was to send a gentleman from the Court to visit him, when he was confined to his bed and near death ; and this mark of favour so delighted him, that he seemed ready to sing *Nunc dimittis.* But it was a false peace, and the lifting up of the soul that goes before a fall ; and like another Aman, he was bidden not to a banquet, but to execution, and that for ever. So with his mouth full of the Queen's praises, and his great obligations to her Majesty, he died a miserable death, and anguish took the place of his joy. The joy of the hypocrite is but for an instant.

"This man's successor in the office of persecuting and harassing the servants of God, was William [Waad or] Wade, now Governor of the Tower of London, but at that time Private Secretary of the Lords of the Council. For the members of the Council choose always to have a man in their service, to whose cruelty anything particularly odious may be attributed, instead of its being supposed to be done by their warrant. This Wade then sent for me, and first of all showed me the blank paper that I had given the boys, and asked me if I recognized it. I answered : 'No, I do not.' And in fact I did not recognize it, for I did not know the boys had been taken. Then he dipped the paper in a basin of water, and showed me the writing, and my name subscribed in full. When I saw it, I said : 'I do not acknowledge the writing. Any one may easily have counterfeited my handwriting and forged my signature ; and if such boys as you speak of have been taken, they may perhaps in their terror say anything that their inquisitors want them to say, to their own prejudice and that of their friends ; a thing I will never do. At the same time, I do not deny that it would be a good deed to send such boys abroad to be better educated ; and I would gladly do it, if I had the means ; but closely confined as I am in prison, I cannot do anything of the kind, though I should like to do it.'

" He replied to me with a torrent of abuse for denying my signature and handwriting, and said : 'In truth, you have far too much liberty ; but you shall not enjoy it long.' Then he rated the gaoler soundly, for letting me have so much freedom."

Father Bartoli in his *Inghilterra,*[1] has the following passage about Father Gerard, whom he knew personally at Rome. "At his first entrance into this prison (the Clink) he procured himself a habit of the Society, and continued to wear it from that time forward, even in the face of all London, when he was being taken to his different examinations ; so that the people crowded to see a Jesuit in his habit, while the preachers were all the more exasperated at what they thought an open defiance of them."

This proceeding at that time was not anything very exceptional, for Father Weston in his narrative[2] gives it as one of the signs that warned Catholics that Anthony Tyrrel was wavering in his faith, that without any necessity, in the Clink prison, he would wear secular dress. His own clerical costume in prison he mentions as a matter of course. "On the succeeding day I set out, having changed my habit for secular clothes."

Father Gerard thus mentions his own practice. " I was sent for on two or three other occasions, to be examined ; and whenever I came out of this prison I always wore a Jesuit's cassock and cloak, which I had had made as soon as I came among Catholic fellow-prisoners. The sight of this dress raised mocks from the boys in the streets, and put my persecutors in a rage. On the first occasion, they said I was a hypocrite. I replied : 'When I was arrested,

[1] Lib. v. cap. 13. [2] *Troubles*, Second Series, pp. 204, 209.

you called me a courtier, and said that I had dressed myself in that fashion in order to· disguise my real character, and to be able to deal with persons of rank in safety and without being recognized. I told you then that I did not like a layman's dress, and would much rather wear my own. Well, now I am doing so ; and you are in a rage again. In fact, you are not satisfied with either piping or mourning, but you seek excuses for inveighing against me.'

" To this they answered : ' Why did you not go about in this dress before, instead of wearing a disguise, and taking a false name ? A thing no good man would do.'

" I replied : ' I am aware you would like us not to do so, in order that we might be arrested at once, and not be able to do any good in the work of rescuing and gaining souls. But do you not know that St. Raphael personated another, and took another name, in order that, not being known, he might better accomplish God's work for which he had been sent.'

" At another time I was examined before the Dean of Westminster, the dignitary who has taken the place of the former Abbot of the great royal monastery there. Topcliffe and some other commissioners were present. Their object was to confront me with the good widow, my host's mother, of whom I have before spoken ; and who was confined at this time in a prison[1] near the church at Westminster ; for she was not yet condemned to death ; that happened later. They wanted to see if she recognized me. So when I came into the room where they brought me, I found her already there. When she saw me coming in with the gaolers, she almost jumped for joy : but she controlled herself, and said to them : ' Is that the

[1] The Gatehouse prison, near the west end of the Abbey, "is so called of two gates, the one out of the College court towards the north, on the east side whereof was the Bishop of London's prison for clerks convict ; and the other gate, adjoining the first, but towards the west, is a gaol or prison for offenders thither committed." Stow, p. 176.

person you spoke of ?   I do not know him ; but he looks like a priest.'

" Upon this she made me a very low reverence, and I bowed in return.   Then they asked me if I did not recognize her.

" I answered : 'I do not recognize her.'[1]   At the same time, you know this is my usual way of answering, and I will never mention any places, or give the names of persons that are known to me (which this lady however is not) ; because to do so, as I told you before, would be contrary both to justice and charity.'

" Then Topcliffe said : ' Tell the truth: have you reconciled any person to the Church of Rome ? '

" I quite understood his blood-thirsty intention, that being a thing expressly prohibited under penalty of high treason, as I mentioned before in the case of Master Rigby who was martyred ; but then I knew I was already as much compromised on account of my priesthood, and therefore I answered boldly : 'Yes, in truth I have received some persons, and I am sorry that I have not done this good service to more.'

" 'Well,' said Topcliffe, 'how many would you like to have reconciled, if you could ?   A thousand ? '

" ' Certainly,' I said, 'a hundred thousand, and many more still, if I could.'

" 'That would be enough,' said Topcliffe, 'to levy an army against the Queen.'

" 'Those whom I reconciled,' said I, 'would not be against the Queen, but all for her ; for we hold that obedience to superiors is of obligation.'

" 'No such thing,' said Topcliffe, 'you teach rebellion.

---

[1] We must here refer our readers to a note on a former passage (p. 163). It will be noticed that when such answers as the above are given, the speaker often adds something to show the questioner that he has no right to expect a true answer, and consequently no ground for trusting the present answer to be a true one.

See, I have here a Bull of the Pope, granted to Sanders[1] when he went to Ireland to stir up the Queen's subjects to rebellion. See, here it is. Read it.'

" I answered : 'There is no need to read it. It is likely enough that the Pontiff, if he sent him, gave him authority. But *I* have no power to meddle at all in such matters. We are forbidden to have anything to do with such things. I never have, and never will.'

" 'Take and read it,' he said : 'I will have you read it.'

" So I took it, and seeing the name of Jesus on the top, I reverently kissed it.

" 'What,' said Topcliffe, 'you kiss a Bull of the Pope, do you ?'

" 'I kissed,' said I, 'the name of Jesus, to which all love and honour are due. But if it is a Bull of the Pope, as you say, I reverence it also on that score.'

" And so saying, I kissed the printed paper again. Then Topcliffe, in a furious passion, began to abuse me with indecent accusations.

" At this insolence, to own the truth, I somewhat lost command of myself ; and though I knew that he had no grounds which seemed probable even to himself for what he said, but had uttered it from pure malice, I exclaimed : " I call the great and blessed God to witness, that all your insinuations are false.'

" And, as I spoke, I laid my hand on the book that was open before me on the table. It was a copy of the Holy Bible, but according to their corrupt translation into the vulgar tongue. Then Topcliffe held his peace ; but the Dean took up the word.

" 'Are you willing,' said he, 'to be sworn on our Bible?' The better instructed Catholics, who can show the dishonesty of that translation, usually refuse to do this.

" I replied : 'In truth, under the necessity of rebutting

---

[1] The celebrated theologian and controversialist, Dr. Sanders, was sent as Papal Legate into Ireland by Gregory XIII. in 1579.

this man's false charges at once, I did not take notice what version this was. However, there are some truths, as for instance the Incarnation and Passion of Christ, that have not been corrupted by mis-translation; and by these I call the truth of God to witness. There are many other things falsely rendered, so as to involve heresies; and these I detest and anathematize.'

"So saying, I laid my hand again upon the book, and more firmly than before. Then the old man was angry, and said : ' I will prove that you are a heretic.'

"I replied : 'You cannot prove it.'

"'I will prove it,' he said, 'thus: Whoever denies Holy Scripture is a heretic : you deny this to be Holy Scripture : *Ergo.*'

"I replied : 'This is no true syllogism; it shifts from general to particular, and so has four terms.'

"The old man answered : 'I could make syllogisms before you were born.'

"'Very likely,' I said ; 'but the one you have just produced is not a true one.'

"However, the good old man[1] would not try a new middle-term, and made no further attempt to prove me a heretic. But one urged one thing, and another another, not in the way of argument, but after their usual plan, asking me such questions as they knew very well I did not like to answer ; and then, in the end, they sent me back to prison.

[1] Gabriel Goodman, Dean of Westminster from 1561 to 1601.

NOTE TO CHAPTER XVII.

AMONGST Father Gerard's converts at this time there was one whose history is thus recorded in the Chronicle of St. Monica's, Louvain. " Unto this conversion and calling to religion of our first subprioress, Sister Elizabeth Shirley [whom Father Gerard in one of his letters calls his cousin], we will adjoin another of the elders, to wit, Sister Anne Brumfield, because it showeth evidently with what a powerful hand Almighty God calleth some unto Him amidst all the pleasures of the world, and how the Divine Wisdom, having in the forementioned disposed things sweetly, in this disposed them strongly. She was daughter to Edward Brumfield, Esquire in the county of Surrey, who living long a schismatic, yet some two years before his death was reconciled and died a good Catholic. After whose decease his widow, named Catherine Fromans before her marriage, being a gentlewoman of very fine behaviour and having good friends, was called to the Court of Queen Elizabeth and made mother to the Maids of Honour. Not being a Catholic as her deceased husband, but only well-minded, she then took this her daughter Anne to the Court at the age of sixteen, where for four years she gave herself wholly to the pleasures and delights of the world, yet that so being of a high mind and aiming at greater matches than her degree, she never was enthralled in the love of any man amidst the occasions of such a Court as that was, for Almighty God, Who intended to satisfy her aspiring mind with no less than Himself and to bring her into a higher estate than [that] of any worldly nobility, permitted not His future spouse to be defiled with sensual love : but behold, against the time of a great marriage in the Court, when she supposed to have had abundant pleasure and follies, suddenly all is turned quite contrary, for so great a cloud of affliction invadeth her mind, and so deep a melancholy accompanied with horrible and desperate temptations, that all the pleasures of the Court were turned now into sorrows, her feasting into mourning, her tears poured forth amain whenever she could get out of company, and being once gotten alone, which was very hard to do in that place, and lamenting according to her custom her great misfortune that she should take comfort in nothing and knew not what should help her, it came suddenly to her mind that she must leave the world and become a nun, having heard some speech in her infancy of Religious Houses and nuns in old time, as also having been taught her *Pater noster*, *Ave Maria*, Creed, and Jesus Psalter, all which prayers worldly pleasures had now brought to oblivion. She finding this notion in her mind, and not knowing how to compress the same, being as yet no Catholic, neither having notice of Religious Houses, notwithstanding one day she disclosed it unto a person who put her quite out of thinking upon religion. Thereupon her mother, desirous to help her, seeing [her] to spend the nights in tears as she lay by her, would give her to read a book of Catholic prayer; so that now affliction made her call to mind her old prayers. But nothing availed to comfort her; the Court was loathsome, all things disgustful, and she knew not what ailed her. Her mother hereupon sends her into the country to a married sister of hers, to see if that would help her, but all recreation made her worse and worse, so that at length she thought by main violence to get her pleasure again in the world. She therefore desired her mother to send for her to the Court, which she did, but our Lord would have the mastery, and therefore coming back to Court again, her afflictions are renewed, no contentment can enter her mind, insomuch that looking out of window she thought a dog more happy than herself because it had not trouble of mind. Almighty God forgot her not in this case, but one day a gentleman that was a Catholic, though unknown, coming to the Court and seeing her so sad and melancholy, asked what she wanted. Whereunto she answered she knew not what to do, nor what would help her, she was in such affliction of mind. He answered that he would bring her to one who should help her. She regarded not then his words, being overwhelmed with affliction; but some days after, he coming there again, she desired him for God's sake to bring her to one as he had said the other day, who thereupon brought her to Father Garret [Gerard], who instructed her in Catholic religion and reconciled her, whereupon her mind was

so quieted that she became contented. But yet she could take
no pleasure in the world, therefore [she] left the Court, and lived
as the said Father appointed order for her. At length she discovered to him how she was moved to undertake a religious
life, and he very much applauded her mind and animated her
therein. Then considering what Order to choose, she had most
mind to the Clarisses' Order, until one day she felt it sensibly,
as it were, said in her mind that she must go to St. Ursula's,
for she had long before heard one speak of such a cloister in
Louvain, whereupon Father Garret sought for means to help her
over, but being taken and clapped up in the Tower, he left order
with Father Garnet, his Provincial, to help her, which he did,
and sent her over with another, to wit Sister Mary Welch, so
that the day twelvemonth that she was reconciled to the Church,
she was on the sea for religion."

CHAPTER XVIII.

"On another occasion they examined me, and all the other Catholics that were confined in the same prison with me, in a public place called Guildhall, where Topcliffe and several other commissioners were present. When they had put their usual questions, and received from me the usual answers, they came to the point; intending, I imagine, to sound us all as to our feelings towards the State, or else to entrap us in some expressions about the State, that might be made matter of accusation. They asked me then, whether I acknowledged the Queen as the true governor and Queen of England.

"I answered, 'I do acknowledge her as such.'

"'What,' said Topcliffe, 'in spite of Pius V.'s excommunication?'

"I answered, 'I acknowledge her as our Queen, notwithstanding I know there is such an excommunication.'

"The fact was, I knew that the operation of that excommunication had been suspended for all in England by a declaration of the Pontiff, till such time as its execution became possible.

"Topcliffe proceeded: 'What would you do in case the Pope sent an army into England, asserting that the object was solely to bring back the kingdom to the Catholic religion, and protesting that there was no other way left of introducing the Catholic faith, and, moreover,

P

commanding all in virtue of his Apostolical authority to aid his cause? Whose side would you then take, the Pope's or the Queen's?'

"I saw the man's malicious cunning, and that his aim was, that whichever way I answered I might injure myself, either in soul or body, and so I worded my reply thus: 'I am a true Catholic, and a true subject of the Queen. If, then, this were to happen, which is unlikely, and which I think will never be the case, I would act as became a true Catholic and a true subject.'

"'Nay, nay,' said he, 'answer positively and to the point.'

"'I have declared my mind,' said I, 'and no other answer will I make.'

"On this he flew into a most violent rage, and vomited out a torrent of curses, and ended by saying, 'You think you will creep to kiss the Cross this year; but before the time comes, I will take good care you do no such thing.'

"He meant to intimate, in the abundance of his charity, that he would take care I should go to Heaven by the rope before that time. But he had not been admitted into the secrets of God's sanctuary, and did not know my great unworthiness. Though God had permitted him to execute his malice on others, whom the Divine Wisdom knew to be worthy and well-prepared, as on Father Southwell, and others, whom he pursued to the death, yet no such great mercy of God came to me from his anger. Others, indeed, for whom a kingdom was prepared by the Father, were advanced to Heaven by our Lord Jesus through his means; but this heavenly gift was too great for an angry man to be allowed to bestow on me. However, he was really in some sort a prophet in uttering these words, though he meant them differently from the sense in which they were fulfilled.

"What I have mentioned happened about Christmas

[1594]. In the following Lent[1] he himself was thrown
into prison for disrespect to the members of the Queen's
Council, on an occasion, if I mistake not, when he had
pleaded too boldly in behalf of his only son, who had killed
a man with his sword in the great hall of the Court of
Queen's Bench. This took place about Passion Sunday.
We then, who were in prison for the faith, seeing our
enemy Aman about to be hanged on his own gibbet, began
to lift up our heads, and to use what liberty we had a little
more freely, and we admitted a greater number to the
sacraments, and to assist at the services and holy rites of
the Church. Thus it was that on Good Friday [1595] a
large number of us were together in the room over mine—
in fact, all the Catholics in the prison, and a number of
others from without. I had gone through all the service,
and said all the prayers appointed for the day, up to the
point where the priest has to lay aside his shoes. I had
put them off, and had knelt down, and was about to creep
towards the Cross and make the triple adoration of it,
when, just as I had moved two paces, the head gaoler
came and knocked at the door of my room underneath,
and as I did not answer from within he began to batter
violently at the door and make a great noise. As soon
as I heard it, I knew that the chief gaoler was there,
because no other would have ventured to behave in that
way to me: so I sent some one directly, to say that I
would come without delay, and then, instead of going on
with the adoration of the material cross, I hastened to the

---

[1] "From the Marshalsea this Monday in Easter-week, 1595. The humble
prisoner of her Majesty Ryc. Topcliffe" to the Lords of the Privy Council,
enclosing copies in his hand of two letters to the Queen, one dated the 15th of
April 1595, the other "At the Marshalsea this Good or evil Friday,
1595." In the last-mentioned letter, Topcliffe wrote to Elizabeth: "In all
prisons rejoicings; and it is like that the fresh dead bones of Father
Southwell at Tyburn and Father Walpole at York, executed both since
Shrovetide, will dance for joy." Brit. Mus., *Harleian MSS.*, 6698, f. 184.
The fullest and best account of Richard Topcliffe is to be found in Dr. Jessopp's
One Generation of a Norfolk House, p. 78.

spiritual cross that God presented to me, and taking off
the sacred vestments that I was wearing, I went down
with speed, for fear the gaoler might come up after me,
and find a number of others, who would have thus been
brought into trouble. When he saw me, he said in a loud
tone of voice, 'How comes it that I find you out of your
room, when you ought to be kept strictly confined to
it?'

"As I knew the nature of the man, I pretended in
reply to be angry, that one who professed to be a friend
should have come at such a time as that, when if ever we
were bound to be busy at our prayers.

"'What,' said he, 'you were at mass, were you? I
will go up and see.'

"'No such thing,' I said; 'you seem to know very
little of our ways: there is not a single mass said to-day
throughout the whole Church. Go up if you like; but
understand that, if you do, neither I nor any one of the
Catholics will ever pay anything for our rooms. You may
put us all, if you like, in the common prison of the poor
who do not pay. But you will be no gainer by that;
whereas, if you act in a friendly way with us, and do not
come upon us unawares in this manner, you will not find
us ungrateful, as you have not found us hitherto.'

"He softened down a little at this, and then I said,
'What have you come for now, I pray?'

"'Surely,' said he, 'to greet you from Master Topcliffe.'

"'From him?' I said, 'and how is it that he and I
are such great friends? Is he not in such a prison? He
cannot do anything against me just now, I fancy.'

"'No,' said the gaoler, 'he cannot. But he really
sends to greet you. When I visited him to-day, he asked
me how you were. I replied that you were very well.
'But he does not bear his imprisonment,' said Master
Topcliffe, 'as patiently as I do mine. I would have you
greet him then in my name, and tell him what I have said.'

So I have come now for the purpose of repeating his message to you.'

" 'Very well,' I replied. ' Now tell him from me, that by the grace of God I bear my imprisonment for the cause of the faith with cheerfulness, and I could wish his cause were the same.'

"Thereupon the gaoler went away, rating his servant, however, for not having kept me more closely confined. And thus Topcliffe really accomplished what he had promised, having checked me in the very act of adoration, although without thinking of what he said, and with another intent at the time. Thus was Saul among the prophets. However, he did not prevent my going up again and completing what I had begun.

"The man who had charge of my room would not do anything in our rooms without my leave. And after my first gaoler, who soon died, the others who succeeded were well disposed to oblige me. One of them, who had the gaolership by inheritance, I made a Catholic. He immediately gave up his post and sold the right of succession, and became the attendant of a Catholic gentleman, a friend of mine, and afterwards accompanied his son to Italy, and got a vocation to the religious state. At present he is a prisoner in the very prison where he had been my gaoler. The next who had the charge of me after him, being a married man with children, was kept by fear of poverty from becoming a Catholic ; but yet he was afterwards so attached to myself and all our friends, that he received us into his own house, and sometimes concealed there such Catholics as were more sorely pressed than others by the persecution. And when I was to be got out of the Tower of London, with serious risk to all who aided the enterprize, he himself in person was one of three who exposed themselves to such great danger. And although he was nearly drowned the first night of the attempt, he rowed the boat the next night as before, as

I shall hereafter relate. For not long after what I just now mentioned, I was removed from that prison to the Tower of London : the occasion of which was the following.

"There was in the prison with me a certain priest,[1] to whom I had done many good services. When he first came to England, I had lodged him in an excellent house with some of my best friends ; I had made Catholics of his mother and only brother ; I had secured him a number of friends when he was thrown into prison, and had made him considerable presents. I had always shown him affection, although, perceiving that he was not firm and steady in spirit, but rather hankered too much after freedom, I did not deal confidently with him, as with others in the prison, especially Brother Emerson and John Lilly. Nevertheless this good man, from some motive or other, procured my removal ; whether in the desire and expectation that, if I were gone, all whom he saw coming to me would thenceforth come to him, or in order to curry favour with our enemies, and obtain liberty or some such boon for himself, is not certain. Be that as it may, he reported to our enemies, that he was standing by, when I handed a packet of letters dated from Rome and Brussels to a servant of Father Garnet's, of the name of Little John [Nicholas Owen], about whom I have before spoken. This latter, after having been arrested in my company, as I have related, and subjected to various examinations, but without disclosing anything, had been released for a sum of money which some Catholic gentlemen paid. For his services were indispensable to them and many others, as he was a first-rate hand at contriving priests' hiding-places. The priest then reported that I had given this man letters, and

---

[1] William Atkinson, the apostate priest, in a letter to Blackwell the arch-priest, dated April 9, 1602, said that he had been in prison with Father Gerard. Bartoli, *Inghilterra*, p. 416. This man dared to offer to poison the Earl of Tyrone in a sacred host. P.R.O., *Domestic, Elizabeth*, vol. ccli. n. 49.

that I was in the habit of receiving letters from beyond the sea addressed both to my Superior and to myself.

"Acting on this information, the persecutors sent a Justice of the Peace to me one day, with two Queen's messengers, or pursuivants as they call them. These came up to my room on a sudden with the head-gaoler ; but by God's Providence they found no one with me at the time except two boys, whom I was instructing with intention to send them abroad : one of whom, if I remember right, escaped, the other they imprisoned for a time. But they found nothing else in my room that I was afraid of being seen ; for I was accustomed to keep all my manuscripts and all other articles of importance in some holes made to hide things. All these holes were known to Brother Emerson ; and so after my removal he took out everything, and among the rest a reliquary that I have with me now, and a store of money that I had in hand for the expenses of my house in town, of which I have before spoken, to the amount of thirteen hundred florins [130*l.*]. This money he sent to my Superior, who took charge of the house from that time till I was got out of prison.

"When these officials came in they began to question me ; and when the examination was over, which it soon was, as they could get nothing from me of what they wanted to know, they began to search the room all over, to find letters or something else, that might serve their turn and injure me. While the Justice of the Peace was rummaging my books, one of the pursuivants searched my person, and opening my doublet, he discovered my hair-shirt. At first he did not know what it was, and said : 'What is this ?'

"'A shirt,' I replied.

"'Ho, ho !' said he, 'it is a hair-shirt.' And he caught hold of it, and wanted to drag it off my body by force.

"This insolence of the varlet, to confess my imperfection honestly, excited me more than anything I have ever had to endure from my enemies, and I was within a little of thrusting him violently back; but I checked myself by God's grace, and claimed the Justice's protection, who immediately made him give over. So they sought, but found nothing that they sought for in my room except myself; and me they took at once, and went straight to the Tower of London with me, and there handed me to the Governor, whose title is King's Lieutenant. He was a knight of the name of Barkeley. He conducted me at once to a large high tower of three stories, with a separate lock-up place in each, one of a number of different towers contained within the whole inclosure. He left me for the night in the lowest part, and committed the custody of my person to a servant in whom he placed great confidence. The servant brought a little straw at once, and throwing it down on the ground went away, fastening the door of my prison, and securing the upper door both with a great bolt and with iron bars. I recommended myself therefore to God, Who is wont to go down with His people into the pit, and Who never abandoned me in my bondage, as well as to the most Blessed Virgin, the Mother of Mercy, and to my Patron Saints and Guardian Angel; and after prayer I lay down with a calm mind on the straw, and slept very well that night [April 12, 1597].

"The next day I examined the place, for there was some light, though dim; and I found the name of Father Henry Walpole, of blessed memory,[1] cut with a knife on the wall, and not far from there I found his oratory, which was a space where there had been a narrow window, now blocked up with stones. There he had written on either side with chalk the names of the different choirs of Angels, and on the top above the Cherubim and Seraphim the name of Mary Mother of God, and over that the

[1] Henry Walpole S.J. was executed at York, April 7, 1595, for his priesthood.

name of Jesus, and over that again in Latin, Greek, and Hebrew, the name of God. It was truly a great consolation to me, to find myself in this place, hallowed by the presence of so great and so devoted a martyr, the place too in which he was frequently tortured, to the number, as I have heard, of fourteen times. Probably they were unwilling to torture him in public and in the ordinary place, because they did it oftener than they would have it known. And I can well believe that he was racked that number of times, for he lost through it the proper use of his fingers. This I can vouch for from the following circumstances. He was carried back to York, to be executed in the place where he was taken on his first landing in England, and while in prison there he had a discussion with some ministers which he wrote out with his own hand.[1] A part of this writing was given to me, together with some meditations on the Passion of Christ, which he had written in prison before his own passion. These writings however I could scarcely read at all, not because they were written hastily, but because the hand of the writer could not form the letters. It seemed more like the first attempts of a child, than the handwriting of a scholar and a gentleman such as he was. Yet he used to be at Court before the death of Father Campion,[2] in whose honour he also wrote some beautiful verses in the English tongue,[3] declaring that he and many others had received the warmth of life from that blessed martyr's blood, and had been animated by it to follow the more perfect counsels of Christ.

[1] It was Father Walpole's custom to make notes of his conferences with ministers. In the Public Record Office (*Domestic, Elizabeth*, vol. ccxlviii. n. 51) there is an interesting record in his own hand of his discussions while he was in the custody of Outlaw the pursuivant, at York.

[2] Edmund Campion S.J. suffered at Tyburn, December 1, 1581, for a pretended conspiracy at Rome and Rheims. The Act of Elizabeth (1585), which made the mere presence of a priest in England high treason, had not yet been passed.

[3] These are the verses commencing "Why do I use my paper, pen and ink?" mentioned *supra*, p. 158.

"When therefore I found myself in Father Walpole's cell, I rejoiced exceedingly thereat : but I was not worthy to be the successor of such a man in his place of suffering. For on the day following my gaoler, either because he thought to do me a favour, or in consequence of his master's orders, brought me into the upper room, which was sufficiently large and commodious for a prisoner. I told him that I preferred to stay in the lower dungeon, and mentioned the reason, but as he showed himself opposed to this, I asked him to allow me to go there sometimes and pray. This he promised me, and in fact frequently permitted. Then he inquired of me if he could go for me anywhere to any friends of mine who would be willing to send me a bed. For it is the custom in this prison that a bed should not be provided, but that a prisoner should provide himself a bed and other furniture, which afterwards goes to the Lieutenant of the Tower, even though the prisoner should be liberated. I replied that I had no friends to whom I could send, except such as I left in the prison from which I had been brought :[1] these, perhaps, if he would call there, would give me a plain bed by way of alms. The gaoler therefore went to the Catholics detained in the Clink, who immediately sent me a bed such as they knew I wished for ; that is, a mattrass stuffed with wool and feathers after the Italian fashion. They sent also a coat and some linen for me ; and asked him always to come there for anything I wanted, and promised to give money or anything else, provided he brought a note signed by me of things I needed. They also gave him money at that time for himself, and besought him to treat me kindly."

[1] This was said of course, because it was dangerous to mention the names of any friends who were still at liberty. It could do no harm to mention those already in prison.

CHAPTER XIX.

TORTURE.

1597.

"On the third day immediately after dinner came my gaoler to me, and with sorrowful mien told me that the Lords Commissioners had come, and with them the Queen's Attorney General, and that I must go down to them.

"'I am ready,' I replied; 'I only ask you to allow me to say a *Pater* and *Ave* in the lower dungeon.'

"This he allowed, and then we went together to the house of the Lieutenant, which was within the Tower walls. There I found five men, none of whom had before examined me except Wade, who was there for the purpose of accusing me on all points.

"The Queen's Attorney General then took a sheet of paper, and began to write a solemn form of juridical examination."

The examination of Father Gerard on this occasion is preserved in the Public Record Office.[1] The Commissioners were Sir Richard Barkeley, Lieutenant of the Tower, Sir Edward Coke, then Attorney General, Thomas Fleming, a Privy Councillor, Sir Francis Bacon, afterwards Lord Chancellor, and William Wade or Waad, afterwards Justice Young's successor, and subsequently Lieutenant of the Tower, then Secretary to the Lords of the Council.

"The examination of John Gerard, priest, taken this 14th day of April 1597.[1]

[1] P.R.O., *Domestic, Elizabeth*, vol. cclxii. n. 123.

" Being demanded whether he received any letters from the parts beyond the seas or no, confesseth that within these four or five days he received[1] from Antwerp (as he supposeth) letters inclosed and sealed up. But how many letters were inclosed therein he knoweth not, and saith that the said letters were directed to him by the name of Standish ; and being demanded from whom those letters were sent,[2] saith that he knoweth not from whom the same were sent, and denieth that he read them or that he knoweth the contents of the same, and at the first he said that he burnt them, but afterwards retracted that and confesseth that he sent them over to whom the same appertained, but[3] refuseth to declare to whom the same were delivered over, and refuseth also to declare who brought the same to him, or by whom he conveyed them over.   He confesseth that he received within this year past other letters from the parts beyond the seas, and two or three of them he confesseth he did read, and saith that those letters contained matter concerning maintenance of scholars beyond sea, but refuseth to declare who sent those letters or by whom the same were brought, and saith that some of those letters were sent from St. Omers ; and two or three other letters which he received from the parts beyond the seas he conveyed over to some other within this realm, but denieth that he knew the contents of those letters and refuseth to tell who sent or brought the same or to whom the same were conveyed, but saith that the same were sent over to him to whom the said last letters which he received were conveyed unto. And being demanded whether he sent not those letters to Garnet his Superior, saith that he will name no name ; but saith that those letters came to him because he had more opportunity to receive them and to convey them over. And confesseth that the party to whom he sent those letters is a priest,

---

[1] As he supposed, *erased.*   [2] Denieth that, *erased.*
[3] Denieth that, *erased.*

and being demanded how it is possible that he should
know to whom the said last letters appertained, considering
that he saith that he neither knoweth from whom the same
were sent, nor knoweth the contents of the same, especially
the said letters being directed to himself by the name of
Standish, saith that he[1] thinketh that some within this
realm have greater[2] care and authority to provide for such
scholars as be beyond sea than he, and saith that he sent
those last letters as he had done other to that person,
taking the same to contain no other matter but only concerning[3] maintenance of scholars and such as be sent from
hence for the like matters. And being demanded whether
he opened not the outermost sealed of those last letters,
confesseth that he did ; and being also demanded to whom
the letters within inclosed were directed, saith that he
remembereth not[4] the name, but saith that he thinketh it
was to the said former person, and saith that there was
nothing written within the outermost paper, and thinketh
that there were two letters within that which he conveyed
over. And saith that the letters within were not directed
as the outermost was, but saith that he remembereth not[5]
by what name the same were directed.

"*I refuse not for any disloyal mind I protest as I look
to be saved but for that I take these things not to have concerned any matter of State with which I would not have
dealt nor any other but matters of devotion as before.*

"And being demanded whether this subscription is
his usual manner of writing,[6] saith that he useth the same
in his subscriptions to his examinations, and saith that

---

[1] Thinketh that some *substituted for* knoweth who.
[2] Care *substituted for* charge.
[3] Concerning scholars. Maintenance of, &c., *interlined*.
[4] The name . . . person *interlined in place of* to whom.
[5] By what name *substituted for* to whom.
[6] "He had hoped . . . to find out my handwriting, so that some of the
papers found in the houses of the Catholic might be proved to be mine. I
foresaw this, and wrote in a feigned hand." This Father Gerard wrote of
an examination when he was in the Counter (p. 188).

the cause thereof is that he would bring no man to trouble and that he will not acknowledge his own hand, and saith that he never wrote any letter to any man in this hand, saving once to Mr. Topcliffe. And being demanded what was the cause that moved him to have escaped out of prison of late, saith that the cause was that he might have more opportunity to have won souls. And being demanded who procured the counterfeit keys for him by means whereof he should have escaped, refuseth to tell who it was, for that as he saith he will not discover anything against any other that may bring them to trouble.

"JHON GERRARD.

" Examined by us,   RY. BARKELEY.

EDW. COKE.

THO. FFLEMYNGE.

FR. BACON.

W. WAAD."

Endorsed—" Jo. Jerrard."

On the back of a playing card (the seven of spades) which is attached to the original document, is written in Sir Edward Coke's handwriting:

" Polewhele   1

Walpole   1

Pat Cullen   1

Annias   31

Willms   1

Squier

Jarrard   1 "

Polewhele, Patrick Cullen or O'Collun, Williams, and Squire were all executed for high treason, the latter on the accusation of having, at Father Walpole's instigation, poisoned the pommel of Elizabeth's saddle. Annias apostatized after two years' imprisonment.

We now return to the impression that remained on Father Gerard's memory of this examination, when he wrote his Life some twenty years afterwards.

"They did not ask anything at that time about private Catholics, but only about matters of State, to which I answered as before in general terms, namely, that all such things were strictly forbidden to us of the Society; that I had consequently never mixed myself up with political matters, sufficient proof whereof I said was to be found in the fact that though they had had me in custody for three years, and had constantly examined me, they had never been able to produce a single line of my writing, nor a single trustworthy witness, to show that I had ever injured the State in a single point.

"They then inquired what letters I had lately received from our fathers abroad. Here it was I first divined the reason of my being transferred to the Tower. I answered, however, that if I had ever received any letters from abroad, they never had any connection with matters of State, but related solely to the money matters of certain Catholics who were living beyond seas.

"'Did not you,' said Wade, 'receive lately a packet of letters; and did you not deliver them to such a one for Henry Garnet?'

"'If I have received any such,' I answered, 'and delivered them as you say, I only did my duty. But I never received nor delivered any, but what related to the private money matters of certain religious or students, who are pursuing their studies beyond seas, as I have before said.'

"'Well,' said they, 'where is he to be found to whom you delivered the letters, and how is he called?'

"'I do not know,' I answered, 'and if I did know, I neither could nor would tell you,' and then I alleged the usual reasons.

"'You tell us,' said the Attorney General, 'that you do not wish to offend against the State. Tell us, then, where this Garnet is. For he is an enemy of the State, and you are bound to give information of such people.'

"'He is no enemy of the State,' I replied, 'but, on the contrary, I am sure that he would be ready to lay down his life for the Queen and the State. However, I do not know where he is, and if I did know I would not tell you.'

"'But you shall tell us,' said they, 'before we leave this place.'

"'Please God,' said I, 'that shall never be.'

"They then produced the warrant which they had for putting me to the torture, and gave it me to read; for it is not allowed in this prison to put any one to the torture without express warrant. I saw the document was duly signed, so I said, 'By the help of God I will never do what is against justice and against the Catholic faith. You have me in your power; do what God permits you, for you certainly cannot go beyond.'

"Then they began to entreat me not to force them to do what they were loth to do, and told me they were bound not to desist from putting me to the torture day after day, as long as my life lasted, until I gave the information they sought from me.

"'I trust in God's goodness,' I answered, 'that He will never allow me to do so base an act as to bring innocent persons to harm. Nor, indeed, do I fear what you can do to me, since all of us are in God's hands.'

"Such was the purport of my replies, as far as I can remember.

"Then we proceeded to the place appointed for the torture. We went in a sort of solemn procession, the attendants preceding us with lighted candles, because the place was underground and very dark, especially about the entrance.[1] It was a place of immense extent, and in it were ranged divers sorts of racks, and other instruments

---

[1] It is said that there is an underground passage from the Lieutenant's lodgings to the vaults of the White Tower, where it would appear Father Gerard was tortured.

of torture. Some of these they displayed before me, and told me I should have to taste them every one. Then again they asked me if I was willing to satisfy them on the points on which they had questioned me. 'It is out of my power to satisfy you,' I answered; and throwing myself on my knees, I said a prayer or two.

"Then they led me to a great upright beam or pillar of wood which was one of the supports of this vast crypt. At the summit of this column were fixed certain iron staples for supporting weights. Here they placed on my wrists gauntlets of iron, and ordered me to mount upon two or three wicker steps;[1] then raising my arms, they inserted an iron bar through the rings of the gauntlets and then through the staples in the pillar, putting a pin through the bar so that it could not slip. My arms being thus fixed above my head, they withdrew those wicker steps I spoke of, one by one, from beneath my feet, so that I hung by my hands and arms. The tips of my toes, however, still touched the ground,[2] so they dug away the ground beneath; for they could not raise me higher, as they had suspended me from the topmost staples in the pillar.

"Thus hanging by my wrists, I began to pray, while those gentlemen standing round asked me again if I was willing to confess. I replied, 'I neither can nor will,' but so terrible a pain began to oppress me that I was scarce able to speak the words. The worst pain was in my breast and belly, my arms and hands. It seemed to me that all the blood in my body rushed up my arms into my hands; and I was under the impression at the time that the blood actually burst forth from my fingers and

---

[1] Scirpicula quædam duo vel tria ex juncis facta.—*MS.* It is not easy to understand exactly what these were.

[2] Father Gerard's great stature could not be more clearly indicated. This would of course involve a greater weight of body, and consequently greater severity in this mode of torture. "Erat enim," says Father More in his History, "pleno et procero corpore."

Q

at the back of my hands. This was, however, a mistake; the sensation was caused by the swelling of the flesh over the iron that bound it.

"I felt now such intense pain (and the effect was probably heightened by an interior temptation), that it seemed to me impossible to continue enduring it. It did not, however, go so far as to make me feel any inclination or real disposition to give the information they wanted. For as the eyes of our merciful Lord had seen my imperfection, He did 'not suffer me to be tempted above what I was able, but with the temptation made also a way of escape.' Seeing me, therefore, in this agony of pain and this interior distress, His infinite mercy sent me this thought: 'The very furthest and utmost they can do is to take away thy life; and often hast thou desired to give thy life for God: thou art in God's hands, Who knoweth well what thou sufferest, and is all-powerful to sustain thee.' With this thought our good God gave me also out of His immense bounty the grace to resign myself and offer myself utterly to His good pleasure, together with some hope and desire of dying for His sake. From that moment I felt no more trouble in my soul, and even the bodily pain seemed to be more bearable than before, although I doubt not that it really increased from the continued strain that was exercised on every part of my body.

"Hereupon those gentlemen, seeing that I gave them no further answer, departed to the Lieutenant's house, and there they waited, sending now and then to know how things were going on in the crypt. There were left with me three or four strong men, to superintend my torture. My gaoler also remained, I fully believe out of kindness to me, and kept wiping away with a handkerchief the sweat that ran down from my face the whole time, as indeed it did from my whole body. So far, indeed, he did me a service; but by his words he rather added to my distress, for he never stopped entreating and beseeching me to have pity on myself, and tell these gentlemen what they wanted to know; and so many human reasons did he allege, that I verily believed he was either instigated directly by the devil under pretence of affection for me, or had been left there purposely by the persecutors to influence me by his show of sympathy. In any case, these shafts of the enemy seemed to be spent before they reached me, for though annoying, they did me no real hurt, nor did they seem to touch my soul or move it in the least. I said, therefore, to him, 'I pray you to say no more on that point, for I am not minded to lose my soul for the sake of my body.' Yet I could not prevail with him to be silent. The others also who stood by said, 'He will be a cripple all his life, if he lives through it; but he will have to be tortured daily till he confesses.' But I kept praying in a low voice, and continually uttered the Holy Names of Jesus and Mary.

"I had hung in this way till after one of the clock as I think, when I fainted. How long I was in the faint I know not—perhaps not long; for the men who stood by lifted me up, or replaced those wicker steps under my feet, until I came to myself; and immediately they heard me praying they let me down again. This they did over and over again when the faint came on, eight or nine times before five of the clock. Somewhat before five came Wade again, and drawing near, said, 'Will you yet obey the commands of the Queen and the Council?'

"'No,' said I, 'what you ask is unlawful, therefore I will never do it.'

"'At least, then,' said Wade, 'say that you would like to speak to Secretary Cecil.'

"'I have nothing to say to him,' I replied, 'more than I have said already; and if I were to ask to speak to him, scandal would be caused, for people would imagine that I was yielding at length, and was willing to give information.'

"Upon this Wade suddenly turned his back in a rage and departed, saying in a loud and angry tone, 'Hang there, then, till you rot!'

"So he went away, and I think all the Commissioners then left the Tower; for at five of the clock the great bell of the Tower sounds, as a signal for all to leave who do not wish to be locked in all night. Soon after this they took me down from my cross, and though neither foot nor leg was injured, yet I could hardly stand.

"I was helped back to my cell by the gaoler, and meeting on the way some of the prisoners who had the range of the Tower, I addressed the gaoler in their hearing, saying I wondered how those gentlemen could insist so on my telling them where Father Garnet was, since every one must acknowledge it to be a sin to betray an innocent man, a thing I would never do, though I should die for it. This I said out loud, on purpose that the authorities might not have it in their power to publish a report about me, that I had made a confession, as they often did in other cases. I had also another reason, which was that word might reach Father Garnet (through these persons spreading abroad what they heard me say), that it was about him I was chiefly examined, in order that he might look to himself. I noticed that my gaoler was very unwilling I should speak thus before the others, but I did not stint for that. My gaoler appeared sincerely to compassionate my state, and when we reached my cell he laid me a fire, and brought me some food, as supper time had nearly come. I scarcely tasted anything, but laid myself on my bed, and remained quiet there till the next morning.

"Early next morning, however, soon after the Tower gates were opened, my gaoler came up to the cell and told me that Master Wade had arrived, and that I must go down to him. I went down, therefore, that time in a sort of cloak with wide sleeves, for my hands were so swollen that they would not have passed through ordinary sleeves. When I had come to the Lieutenant's house, Wade addressed me thus : ' I am sent to you on the part of the Queen and of Master Secretary Cecil, the first of whom assures you on the word of a Sovereign, the other on his word of honour, that they know for certain that Garnet *is* in the habit of meddling in political matters, and that he is an enemy of the State. Consequently, unless you mean to contradict them flatly, you ought to submit your judgment, and produce him.'

" ' They cannot possibly know this,' I replied, ' by their own experience and of certain knowledge, since they have no personal knowledge of the man. Now I have lived with him, and know him well, and I know him to be no such character as you say.'

" ' Well, then,' returned he, ' you will not acknowledge it, nor tell us what we ask ? '

" ' No, certainly not,' said I, ' I neither can nor will.'

" ' It would be better for you if you did,' he replied. And thereupon he summoned from the next room a gentleman who had been there waiting, a tall and commanding figure, whom he called the Superintendent of Torture. I knew there was such an officer, but this man was not really in that charge, as I heard afterwards, but was Master of the Artillery in the Tower. However, Wade called him by this name to strike the greater terror into me, and said to him, ' I deliver this man into your hands. You are to rack him twice to-day, and twice daily until such time as he chooses to confess.' The officer then took charge of me, and Wade departed.

" Thereupon we descended with the same solemnity as before into the place appointed for torture, and again they put the gauntlets on the same part of my arms as before : indeed, they could not be put on in any other part, for the flesh had so risen on both sides that there were two hills of flesh with a valley between, and the gauntlets would not meet anywhere but in the valley.

Here, then, were they put on, not without causing me much pain. Our good Lord, however, helped me, and I cheerfully offered Him my hands and my heart. So I was hung up again as I before described; and in my hands I felt a great deal more pain than on the previous day, but not so much in my breast and belly, perhaps because this day I had eaten nothing.

"While thus hanging I prayed, sometimes silently, sometimes aloud, recommending myself to our Lord Jesus and His Blessed Mother. I hung much longer this time without fainting, but at length I fainted so thoroughly that they could not bring me to, and they thought that I either was dead or soon would be. So they called the Lieutenant, but how long he was there I know not, nor how long I remained in the faint. When I came round, however, I found myself no longer hanging by my hands, but supported sitting on a bench, with many people round me, who had opened my teeth with some iron instrument and were pouring warm water down my throat. Now when the Lieutenant saw I could speak, he said, 'Do you not see how much better it is for you to yield to the wishes of the Queen than to lose your life this way?'

"By God's help I answered him with more spirit than I had ever before felt: 'No, certainly I do not see it. I would rather die a thousand times than do what they require of me.'

"'You will not, then?' he repeated.

"'No, indeed I will not,' I answered, 'while a breath remains in my body.'

"'Well, then,' said he, and he seemed to say it sorrowfully, as if reluctant to carry out his orders, 'we must hang you up again now, and after dinner too.'

"'Let us go, then, in the name of God,' I said; 'I have but one life, and if I had more I would offer them all for this cause.' And with this I attempted to rise in order to go to the pillar, but they were obliged to support

me, as I was very weak in body from the torture. And
if there was any strength in my soul, it was the gift of
God, and given, I am convinced, because I was a member
of the Society, though a most unworthy one. I was suspended, therefore, a third time, and hung there in very
great pain of body, but not without great consolation of
soul, which seemed to me to arise from the prospect of
dying. Whether it was from a true love of suffering for
Christ, or from a sort of selfish desire to be with Christ,
God knows best ; but I certainly thought that I should
die, and felt great joy in committing myself to the will
and good pleasure of my God, and contemning entirely
the will of men. Oh, that God would grant me always
to have that same spirit (though I doubt not that it wanted
much of true perfection in His eyes), for a longer life
remains to me than I then thought, and He granted me
a reprieve to prepare myself better for His holy presence.

"After a while the Lieutenant, seeing that he made
no way with me by continuing the torture, or because the
dinner hour was near at hand, or perhaps through a natural
feeling of compassion, ordered me to be taken down. I
think I hung not quite an hour this third time. I am
rather inclined to think that the Lieutenant released me
from compassion ; for, some time after my escape, a
gentleman of quality told me he had it from Sir Richard
Barkeley himself (who was this very Lieutenant of whom
I speak), that he had of his own accord resigned the office
he held, because he would no longer be an instrument in
torturing innocent men so cruelly. And in fact he gave
up the post after holding it but three or four months, and
another Knight was appointed in his stead, in whose time
it was that I made my escape.

"So I was brought back to my room by my gaoler,
who seemed to have his eyes full of tears, and he assured
me that his wife had been weeping and praying for me
the whole time, though I had never seen the good woman

in all my life. Then he brought me some food, of which
I could eat but little, and that little he was obliged to cut
for me and put into my mouth. I could not hold a knife
in my hands for many days after, much less now, when
I was not even able to move my fingers, nor help myself
in anything, so that he was obliged to do everything for
me. However, by order of the authorities, he took away
my knife, scissors, and razors, lest I should kill myself, I
believe : for they always do this in the Tower as long as
the prisoner is under warrant for torture. I expected,
therefore, daily to be sent for again to the torture-chamber,
according to order ; but our merciful God, while to other
stronger champions, such as Father Walpole and Father
Southwell, He gave a sharp struggle that they might overcome, gave His weak soldier but a short trial, that he
might not be overcome. They, indeed, being perfected
in a short time fulfilled a long space ; but I, unworthy
of so great a good, was left to run out my days, and so
supply for my defects by washing my soul with my tears,
since I deserved not to wash it with my blood. God so
ordained it, and His Holy Will be done."

Father Garnet in his letters mentions Father Gerard's
torture for the first time when writing on the 23rd of April
1597 to Father Persons at Rome.[1] "John Gerard hath
been sore tortured in the Tower : it is thought it was for
some letters directed to him out of Spain." This was
prompt and accurate news as far as it went ; and between
this date and the next some details had reached Father
Garnet, for on the 7th of May, 1597, he wrote[2] to the
General (we translate from the Italian) : "Of John Gerard
I have already written to you where he is. He hath been
twice hanged up by the hands, with great cruelty of others,
and not less suffering of his own. The inquisitors here

[1] Stonyhurst MSS., Father Grene's *Collectan. P.* vol. ii. f. 547.
[2] *Ibid., Angl. A.* vol. ii. n. 27 ; *Collectan. P.* vol. ii. f. 604.

say that he is very obstinate, and that he has a great
alliance with God or the devil, as they cannot draw the
least word out of his mouth, except that in torment he
cries 'Jesus.' They took him lately to the rack, and the
torturers and examiners were there ready ; but he suddenly,
when he entered the place, knelt down and with a loud
voice prayed to our Lord that, as He had given grace and
strength to some of His saints to bear with Christian
patience being torn to pieces by horses for His love, so
He would be pleased to give him grace and courage, rather
to be dragged into a thousand pieces than to say anything
that might injure any person or the Divine glory. And
so they left him without tormenting him, seeing him so
resolved." On the 10th of June (in the copy it is *Jan.*,
evidently a mistake) Father Garnet writes :[1] " I wrote
unto you heretofore of the remove of Mr. Gerard to the
Tower : he hath been thrice hanged up by the hands,
every time until he was almost dead, and that in one day
twice. The cause was (as I now understand perfectly) for
to tell where his Superior was, and by whom he had sent
him letters which were delivered him from Father Persons,
and he was discovered by one of his fellow-prisoners.
The Earl of Essex saith he must needs honour him for
his constancy." Again, a letter from Father Garnet to
the General, in Latin, dated the 11th of June, 1597, runs
thus :[2] " I have written to you more than once of our
Mr. John Gerard, that he has been thrice tortured, but
that he hath borne all with invincible courage. We have
also lately heard for certain that the Earl of Essex praised
his constancy, declaring that he could not help honouring
and admiring the man. A Secretary of the Royal Council
denies that the Queen wishes to have him executed. To
John this will be a great trouble."

[1] Stonyhurst MSS., Father Grene's *Collectan. P.* vol. ii. f. 548.
[2] *Ibid.* f. 601.

CHAPTER XX.

"I REMAINED therefore in my cell, spending my time principally in prayer. And now again I made the Spiritual Exercises, as I had done at the beginning of my imprisonment, giving four or five hours a day to meditation for a whole month. I had a breviary with me, so that I was able to say my Office ; and every day I said a dry mass, (*i.e.*, such as is said by those who are practising mass before the priesthood), and that with great reverence and desire of communicating, especially at that part where I should have communicated if the Sacrifice had been real. And these practices consoled me in my tribulation.

"At the end of three weeks, as far as I can remember, I was able to move my fingers, and help myself a little, and even hold a knife. So when I had finished my retreat I asked leave to have some books, but they only allowed me a bible, which I obtained from my friends in my former prison. I sent to them for some money, by means of which I saw that I should be able to enlist the sympathies of my gaoler, and induce him to allow me things, and even to bring me some books. My friends sent me by him all that I asked for. I got my gaoler to buy some large oranges, a fruit of which he was very fond. But besides gratifying him with a present of them, I meditated making another use of them in time.

"I now began to exercise my hands a little after dinner.

Supper I never took, though it was allowed : indeed, there was no stint of food in the prison, all being furnished at the Queen's expense; for there were given me daily six small rolls of very good bread. There are different scales of diet fixed in the prison according to the rank of the prisoner; the religious state indeed they take no account of, but only human rank, thus making most of what ought to be esteemed the least. Well, the exercise which I gave my hands was to cut the peels of these oranges into the form of crosses, and sew them two and two together. I made many of these crosses, and many rosaries also strung on silken cord. Then I asked my gaoler if he would carry some of these crosses and rosaries to my friends in my old prison. He, seeing nothing in this to compromise him, readily under- took to do so. In the meantime I put by some of the orange-juice in a small jug. I was now in want of a pen, but I dared not openly ask for one : nay, even if I had asked and obtained my request, I could at this time scarcely have written, or but very badly; for though I could hold a pen, yet I could hardly feel that I had anything in my fingers. The sense of touch was not recovered for five months, and even then not fully, for I was never without a certain numbness in my hands up to the time of my escape, which was more than six months after. So I begged for a quill to make myself a tooth- pick, which he readily brought me. I made this into a pen fit for writing, then cutting off a short piece of the pointed end, I fixed it on a small stick. With the rest of the quill I made a tooth-pick, so long that nothing appeared to have been cut off, and this I afterwards showed my gaoler. Then I begged for some paper to wrap up my rosaries and crosses, and obtained his leave also to write a line or two with pencil on the paper, asking my friends to pray for me. All this he allowed, not suspecting that he was carrying anything but what he knew.   But I had managed to write on the paper with some orange-juice, telling my friends to write back to me in the same way, but sparingly at first ; asking them also to give the bearer a little money and promise him some as often as he should bring any crosses or rosaries from me with a few words of my writing to assure them that I was well.

"When they received the paper and the rosaries, knowing that I should if possible have written something with orange-juice, as I used to do with them, they immediately retired to a private room and held the paper to a fire.   Thus they read all I had written, and wrote back to me in the same way, sending me some comfits or dried sweetmeats wrapped up in the paper on which they had written.   We continued this method of communication for about half a year ; but we soon proceeded with much greater confidence when we found that the man never failed to deliver our missives faithfully.   For full three months however he had no idea that he was conveying letters to and fro.   But after three months I began to ask him to allow me to write with a pencil at greater length, which he permitted.   I always gave him these letters open, that he might see what I wrote ; and I wrote nothing but spiritual matters that he could see, but on the blank part of the paper I had written with orange-juice directions and particular advice for my different friends, about which he knew nothing.

"As it happened indeed, I need not have been so circumspect ; for the man, as I found out after some time, could not read.   He pretended, however, that he was able, and used to stand and look over my shoulder while I read to him what I had written with pencil.   At length it occurred to me that possibly he could not read ; so in order to make the trial, while he was looking over the paper I read it altogether in a different way from what I had written it.   After doing this on two or three

occasions without his taking any notice, I said openly to
him with a smile, that he need not look over my shoulder
any more. He acknowledged indeed that he could not
read, but said that he took great pleasure in hearing what
I read to him. After this he let me write what I would,
and carried everything as faithfully as ever. He even
provided me with ink, and carried closed letters to and
fro between my friends and me. For seeing that I had
to do with very few, and those discreet and trustworthy
people, and thinking that neither I nor they were likely
to betray him, he did just what we asked him for a
consideration, for he always received a stipulated payment.
He begged me, however, not to require him to go so often
to the Clink prison, lest suspicion should arise from these
frequent visits, which might cause harm not only to him
but to me: he proposed therefore that some friend of
mine should meet him near the Tower and deliver the
letters to him. But I was loth to risk the safety of any
one by putting him thus in the man's power. It made
no difference to those already in custody; they could
without much additional danger hold correspondence with
me, and send me anything for my support by way of alms.
Besides I knew that my messenger would not be likely
to speak of the letter he carried, as this would be as
dangerous for himself as for those to whom he carried
them.

"Nay, even if he had wished he could not have done
much injury either to me or my friends, because I took
good care never to name any of them in my letters. But
before I was in prison and after, I invariably used pseu-
donyms which were understood by those to whom I wrote:
thus, I called one 'brother,' another 'son,' another 'nephew,'
or 'friend,' and so of their wives, calling this one 'sister,'
that 'niece,' or 'daughter.' In this way no one not in
the secret could possibly tell whom I meant, even if the
letters had been intercepted, which they never were. I

may add that even if the letters had been betrayed and
read, they could never have been made further use of by
the enemy, in allowing them to be carried to their desti-
nation to lure the correspondents on till they should
compromise themselves, as was sometimes done. For I
never wrote now with lemon-juice, as I did once in the
Clink; which letter was betrayed to the persecutor Wade,
as I before related. The reason of my doing so then was
because that was a kind of circular letter which had to be
read in one place and then carried to another. Now
lemon-juice has this property, that what is written in it
can be read in water quite as well as by fire, and when the
paper is dried the writing disappears again till it is steeped
afresh, or again held to the fire. But anything written
with orange-juice is at once washed out by water and
cannot be read at all in that way; and if held to the fire,
though the characters are thus made to appear and can be
read, they will not disappear; so that a letter of this sort
once read can never be delivered to any one as if it had
not been read. The party will see at once that it has
been read, and will certainly refuse and disown it if it
should contain anything dangerous. It was in this way
I knew that my letters always reached my friends and that
theirs reached me in safety. And so our correspondence
continued,—I obtaining sure information of all my friends,
and they receiving at my hands the consolation they
sought.

"In order however that matters might go on still more
securely, I managed through some of my friends that
John Lilly's release should be purchased: and from that
time I always got him to bring to my gaoler everything
that reached me from the outside. It was through his
means too a little later that I escaped from the Tower,
although nothing certainly was farther from my thoughts
when I thus secured his services: all I had in view was
to be able to increase my correspondence with safety.

This went on for about four months, and after the first month I gave a good time to study by means of books secretly procured. But at this time an event occurred which caused me great anxiety.

"Master Francis Page, of whom I have before spoken, was now living with my former host [Mr. Wiseman], who had been released from prison. After my removal to the Tower, he got to learn in what part of it I was confined: and out of respect for me used to come daily to a spot from whence he could see my window, in order to get the chance some day of seeing me there. At last it so happened that going one day to the window (it was a warm day in summer), I noticed a gentleman at some distance pull off his hat as if to me; then he walked to and fro, and frequently stopped and made pretence of arranging his hair or doing something about his head, in order to have the opportunity of doffing his hat to me without attracting the attention of others. At last I recognized him by the clothes that he was accustomed to wear, and made him a sign of recognition, and giving him my blessing I withdrew at once from the window, lest others should see me and have suspicion of him. But the good man was not content with this; daily did he come for my blessing, and stopped some time walking to and fro, and ever as he turned he doffed his hat, though I frequently made signals to him not to do so. At length he was noticed doing this, and one day as I was looking I saw him to my great grief seized and led away. He was brought to the Lieutenant of the Tower, who examined him about me and my friends. But he denied everything, and said that he simply walked there for his amusement, it being a fine open space close to the River Thames. So they kept him a prisoner[1] for some days, and meanwhile by inquiry found that he was living with

---

[1] In the Beauchamp tower he has left a sharply-cut inscription: "*En Dieu est mon esperance.* F. PAGE."

my former host.   This increased their suspicion that he had been sent there to give me some sign.   But as he constantly denied everything, they at last had recourse to me, and sent for me to be examined.   Now as I was going to the examination Master Page was walking up and down with my gaoler in the hall, through which I was taken to the chamber where the authorities awaited me.   Immediately I was introduced the examiners said to me: 'There is a young man here named Francis Page who says he knows you and desires to speak with you.'

"'He can do so if he wishes,' I replied ; 'but who is this Francis Page?   I know no such person.'

"'Not know him?' said they, 'he at any rate knows you so well that he can recognize you at a distance, and has come daily to salute you.'

"I however maintained I knew no such man.   So when they found they could twist nothing out of me either by wiles or threats, they sent me back.   But as I passed again through the hall where Master Page was with the others, I looked round from one to another, and said with a loud voice, 'Is there any one here of the name of Francis Page, who says he knows me well, and has often come before my window to see me?   Which of all these is he?   I know no such person, and I wonder that any one should be willing to injure himself by saying such things.'

"All this while the gaoler was trying to prevent my speaking, but was unable.   I said this not because I had any idea that he had acknowledged that he knew me, but for fear they might afterwards tell him of me what they had told me of him.   And so it turned out.   For they had told him already that I had acknowledged I knew him, and they had only sent for me then that he might see me go in, intending to tell him I had confirmed all I said before.   But now they could not so impose on him.   For when he was summoned, he immediately told

them what I had said publicly in the hall as I passed
through. The men in their disappointment stormed
against the gaoler and me, but being thus baffled could
not carry out their deception.

"A little later they released Master Page for money,
who soon crossed the sea, and after going through his
studies in Belgium was made priest.[1] Thence he returned
afterwards to England and remained mostly in London,
where he was much beloved, and useful to many souls.
One of his penitents was that Mistress Line whose martyrdom I have above related. In her house he was once
taken as I said, but that time he escaped. A little after
he obtained his desire of being admitted into the Society,
but before he could be sent over to Belgium for his
noviceship, he was again taken, and being tried like gold
in the furnace, and accepted as the victim of a holocaust,
he washed his robe in the blood of the Lamb, and is
now in the possession of his reward. And he sees me
now no longer detained in the Tower while he is walking
by the water of the Thames, but rather he beholds me
on the waters still tossed by various winds and storms
while he is secure of his own eternal happiness, and
solicitous as I hope for mine. Before all this however he
used to say that he was much encouraged and cheered
by hearing what I said as I passed through the hall, as it
enabled him to detect and avoid the snares of the enemy.

"During the time I was detained in the Tower, no
one was allowed to visit me, so that I could afford no
help to souls by my words; by letter however I did what
I could with those to whom I could venture to trust the
secret of how they might correspond with me. Once
however after John Lilly's release, as he was walking in
London streets, two ladies, mother and daughter, accosted
him, and begged him if it was by any means possible to

---

[1] In the Ordination list in the First Douay Diary there is the entry,
"Anno millesimo sexcentesimo, Aprilis 1°, Franciscus Pageus Londinen. M."

R

bring them where they could see me. He knowing the
extreme danger of such an attempt endeavoured to dissuade them, but they gave him no peace till he promised
to open the matter to the gaoler, and try to get him to
admit them, as if they were relations of his. Gained over
by large promises the man consented ; the ladies had
also made a present of a new gown to his wife. They
therefore dressing themselves as simple London citizens,
the fashion of whose garments is very different from that
of ladies of quality, came with John Lilly, under pretence
of visiting the gaoler's wife, and seeing the lions that are
kept in the Tower, and the other animals there which
the curious are in the habit of coming to see. After
they had seen all the sights, the gaoler led them within
the walls of the Tower, and when he found a good opportunity introduced them into my room, exposing himself
to a great danger for a small gain. When they saw me
they could not restrain themselves from running and
kissing my feet, and even strove with one another who
should first kiss them. For my part I could not deny
them what they had bought so dear, and then begged for
so earnestly, but I only allowed them to offer this homage
to me as to the prisoner of Christ, not as to the sinner
that I am. We conversed a little, then leaving with me
what they had brought for my use, they returned in safety
much consoled, for they thought they should never see
my face again, inasmuch as they had heard in the city
that I was to be brought to trial and executed.

"Once also Father Garnet sent me similar happy
news, warning me in a letter full of consolation to prepare
myself for death. And indeed I cannot deny that I
rejoiced at the things that were said to me ; but my
great unworthiness prevented me from going into the
House of the Lord. In fact the good Father, though
he knew it not, was to obtain this mercy before me ;
and God grant that I may be able to follow him even

at a distance to the cross which he so much loved and honoured. God gave him the desire of his heart; for it was on the feast of the Invention of the Holy Cross that he found Him whom his soul loved. On this same feast of the Holy Cross and anniversary day of this holy Father's martyrdom, I received, by his intercession I fully believe, two great favours of which I will speak further at the close of this narration; to which close indeed it behoves me to hasten, for I am conscious that I have been more diffuse than such small matters warranted.

"What Father Garnet warned me of by letter the enemy threatened also by words and acts about that time. For those who had come before with authority to put me to the torture, now came again, but with another object, viz., to take my formal examination in preparation for my trial. So the Queen's Attorney-General questioned me on all points, and wrote everything down in that order which he meant to observe in prosecuting me at the assizes, as he told me. He asked me therefore about my priest-hood, and about my coming to England as a priest and a Jesuit, and inquired whether I had dealt with any to reconcile them to the Pope, and draw them away from the faith and religious profession which was approved in England. All these things I freely confessed that I had done; answers which furnished quite sufficient matter for my condemnation according to their laws. When they asked, however, with whom I had communicated in political matters, I replied that I had never meddled with such things. But they urged the point, and said it was impossible that I, who so much desired the conversion of England, should not have tried these means also, as being very well adapted to the end. To this I replied, as far as I recollect, in the following way:

"'I will tell you my mind candidly in this matter, and about the State, in order that you may have no doubt about my intent, nor question me any more on the sub-

ject ; and in what I say, lo ! before God and His holy
angels I lie not, nor do I add aught to the true feeling of
my heart.   I wish, indeed, that the whole of England
should be converted to the Catholic and Roman faith, that
the Queen too should be converted and all the Privy
Council, yourselves also, and all the magistrates of the
realm ; but so that the Queen and you all without a single
exception should continue to hold the same powers and
dignities that you do at present, and that not a single
hair of your head should perish, that so you may be happy
both in this life and the next.   Do not think, however,
that I desire this conversion for my own sake, in order to
regain my liberty and follow my vocation in freedom.
No ; I call God to witness that I would gladly consent to
be hanged to-morrow, if all this could be brought about
by that means.   This is my mind and my desire, consequently I am no enemy of the Queen's nor of yours, nor
have I ever been so.'

   " Hereupon Mr. Attorney kept silence for a time, and
then he began afresh to ask me what Catholics I knew ;
did I know such and such ?   I answered, ' I do not know
them.'   And I added the usual reasons why I should still
make the same answer even if I did know them, showing
that this was not telling a falsehood.   Upon this he
digressed to the question of equivocation,[1] and began to
inveigh against Father Southwell, because on his trial he
denied that he knew the woman who was brought forward

---

   [1] Our readers cannot fail to remember the passage in Shakspeare's *Macbeth*,
which is most evidently aimed against the Catholic martyrs.   The castle porter,
Act. II. Sc. 3, imagines himself porter at Hell gate, and soliloquizes : "Knock,
knock ! who's there? . . . Faith, here's an *equivocator*, that could swear in
both the scales against either scale : *who committed treason enough for God's
sake*, yet could not equivocate to Heaven."   If these words were Shakspeare's,
they would be sufficient by themselves to settle the question of his Catholicity.   No Catholic could speak thus of those who died for their faith.   The
Cambridge Editors (Clarendon Press Series) reject the passage, and they quote
Coleridge's criticism : " This low soliloquy of the porter, and his few speeches
afterwards, I believe to have been written for the mob by some other hand."

to accuse him.[1] She swore that he had come to her
father's house and was received there as a priest; this
he positively denied, though he had been taken in that
house and was found in a hiding-place, having been betrayed by this wretched woman. A dutiful daughter truly,
who thus betrayed to death both her spiritual and her
natural father! Christ our Lord, however, came not to
send peace, but a sword to divide between the good and
the bad; and in this case He divided the bad daughter
from the good parents. Good Father Southwell, then,
though he marvelled at the impudence of this miserable
wench, yet denied what she asserted, and gave good
reasons for his denial, well knowing and thoroughly
proving that it was not lawful for him to do otherwise,
lest he should add to the injury of those who were already
suffering for the faith, and for charity shown to him.
Taking this occasion, therefore, he showed very learnedly
that it was lawful in some cases, nay, even necessary,
perhaps, to use equivocation; which doctrine he established and confirmed by strong arguments and copious
authorities, drawn as well from Holy Scripture as from
the writings of the Doctors of the Church.

"The Attorney-General inveighed much against this,
and tried to make out that this was to foster lying, and
so destroy all reliable communications between men, and
therefore all bonds of society. I, on the other hand, maintained that this was not falsehood, nor supposed an intention of deceiving, which is necessary to constitute a lie,
but merely a keeping back of the truth, and that where
one is not bound to declare it: consequently there is no
deception, because nothing is refused which the other has
a right to claim. I showed, moreover, that our doctrine
did in no way involve a destruction of the bonds of society,

---

[1] This was the wretched Anne Bellamy, a young Catholic gentlewoman,
who when in prison was ruined by Topcliffe and married by him to Nicholas
Jones, the underkeeper of the Gatehouse. *Troubles*, Second Series, pp. 51—64.

because it is never allowed to use equivocation in making contracts, since all are bound to give their neighbour his due, and in making of contracts truth is due to the party contracting. It should be remarked also, I said, that it is not allowed to use equivocation in ordinary conversation to the detriment of plain truth and Christian simplicity, much less in matters properly falling under the cognizance of civil authority,[1] since it is not lawful to deny even a capital crime if the accused is questioned juridically. He asked me, therefore, what I considered a juridical questioning. I answered that the questioners must be really superiors and judges in the matter of examination ; then, the matter itself must be some crime hurtful to the common weal, in order that it may come under their jurisdiction ; for sins merely internal were reserved for God's judgment. Again, there must be some reliable testimony previously brought against the accused ; thus, it is the custom in England that all who are put on their trial, when first asked by the judge if they are guilty or not, answer 'Not guilty,' before any witness is brought against them, or any verdict found by the jury ; and though they answer the same way, whether really guilty or not, yet no one accuses them of lying. Therefore I laid down this general principle, that no one is allowed to use equivocation except in the case when something is asked him either actually or virtually, which the questioner has no right to ask, and the declaration of which will turn to his own hurt, if he answers according to the intention of the questioner. I showed that this had been our Lord's practice and that of the saints. I showed that it was the practice of all prudent men, and would certainly be followed by my interrogators themselves in case they

---

[1] In subornata gubernatione Reipublicæ.—*MS.* There is clearly some blunder here. Probably we ought to read "subordinata": yet even so, the phrase is not very intelligible. We have judged of the sense intended, by the context.

were asked about some secret sin, for example, or were asked by robbers where their money was hid.

"They asked me, therefore, when our Lord ever made use of equivocation; to which I replied, 'When He told His Apostles that no one knew the Day of Judgment, not even the Son of Man: and again when He said that He was not going up to the Festival at Jerusalem, and yet He went; yea, and He knew that He should go when He said He would not.'

"Wade here interrupted me, saying, 'Christ really did not know the Day of Judgment, as Son of Man.'

"'It cannot be,' said I, 'that the Word of God Incarnate, and with a human nature hypostatically united to God, should be subject to ignorance; nor that He Who was appointed Judge by God the Father should be ignorant of those facts which belonged necessarily to His office; nor that He should be of infinite wisdom, and yet not know what intimately concerned Himself.' In fact these heretics do not practically admit what the Apostle teaches (though they boast of following his doctrines), viz., that all the fulness of the Divinity resided corporally in Christ, and that in Him were all the treasures of the wisdom and knowledge of God. It did not, however, occur to me at the moment to adduce this passage of St. Paul.

"They made no reply to my arguments, but the Attorney-General wrote everything down, and said he should use it against me at my trial in a short time. But he did not keep his word. For I was not worthy to enter under God's roof, where nothing defiled can enter. I have therefore still to be purified by a prolonged sojourn in exile, and so at length, if God please, be saved as by fire.

"This my last examination was in Trinity Term, as they call it. They have four terms in the year, during which many come up to London to have their causes tried, for these are times that the Law Courts are open. It is during these terms, on account of the great confluence of people, that they bring those priests to trial whom they have determined to prosecute ; and probably this was what they proposed to do in my case—but man proposes and God disposes, and He had disposed otherwise. When this time, therefore, had passed away, there was no longer any probability that they would proceed against me publicly. I turned my attention consequently to study in this time of enforced leisure, as I thought they had now determined only to prevent my communication with others, and that this was the reason they had transferred me to my present prison as being more strict and more secure."

Midsummer day came, when the Lieutenant of the Tower as usual sent in his quarterly bill to the Exchequer "for the diets and charges of certain prisoners in his custody from the Feast of the Annunciation of our Lady the Virgin 1597, until the Feast of St. John the Baptist then next following." This paper,[1] which bears the signatures of the Lords of the Privy Council, gives us the date of Father Gerard's transfer to the Tower. "*Item*, for the diet and charges of John Gerratt gent. from the 12th day of April 1597 until the feast of St. John Baptist next ensuing, being 10 weeks and a half, the sum of 6*l.* 13*s.* 4*d.*

"*Item*, for his keeper during the same time at 6*s.* 8*d.* the week   .   .   .   . 3*l.* 6*s.* 8*d.*

"*Item*, for fuel and lights during the same time at 6*s.* 8*d.* the week.   .   .   . 3*l.* 6*s.* 8*d.*

"*Item*, for his washing during the same time   .   .   .   .   .   . 5*s.*"

It would have been interesting to see how the Lieutenant expressed himself when he sent in his Michaelmas bill, but unfortunately the paper is lost. By that time Father Gerard had ceased to be one of the prisoners in his custody.

[1] P.R.O., Pell Office, Exchequer Papers, Tower Bills : parcel 1, 1572—1605.

NOTE TO CHAPTER XX.

IT seems desirable to treat at greater length than would be possible in a simple footnote the question of the equivocation which was practised under certain circumstances by Father Gerard, as he has himself related in various parts of his Narrative. On examination we shall see that his practice was not merely in accordance with the rules of morality, but was absolutely inevitable if he would avoid a great wrong to others, and that so far from leading us to distrust his veracity, on the contrary, it is a proof to us of the clearness with which he kept before his mind the obligations of the law of truthfulness between man and man, and the fidelity of his practice to that law.

It is quite true that he, and many others, considered themselves justified, when their own lives or those of innocent persons were at stake, in the use of assertions that were simple falsehoods in the ordinary sense of the terms employed. These they called equivocations; and we find no trace in the period of which we are writing of the modern sense of the word, that is, of a true expression which is really beside the point, though it is so employed that it is very unlikely to be seen to be so by the person to whom it is addressed, who thus is said rather to be suffered to deceive himself than to be deceived. Practically the distinction is hard to draw, and it has the disadvantage of seeming to make the morality of the expression depend on the quickness and readiness of the person in danger, who may be able to think of phrases containing a real ambiguity but which yet would throw the hearers off the right scent.

According to modern feeling, Father Gerard would have been quite justified in examining the trees and hedges in search of a falcon he had not lost, and inquiring of all he met whether they had heard the tinkling of the bird's bells, although it was to make them think that he had lost a falcon,[1] or in other words, to

---

[1] *Supra*, p. 38.

deceive them; but by the same modern feeling he would be held to be guilty of a lie when he said that he was the servant of a lord in a neighbouring county, although he might have worn that lord's livery as a disguise if he could have obtained it, which would have been a more effectual deception than any words.

Again, according to modern judgment, John Lilly would be held guilty of a lie when he said[1] of Gerard's books and manuscripts, "They are mine;" but quite guiltless when, with the same intention of making the magistrates believe him to be a priest when he was not, he said, "I do not say I am a priest, that is for you to prove." Yet the latter expression was far more likely to deceive than the former. It was more like what a priest, under the circumstances, would have said. Present feeling would condemn him of a lie for saying simply that the books were his, when it would acquit him if he had thought of using far more deceptive expressions, such as, "I am not bound to compromise myself by saying whose they are."

The only difference between modern morality and that on which Father Gerard acted was that now-a-days men say, "Have recourse to evasions." Then men said, "Say what you like, it is their fault if they think it true." It is evident that of the two courses of proceeding, the plain-spoken old way is the least open to abuse. No one certainly would have recourse to it excepting from a well-weighed plea of a sorrowful necessity. Whereas, on the other hand, evasions are not startling, and the conscience may lay but little stress on the presence or absence of justifying circumstances. For it is most necessary to bear seriously in mind that all Catholic divines then held, and now hold, that to make use of equivocation, excepting under those peculiar circumstances that make it lawful, is in itself a sin, and thus no escape from the sin of lying. So Father Garnet plainly said when on his trial,[2] "As I say it is never lawful to equivocate in matters of faith, so also in matters of human conversation, it may not be used promiscually or at our pleasure, as in matters of contract, in matters of testimony, or before a competent judge, or

[1] *Infra*, p. 324.   [2] *Condition of Catholics*, p. 244.

to the prejudice of any third person ; in which case we judge it altogether unlawful."

It is but fair that, in reading the narrative of times when many lives hung on successful disguise and concealment, we should remember that the modern sense of equivocation was then unknown. Protestant moralists have spoken out their minds plainly enough on this subject.

" Great English authors, Jeremy Taylor, Milton, Paley, Johnson, men of very distinct schools of thought, distinctly say that under certain extreme circumstances it is allowable to tell a lie. Taylor says : 'To tell a lie for charity, to save a man's life, the life of a friend, of a husband, of a prince, of a useful and a public person, hath not only been done at all times, but commended by great and wise and good men. Who would not save his father's life, at the charge of a harmless lie, from persecutors or tyrants ? ' Again, Milton says : 'What man in his senses would deny that there are those whom we have the best ground for considering that we ought to deceive, as boys, madmen, the sick, the intoxi- cated, enemies, men in error, thieves ? I would ask, by which of the Commandments is lying forbidden ? You will say, by the ninth. If then my lie does not injure my neighbour, certainly it is not forbidden by this Commandment.' Paley says : ' There are falsehoods which are not lies, that is, which are not criminal.' Johnson : ' The general rule is, that truth should never be violated ; there must, however, be some exceptions. If, for instance, a murderer should ask you which way a man is gone.' " [1]

This *language* would not have been used by Catholics. With them the word " lie " signified a simple falsehood ; and an " equivocation " was a false expression used under such circum- stances that if they to whom it was addressed were deceived by it,

[1] *Apologia pro Vita sua*, by John Henry Newman, D.D. London, 1864, p. 418. The reader's attention is earnestly called to Cardinal Newman's treatment of this subject, both at the page quoted, and in the Appendix, p. 72. To the Protestant authors quoted above may be added Mr. Froude (*History of England*, vol. ii. ch. vi. p. 57, note). " It seems obvious that a falsehood of this sort is different in kind from what we commonly mean by unveracity, and has no affinity with it. . . . Rahab of Jericho did the same thing which Dalaber did" [a Protestant, who gave false answers and swore to them, to save Garret, his fellow] " and on that very ground was placed in the catalogue of saints."

it was their own fault. They had then no right to the truth, and even in some cases it would have been a sin to tell them the truth. In substance, however, though not in form, the doctrine of Gerard, Southwell, and Garnet, was the same as that of Taylor, Milton, and Johnson.

But to confine ourselves to the practice of Father Gerard, this doctrine is not necessary for his defence, and if his conduct be fairly examined, he will be held, even from the modern point of view, to have done no wrong. Protestant moralists, as we have seen, permit men under certain circumstances to tell a lie with intent to deceive. And Catholic moralists permit under such circumstances assertions which would lead the hearers to deceive themselves by neglecting to advert to the limit of the speaker's obligation to tell the truth. But with regard to Father Gerard's legal interrogations, we may waive the question whether they are right or wrong in their morality, for we see clearly that he so expressed himself as to show that his words were not intended to be believed.

The first instance that occurs in Father Gerard's Life, is that when, after his apprehension, on being questioned he declared that he was quite unacquainted with the family of the Wisemans, and those who were examining him betrayed their informer by crying out, "What lies you tell! Did you not say so-and-so before such a lady as you read your servant's letter?" Then he adds, "But I still denied it, *giving them good reasons however why, even if it had been true, I could and ought to have denied it.*" [1]

Another time [2] he was confronted with three servants of Lord Henry Seymour, who avouched that he had dined with their mistress and her sister, the Lady Mary Percy, that it was in Lent, and they told how their mistress ate meat, while Lady Mary and Father Gerard ate nothing but fish. "Young flung this charge in my teeth with an air of triumph, as though I could not help acknowledging it, and thereby disclosing some of my acquaintances. I answered that I did not know the men whom he had brought up.

[1] *Supra,* p. 163.   [2] *Supra,* p. 195.

"'But we know you,' said they, 'to be the same that was at such a place on such a day.'

"'You wrong your mistress,' said I, 'in saying so. I, however, will not so wrong her.'

"'What a barefaced fellow you are!' exclaimed Young.

"'Doubtless,' I answered, 'were these men's statements true. *As for me, I cannot in conscience speak positively in the matter, for reasons that I have often alleged; let them look to the truth and justice of what they say.*'"

A third instance is the interview [1] between Father Gerard and the widow Wiseman, in the presence of the Dean of Westminster, Topcliffe, and others. "They wanted to see if she recognized me. So when I came into the room where they brought me, I found her already there. When she saw me coming in with the gaolers, she almost jumped for joy; but she controlled herself, and said to them: 'Is that the person you spoke of? I do not know him; but he looks like a priest.'

"Upon this she made me a very low reverence, and I bowed in return. Then they asked me if I did not recognize her?

"I answered: 'I do not recognize her. *At the same time, you know this is my usual way of answering, and I will never mention any places, or give the names of any persons that are known to me* (which this lady, however, is not); *because to do so, as I have told you before, would be contrary both to justice and charity.*'"

Lastly, when examined by the Attorney-General as to what Catholics he knew: "Did I know such and such? I answered: 'I do not know them.' *And I added the usual reasons why I should still make the same answer even if I did know them,* [2] *showing that this was not telling a falsehood.*"

In every one of these instances words are carefully introduced to show that the denials in question were uttered not with the intent of deceiving the hearers (though even that, according to the grave Protestant authorities recently quoted, would have been lawful), nor of allowing them to deceive themselves if they did not choose to advert to the circumstances in which the denials

---

[1] *Supra*, p. 218.
[2] *Ostendi non esse hoc falsum dicere.* MS.

were made (as Catholic divines would have permitted);[1] but avowedly in order that they might not be available as legal evidence against the speaker or his friends.

To Father Gerard's defence of himself it may be as well to add that of Father Southwell,[2] who was assailed by Sir Edward Coke.

"The Father would have spoken further on this point [obedience to the laws] had they not attacked him on another, objecting to him a statement of Anne Bellamy's, who deposed that Father Robert had instructed her, that if asked by searchers or persecutors if there was a priest in the house, she could say 'No,' though she knew there was one : nay, that if asked on oath,

---

[1] Sir Walter Scott's words have been often quoted, and they are fair specimens of what an honourable man considers lawful. As they were no hasty and unconsidered expressions, they are deserving of insertion in this place. Lockhart calls them "a style of equivoque which could never seriously be misunderstood." To John Murray Scott wrote : "I give you heartily joy of the success of the Tales, although I do not claim that paternal interest in them which my friends do me the credit to assign me. I assure you I have never read a volume of them until they were printed, and can only join with the rest of the world in applauding the true and striking portraits which they present of old Scottish manners. *I do not expect implicit reliance to be placed on my disavowal, because I know very well that he who is disposed not to own a work must necessarily deny it, and that otherwise his secret would be at the mercy of all who choose to ask the question, since silence in such a case must always pass for consent, or rather assent.* But I have a mode of convincing you that I am perfectly serious in my denial—pretty similar to that by which Solomon distinguished the fictitious from the real mother—and that is, by reviewing the work, which I take to be an operation equal to that of quartering the child." And, in a letter written two years later, he says : "I own I did mystify Mrs. —— a little about the report you mention; and I am glad to hear the finesse succeeded. She came up to me with a great overflow of gratitude for the delight and pleasure, and so forth, which she owed to me on account of these books. Now, as she knew very well that I had never owned myself the author, this was not *polite* politeness, and she had no right to force me up into a corner and compel me to tell her a word more than I chose, upon a subject which concerned no one but myself—and I have no notion of being pumped by any old dowager Lady of Session, male or female. So I gave in dilatory defences, under protestation to add and eik ; for I trust, in learning a new slang, you have not forgot the old. In plain words, I denied the charge, and as she insisted to know who else *could* write these novels, I suggested Adam Fergusson as a person having all the information and capacity necessary for that purpose. But the inference that he *was* the author was of her own deducing ; and thus ended her attempt, notwithstanding her having primed the pump with a good dose of flattery." Lockhart's *Memoirs of Sir Walter Scott*, 1844, pp. 338, 389.

[2] We translate partly from Bartoli, *Inghilterra*, lib. v. c. 9, and partly from More, *Hist. Prov.* lib. v. c. 29.

she could swear there was not. No sooner was this brought out than the judges and officers of the court showed themselves highly scandalized, and were for stopping their ears :[1] as if, forsooth, the seeking for Catholic priests to put them to a traitor's death, or force them to apostatize, were a proceeding so clearly and so indubitably just, as to make it as clearly and indubitably unjust to hide them from such an ordeal, or to deny them to their pursuers : nor, indeed, would the harm be confined to the cruel execution of the priest, but with him the whole of the family in whose house he was found would be liable to the same death of traitors. Coke, therefore, the Attorney-General, made the most he could of this matter, insisting that such a pernicious doctrine tended to destroy all truth, and all reliance of men in each other's veracity, and if allowed to prevail, would upset all good government. Topcliffe also inveighed against it so exorbitantly, that Judge Popham silenced him. Father Robert then, as soon as he was allowed to reply, explained briefly what he had said to the witness, whose statement was not altogether exact, and addressing the Judge, said :

" ' If you will have the patience to listen to me, I shall be able to prove to you from the Holy Scriptures, from the Fathers, from theologians, and from reason, that in case a demand is made against justice and with the view of doing grievous harm to an innocent person, to give an answer not according to the intent of the questioner is no offence against either the divine law or the natural law. Nay, I will prove that this doctrine in no wise threatens the good government of states and kingdoms : and that, where the other necessary conditions of an oath are present, there is nothing wrong in confirming such an answer in that manner. Now I ask you, Mr. Attorney, Supposing the King of France (which God forbid) were to invade this country successfully, and having obtained full possession of this city, were to make search for her Majesty the Queen, whom you knew to be hidden in a secret apartment of the palace : supposing,

---

[1] Father Bartoli here asks us to contrast the pious horror expressed by the officials at Father Southwell's doctrine with the fact related by Father Gerard (*supra*, p. 194) of the magistrate Young swearing on the Scriptures to what he knew to be false.

moreover, that you were seized in the palace and brought before the King, and that he asked you where the Queen was, and would receive no profession of ignorance from you except on oath : what would you do ? To palter or hesitate is to show that she is there : to refuse to swear is equivalent to a betrayal. What would you answer ? I suppose, forsooth, you would point out the place ! Yet who of all who now hear me would not cry out upon you for a traitor ? You would then, if you had any sense, swear at once, either that you knew not where she was, or that you knew she was not in the palace, in order that your knowledge might not become instrumental to her harm.   Of this kind, in fact, was the answer of Christ in the Gospel, when He said that concerning the Day of Judgment no one had any knowledge, neither the angels in Heaven, nor the Son : that is, according to the interpretation of the Fathers, such knowledge that He could communicate to others.   Now this is the condition of Catholics in England : they are in peril of their liberty, their fortunes, and their lives, if they should have a priest in their houses.   How can it be forbidden them to escape these evils by an equivocal answer, and to confirm this answer, if necessary, by an oath ?   For in such a case, three things must be remembered : first, that a wrong is done unless you swear ; secondly, that no one is obliged to answer everybody's questions about everything ; thirdly, that an oath is always lawful, if made with truth, with judgment, and with justice, all which are found in this case.'[1]

" He went on to exemplify his position by supposed queries of robbers and highwaymen ; but he was interrupted by abuse."

Father Garnet has defended himself at sufficient length in his speech on his trial ;[2] but as he there refers to his previous answers, we have thought it best to give insertion here to an autograph paper of his preserved in the Public Record Office.[3]

---

[1] This last consideration applies, of course, not to the general question of equivocation (for in that case it would involve a *petitio principii*), but to the sub-question whether supposing a simple equivocation lawful (*i.e.*, allowing it to be no violation of veracity in some cases), it could ever be lawful to add to it the confirmation of an oath. Father Southwell maintains reasonably, that whatever it is lawful to say, it is lawful also to swear to, provided the other conditions for an oath are present.

[2] *Condition of Catholics*, p. 244.   [3] *Gunpowder Plot Book*, n. 217A.

"Concerning equivocation, which I seemed to condemn in moral things, my meaning was in moral and human conversation, in which the virtue of verity is required among friends, for otherwise it were injurious to all humanity. Neither is equivocation at all to be justified, but in case of necessary defence from injustice or wrong, or the obtaining some good of great importance, when there is no danger of harm to others, as in the case of Cowetry,[1] wherein I suppose it is a great advantage to me for to be admitted, and no harm can ensue to the city. For the city seeketh nothing but to be free from the sickness, and if it were possible that the city knew me to be free of certainty, they would admit me presently, which is confirmed by the custom of places beyond [sea], where, though they know a man to come from a place infected, yet after they have kept him in some several place, with convenient diet, for forty days, they admit him.

"As for Mr. Tresham's equivocation, I am loth to judge ; yet I think ignorance might excuse him, because he might think it lawful in that case to equivocate for the excuse of his friend, yet would I be loth to allow of it or practise it : he being not then urged, but voluntarily offering it himself, contrary to that which he had before set down, and especially being in case of manifest treason, as I will after explain. But in case a man be urged at the hour of his death, it is lawful for to equivocate, *with such due circumstances as are required in his life.* An example we may bring in another matter. For the divines hold that in some cases a man may be bound to conceal *something in his confession,* because of some great harm which may ensue of it. And as he may do so in his life, so may he at his death, if the danger of the harm continue still.

"The case being propounded, supposing that I knew Gerard acquainted with this treason, and having been often demanded thereof, I still denying it, by way of equivocation, whether at the hour of my death, either natural or by course of justice, I may by equivocation seek to clear him again.

"I answer, that in case I be not urged I may not, but I must leave the matter in case in which it stand ; but if I be urged, then

---

[1] If this word is "Coventry," there may possibly be here a clue to the origin of our phrase "sent to Coventry."

S

I may clear him by equivocation, whereas otherwise my silence would be accounted an accusation. But all this I understand when the case is such that I am bound to conceal Gerard's treason, as if I had heard it in confession. For this is a general rule, that in cases of true and manifest treason,[1] a man is bound voluntarily in utter and very truth by no way to equivocate, if he know it not by way of confession, in which case also he is bound to seek all lawful ways to discover, *salvo sigillo.*

" 29° Martii.   " HENRY GARNETT.

"All the Doctors that hold equivocation to be lawful do maintain that it is not lawful when the examinate is bound to tell the simple truth, that is, according to the civil law, when there is a competent judge, and the cause subject to his jurisdiction, and sufficient proofs. But in case of treason a man is bound to confess of another without any witness at all, yea, voluntarily to disclose it; not so of himself.

"And how far the common law bindeth in cases that are not treason a man to confess of himself, I know not. In the civil law, it is sufficient to have *semiplenam probationem,* that is, *unum testem omni exceptione majorem,* or *manifesta indicia.*

"Our law I take to be more mild, and that a man may put all to witnesses without confessing, except in cases of treason. For, according to our law, *non pervertitur judicium tacendo vel negando,*

---

[1] "One necessary condition," says Father Garnet in another paper (P.R.O., *Domestic, James I.,* vol. xx. n. 2), "required in every law is that it be just. For if this condition be wanting, that the law be unjust, then is it *ipso facto* void and of no force, neither hath it any power to oblige any. And this is a maxim, not only of divines, but of Aristotle and all philosophers. Hereupon ensueth that no power on earth can forbid or punish any action which we are bound unto by the law of God, which is the true pattern of all justice. So that the laws against recusants, against receiving of priests, against confession, against mass, or other rites of Catholic religion, are to be esteemed as no laws by such as steadfastly believe these to be necessary observances of the true religion.

"Likewise Almighty God hath absolute right for to send His preachers of His Gospel to any place in the world. 'Euntes docete omnes gentes.' So that the law against priests coming into the realm sincerely to preach, is no law, and those that are put to death by virtue of that decree are verily martyrs because they die for the preaching of true religion.

"Being asked what I meant by true treason, I answer that that is a true treason which is made treason by any just law, and that is no treason at all which is made treason by an unjust law."

as in the civil law, where is required *reus confitens*. But generally, when a man is bound to confess, there is no place of equivocation. And when he is not bound to confess according to the laws of each country, then may he equivocate."

In the last paper Father Garnet is not speaking of equivocation used in defence of an innocent person, but of what we may call the persistent plea of "Not guilty," and he there draws an interesting distinction between the Roman civil law and our own, which he calls "more mild," in that it professed to regard a prisoner as innocent till he is proved to be guilty. Happily this is our practice now, as well as our profession, and our quotations are needed to enable us to form judgments of conduct in times that have happily passed away.

The prisoner's usual plea of "Not guilty" is the real parallel to the denials of Father Gerard and others in similar positions. Being called on to plead "Guilty or not guilty," is the only form in which the *question* is now put to a person accused. But in those days the question was put over and over again, and in every variety of form. To deny was really to plead "Not guilty," and if this was lawful once, it was lawful whenever they were forced to repeat it. Not only was it a capital offence to be a priest within the realm, but it was high treason to be reconciled to the Church, or to be absolved by a priest, or to harbour or comfort one. Thus the interrogations addressed to prisoners were always intended to make them criminate themselves or others; that is, in the one case to cause them to plead guilty, so that they might be condemned to death on their own confessions; or, in the other case, to force them to become Queen's evidence, and be accessory to the infliction upon others of the extremest penalties enacted by an unjust law.

But with regard to Father Gerard's general truthfulness, and in particular with regard to the trustworthiness of his evidence respecting the Gunpowder Plot, even if the lawfulness of his denials under examination were not admitted, all that we should be concerned to show is, that untrue statements, made by a man under circumstances which, rightly or wrongly, he considers to justify him in making them, furnish no presumption whatever that, under other circumstances, affording to his conscience no such justification, his word cannot be trusted. It is an evident instance of the maxim that the exception proves the rule. Restraining himself carefully within the limits of what he held to be lawful under circumstances of extreme difficulty and great personal danger, are we not rather to conclude that, under far less pressure, he will as carefully confine himself to the laws imposed by his conscience?   Clearly there is nothing in Father Gerard's practice under examination to cause us to hesitate in placing implicit trust in his word when he speaks as an historian ; and in addition we are sure that no one will rise from the perusal of the exculpatory letters which will be found in a later chapter, without a full conviction of his innocence and truthfulness.

CHAPTER XXI.

ESCAPE FROM THE TOWER.

1597.

"I THUS endeavoured to conform myself to the decrees of God and the tyranny of man; when lo! on the last day of July [1597], the anniversary of our holy Father Ignatius' departure from this life, while I was in meditation, and was entertaining a vehement desire of an opportunity for saying Mass, it came into my head that this really might be accomplished in the cell of a certain Catholic gentleman [John Arden], which lay opposite mine on the other side of a small garden within the Tower. This gentleman[1] had

---

[1] We find from an extract of one of Father Garnet's letters in the Stonyhurst MSS. that this gentleman's name was Arden. "Oct. 8, 1597. Upon St. Francis' day at night broke out of the Tower one Arden, and Mr. Gerard the Jesuit: there is yet no great inquiry after him." Father Grene's *Collectan. P.* vol. ii. f. 548. Father Bartoli also and Father More mention Arden as the name of Father Gerard's companion. In the Lieutenant's Midsummer bill to the Exchequer we have the name of John Ardente as that of one of Father Gerard's fellow prisoners. In August, 1588, "John Ardent gent." was reported by the Lieutenant as then "prisoner one year six months, condemned of treason," committed Jan. 28, 158⁴⁄₇, and maintained at the Queen's charge, but a note is added to his name in Lord Burghley's hand, "to the King's Bench." P.R.O., *Domestic, Elizabeth*, vol. ccxv. n. 19.

There was also a Francis Arden, who was committed to the Tower, according to Rishton, on Lady Day, 1584. A paper entitled "What course is meet to be held in the causes of certain prisoners remaining in the Tower," dated May 27, 1585, says of him, "Francis Arden, indicted of treason, but the matter not full enough against him, to be removed to her Majesty's Bench." *Ibid.* vol. clxxviii. n. 74. Later on he was tried, condemned, and retransferred to the Tower, as we learn from the term of his imprisonment in a subsequent list of prisoners in the Tower, Oct. 24, 1589, in which he is mentioned as "prisoner two years and three quarters, condemned

been detained ten years in prison. He had been indeed condemned to death, but the sentence was not carried out. He was in the habit of going up daily on the leads of the building in which he was confined, which he was allowed to use as a place of exercise; here he would salute me, and wait for my blessing on bended knees.

"On examining this idea of mine more at leisure, I concluded that the matter was feasible, if I could prevail on my gaoler to allow me to visit this gentleman. For he had a wife who had obtained permission to visit him at fixed times, and bring him changes of linen and other little comforts in a basket; and as this had now gone on many years, the officers had come to be not so particular in examining the basket as they were at first. I hoped therefore that there would be a possibility of introducing gradually by means of this lady all things necessary for the celebration of Mass, which my friends would supply. Resolving to make the trial, I made a sign to the gentleman to attend to what I was going to indicate to him. I then took pen and paper and made as if I was writing somewhat; then, after holding the paper

of treason," and in the margin "Referred to her Majesty." *Ibid.* vol. ccxxvii. n. 37.

Francis Arden was probably a relation of Edward Arden, who was hanged Dec. 23 (Stowe says Dec. 20), 1583, "protesting his innocence of every charge, and declaring that his only crime was the profession of the Catholic religion." Rishton's *Diary in the Tower.* In a curious paper (*Domestic, Elizabeth,* vol. ccix. n. 3), dated March 1, 158$\frac{7}{8}$, Robert Ardern of Burwycke gives information to the Earl of Leicester against "Mr. Ardern of Cotesford, a gentleman of Oxfordshire," in which paper mention is made of a man that "was Ardern's keeper that is prisoner in the Tower." Robert Arden was in the Marshalsea with Father Gerard in 1584, "sent in the 10th of Dec., 1582." *Ibid.* vol. clxx. n. 11.

Eleven years before Father Gerard's escape with John Arden, there was a rumour current that one of the Ardens had broken prison. Sir Amias Poulet wrote from Fotheringay, where poor Queen Mary was then within a few days of her death, to Mr. Secretary Davison, Jan. 27, 158$\frac{6}{7}$. "There is a great alarm in the county and in counties adjoining, upon the rumour of the escape of one Arden a traitor." Poulet's *Letter-books,* p. 353.

to the fire, I made a show of reading it, and lastly I wrapped up one of my crosses in it, and made a sign of sending it over to him. I dare not speak to him across the garden, as what I said would easily have been heard by others. Then I began treating with my gaoler to convey a cross or a rosary for me to my fellow-prisoner, for the same man had charge of both of us, as we were near neighbours. At first he refused, saying that he durst not venture, as he had had no proof of the other prisoner's fidelity in keeping a secret. 'For if,' said he, 'the gentleman's wife were to talk of this, and it should become known I had done such a thing, it would be all over with me.' I reassured him, however, and convinced him that such a result was not likely, and, as I added a little bribe, I prevailed upon him as usual to gratify me. He took my letter, and the other received what I sent; but he wrote me nothing back as I had requested him to do. Next morning, when he made his appearance on the leads, he thanked me by signs, and showed the cross I had sent him.

"After three days, as I got no answer from him, I began to suspect the real reason, viz., that he had not read my letter. So I called his attention again, and went through the whole process in greater detail. Thus, I took an orange and squeezed the juice into a little cup, then I took a pen and wrote with the orange-juice, and holding the paper some time before the fire, that the writing might be visible, I perused it before him, trying to make him understand that this was what he should do with my next paper. This time he fathomed my meaning, and thus read the next letter I sent him. He soon sent me a reply, saying that he thought the first time I wanted him to burn the paper, as I had written a few visible words on it with pencil; therefore he had done so. To my proposal moreover he answered, that the thing could be done, if my gaoler would allow me to visit him in the evening and remain with him the next day; and that his wife would bring all the furniture that should be given her for the purpose.

"As a next step I sounded the gaoler about allowing me to visit my fellow-prisoner, and proposed he should let me go just once and dine with him, and that he, the gaoler, should have his share in the feast. He refused absolutely, and showed great fear of the possibility of my being seen as I crossed the garden, or lest the Lieutenant might take it into his head to pay me a visit that very day. But as he was never in the habit of visiting me, I argued that it was very improbable that the thing should happen as he feared; after this, the golden arguments I adduced proved completely successful, and he acceded to my request. So I fixed on the Nativity of the Blessed Virgin; and in the meanwhile I told my neighbour to let his wife call at such a place in London, having previously sent word to John Lilly what he should give her to bring. I told him, moreover, to send a pyx and a number of small hosts, that I might be able to reserve the Blessed Sacrament. He provided all I told him, and the good lady got them safely to her husband's cell. So on the appointed day I went over with my gaoler, and stayed with my fellow-prisoner that night and the next day; but the gaoler exacted a promise that not a word of this should be said to the gentleman's wife. The next morning, then, I said Mass, to my great consolation; and that Confessor of Christ communicated, after having been so many years deprived of that favour. In this Mass I consecrated also two and twenty particles, which I reserved in the pyx with a corporal; these I took back with me to my cell, and for some days renewed the Divine banquet with ever-fresh delight and consolation.

"Now while we were together that day, I—though nothing was less in my thoughts when I came over than any idea of escape (for I sought only our true deliverer

Jesus Christ, as He was prefigured in the little ash-baked loaf of Elias, that I might with more strength and courage travel the rest of my way even to the mount of God)— seeing how close this part of the Tower was to the moat by which it was surrounded, began to think with myself that it were a possible thing for a man to descend by a rope from the top of the building to the other side of the moat. I asked my companion therefore what he thought about it, and whether it seemed possible to him.

"'Certainly,' said he, 'it could be done, if a man had some true and real friends to assist him, who would not shrink from exposing themselves to danger to rescue one they loved.'

"'There is no want of such friends,' I replied, 'if only the thing is feasible, and worth trying.'

"'For my part,' said he, 'I should only be too glad to make the attempt; since it would be far better for me to live even in hiding, where I could enjoy the sacraments and the company of good men, than to spend my life here in solitude between four walls.'

"'Well then,' I answered, 'let us commend the matter to God in prayer; in the meanwhile I will write to my Superior, and what he thinks best we will do.'

"I returned that night to my cell, and wrote a letter to Father Garnet by John Lilly, putting all the circumstances before him. He answered me that the thing should be attempted by all means, if I thought it could be done without danger to my life in the descent.

"Upon this I wrote to my former host [Mr. Wiseman], telling him that an escape in this way could be managed, but that the matter must be communicated to as few as possible, lest it should get noised about and stopped. I appointed moreover John Lilly and Richard Fulwood, the latter of whom was at that time serving Father Garnet, if they were willing to expose themselves to the peril, to come on such a night to the outer bank of the

moat opposite the little tower in which my friend was
kept, and near the place where Master Page was apprehended, as I described before.   They were to bring with
them a rope, one end of which they were to tie to a stake,
then we from the leads on the top of the tower would
throw over to them a ball of lead with a stout string
attached, such as men use for sewing up bales of goods.
This they would find in the dark by the noise it would
make in falling, and would attach the string to the free
end of their rope, so that we who retained one end of
the string would thus be able to pull the rope up.
I ordered, moreover, that they should have on their
breasts a white paper or handkerchief, that we might
recognize them as friends before throwing our string, and
that they should come provided with a boat in which we
might quickly make our escape.

"When these arrangements had been made and a
night fixed, yet my host wished that a less hazardous
attempt should first be made, namely, by trying whether
my gaoler could be bribed to let me out, which he could
easily do by permitting a disguise.   John Lilly. therefore
offered him on the part of a friend of mine a thousand
florins [100*l.*] on the spot, and a hundred florins [10*l.*]
yearly for his life, if he would agree to favour my escape.
The man would not listen to anything of the kind, saying
he should have to live an outcast if he did so, and should
be sure to be hanged if ever he was caught.   Nothing therefore could be done with him in this line.   So we went
on with our preparations according to our previous plan;
and the matter was commended to God with many
prayers by all those to whom the secret was committed.
One gentleman indeed, heir to a large estate, made a vow
to fast once a week during his life if I escaped safely.
When the appointed night came, I prevailed on the gaoler
by entreaties and bribes to allow me to visit my friend.
So he locked us both in together with bolts and bars of

iron as usual, and departed. But as he had also locked
the inside door that led to the roof, we had to loosen the
stone, into which the bolt shot, with our knives, or otherwise we could not get out. This we succeeded in doing
at length, and mounted the leads softly and without a
light, for a sentinel was placed in the garden every night,
so that we durst not even speak to each other but in a
very low whisper.

"About midnight we saw the boat coming with our
friends, namely, John Lilly, Richard Fulwood, and another
who had been my gaoler in the former prison, through
whom they procured the boat, and who steered the boat
himself. They neared the shore; but just as they were
about to land, some one came out of one of the poor
cottages thereabouts to do somewhat, and seeing their
boat making for the shore, hailed them, taking them
for fishermen. The man indeed returned to his bed
without suspecting anything, but our boatmen durst not
venture to land till they thought the man had gone to
sleep again. They paddled about so long however that
the time slipped away, and it became impossible to
accomplish anything that night; so they returned by
London Bridge. But the tide was now flowing so
strongly that their boat was forced against some piles
there fixed to break the force of the water, so that they
could neither get on nor get back. Meanwhile the tide
was still rising, and now came so violently on the boat
that it seemed as if it would be upset at every wave.
Being in these straits they commended themselves to
God by prayers, and called for help from men by their
cries.

"All this while we on the top of the tower heard them
shouting, and saw men coming out on the bank of the
river with candles, running up and getting into their
boats to rescue those in danger. Many boats approached
them but none durst go up to them, fearing the force

of the current.[1] So they stood there in a sort of circle
round them, spectators of their peril, but not daring to
assist.   I recognized Richard Fulwood's voice in the
shouts, and said, 'I know it is our friends who are in
danger.' My companion indeed did not believe I could
distinguish any one's voice at that great distance;[2] but
I knew it well, and groaned inwardly to think that such
devoted men were in peril of their lives for my sake.
We prayed fervently therefore for them, for we saw that
they were not yet saved, though many had gone to assist
them.   Then we saw a light let down from the bridge,[3]
and a sort of basket attached to a rope, by which they
might be drawn up, if they could reach it. This it seems
they were not able to do. But God had regard to the
peril of his servants, and at last there came a strong sea
boat with six sailors, who worked bravely, and bringing
their boat up to the one in danger took out Lilly and
Fulwood. Immediately they had got out, the boat they
had left capsized before the third could be rescued, as
if it had only kept right for the sake of the two who
were Catholics. However by God's mercy the one who
was thrown into the river caught a rope that was let down
from the bridge, and was so dragged up and saved. So
they were all rescued, and got back to their homes.

"On the following day [October 4, 1597] John Lilly
wrote me by the gaoler as usual. What could I expect
him to say but this:—'We see, and have proved it by
our peril, that it is not God's will that we should proceed
any further in this business.' But I found him saying
just the contrary. For he began his letter as follows:—

[1] The number of piers in old London Bridge was so large, and offered so
great an obstruction to the water, that it was always a service of danger to pass
under the arches while the tide was running: and often the river formed a
regular cataract at this part.

[2] The distance would be something over half a mile.

[3] Our readers will remember that at this time each side of the bridge was
lined with houses, which looked sheer down into the river.

'It was not the will of God that we should accomplish our desire last night, still He rescued us from a great danger, that we might succeed better the next time. What is put off is not cut off:[3] so we mean to come again to-night with God's help.'

" My companion on seeing such constancy joined with such strong and at the same time pious affection, was greatly consoled and did not doubt success. But I had great ado to obtain leave from the gaoler to remain another night out of my cell; and had misgivings that he would discover the loosening of the stone when he locked the door again. He however remarked nothing of it.

" In the meantime I had written three letters to be left behind. One was to the gaoler, justifying myself for taking this step without a word to him; I told him I was but exercising my right, since I was detained in prison without any crime, and added that I would always remember him in my prayers, if I could not help him in any other way. I wrote this letter with the hope that if the man were taken into custody for my escape it might help to show that he was not to blame. The second letter was to the Lieutenant, in which I still further exonerated the gaoler, protesting before God that he knew nothing whatever about my escape, which was of course perfectly true, and that he certainly would not have allowed it if he had suspected anything. This I confirmed by relating the very tempting offer which had been made him and which he had refused. As to his having allowed me to go to another prisoner's cell, I said I had extorted it from him with the greatest difficulty by repeated importunities, and therefore it would not be right that he should suffer death for it. The third letter was to the Lords of the Council, in which I stated first the causes which moved me to the recovery of my

[3] *Quod differtur non aufertur.* MS.

liberty of which I had been unjustly deprived. It was not so much the mere love of freedom, I said, as the love of souls which were daily perishing in England that led me to attempt the escape, in order that I might assist in bringing them back from sin and heresy. As for matters of State, as they had hitherto found me averse to meddling with them, so they might be sure that I should continue the same. Besides this, I exonerated the Lieutenant and gaoler from all consent to or connivance at my escape, assuring them that I had recovered my liberty entirely by my own and my friends' exertions. I prepared another letter also, which would be taken next morning to my gaoler, not however by John Lilly, but by another, as I shall narrate presently.

"At the proper hour we mounted again on the leads. The boat arrived and put to shore without any interruption. The schismatic, my former gaoler, remained with the boat, and the two Catholics came with the rope. It was a new rope, for they had lost the former one in the river on occasion of their disaster. They fastened the rope to a stake, as I had told them ; they found the leaden ball which we threw, and tied the string to the rope. We had great difficulty however in pulling up the rope, for it was of considerable thickness, and double too. In fact Father Garnet ordered this arrangement, fearing lest otherwise the rope might break by the weight of my body. But now another element of danger showed itself, which we had not reckoned on : for the distance was so great between the tower and the stake to which the rope was attached, that it seemed to stretch horizontally rather than slopingly ; so that we could not get along it merely by our weight, but would have to propel ourselves by some exertion of our own. We proved this first by a bundle which we had made of books and some other things wrapped up in my cloak. This bundle we placed on the double rope to see if it would slide down of itself, but it stuck at once. And it was well it did; for if it had gone out of our reach before it stuck, we should never have got down ourselves. So we took the bundle back and left it behind.

"My companion, who had before spoken of the descent as a thing of the greatest ease, now changed his mind, and confessed it to be a thing very difficult and full of danger. 'However,' said he, 'I shall most certainly be hanged if I remain now, for we cannot throw the rope back without its falling into the water, and so betraying both us and our friends. I will therefore descend, please God, preferring to expose myself to danger with the hope of freedom, rather than to remain here with good certainty of being hanged.' So he said a prayer, and took to the rope. He descended fairly enough, for he was strong and vigorous, and the rope was then taut; his weight however slackened it considerably, which made the danger for me greater, and though I did not then notice this, yet I found it out afterwards when I came to make the trial.

"So commending myself to God, to our Lord Jesus, to the Blessed Virgin, to my Guardian Angel, and all my patrons, particularly Father Southwell, who had been imprisoned near this place for nearly three years before his martyrdom, and Father Walpole, I took the rope in my right hand and held it also with my left arm; then I twisted my legs about it, to prevent falling, in such a way that the rope passed between my shins. I descended some three or four yards face downwards, when suddenly my body swung round by its own weight and hung under the rope. The shock was so great that I nearly lost my hold, for I was still but weak, especially in the hands and arms. In fact, with the rope so slack and my body hanging beneath it, I could hardly get on at all. At length I made a shift to get on as far as the middle of the rope, and there I stuck, my breath and my strength failing me, neither of which were very copious to begin with. After a little time, the saints assisting me, and my good friends below drawing me to them by their prayers, I got on a little further and stuck again, thinking I should never be able to accomplish it. Yet I was loth to drop into the water as long as I could possibly hold on. After another rest therefore I summoned what remained of my strength, and helping myself with legs and arms as well as I could, I got as far as the wall on the other side of the moat. But my feet only touched the top of the wall, and my whole body hung horizontally, my head being no higher than my feet, so slack was the rope. In such a position, and exhausted as I was, it was hopeless to expect to get over the wall by my own unaided strength. So John Lilly got on to the wall somehow or other (for, as he afterwards asserted, he never knew how he got there), took hold of my feet, and by them pulled me to him, and got me over the wall on to the ground. But I was quite unable to stand, so they gave me some cordial waters and restoratives which they had brought on purpose. By the help of these I managed to walk to the boat, into which we all entered. They had, however, before leaving the wall, untied the rope from the stake and cut off a part of it, so that it hung down the wall of the Tower. We had previously, indeed, determined to pull it away altogether, and had with this object passed it round a great gun on the Tower without knotting it. But God so willed it that we were not able by any exertion to get it away; and if we had succeeded it would certainly have made a loud splash in the water, and perhaps have brought us into a worse danger. On entering the boat we gave hearty thanks to God Who had delivered us from the hand of the persecutor, and from all the expectation of the people;[1] and we also returned our best thanks to those who had

---

[1] Acts xii. 11.

exposed themselves to such labours and perils for our sakes."

Father Gerard has now told the story of his torture in the Tower and of his escape from that famous State prison. However eager we might be to identify the places mentioned by him, it was impossible that we should permit ourselves to check the interest of the story by breaking its thread. Now that the tale is told we may pause to visit the Tower of London [1] to ascertain which was the cell occupied by Father Gerard and which was the point where he succeeded in crossing the moat. He has mentioned a sufficient number of circumstances to make this identification possible, and as far at least as the cells are concerned which were honoured by the imprisonment of Father Henry Walpole and himself, they are happily in excellent condition, and but little changed.

He has told us that, when brought to the Tower, he was conducted by Sir Henry Barkeley, the Lieutenant, "to a large high tower of three storeys, with a separate lock-up place in each, one of a number of different towers contained within the whole inclosure. He left me," said Father Gerard, "in the lowest part," and the warder, after throwing some straw on the ground, "fastened the door of my prison and secured the upper door both with a great bolt and iron bars. The next day I examined the place, for there was some light though dim, and I found the name of Father Henry Walpole, of blessed memory, cut with a knife on the wall, and not far from there I found his oratory, which was a space where there had been a narrow window, now blocked up with stones. There he had written on either side with chalk the names of the different choirs of angels, and on the top, above the cherubim and seraphim, the name of the Mother of

---

[1] This examination of the localities in the Tower of London was published in the *Month* for December, 1874.

T

God, and above that again, in Latin, Greek, and Hebrew, the name of God."

The place thus described was the Salt Tower, an ancient tower, the origin of the name of which is unknown, and which seems at one time to have shared with the White Tower the honour of being called after "Julyus Sesar."[1] The tower has received a new external face of stone, but the interior is as nearly in its ancient state as is compatible with its present use as a dwelling-house. A door has been opened at the bottom of the tower, which did not exist in Father Gerard's time, when the entrance to it was from the ballium wall or inner line of fortification, of which the Salt Tower formed the south-east angle. Father Gerard took no account of what is now called the cellar, and the interior face of the stones of its walls shows no sign of ever having been scored by a prisoner's knife. Besides this there are three ancient storeys. What we should now call the first floor is the cell to which Father Gerard descended from the door by which he entered the tower, and which he calls "the lower dungeon" where Father Walpole's "oratory" was. The room is "sufficiently large and commodious for a prisoner," being internally a pentagon about sixteen feet across. It is no longer dimly lighted, for a modern two-light Gothic window has taken the place of one of the ancient loopholes, through which the cell received of old such light and air as it had. There were five of these narrow openings in the enormously thick walls of the circular tower, and as Father Gerard says that one at least of these was blocked up with stones, the place may well have been dim.

There are many inscriptions remaining on the walls of the cell, interesting enough in their way; but there is one in particular, that has not been noticed in any of the books written on the Tower, the sight of which is enough

[1] Survey of 1532, quoted in Bayly's *History of the Tower*.

to make one's heart leap into one's mouth.   These are the
words, thickly coated with whitewash,

that testified that in this cell Father Walpole had been
imprisoned.   The name of the martyr is to be seen where
Father Gerard saw it, by the window, though of course
the holy words that he had written close by in chalk have
long ago been effaced.   A very fine old fireplace faces
you as you enter the cell, and the window once thus
sanctified is the next to it on your left.   "It was truly a
great consolation to me," says Father Gerard, and his
words find their echo still, "to find myself in this place,
hallowed by the presence of so great and so devoted a
martyr, the place too in which he was frequently tortured,
to the number, as I have heard, of fourteen times.   Probably they were unwilling to torture him in public and
in the ordinary place, because they did it oftener than
they would have it known."   There are other thoughts
that mingle in our minds with those expressed by Father
Gerard, for he did not know that which to our grief the
State Papers make known to us, that the cruel, oft-repeated
torture did its wicked work, and wrenched from the broken
spirit what the conscience condemned.   But though they
extorted what was wrong, the torturers evidently did not
get all that they wanted, so that that which they got was
valueless in their eyes.   So they sent him to York to be
tried for the crime of his priesthood, and the guilt of the
words extorted by torture was washed away in the baptism
of blood.

Father Gerard's prison was the cell overhead. It must be visited in order to ascertain which was the tower where Father Gerard said mass and from the top of which he afterwards escaped. It "lay opposite to mine," he says, "on the other side of a small garden within the Tower." So far the description is verified by either of two small towers in the outer line of fortification. The Salt Tower, the Well Tower, and the Cradle Tower were at the corners of a small triangular garden called the Queen's Privy Garden—the King's Gallery, which Oliver Cromwell afterwards pulled down, at that time dividing the King's Garden from the Queen's. The Well Tower, which still exists, is the nearest of the two to the Salt Tower, but externally no window now exists by which the Well Tower could have been seen from a cell in the Salt Tower, and the question was whether the new face of stonework had closed an ancient window, and this an internal examination alone could show. It was plain at a first glance that there was no such window. A fireplace, immediately over the broad chimney-place in the cell below, occupies the whole site of the tower that turns towards the Well Tower; while through the deep em-brasure on the right hand the little modern artillery tower that covers the remains of the old Cradle Tower can be plainly seen.

It was then in the Cradle Tower that John Arden was immured. When on the leads of his tower, he would not be so high as Father Gerard was in his cell half-way up the Salt Tower. "Here he would salute me," says Father Gerard, "and wait for my blessing on bended knees." From this loophole Arden learnt by signs that there was writing on the apparently blank pages in which the crosses and rosaries of orange peel were wrapped, and that it could be made legible by being held to the fire. "I dared not speak to him across the garden"—the two towers were about five and forty yards apart—"as what I

said would easily have been overheard by others." There
it was, then, in the little Cradle Tower that on the
Nativity of the Blessed Virgin, now nearly three centuries
ago, the mass was said, "that confessor of Christ communicated, after having been so many years deprived of
that favour," and thence that Father Gerard returned to the
Salt Tower, with a beating heart, bearing with him a pyx
containing two and twenty particles, and thus "for many
days renewed the divine banquet with ever fresh delight
and consolation."

Reluctantly we leave the cell where the Hidden God
did not disdain to come to console the prisoner for His
Name's sake, and we go out into into the paved yard
which was once the Queen's Garden. The Cradle Tower
attracts us, and we see that its remains are very interesting.
In the lower part of it there is an arch which spanned a
water-way entrance,[1] which served for the admission into
the Tower precincts of arrivals by the river, whose importance did not call for the unclosing of the Traitors'
Gate. This Cradle Tower was parted from its neighbour,
called the Lanthorn, by a gateway through which ran the
outer ward. That Lanthorn Tower, till Oliver Cromwell
destroyed it, contained the King's bedchamber, and many
an uneasy head has lain there the night before it was
burdened with the Crown of England; but the site of
that royal chamber has less interest for us at this moment
than the modern little turret that covers the beautiful
vaulting of the old Cradle Tower. We look over the
parapet, and see before us the moat, the Tower wharf,
and the River Thames beyond. Fill the moat with water,
as it fills even yet in time of floods, build a wall along the
wharf on the other side of the moat, and you see things

---

[1] Mr. Hepworth Dixon in *Her Majesty's Tower* gives a view in which a
footbridge crosses the moat from the Cradle Tower and a pathway leads to
the river-bank. This is evidently owing to a misunderstanding of the water-
gate which is shown in the contemporary engraving.

much as John Gerard and John Arden saw them when they debated the feasibility of close prisoners escaping from the Tower of London. It is the one spot where their enterprise was possible. Opposite to the Well Tower on your left were buildings along the moat, as the old bird's-eye view taken in 1597 shows, which would have hindered escape there. The moat, too, is a trifle narrower opposite to the Cradle. Both the Well and the Cradle are built some nine or ten feet projecting into the moat, and the remaining width of moat opposite the Cradle is only thirty feet. There was a wall, as we have said, dividing the wharf from the moat. Over this the prisoners threw a leaden ball to which twine was attached. Their faithful friends tied the bight of a rope to it, fastening the ends to a stake, and a gun on the tower served to hold the double rope. The Cradle Tower was a very low one, probably not more than a few feet higher than the opposite wall, and the main difficulty of the escape consisted in this, that the rope was nearly horizontal and there was the greatest danger of falling into the water. The portion of the wharf that they at length reached was that which was visible from Father Gerard's cell, where Francis Page used to walk up and down, and stop and doff his hat and look for Father Gerard's blessing until at last he was noticed and Mr. Lieutenant took him in charge. To this .part of the wharf a modern drawbridge now gives access between the Well and the Cradle Towers, opposite to the Salt Tower ; and so, looking back upon them as we leave them and mentally reproducing the scenes of our story, we take our leave of the cruel Tower of London.

NOTE TO CHAPTER XXI.

The following inscriptions are still to be seen in the soffit of one of the windows of Father Gerard's cell, and as they are anterior in date to the time of his imprisonment his eye has often scanned them.

EGREMOND RADCLYFF
1576 POUR PARV

F	EMONGSTE THE WORLDLY SOROWES ALL
1553	TO MAN MORE GRIEF THERE CANNOT BE
Digbi	THEN FROM FELISCITE TO FAWLE
	INTO THIS CAPTIVITE

R buxton   GODSA

1566   IOHN COLLETON PRISTE   CHETWODE

1581   22 July   ffixer

Father Gerard probably recognized all these his predecessors in captivity. We do not know who the F. Digby was, whose limping verse, in exquisitely cut letters, tells us that he held his captivity there after his former felicity to be the greatest possible grief that could befall him. The year that he has noted is that of the death of Edward the Sixth, of Lady Jane Grey's short reign, and of Mary's accession. Chetwode we do not know, nor Buxton; but John Fixer was one of a party of twelve priests who left Seville for England at the end of 1590, of which number three, John Cecil *alias* Snowden, James Young *alias* Dingley *alias* Christopher, and this John Fixer *alias* Wilson, are shown by Lord Burghley's letters in the Public Record Office to have become spies and traitors. "Godsa" is probably the beginning of the name of a Douay priest, named John Godsalfe, who was imprisoned.

John Colleton, or Collington, and Thomas Ford were the two priests who lay side by side with Father Campion in the hiding-place at Lyford, and were taken with him on the 17th of July, 1581. We do not know which cell it was in which Campion was confined, but we learn from Bayly that Thomas Ford, who was afterwards martyred, was imprisoned in the Broad Arrow Tower. The date of the 22nd of July, which Colleton has left on the wall of the Salt Tower, is the very day when they were handed over to the custody of the Lieutenant of the Tower. Colleton was therefore confined here in the first instance. He was afterwards transferred to the Beauchamp Tower, where his name appears again; probably after his acquittal at Father Campion's trial on the *alibi* proved by Mr. Lancaster, who witnessed "that he was with him in Grays Inn the very day that he was charged with plotting at Rheims." The Douay Diary gives his name as sent into banishment in January, 1585, one of the seventy-two priests who were transported at the same time. He soon returned to England, and lived till 1635. He was the first Dean of the Bishop of Chalcedon's Chapter.

Egremont Radcliffe, Bayly tells us, was the only son of Henry Radcliffe, second Earl of Essex, by his second wife, Anne, daughter of Sir Philip Calthorpe of Norwich, knight. His life was an unhappy one, and it was unhappily ended. Having been engaged in the rebellion of the North in 1569, he fled to Spain and Flanders, but pining for home he wrote earnest letters to ask Burghley's intercession with Elizabeth. His enemy, however, was his own half-brother, the Earl of Sussex, then Lord Chamberlain to the Queen. He crept nearer and nearer to England, as the dates of his letters show, first to Bruges, then to Calais; and at last, despite a warning that Elizabeth sent him, he landed without leave, and was at once sent to the Tower of London. He was at one time in the Beauchamp Tower, where, as in the Salt Tower, he has cut his name and his motto *Pour parvenir.* On being banished once more, he entered the service of Don John of Austria, but—it is said, by Walsingham's contrivance— he was executed for conspiring against Don John's life. Sanders has the worst opinion of him, calling him "an assassin, with daring enough for any deeds of the kind." He was executed by the Prince of Parma after Don John's death, and at his execution he is said to have confessed that he was sent over to murder Cardinal Allen.

These are all that remain of the inscriptions of prisoners in

Father Gerard's cell. In Father Walpole's cell we find the following.

+ HARMAN BARRESTER	MICHAEL MOODY
IHS	Mar. 15, 1587
EDWARDVS HYRSTE	WILLIAM BLO
1587 January 24	I. LYON 1574
Custos MM hoc scripsit	JOHN BAPTISTE
HARRY CLARKE in anno	CRISTOFER PERNE
1553	P CRISTOFER
HVMFRY HOLT 1553	Mense Maii 1552 HVMFRY
	MICHEL

These are of less interest, as we do not know the names. Michael Moody alone is recognizable, for he was committed to the Tower on account of the fictitious plot of the younger Stafford, the Ambassador's brother, against Elizabeth's life, which was invented in order to hasten the execution of Mary, Queen of Scots. On the left hand side of the room there was a shield bearing three crosses, and a long memorial in French, which was whitewashed over when Bayly wrote.

Besides these inscriptions there is a carving, and a very curious one, in the cell. It is a circle intersected by many lines, inclosed in a square divided into degrees, and at the side are the signs of the Zodiac arranged in seven columns. In the middle the word "afternoon" is still decipherable. The inscription on it is—

HEW . DRAPER . OF . BRISTOW . MADE . THYS
SPHEER . THE . 30 . DAYE . OF . MAYE . ANNO . 1561

In another part of the room there is a globe carved by the same man. He was committed March 20, 1560, "accused by John Man, an astronomer, on a suspect of [being] a conjurer or sorcerer, and thereby to practise matter against Sir William St. Lowe [spelt also Sentlo] and my lady." So writes Sir Edward Warner, Lieutenant of the Tower, to the Lords of the Privy Council, dating his letter four days before poor Draper dated his inscription. The Lieutenant adds, " He is presently very sick. He seemeth to be a man of good wealth, and keepeth a tavern at Bristowe [Bristol], and is of his neighbours well reported."

CHAPTER XXII.

AT LARGE AGAIN.

1597.

"WE went some considerable distance in the boat before landing. After we had landed I sent the gentleman, my companion, with John Lilly, to my house, of which I have before spoken, which was managed by that saintly widow, Mistress Line. I myself, however, with Richard Fulwood went to a house which Father Garnet had in the suburbs ;[1] and there Little John and I, a little before daylight, mounted our horses, which he had ready there for the purpose, and rode straight off to Father Garnet, who was then living a short distance in the country. We got there by dinner-time, and great rejoicing there was on my arrival, and much thanksgiving to God at my having thus escaped from the hands of my enemies in the name of the Lord.

"In the meanwhile I had sent Richard Fulwood with a couple of horses to a certain spot, that he might be ready to ride off with my gaoler, if he wished to consult his immediate safety. For I had a letter written, of which I made previous mention, which was to be taken to him early in the morning at the place where he was accustomed to meet John Lilly. Lilly, however, did not carry the letter, for I had bidden him remain quiet within doors,

---

[1] Father Tesimond in the Narrative of his coming on the English Mission, says that when he came to England in this very year 1597, Father Garnet was living at a house called Morecroftes in Uxbridge, twelve or thirteen miles from London. The house in the suburbs was in Spitalfields. *Troubles*, First Series, pp. 177, 179.

until such time as the storm which was to be expected
had blown over. So another person took the letter, and
gave it to the gaoler at the usual meeting place. He was
indeed surprised at another's coming, but took the letter
without remark, and was about to depart with the intention
of delivering it to me as usual ; but the other stopped him,
saying :

"'The letter is for you, and not for any one else.'

"'For me ?' said the gaoler : 'from whom, then, does
it come ?'

"'From a friend of yours,' replied the other, 'but who
he is I don't know.'

"The gaoler was still more astonished at this, and said,
'I cannot myself read : if, then, it is a matter which requires immediate attention, pray read it for me.'

"So the man that brought the letter read it for him.
It was to the effect that I had made my escape from
prison ; and here I added a few words on the reasons of
my conduct, for the purpose of calming his mind. Then
I told him that though I was no wise bound to protect
him from the consequences, as I had but used my just
right, yet as I had found him faithful in the things which
I had entrusted him with, I was loth to leave him in the
lurch : if, therefore, he was inclined to provide for his own
safety immediately, there was a horse waiting for him with
a guide who would bring him to a place of safety, sufficiently distant from London, where I would maintain him
for life, allowing him two hundred florins [20*l.*] yearly,
which would support him comfortably. I added that if he
thought of accepting this offer, he had better settle his
affairs as quickly as possible, and betake himself to the
place which the bearer of the letter would show him.

"The poor man was, as may well be supposed, in a
great fright, and accepted the offer ; but as he was about
to return to the Tower to settle matters and get his wife
away, a mate of his met him, and said, 'Be off with you,

as quick as you can, for your prisoners have escaped, and Master Lieutenant is looking for you everywhere. Woe to you if he finds you!' So returning all in a tremble to the bearer of the letter, he besought him for the love of God to take him at once to where the horse was waiting for him. He took him, therefore, and handed him over to Richard Fulwood, who was to be his guide. Fulwood took him to the house of a friend of mine residing at the distance of a hundred miles from London, to whom I had written, asking him, if such a person should come, to take him in and provide for him : I warned him, however, not to put confidence in him, nor to acknowledge any acquaintance with me. I told him that Richard Fulwood would reimburse him for all the expenses, but that he must never listen to the man if at any time he began to talk about me or about himself.

"Everything was done as I had arranged ; my friend received no damage, and the gaoler remained there out of danger. After a year he went into another county, and becoming a Catholic, lived there comfortably for some five years with his family on the annuity which I sent him regularly according to promise. He died at the end of those five years, having been through that trouble rescued by God from the occasions of sin, and, as I hope brought to Heaven. I had frequently in the prison sounded him in matters of religion ; and though his reason was perfectly convinced, I was never able to move his will My temporal escape, then, I trust, was by the sweet disposition of God's merciful Providence the occasion of his eternal salvation.

"The Lieutenant of the Tower, when he could not find either his prisoners or their gaoler, hastened to the Lords of the Council with the letters which he had found. They wondered greatly that I should have been able to escape in such a way ; but one of the chief members of the Council, as I afterwards heard, said to a gentleman who was in attendance, that he was exceedingly glad I had got off. And when the Lieutenant demanded autho rity and assistance to search all London for me, and any suspected places in the neighbourhood, they all told him it would be of no use. 'You cannot hope to find him, said they; 'for if he had such determined friends as to accomplish what they have, depend upon it they will have made further arrangements, and provided horses and hiding-places to keep him quite out of your reach.' They made search, however, in one or two places, but no one of any mark was taken that I could ever hear of.

"For my part, I remained quietly with Father Garnet for a few days, both to recruit myself and to allow the talk about my escape to subside. Then my former hosts [the Wisemans], who had proved themselves such devoted friends, urged my return to them, first to their London house close to the Clink Prison, where they were as yet residing. So I went to them, and remained there in secrecy, admitting but very few visitors; nor did I ever leave the house except at night, a practice I always observed when in London, though at this time I did even this very sparingly, and visited only a few of my chief friends.

"At this time I also visited my house, which was then under the care of Mistress Line, afterwards martyred. Another future martyr was then residing there of whom I have previously spoken, namely, Mr. Robert Drury, priest. In this house about this time I received one who had been chaplain to the Earl of Essex in his expedition against the Spanish King, when he took Cadiz. He was an eloquent man and learned in languages, and when converted to the Catholic faith he had abandoned divers great preferments, nay, had likewise endured im- prisonment for his religion. Hearing that he had an opportunity of making his escape, I offered that he should come to my house. There I maintained him for two or three months, during which time I gave him the Spiritual Exercises. In the course of his retreat he came to the determination of offering himself to the Society : upon which I asked him to tell me candidly how he, who had been bred up in Calvin's bosom, as it were, had been accustomed to military life, and had learnt in heresy and had long been accustomed to prefer his own will to other people's, could bring himself to enter the Society, where he knew, or certainly should know, that the very opposite principles prevailed. To this he replied, ' There are three things in fact which have especially induced me to take this step. First, because I see that heretics and evil livers hold the Society in far greater detestation than they do any other religious order ; from which I judge that it has the Spirit of God in an especial degree, which the spirit of the devil cannot endure, and that it has been ordained by God to destroy heresy, and wage war against sin in general. Secondly, because all ecclesiastical dignities are excluded by its Constitutions, whence it follows that there is in it a greater certainty of a pure intention ; and as its more eminent members are not taken from it for the Episcopate, it is more likely to retain its first fervour and its high estimation for virtue and learning. Thirdly, because in it obedience is cultivated with particular care, a virtue for which I have the greatest veneration, not only on account of the excellent effects produced thereby in the soul, but also because all things must needs go on well in a body where the wills of the members are bound together, and all are directed by God.'

"These were his reasons ; so I sent him into Belgium, that he might be forwarded to Rome by Father Holt, giving him three hundred florins [30*l.*] for his expenses."

This chaplain to the Earl of Essex was evidently the well known William Alabaster, who apostatized after this was written. The Earl's chaplains on this expedition were Mr. Sharpe, Mr. Hopkins, Mr. Alabaster, and Mr.

Whalley.[1] In the examination of William Alabaster before Sir John Peyton and Attorney General Coke, he says, "After Gerard the priest escaped out of the Tower, I had conference with him, and received 30*l.* in Brussels by credit." [2]

"I gave the Spiritual Exercises also to some others in that house before I gave it up, among whom was a good and pious priest, named Woodward, who also found a vocation to the Society, and afterwards passed into Belgium with the intention of entering it ; but as there was a great want of English priests in the army at the time, he was appointed to that work, and died in it, greatly loved and reverenced by all.

"I did not, however, keep that house long after the recovery of my liberty, because it was now known to a large number of persons, and was frequented during my imprisonment by many more than I should have permitted if I had been free. My principal reason, however, for giving it up was because it was known to the person who had been the cause of my being sent to the Tower. He had indeed expressed his sorrow for his act, and had written to me to beg my pardon, which I freely gave him ; yet as he was released from prison soon after my escape, and I found that those among whom he had lived had no very good opinion of his character, I did not think it well that a thing involving the safety of many should remain within his knowledge. Mistress Line, also, a woman of singular prudence and virtue, was of the same mind. So I determined to make other arrangements as soon as possible.

"Now a little before this, had begun the movement of opposition against the Archpriest. Hence it happened that some priests who were in the habit of resorting to

[1] Birch's *Elizabeth*, vol. ii. p. 17.
[2] P.R.O., *Domestic, Elizabeth*, vol. cclxxv. n. 32. See *Records*, vol. i. pp. 66, 622.

my house and residing there for a time, began to swerve somewhat from the more perfect course, and yet always expected to be received to board and lodging in a house where they knew Mistress Line resided. The consequence was that this asylum of mine, which should have been reserved for the use of myself and my chief friends, was the resort of a great number of persons, many of whom were no great friends of mine, nor too much to be trusted. These circumstances, no less than those I mentioned above, confirmed me in my resolution of making a total change in my arrangements.

"It seemed best, therefore, in order to remove all idea of so general a place of resort, that Mistress Line should lodge for a space by herself in a hired room of a private house; while I, who did not wish to be without a place in London where I could safely admit some of my principal friends, and perhaps house a priest from time to time, joined with a prudent and pious gentleman, who had a wife of similar character, in renting a large and spacious house between us. Half the house was to be for their use, and the other half for mine, in which I had a fair chapel well provided and ornamented. Hither I resorted when I came to London, and here also I sent from time to time those I would, paying a certain sum for their board. In this way I expended scarce half the amount I did formerly under the other arrangement, when I was obliged to maintain a household whether there were any guests in the house or not; though indeed it was seldom that the house was empty of guests.

"I made this new provision for my own and my friends' accommodation just in good time; for most certainly had I remained in my former house I should have been taken again. The thing happened in this wise. The priest[1]

---

[1] Of Atkinson our latest notices are in letters of Father Richard Blount to Father Persons. One is dated May 5, 1602. "Atkinson the apostate was this day twice taken by the constables for a rogue to be sent into Flanders

who, as I have related, got me promoted from a more
obscure prison to a nobler one, began to importune me
with continual letters that I would grant him an interview.
Partly by delaying to answer him, partly by excusing
myself on the score of occupation, I put him off for about
half a year. At length he urged his request very pressingly, and complained to me by letter that I showed
contempt of him. I sent him no answer, but on a convenient occasion, knowing where he lodged, I despatched
a friend to him to tell him that if he wished to see me,
he must come at once with the messenger. I warned the
messenger, however, not to permit any delay, nor to allow
him to write anything nor address any one on the way
if he wished to have an interview with me. I arranged,
moreover, that he should be brought not to any house,
but to a certain field near one of the Inns of Court, which
was a common promenade, and that the messenger should
walk there alone with him till I came. It was at night,
and there was a bright moon. I came there with a couple
of friends, in case any attempt should be made against me,
and making a half circuit outside, entered the field near
the house of a Catholic which adjoined it; and our good
friend catching first sight of me near this house, thought
perhaps that I came out of it, and in fact the Archpriest
was lodging in it at the time. However that may be, I

---

with other soldiers, which are now pressing in all haste, but was still discharged by the Chief Justice; and now the third time is apprehended by
warrant from the same Chief Justice and lieth loaded with irons in the dungeon
at Newgate." In another letter dated December 7, 1606, Father Blount says,
"These naughty priests afflict us much, for besides Skydmore, the Bishop of
Canterbury's man, Rowse, Atkinson, Graverer and other relapsed, which
openly profess to betray their brethren, others are no less dangerous which
persuade a lawfulness of going to sermons and to service." This Atkinson
was the cause of the death of at least one martyr. Sir Robert Cecil endorsed
the letter quoted in a former note "Atkinson's letter, the priest that discovered
Tychburn and was brought me by Mr. Fowler." Thomas Tichbourne suffered
for his priesthood at Tyburn, April 20, 1602. Bishop Challoner says 1601,
but the error has been obligingly pointed out to us by Canon Toole of Manchester.

U

found him there walking and waiting for me, and when I had heard all he had to say, I saw there was nothing which he had not already said in his letters, and to which he had not had my answer. My suspicion was therefore increased, and certainly not without reason. For within a day or two that corner house near which he saw me enter the field, and my old house which I had lately left (though he knew not I had left it), were both of them surrounded and strictly searched on the same night and at the same hour. The Archpriest was all but caught in the one ; he had just time to get into a hiding-place, and so escaped. The search lasted two whole days in the other house, which the priest knew me to have occupied at one time. The Lieutenant of the Tower and the Knight-Marshal conducted the searches in person, a task they never undertake unless one of their prisoners has escaped. From these circumstances it is sufficiently clear, both whom they were in search of, and from whom they got their information."

The Lieutenant of the Tower was no doubt in search of Father Gerard, but the Knight-Marshal was anxious to find the Archpriest. In a letter[1] from John Chamberlain to Dudley Carleton, dated January 17, 159⅘, which date will give us a clue to the time when these searches took place, the writer says, "The Queen is very angry with Sir Thomas Gerard for the escape of one Blackwell, an archpriest, out of the Marshalsea." Queen Elizabeth's Knight-Marshal[2] was Sir Thomas Gerard, who has been already mentioned as created by King James Lord Gerard of Gerard's Bromley.

---

[1] P.R.O., *Domestic, Elizabeth*, vol. cclxx. n. 16.

[2] The Knight-Marshal had jurisdiction within the precincts of the Court, that is within twelve miles from the lodging of the Sovereign, even on a progress. The Marshalsea was the prison originally attached to the King's house, and at first was intended only for the committal of persons accused of offences within the jurisdiction of the Knight-Marshal. It stood in High-street, Southwark, on the south side, between King-street and Mermaid-court, over against Union-street. Cunningham's *Handbook of London*, p. 316.

The following description[1] of Blackwell the Archpriest was given about this time. " The Archpriest is of comely stature, not very low, grey-haired, and about the age of 58 or 60. His beard grey, and on his upper lip a red spot of hair differing in colour from grey. He is lean-faced, a little hollow-eyed, fair, and well-spoken."

Perhaps the very search for him mentioned by Father Gerard is that which is thus related in the Life[2] of Anne Countess of Arundel. " How willing and desirous she was to have helped any of the Clergy on just occasions is manifest by what she did for the delivery of Mr. Blackwell the first archpriest. For he being forced for his own and the gentlewoman's security he lived with, to hide himself in a secret place of the house when search was made after [him] by the heretics, and being in great danger of being taken or famished by reason that all the Catholics of the house were carried away to prison, and heretic watchmen put into the house to keep it and hinder any from helping him, she, having notice of his distress, dealt so with the officer who had the principal charge of that business, that after three days he was content two of her servants should come to that house at the time when the guard was changed, take Mr. Blackwell out of the hiding-place and convey him away, as they speedily did, bringing him betwixt them, he not being able to go alone, to their lady's house, where after some days for refreshing he had stayed, she sent him safe to the place he desired to go. She was so well pleased with the officer who permitted his escape, that besides a good sum of money given at that time, she sent him every year as long as he lived a venison pasty to make merry with his friends at Christmas."

Father Gerard resumes, " But when they found me not

---

[1] P.R.O., *Domestic, Elizabeth*, vol. cclxi. n. 97.
[2] *The Lives of Philip Howard, Earl of Arundel, and of Anne Dacres, his wife*, p. 216.

(nor indeed did they find the priest who was then in the house living with a Catholic to whom I had let it), they sent pursuivants on the next day to the house of my host, who had by this time returned to his country seat [at Braddocks], but by God's mercy they did not find him there either. It was well, therefore, that I acted cautiously with the above-mentioned priest, and also that I had so opportunely changed my residence in London."

About this time Father General thought of sending Father Gerard out of England, evidently from fear lest, owing to his zeal, he should be recaptured and be still more hardly dealt with, for on March 31, 1598, Father Garnet wrote[1] to Rome, probably to Father Persons: "Father Gerard is much dismayed this day when I wrote to him to prepare himself to go. He came to me of purpose. Indeed he is very profitable to me, and his going would be wondered at. I hope he will walk warily enough. . . . You know my mind ; if you think it good, I desire his stay. All the rest are well."

"I saw also," says Father Gerard himself, "that it would soon be necessary for me to give up my present residence in the country, and betake myself elsewhere ; otherwise those good and faithful friends of mine [the Wisemans] would always be suffering some annoyance for my sake. I proposed the matter, therefore, to them, but they refused to listen to me in this point, though in all other things most compliant. But I thought more of their peace than of their wishes, however pious these wishes were ; and therefore I laid the matter before my Superior, who approved my views. So I obtained from Father Garnet another of ours, a pious and learned man whom I had known at Rome, and who at present was companion to Father Oldcorne of blessed memory : this was Father Richard Banks, now professed of four vows. I took him to live with me for a time, that I might by degrees intro-

[1] Stonyhurst MSS., Father Grene's *Collectan. P.*, vol. ii. p. 551.

duce him into the family in my place ; and in the meantime I made more frequent excursions than usual."

And thus we have, in the list of Jesuits[1] with which
some well informed spy furnished the Earl of Salisbury
in 1601 or 1602, " Mr. Bankes, with Mr. Wiseman, of
Brodocke, in Essex." The mention of Father Gerard in
the same list is, " John Gerard with Mrs. Vaux and young
Mr. Hastings."

---

[1] *Troubles*, First Series, p. 191.

CHAPTER XXIII.

ELIZABETH VAUX.

1598.

"IN one of these excursions I visited a noble family, by whom I had long been invited and often expected, but I had never yet been able to visit them on account of my pressing occupations. Here I found the lady of the house, a widow, very pious and devout, but at this present overwhelmed with grief at the loss of her husband. She had indeed been so affected by this loss that for a whole year she scarce stirred out of her chamber, and for the next three years which had intervened before my visit, had never brought herself to go to that part of the mansion in which her husband had died. To this grief and trouble were added certain anxieties about the bringing up of her son, who was yet a child under his mother's care. He was one of the first barons of the realm ; but his parents had suffered so much for the faith, and had mortgaged so much of their property to meet the constant exactions of an heretical government, that the remaining income was scarcely sufficient for their proper maintenance. But a wise woman builds up a house and is proved in it."

This lady was Elizabeth, daughter of Sir John Roper, who was raised to the peerage in 1616 as Lord Teynham. In 1590[1] she married George, the second son of William, Lord Vaux of Harrowden, but her husband died in 1594, during the lifetime of his father. When in the following year her father-in-law also died, she was left in charge of

[1] P.R.O., *Domestic, Elizabeth*, vol. ccxxxiii. n. 3.

her infant son Edward, fourth Baron Vaux of Harrowden. The family was conspicuous for its Catholicity, and suffered accordingly. William Lord Vaux wrote[1] to Lord Burghley, February 18, 1592, signing himself, "infortunatest peer of Parliament for poverty that ever was, W. Harowden;" and in the letter he says, "My parliament robes are at pawn to a citizen, where I have offered large interest (unable to disburse the principal) to borrow them for some few days, also offering my bond with surety to redeliver them, nevertheless I cannot obtain them."

William Lord Vaux had three sons, Henry, George, and Ambrose. The eldest, Henry, was one of that zealous band of young Catholic gentlemen who received Fathers Campion and Persons on their arrival in England in 1580. It is he who is meant, apparently, and who is named with Father Gerard, in the list[2] of "Persons to be sought after. August 9, 1586. The son of Sir Thomas Gerard. The Lord Vaux his son." It is not known when he died, but Father Persons, in his MS. Life of Campion,[3] written in 1594, thus speaks of him. "That blessed gentleman and saint, Mr. Henry Vaux, whose life was a rare mirror of religion and holiness unto all that knew him and conversed with him. He died most sweetly and comfortably in England, having resigned long before his death, and in his perfect health, his inheritance to the Barony to his younger brother, reserving only a small annuity to himself whereby to live in study and prayer all the days of his life without marrying as he full[y] resolved to do : and in like manner died his brother-in-law Mr. Brooks, son and heir to his father, and a great admirer and follower of Mr. Henry Vaux his virtues, as he might in the state of wedlock wherein he was."[4]

[1] Ellis' *Original Letters*, 3rd series, vol. iv. p. 109.
[2] Brit. Mus. *Harleian MSS.* 360, f. 8.
[3] Stonyhurst MSS. Father Grene's *Collectan. P.* f. 126.
[4] "Ad hunc Henricum videtur scripta prima epistola Campiani in edit. Antwerp. 1631." *Marginal note* by Father Grene, *Collectan. P.* f. 151.

Ambrose, the third son, was a Knight of the Holy
Sepulchre.   John Withie[1] in 1635 calls him, in error,
Prior of St. John of Jerusalem.   He did not belong to the
Order of Malta.   The account of his knighthood is given
in the MS. Chronicle of St. Monica's Convent at Louvain.
After saying that Anthony Copley, the third son of Sir
Thomas Copley, was banished with Sir Griffin Markham,
it continues, " he gave himself after his coming on this side
the seas to devotion, and took a voyage to the Holy
Land together with Mr. Ambrose Vaux, and coming to
Jerusalem, they were both knighted at our Lord's
Sepulchre; as the manner is that when such pilgrims
there as can show sufficient proofs to be of noble
extraction and capable of knighthood, if they will undertake to observe the points there proposed, for to defend
the honour of God in the manner set down, the Guardian
of the Franciscan Convent there dubbeth them Knights.
After they had performed their devotions, visiting the
holy places, in their return home he died by the way,
and Sir Ambrose Vaux coming home brought news of
his death."   In the Pilgrim-book of the English College
at Rome[2] a visit of his on the 12th of August, 1609, is
recorded.

Anne Vaux and Eleanor, the widow of Edward
Brooksby, or Brooks, as Father Persons calls him, of
whom such frequent mention is made as Father Garnet's
hostesses, were half sisters of George Vaux.   Their mother,
William Lord Vaux's first wife, was Elizabeth, daughter
of John Beaumont of Gracedieu in Leicestershire, while
the mother of George Vaux was Mary, sister of Sir
Thomas Tresham, of Rushton in Northamptonshire.   The

---

[1] Brit. Mus. *Harleian MS.* 1073.   *Book of Arms* by John Withie, who is
also in error when he says that Henry Vaux " died a prisoner in the Tower of
London."

[2] " Die 12 Augusti [1609] exceptus fuit Dominus Ambrosius Vaux generosus
et nobilis, quem famulus suus post tres dies assequutus pariter exceptus fuit
Joannes.

Catholicity of the whole family, and of all those connected with it, was undoubted, excepting it would seem George Vaux, who "became a Catholic before his death." Before going with Father Gerard to Mrs. Vaux's house, we may avail ourselves of the insight we obtain into her father-in-law's London house from the confession[1] of a spy called Ralph Myller, dated October 9, 1584. "This examinate did afterwards meet one Robert Brown, who hath an uncle a priest with the Lord Vaux, who is a little man with white head, and a little brown hair on his face, goeth in an ash-coloured doublet coat and a gown faced with cony, and he was made priest long sithence at Cambray, as this examinate thinketh. This examinate spoke with the Lord Vaux and with his lady at Hackney, after that his son Mr. George and the said Robert Browne had told him that this examinate was a tailor of Rheims; and on Sunday was fortnight, this examinate did hear mass there, whereat were present about eighteen persons, being my lord's household, and the priest last before-named said the mass. The said priest lieth in a chamber beyond the hall, on the left hand [of] the stair that leadeth to the chambers, and the mass is said in the chapel, being right over the port entering into the hall; and the way to it is up the stair aforesaid, on the left hand, at the further end of the gallery; and there is a very fair crucifix of silver."

It may seem rash with so few data as those given by Father Gerard to name the Jesuit Father who was with Mrs. Vaux before his arrival; but as there were but fifteen Fathers in England at the time,[2] and we know the whereabouts of them all, it may perhaps be allowable to conjecture that it was Father Richard Cowling, a Yorkshireman,[3] who came on the English mission in April 1596. Lord Salisbury's "Note of Jesuits that lurk

---

[1] P.R.O., *Domestic, Elizabeth,* vol. clxxiii. n. 64.
[2] *Troubles,* 1st series, p. 191.   [3] *Ibid.* 3rd series, p. 280.

in England" in 1601-2 assigns him to Mr. Bentley's in Northamptonshire.

Father Gerard says, "I found residing with this family one of our Fathers, a learned man and a good preacher: he had been a year in the house, but some of the household were prejudiced against him. The mistress, however, always showed him the utmost reverence, and was assiduous in approaching the Sacraments. On my arrival this good widow seemed to see her wishes fulfilled, and not only welcomed me most charitably, but appeared so changed from grief to joy, that some of her household represented to me that if I would come there oftener, still more if I could reside there permanently, they were assured she would lay aside that long-continued grief, and that both she herself and her affairs would soon be in a better condition. This I think they had from the mistress herself. For she soon took an opportunity of praising the happiness of my hosts, of whom she had heard much, not only about their domestic chapel and altar furniture, but also about their virtue and patience, which had been so tried in the fire of persecution. She added that she marvelled not that they went forward so steadfastly since they had such a guide; she also would be able to do the like, had she but like opportunity; then all her affairs would go well.

"I saw how much she was deceived in me, and how she thought of me above what was in me; I answered her therefore that she had even more and greater helps than they had, which was indeed but the truth. She rejoined that she had indeed a good and pious director whom she both much reverenced and loved; but that as he had never lived in the world, having always been with those who gave themselves to study, he was not so well able to judge what was best to be done in worldly affairs, and consequently some in the house were opposed to him.

"'These persons,' said I, 'are evidently not possessed

of the true spirit, which supposes obedience and subordination : and they would treat me in like fashion were I living in the house.'

"'They should soon quit it then,' she replied, 'even if they were ten times as necessary to me as they are.' In fact they had the principal charge of the household under their mistress.

"She besought me to make trial of her, whether or no she would be obedient in all that I might judge to be for the greater glory of God. I felt it impossible to reject such an offer from such a person, made as it was at a time when good reasons made it expedient that I should change my residence. Nay, it seemed to me clearer than noon-day that God's good providence had arranged this, as from the first day of my arrival in England it had directed me hither and thither, but always changing my position for the better, continually affording me additional means of becoming acquainted with greater numbers of persons, and those of higher rank, and of strengthening and guiding them in His service. I replied to her therefore, that I returned her my best thanks, and that I would mention her pious wish to my Superior : I added that there was one thing that inclined me to listen to her proposal, and this was that whereas elsewhere I had only a secular priest as companion, in her house I should have a member of the same Society with myself, and a person whom I much loved.

"On my return to London therefore I proposed the matter to Father Garnet, who was much rejoiced at the offer, knowing the place to be one where much good might be done both directly and indirectly. He said too that the offer had occurred most opportunely, for that there were some Catholics in another county more to the north, where there was no priest of the Society, who had been long petitioning for this very father, at present stationed at that house, and who would much rejoice at the prospect of

having him among them. To this I urged that the place
was large enough for two, and that I very much desired to
have a companion of the Society with me. Father Garnet,
however, had already determined to place another Father
in that residence, on account of the opposition of which I
have spoken ; and was therefore unwilling to let me have
him for companion. I then requested that he would
assign me Father John Percy, with whom I had become
acquainted during my imprisonment, not indeed personally but by frequent interchange of letters. This father
had been brought prisoner from Flanders to Holland,[1]
where he was recognized and tortured ; he was afterwards
thrown into the foul gaol of Bridewell, and after remaining
there some time made a shift to escape from a window
with another priest, letting himself down with a rope.
Mistress Line made him welcome in my house, where he
tarried for a time ; but soon after went down into the
county of York, and dwelt there with a pious Catholic.
In this part he made himself so dear to every one, that

[1] "He was sent to Tournay for his noviceship in 1594, and towards the
end of the second year over application had so injured his head that he had to
be forbidden to use any kind of prayer. Sent to recruit in his native air, he
passed through Holland on his way to England. At Flushing he was taken
by some English soldiers. The letter he was carrying showing who he was,
they threatened him with torture unless he would say who had brought him
over from Rotterdam. He was ready to confess anything about himself, but
he would say nothing of any one else ; so, instead of offering, as he had hoped
to do that day, the Sacrifice of the Body of Christ, he offered that of his own,
to undergo anything rather than betray others. They hung him up by the
hands to a pulley, and then tortured him by twisting a sailor's cord round his
head. During the torture he fixed his mind on the eternity of either pain or
joy, and uttered nothing but "O eternity !" The harm the soldiers tried to
do him turned out a remedy, for the head-ache and singing in the head, from
which he had suffered in the noviceship, diminished from that time and
gradually ceased. He was taken to London in custody and committed to
Bridewell, where his cell was an utterly unfurnished turret. His bed was the
brick floor and a little straw, till he was helped by the care and charity of his
Catholic fellow prisoners, and of our Father Gerard. The latter, who was in
the Clink, kept up a secret correspondence with him, and came to his help
both with his advice and money. After about seven months he succeeded in
making his escape through the tiling, together with two other priests and seven
laymen." Father More, *Historia Provinciæ*, l. viii. c. 23.

though I had Father Garnet's consent, it was a full year before I could get him away from them.

"Since now to the desire of this noble widow was added the approval of Father Garnet, I so settled my affairs as to provide amply for the security and advantage of my former hosts [the Wisemans]. For I left with them Father Banks, a most superior man in every respect : and although at first my old friends did not value him so much, yet as they became better acquainted they found that the good account I had given them was no more than the truth, and soon came to esteem him as a father. I often afterwards visited their house, where I had found so great faith and piety.

"When I was domiciled in my new residence, I began by degrees to wean my hostess' mind from that excessive grief ; showing how that we ought to mourn moderately only over our dead, and not to grieve like those who have no hope. I added that as her husband had become a Catholic before his death, one little prayer would do him more good than many tears : that our tears should be reserved for our own and others' sins, for our own souls stood in need of floods of that cleansing water, and it was to the concerns of our own souls that all our thoughts and labours should be turned. I then taught her the use of meditation, finding her quite capable of profiting by it, for her mental powers were of a very high order. I thus gradually brought her first to change that old style of grief for a more worthy one ; then to give eternal concerns the preference over worldly matters ; and to consider how she might transform her life, which before was good and holy, into better and holier, by endeavouring as much as she could to imitate the life of our Lord and of His saints.

"In the first place therefore she resolved to lead an unmarried life ; secondly to aim at poverty in this sense, that all her actual fortune, and all that she might ever have, should be devoted to the service of God and His

ministers, while she herself should be but their servant to
provide them with what was necessary : lastly, she gave
herself above all to obedience, and determined to reduce
her love of it to practice no less perfectly than if she had
taken a vow : nay, it was her only trouble that it was
forbidden to priests of our Society to receive such vows.
In a word, it was her fixed resolve to imitate as closely as
possible the life of Martha and the other holy women who
followed our Lord, and ministered to Him and His
Apostles. Consequently she was ready to set up her residence wherever I judged it best for our purposes, whether
at London or in the most remote part of the island, as she
often protested to me. I considered however that though
a residence in or near London would be better for the
gaining of souls, yet that it was not at present very safe
for me ; nor indeed could she remain there in private, since
she was well known for a Catholic, and the Lords of the
Council demanded from her frequent accounts of her son,
the Baron, where and how he was educated. Moreover, as
she had the management of her son's estate while he was a
minor, stewards and bailiffs, and other such persons must
have constant communication with her ; so that it was
quite out of the question her living near London under an
assumed name ; yet this was absolutely necessary if a
person wished to carry on the good work in that neighbourhood. It was thus those ladies did with whom Father
Garnet lived so long, who were in fact sisters of this lady's
deceased husband, one unmarried, the other a widow. I
saw therefore no fitter place for her to fix her residence
than where she was among her own people, where she had
the chief people of the county connected with her and her
son, either by blood or friendship.

"The only difficulty which remained was about the
exact spot. The house in which she was actually !iving
was not only old, but antiquated. It had been the residence of her husband's father, who had married a wife

who was a better hand at spending than at gathering, and consequently the house was very poorly appointed for a family of their dignity. There was another and a larger house of theirs at a distance of about three miles, which had been the old family seat. This had also been neglected, so that it was in some part quite ruinous, and not fit for our purpose, namely, to receive the Catholic gentry who might come to visit me. In addition to this, it was not well adapted for defence against any sudden intrusions of the heretics, and consequently we should not be able to be as free there as my hostess wished. Her desire was to have a house where we might as nearly as possible conform ourselves to the manner of life followed in our colleges : and this in the end she brought about.

"She sought everywhere for such a house, and we looked at many houses in the country : but something or other was always wanting to her wishes. At last we found a house which had been built by the late Chancellor of England, who had died childless,[1] and was now to be let for a term of years. It was truly a princely place, large and well-built, surrounded by gardens and orchards, and so far removed from other houses that no one could notice our coming in or going out. This house she took on payment of fifteen thousand florins [1,500*l.*], and began to fit it up for our accommodation. She wished to finish the alterations before we removed thither; but man proposes, and God disposes as He wills, though always for the best, and for the true good of His elect."

[1] Sir Christopher Hatton, who died childless, November 21, 1591, had built a country house at Stoke Pogis, Bucks. Campbell's *Lives of the Chancellors*, 3rd edit. vol. ii. p. 180.

CHAPTER XXIV.

BROTHER JOHN LILLY.

1599.

"WHEN I came to this lady's house, she had a great number of servants, some heretics, others indeed Catholics, but allowing themselves too much liberty. By degrees we got things into better order: some I made Catholics of, others through public and private exhortations became by the grace of God more fervent; in some cases where there did not appear any hope of amendment, I procured their dismissal, and among these was he who had chiefly opposed the former priest of whom I spoke. There was another also whom we could not correct as soon as we wished, and who brought great trouble on us. For on one occasion when we were in London, either from thoughtlessness or loquacity, or because the yoke of a stricter discipline, now begun in the family, sat uneasily upon him, he said to a false brother, that I had lately come to live at his lady's house, and had carried on such doings there; and that I was then at London at such a house, naming the house of which I rented half, as I have before said; he told him also that he had gone to that house with his lady, at a time when she and I were in town on business connected with her son. My hostess had now returned into the country with this servant, leaving me for a short time in town. But the man had left this tale behind him, which soon came to the ears of the Council, how that I had my residence with such a lady, and was at this moment at such a house in London. They instantly therefore commissioned two justices of the peace to search the house.

" I, who had no inkling of such a danger, had remained in town for certain business, and was giving a Retreat to three gentlemen in the house before mentioned. One of these three gentlemen was Master Roger Lee, now Minister in the English College of St. Omers.[1] He was a gentleman of good family, and of so noble a character and such winning manners that he was a universal favourite, especially with the nobility, in whose company he constantly was, being greatly given to hunting, hawking, and all other noble sports. He was indeed excellent at everything, but he was withal a Catholic, and so bent on the study of virtue that he was meditating a retreat from the world, and a more immediate following of Christ. He used frequently to visit me when I was in the Clink prison, and I clearly saw that he was called to greater things than catching birds of the air ; and that he was meant rather to be a catcher of men. I had now therefore fixed a time with this gentleman and good friend of mine, in which he should seek out by means of the Spiritual Exercises the strait path that leads to life, under the guidance of Him Who is Himself the Way and the Life.

" But while he and the others were engaged privately in their chambers in the study of this heroic philosophy, suddenly the storm burst upon us. I too, in fact, after finishing my business in town, had taken the opportunity of a little quiet to begin my own retreat, giving out that I had returned into the country. I was now in the fourth day of the retreat, when about three o'clock in the afternoon John Lilly hurried up to my room and without knocking entered with his sword drawn.

" Surprised at this sudden intrusion, I asked what was the matter.

---

[1] Roger Lee entered the Noviciate of St. Andrew's at Rome October 27, 1600, and died at Dunkirk in 1615, æt. 47. More's *Hist. Prov.* p. 266.

V

"'It is a matter of searching the house,' he replied.

"'What house?'

"'This very house; and they are in it already!'

"In fact they had been cunning enough to knock gently, as friends were wont to do; and the servant opened readily to them, without the least suspicion until he saw them rush in and scatter themselves in all directions.

"While John was telling me this, up came the searching party, together with the mistress of the house, to the very room in which we were. Now just opposite to my room was the chapel, so that from the passage the door of the chapel opened on the one hand, and that of my room on the other. The magistrates then, seeing the door of the chapel open, went in, and found there an altar richly adorned, and the priestly vestments laid out close by, so handsome as to cause expressions of admiration from the heretics themselves. In the meanwhile I in the room opposite, was quite at my wit's ends what to do; for there was no hiding-place in the room, nor any means of exit except by the open passage where the enemy were. However, I changed the cassock which I was wearing for a secular coat, but my books and manuscript meditations which I had there in considerable quantities I was quite unable to conceal.

"We stood there with our ears close to the chink of the door, listening to catch what they said: and I heard one exclaim from the chapel; 'Good God! what have we found here! I had no thoughts of coming to this house to-day!' From this I concluded that it was a mere chance search, and that they had no special warrant. Probably therefore, I thought, they had but few men with them. So we began to consult together whether it were not better to rush out with drawn swords, seize the keys from the searching party, and so escape; for we should have Master Lee and the master of the house to help us, besides two or three men-servants. Moreover, I considered that if we should be taken in the house the master would certainly be visited with a far greater punishment than what the law prescribes for resistance to a magistrate's search.

"While we were thus deliberating, the searchers came to the door of my room and knocked. We made no answer, but pressed the latch hard down, for the door had no bolt or lock. As they continued knocking, the mistress of the house said, 'Perhaps the man-servant who sleeps in that room may have taken away the key. I will go and look for him.'

"'No, no;' said they, 'you go nowhere without us; or you will be hiding away something.'

"And so they went with her, not staying to examine whether the door had a lock or not. Thus did God blind the eyes of the Assyrians that they should not find the place, nor the means of hurting His servants, nor know where they were going.

"When they had got below stairs, the mistress of the house, who had great presence of mind, took them into a room in which some ladies were, viz., the sister[1] of my hostess in the country, and Mistress Line; and while the magistrates were questioning these ladies she ran up to us saying, 'Quick! quick! get into the hiding-place!' She had scarce said this and run down again, before the searchers had missed her and were for remounting the stairs. But she stood in their way on the bottom step, so that they immediately suspected what the case was, and were eager to get past. This, however, they could not do without laying forcible hands on the lady, a thing which as gentlemen they shrank from doing. One of them, however, as she stood there purposely occupying the whole width of the stair-way, thrust his head past her, in hopes of seeing what was going on above stairs. And indeed he almost caught sight of me as I passed along to the

---

[1] Elizabeth Vaux's sister was Mary Lady Lovel, the foundress of the English Teresian Convent at Antwerp. *Supra*, p. 63.

hiding-place. For as soon as I heard the lady's words of warning, I opened the door, and with the least possible noise mounted from a stool to the hiding-place, which was arranged in a secret gable of the roof. When I had myself mounted, I bade John Lilly come up also : but he more careful of me than of himself, refused to follow me, saying : 'No, Father; I shall not come. There must be some one to own the books and papers in your room ; otherwise, upon finding them, they will never rest till they have found you too.'

"So spoke this truly faithful and prudent servant, so full of charity as to offer his life for his friend. There was no time for further words. I acquiesced reluctantly, and closed the small trap-door by which I had entered ; but I could not open the door of the inner hiding-place, so that I should infallibly have been taken if they had not found John Lilly, and mistaking him for a priest ceased from any further search. For this was what happened— God so disposing it, and John's prudence and intrepidity helping thereto.

"For scarcely had he removed the stool by which I mounted, and had gone back to the room and shut the door, when the two chiefs of the searching party again came up stairs, and knocked violently at the door, ready to break it open if the key were not found. Then the intrepid soldier of Christ threw open the door and presented himself undaunted to the persecutors.

"'Who are you?' they asked.

"'A man, as you see:' he replied.

"'But what are you? Are you a priest?'

"'I do not say I am a priest,' replied John ; 'that is for you to prove. But I am a Catholic certainly.'

"Then they found there on the table all my meditations, my breviary, and many Catholic books, and what grieved me most of all to lose, my manuscript sermons and notes for sermons, which I had been writing or compiling for the last ten years, and which I made more account of perhaps than they did of all their money. After examining all these, they asked whose they were.

"'They are mine;' said John.

"'Then there can be no doubt you are a priest. And this cassock—whose is this?'

"'That is a dressing-gown, to be used for convenience now and then.'

"Convinced now they had caught a priest, they carefully locked up all the books and writings in a box, to be taken away with them; then they locked the chapel-door, and put their seal upon it; and taking John by the arm, they led him down stairs, and delivered him into the custody of their officers. Now when he entered with his captors into the room where the ladies were, he, who at other times was always wont to conduct himself with humility and stand uncovered in such company, now on the contrary after saluting them covered his head and sat down. Nay, assuming a sort of authority, he said to the magistrates: 'These are noble ladies; it is your duty to treat them with consideration. I do not indeed know them; but it is quite evident that they are entitled to the greatest respect.'

"I should have mentioned that there was a second priest in the house with me, Father Pollen,[1] an old man, who had quite lately made his noviceship at Rome. He luckily had a hiding-place in his room, and had got into it at the first alarm.

"The ladies therefore now perceiving that I was safe, and that the other priest had also escaped, and seeing also John's assumed dignity, could scarce refrain from showing their joy. They made no account now

---

[1] Father Tesimond relates a search in Sir John Fortescue's house about two years earlier than this, in which also Father Joseph Pollen escaped capture. *Troubles*, First Series, p. 176. This Father was ordained priest at Cambray on Holy Saturday, March 29, 1578. *Ibid*. Third Series, p. 106.

of the loss of property, or the annoyance they should have to undergo from the suspicion of having had a priest in the house. They wondered indeed and rejoiced, and almost laughed to see John playing the priest; for so well did he do it as to deceive those deceivers, and divert them from any further seach.

"The magistrates who had searched the house took away John Lilly with them,[1] and the master of the house also with his two men-servants, under the idea that all his property would be confiscated for harbouring a priest. The ladies, however, represented that they had merely come to pay an after-dinner visit to the mistress of the house, without knowing anything about a priest being there; so they were let off on giving bail to appear when summoned. The same favour was ultimately shown to Master Roger Lee, though it was with greater difficulty the magistrates could be persuaded that he was only a visitor. At last then they departed well satisfied, and locked up their prisoners for the night to wait their morrow's examination.

"Immediately on their departure the mistress of the house and those other ladies came with great joy to give me notice; and we all joined in giving thanks to God Who had delivered us all from such imminent danger by the prudence and fidelity of one. Father Pollen and I removed that very night to another place, lest the searchers should find out their error and return.

"The next day I made a long journey to my hostess' house in the country, and caused much fear, and then much joy, as I related all that God had done for us. Then we all heartily commended John Lilly to God in

---

[1] In the Public Record Office there is a letter which helps us to the date of John Lilly's capture. It is dated July 22, 1599, and purports to be from Francis Cordale to his partner, Balthasar Gybels, at Antwerp. "I wrote to you of one Mr. Heywood's house searched and a man there taken. I have learned his name since to be John Lilly. He is sent to the Tower upon suspicion of helping Gerard the Jesuit out of the same place." *Domestic, Elizabeth,* vol. cclxxi. n. 107.

prayer. And indeed there was reason to do so. For the
magistrates, making full inquiries the next day, found that
John had been an apothecary in London for six or seven
years, and then had been imprisoned in the Clink for eight
or nine more, and that he had been the person who had
communicated with me in the Tower, for the gaoler's wife
after her husband's flight had confessed so much. They
saw therefore clearly that they had been tricked, and that
John was not a priest, but a priest's servant; and they
now began to have a shrewd suspicion, though rather too
late, that I had been hidden at the time in the same house
where they caught him, especially as they found so many
books and writings which they did not doubt were mine.
They sent therefore to search the house again, but they
found only an empty nest, for the birds were flown.

"John was carried to the Tower, and confined there in
chains. Then they examined him about my escape, and
about all the places he had been to with me since. He,
seeing that his dealings with the gaoler were already known
to them, and desirous (if God would grant him such a
favour) to lay down his life for Christ, freely confessed
that it was he who had compassed my deliverance, and
that he took great pleasure in the thought of having done
so; he added that he was in the mind to do the same
again, if occasion required, and opportunity offered. The
gaoler, however, he exonerated, and protested that he was
not privy to the escape. With regard to the places where
he had been with me, he answered (as he had often been
taught to do), that he would bring no one into trouble, and
that he would not name a single place, for to do so would
be a sin against charity and justice. Upon this they said
they would not press him any further in words, but would
convince him by deeds that he must tell them all they
wanted. John replied: 'It is a thing that, with the help
of God, I will never do. You have me in your power; do
what God permits you.'

"Then they took him to the torture-chamber, and hung him in the way I have before described, and tortured him cruelly for the space of three hours. But nothing could they wring from him that they could use either against me or against others; so that from that time they gave up all hope of obtaining anything from him either by force or fear. Consequently they tortured him no more, but kept him in the closest custody for about four months to try and tire him into compliance. Failing also in this, and seeing that their pains availed them nothing, they sent him to another prison [Newgate], where prisoners are usually sent who are awaiting execution; and probably it was their intention to deal that way with him, but God otherwise determined. For after a long detention here, and having been allowed a little communication with other Catholic prisoners, he was asked by a certain priest to assist him in making his escape. Turning his attention therefore to the matter, he found a way by which he delivered both the priest and himself from captivity.

"I ought not, however, to omit an incident[1] that happened during his detention in the Tower, since it is in such things that the dealings of God's Providence are often to be very plainly recognized. While he was under examination about me and others of the Society, Wade, who was at that time the chief persecutor, asked him if he knew Garnet. John said he did not.

"'No?' said Wade, with a sour smile; 'and you don't know his house in the Spital[2] either, I dare say! I don't mind letting you know,' he continued, 'now that I have you safe, that I am acquainted with his residence, and that we are sure of having him here in a day or two to keep you

[1] This story is also told by Father Tesimond. *Troubles*, First Series, p. 179.
[2] Tali loco qui vocatur *Spitell*. M.S. Spitalfields, a district without Bishopgate, once belonging to the Priory and Hospital of St. Mary Spital, founded in 1197, in the parish of St. Botolph. Cunningham's *Handbook of London*, p. 463.

company. For when he comes to London he puts up at that house, and then we shall catch him.'

"John knew well that the house named was Father Garnet's resort, and was in great distress to find that the secret had been betrayed to the enemy; and though kept as close as possible, yet he managed to get an opportunity of sending some little article *wrapped up in blank paper* to a friend in London. His friend on receiving it carefully smoothed out the paper and held it to the fire, knowing that John would be likely to communicate by the means of orange-juice if he had the opportunity: and there he found it written that this residence of Father Garnet's had been betrayed, and that Father Garnet must be warned of it. This was instantly done, and in this way the Father was saved, for otherwise he would assuredly, as Wade had said, have betaken himself to that house in a day or two. Now, however, he not only did not go, but took all his things away: so that when the house was searched a day or two later they found nothing. Had it not been for this providential warning from our greatest enemy, they would have found plenty: they would have found him, his books, altar-furniture, and other things of a similar nature. Father Garnet then escaped this time by John's good help, as I had done previously.

"After his escape John came to me; but though I desired much to keep him, it was out of the question, for he was now so marked a man that his presence would have been a continual danger for me and all my friends. For I was wont in the country to go openly to the houses of Catholic gentlemen, and it might well happen that John might come across persons that knew him, and would know me through him. Whereas but very few of the enemy knew me, for I was always detained in close custody, and none but Catholics saw me in prison; nay, such Catholics only as I knew to be specially trustworthy. I had indeed been examined publicly in London several times, but the persons concerned in the examinations very seldom left town; and if they had done so I should have been warned of it instantly, and should have taken good care never to trust myself in their neighbourhood. So I put John with Father Garnet, to stay in quiet hiding for a time; and when opportunity offered, sent him over to Father Persons, that he might obtain, what he had long hoped for, admission into the Society. He was admitted at Rome, and lived there six or seven years as a lay-brother, much esteemed I believe by everybody. I can on my part testify about him to the greater glory of God,—and that the more allowably because I believe he has died in England before this present writing, whither he returned with a consumption on him,—I can, I say, testify that for nearly six years that he was with me in England, and had his hands full of business for me, though he had to do with all sorts of men in all sorts of places (for while I was engaged upstairs with the gentry or nobility, he was associating downstairs with the servants, often enough very indifferent characters), yet the whole of this time he so guarded his heart and his soul that I never found him to have been even in danger of mortal sin; nay, most constantly in his confessions, unless he had added some venial sins of his past life, I should not have had sufficient matter for the sacrament. Truly his was an innocent soul, and endowed also with great prudence and cleverness.

"But now that I have brought the history of John Lilly to its close, it is time to return to myself, who having just escaped one danger, had like to have fallen into a second and still greater one, had not God again interposed His hand."

John Lilly entered the Society at Rome on the 2nd of February, 1602,[1] in his 37th year. He there remained

---

[1] Bartoli, *Inghilterra*, p. 429.

for seven years and then had to leave Rome on account of his health. Father Persons in a letter[1] from Rome to Father Thomas Talbot, Master of Novices at St. John's, Louvain, dated May 16, 1609, says, "Brother John Lilly departed hence yesterday, May 15, together with Father Nelson, *alias* Neville, and George Dingley, all for your house, and Brother John cometh expressly for your companion and manuductor, and must not be diverted from that by any excuse, if he have his health; nor suffered to write anything of moment, at least for one year."

This note is valuable as throwing light on the date of Father Gerard's autobiography, which it shows to have been written not before the second half of the year 1609. Brother Lilly did not leave Rome till the middle of May, and it was then intended by Father Persons that he should stay at Louvain. He may have reached Louvain in June and have then been found to be so ill that it was considered advisable to try at once whether the air of England might not be beneficial. When Father Gerard wrote he had heard that Lilly had gone to England, but he had not heard certain news of his death; and he had also been informed that Brother Hugh Sheldon had succeeded him in his place with Father Persons at Rome. If, as seems most probable from his reckoning his money in florins, Father Gerard was himself at this time at Louvain, we see that his Autobiography might have been written during the second six months of 1609. That it was not written later is plain from the mention of Robert Drury's martyrdom, which took place on the 26th of February, 160\frac{8}{9}, and this Father Gerard has said[2] was "two years ago from this present writing."

[1] Stonyhurst MSS. *Angl. A.* vol. iii. n. 94; *Records,* vol. i. p. 455.
[2] *Supra,* p. 89.

CHAPTER XXV.

GREAT HARROWDEN.

1598, 1599.

"I MENTIONED just now that one of my hostess' servants told a friend of his, but an enemy of ours, that I habitually resided at his mistress' house, and that at that particular time I was in such a house in London. How this house was searched, and how they seized my companion and my manuscripts, but missed me, I have related. The Council therefore, now knowing my residence in the country, issued a commission to some justices of the peace in that county to search this lady's house for a priest. It had in fact begun to be talked of in the county that she had taken this grand house in order that she might harbour priests there in larger numbers and with greater freedom, because it was more private; and in this people were not far wrong.

"Now at this time, that is, soon after my return from London, we had driven over to the new house to make arrangements for our removal thither, and with the special object of determining where to construct hiding-places. To this end we had Little John [Brother Nicholas Owen] with us, whom I have before mentioned as very clever at constructing these places, and whom Father Garnet had lent to us for a time for this purpose. Having made all the necessary arrangements, we left Little John behind, and Hugh Sheldon also to help him, who is now at Rome with Father Persons in the room of John Lilly. These two, whom we had always found most faithful, were to construct the hiding-places, and to be the only ones beside ourselves to know anything about them. The rest of us however returned the same day to our hostess' old house, and by the advice of one of the servants, God so disposing it, we came back a different way, as being easier for the carriage. Had we returned by the way we went, the searchers would have come early to the house where we were, and most probably catching us entirely unprepared would have found what they came to seek. The fact was that the road by which we went to the new house ran through a town, where some of the enemy were on the watch and had seen us pass: but not seeing us return, they concluded that we were spending the night at the new house, and went there the first thing in the morning to search.

"But the house was so large, that although they had a numerous body of followers, they were not able to surround it entirely, nor to watch all the outlets so narrowly, but what Little John managed to make off safely. Hugh Sheldon they caught, but could get nothing out of him: so they sent him afterwards to prison at Wisbech, and from thence later to some other prison in company with many priests, and at last in the same good company into exile [in 1605].

"When however the justices found that they were wrong, and that the lady had returned home the previous day, they retraced their steps and came as fast as their horses could carry them to the old house. They arrived at our dinner-hour, and being admitted by the carelessness of the porter, got into the hall before we had any warning. Now as the lady of the house was a little indisposed that morning, we were going to take our dinner in my room, viz. Father Percy, myself, and Master Roger Lee, who had been so rudely interrupted before. So when I heard who had come, that they were in the great hall, and that his lordship himself, who was indeed but a boy at that time, could not prevent them from intruding into his room, though he was also unwell, I made a pretty shrewd guess what they had come about, and snatching up such things as wanted hiding I made the best of my way to the hiding-place, together with Father Percy and Master Roger Lee. For it would not do for this latter to have been found here, especially as he had already been found in the house in London where I was known to have been, and would therefore have given good reason to think that I was here also. But we had to pass by the door of the room in which the enemy were as yet waiting, and exclaiming that they would wait no longer. Nay, one of the pursuivants opened the door and looked out ; and some of the servants said afterwards that he must have seen me as I passed. But God certainly interposed ; for it was surely not to be expected from natural causes that men who had come eager to search the house at once, and were loudly declaring they would do so, should stay in a room where they were not locked in, just as long as was necessary for us to hide ourselves, and then come forth as if they had been let loose, intrude upon the lady of the house, and course through all the ·rooms like bloodhounds after their prey. I cannot but think that this was the finger of God, Who would not that the good intentions of this lady should be so soon frustrated, but rather wished by so evident a display of His providence to confirm her in her determinations, and preserve her for many more good works.

"The authorities searched the house thoroughly the whole day, but found nothing. At last they retired disappointed, and wrote to the Council what they had done. We soon discovered who had done the mischief (for he had not done it secretly) and discharged him, but without unkindness. I gave out also that I should quit the place altogether, and for a time we practised particular caution in all points.

"In consequence of this mishap it became impossible for us to remove to the new house. For those same justices, who were pestilent heretics, and several others in the same county, Puritans, declared they would never suffer her ladyship to live at peace if she came there, as her only object was to harbour priests. Being deterred therefore from that place, but not from her design, she set about fitting up her own present residence for the same purpose, and built us separate quarters close to the old chapel, which had been erected anciently by former barons of the family to hear mass in when the weather might make it unpleasant to go to the parish church. Here then she built a little wing of three stories for Father Percy and me. The place was exceedingly convenient, and so free from observation that from our rooms we could step out into the private garden, and thence through spacious walks into the fields, where we could mount our horses and ride whither we would.

"As we lived here safely and quietly, I frequently left Father Percy at home and made excursions to see if I could establish similar centres of operation among other families: and in this Father Roger Lee (to give him his present title) helped me not a little. He first took me to the house of a relation of his, who lived in princely splendour, and whose father was one of the Queen's Council. This young gentleman was a schismatic, that is, a Catholic by conviction, but conforming externally to the State religion; and there seemed no hope of getting him any further, for he contented himself with *velleities*, and was fearful of offending his father. His wife however, who was a heretic, had begun to listen with interest to Catholic doctrine, so that there was hope she might in time be brought into the Church. Their house was full of heretic servants, and there was a constant coming and going of heretic gentry either on business or on visit; it was therefore imperatively necessary that as I could only go there publicly I should well conceal my purpose.

"We paid a visit then to this house, and were made welcome, Master Lee for his own sake, as being much beloved, and I for his. On the first day I looked in vain for an opportunity of a conversation with the lady of the house, for there was always some one by. We were obliged to play at cards to pass the time, as those are wont to do who know not the eternal value of time, or at least care not for it. On the next day however, as the lady of the house stept aside once to the window to set her watch, I joined her there, and after talking a little about the watch, passed on to matters which I had more in view, saying I wished we took as much pains to set our souls in order as we did our watches. She looked up at me in pure surprise to hear such things from my lips ; and as I saw I might never get a better opportunity than the present I began to open a little further, and told her that I had come there with Master Lee specially for her sake, hearing from him that she took interest in matters of religion ; and that I was ready to explain the Catholic doctrine to her, and satisfy all the doubts she could possibly have : moreover, that I could point out the way to a height of virtue which she had hitherto never dreamt of, for that in heresy she could neither find that way, nor any who made account of it. She was struck with what I said, and promised to find some opportunity for further conversation, when we might speak more fully on the matter. I gave her this hint of a higher virtue, because she had been represented to me, as she really was, as a lady of most earnest and conscientious character.

"She found the time according to her promise ; all her difficulties were removed, and she became a Catholic. After reconciling her to the Church, I made some other converts in the same house ; then I got her a Catholic maid, and suggested that she should keep a priest always in the house, to which she gladly assented. This was a thing that might easily be managed, not indeed as it was in our house, where the whole household[1] was Catholic and knew us to be priests; but a priest could well live in the upper part of the house, from which all heretics might be kept away, especially now that some of the servants were Catholics. And indeed the accommodation was such that I do not know any place in England where a priest who wished to be private could live more conveniently. For he could have in the first place a fine room to himself, opening on a spacious corridor of some eighty paces which looked on a garden most expensively laid out : in this corridor moreover was a separate room which would serve excellently as a chapel, and another for his meals, with fire-places and every convenience. It was a pity, I said, that such a place had not a resident priest, where the mistress was a devout Catholic, and the master no enemy to religion. Her husband indeed made no difficulty of receiving priests; nay, he sometimes came to hear me preach, and at last went as far as to be fond of dressing the altar with his own hands, and of saying the Breviary : yet with all this he still remains outside the Ark, liable to be swept off by the waters of the deluge when they break forth, for he presumes too much on an opportunity of doing penance before death.

"The lady then readily fell in with my suggestion of having a priest in her house; so I brought thither Father Antony Hoskins, a man of great ability, who had lately come over from Spain, where he had spent ten years in the Society with remarkable success in his studies. Being placed there, he did a great deal of good on all sides, and remained with them almost up to the present time, when

---

[1] Later on we shall come across two good specimens of the men of this household, Richard Richardson the butler and Francis Swetnam in the bakehouse.

W

at length he has been removed and put to greater things.[1]
He did not, however, stay constantly at home, for he is
a man whom, when once known, many would wish to
confer with, so that he was forced to go about at times.
At present there is another Father in the house, a most
devoted man. But the lady directs herself chiefly by
Father Percy, who this very week addressed me a letter
in the following words: 'Such a one' (meaning this lady
of whom I have been speaking) 'is going on very well.
She has offered her heart to Our Lady of Loretto, to serve
her and her son for ever with all that she possesses; and
in token of this she has had made a beautiful heart of
gold, which she wishes to send to Loretto by the first
opportunity. We desire, therefore, to hear from you by
whom she can send this offering.' Thus he writes about
this lady. In this way, then, by the grace of God, was
this house, with its domestic church, established and confirmed in the faith."

The gentleman, whose father was one of the Queen's
Council, was evidently Sir Francis Fortescue of Salden,
Knight of the Bath, eldest surviving son of Sir John
Fortescue,[2] Master of the Wardrobe to Queen Elizabeth.[3]
The lady of whom Father Gerard is here writing was
therefore Grace, his wife, daughter of Sir John Manners,
second son of Thomas, first Earl of Rutland. Father
Roger Lee was first cousin to Sir Francis Fortescue, their
mothers Cecily and Amicia being daughters and co-
heiresses of Sir Edmund Ashfield, knight, of Ewelm, in
the county of Oxford.[4] The family of the Fortescues of
Salden continued Catholic for generations.

"Master Roger also introduced me to some neighbours

---

[1] He became Vice-prefect of the English Mission, residing in that capacity
at Madrid. *Troubles*, Second Series, p. 281.

[2] *Troubles*, First Series, p. 144.

[3] Sir John died December 23, 1607, æt. 76. Lipscomb's *History of Bucks*,
1847, vol. iii. p. 430.

[4] *Visitations of Oxford*, Harl. Soc. 1871, vol. v. p. 168.

of his : among others to a gentleman of the Queen's court,[1] who had inherited a large estate, and had married a lady who was sole heiress to all her father's property [Mary Mulshaw, of Gothurst, in Buckinghamshire]. Not one of this family was a Catholic, nor even inclined to the Catholic faith. The wife's father, who was the head of the house, was a thorough heretic, and had his thoughts entirely occupied in hoarding money for his daughter, and increasing her revenues. His son-in-law devoted himself wholly to juvenile sports. When in London, he attended at Court, being one of the Queen's gentlemen pensioners ; but in the country he spent almost his whole time in hunting and hawking. Hence it happened that Master Roger Lee, who was a neighbour of his, and fond of similar sports, often joined him on such occasions, and brought his falcons to hawk in company. We two therefore took advantage of this acquaintanceship, and I was introduced to this gentleman's house as a friend and intimate of Master Lee's. We made frequent visits there, and took every opportunity of speaking of Catholic doctrine and practice. I took care, however, that Master Lee should always speak more frequently and more earnestly than I, that no suspicion might arise about my real character. Indeed, so far was this gentleman from having the least suspicion about me, that he seriously asked Master Lee whether he thought I was a good match for his sister, whom he wished to see married well, and to a Catholic, for he looked on Catholics as good and honourable men.

"We had therefore, as I said, frequent converse on matters of salvation ; and the wife was the first to listen with any fruit, at a time when she was living in the country but her husband was up in town. Her parents were now dead, and she was mistress of the house, so that we were

---

[1] In the margin of the MS. is written "Digbæus," in the same hand as the text.

able to deal more directly with her. At last she came
to the point of wishing to be a Catholic, and told me she
should be glad to speak with a priest. I could scarce
forbear a smile at this, knowing that she was already
speaking with one ; I answered, however, that the thing
might be managed, and that I would speak with Master
Lee on the subject. 'In the meantime,' I added, 'I can
teach you the way to examine your conscience, as I myself
was taught to do it by an experienced priest.' So I told
Master Roger that as she was now determined and prepared, he might inform her of my being a priest. This
he did, but she for some time refused to believe it, saying,
'How is it possible he can be a priest ? Has he not lived
among us rather as a courtier ? Has he not played at
cards with my husband, and played well too, which is
impossible for those who are not accustomed to the game ?
Has he not gone out hunting with my husband, and frequently in my hearing spoken of the hunt in proper terms,
without tripping, which no one could do but one who has
been trained to it ?' Many other things she adduced to
show I could not be a priest : to all of which Master Lee
replied, ' It is true that he said and did what you say ; and
unless he had done so, how could he have gained entrance
here, and conversed with you, and by his conversation
brought you to the faith ? For if he had presented himself
as a priest (which he would much prefer, were it feasible),
how would your father, who was then living, have allowed
his introduction, or you yourselves ?'

" She could not but admit the truth of this ; yet she
found it hard to believe that it was so. 'I pray you,' she
said, ' not to be angry with me, if I ask further whether
any other Catholic knows him to be a priest but you.—
Does so-and-so know him ?'

" ' Yes,' he answered, 'and has often gone to confession
to him.'

" Then she mentioned other names, and at last that of

my hostess [Mrs. Vaux], who lived in the neighbourhood, but ten miles off.

"'Does she too know him as a priest, and deal with him as such?'

"'Why,' said Master Lee, 'she not only knows him as a priest, but has given herself, and all her household, and all that she has, to be directed by him, and takes no other guide but him.'

"Then at length she confessed herself satisfied.

"'You will find him, however,' added Master Lee, 'quite a different man when he has put off his present character.'

"This she acknowledged the next day, when she saw me in my cassock and other priestly garments, such as she had never before seen. She made a most careful confession, and came to have so great an opinion of my poor powers that she gave herself entirely to my direction, meditated great things, which indeed she carried out, and carries out still.

"When this matter was thus happily terminated, we all three consulted together, how we could induce her husband to enter also into St. Peter's net. Now it so happened that he had fallen sick in London, and his wife on hearing it determined to go and nurse him. We, however, went up before her, and, travelling more expeditiously, had time to deal with him before she came. I spoke to him of the uncertainty of life, and the certainty of misery, not only in this life but especially in the next, unless we provided against it; and I showed him that we have here no abiding city, but must look for one to come. As affliction oftentimes brings sense, so it happened in his case; for we found but little difficulty in gaining his good-will. And as he was a man of solid sense and excellent heart, he laid a firm foundation from the beginning. He prepared himself well for confession after being taught the way; and when he learnt that I was a priest, he felt no such difficulty in believing it as his wife had done, because he had known similar cases; but he rather rejoiced at having found a confessor who had experience among persons of his rank of life, and with whom he could deal at all times without danger of its being known that he was dealing with a priest. After his reconciliation he began on his part to be anxious about his wife, and wished to consult with us how best to bring her to the Catholic religion. We smiled inwardly at this, but said nothing at that time, determining to wait till his wife came up to town, that we might witness how each loving soul would strive to win the other.

"Certainly they were a favoured pair. Both gave themselves wholly to God's service, and the husband afterwards sacrificed all his property, his liberty, nay, even his life for God's Church, as I shall relate hereafter. For this was that Sir Everard Digby, knight, of whom later on I should have had to say many things, if so much had not been already written and published about him and his companions. But never in any of these writings has justice been done to the sincerity of his intention, nor the circumstances properly set forth which would put his conduct in its true light.

After this they both came to see me at my residence in the country. But while there he was again taken ill, and that so violently and dangerously, that all the Oxford doctors despaired of his life. As, therefore, in all likelihood he had not long to live, he began to prepare himself earnestly for a good death, and his wife to think of a more perfect way of life. For some days she gave herself to learn the method of meditation, and to find out God's will with regard to her future life, how she might best direct it to His glory. To be brief, she came to this determination, that if her husband should die, she would devote herself entirely to good works, observe perpetual chastity and

exact obedience ; that as for her property, which would
be very extensive as they were without children, she would
spend it all in pious uses according to my direction ; she
would herself live where and in what style I judged best
for the advancement of God's honour and the good of her
own soul ; and she added that her desire was to wear poor
clothing wherever she might be, and observe all the rules
of poverty. All this was to be while the persecution might
last in England. If, however, it should cease, and England
should become Catholic, then she would give her house
(a very large and fine one), and all the property her father
left her, for the foundation of a College of the Society :
and this would have been amply sufficient for a first-rate
foundation.

"This was her resolution, but God had otherwise
arranged, and for that time happily. For when all the
Oxford doctors gave up Sir Everard's case as hopeless, I
who loved him much did not lose heart, but without his
knowledge I sent for a certain Cambridge doctor, a
Catholic, and a man of much learning and experience,
whom I had known to cure cases abandoned by other
physicians. On his arrival at our house, where Sir Everard
Digby then was with his wife, after telling him all about
the patient, I got him to examine the sick man himself
and learn from him all about his habit of body and general
constitution. Then I asked him if he thought there was
any hope. He answered, 'If Sir Everard will venture to
put himself entirely in my hands, I have good hopes, with
the help of God, of bringing him round.'

"The patient on hearing this said to me, 'Since this
doctor is known to your reverence, and is chosen by you,
I give myself willingly into his hands.'

"By this doctor, then, he was cured beyond all expectation, and so completely restored to perfect health,
that there was not a more robust or stalwart man in a
thousand. He was a most devoted friend to me, just as

if he had been my twin brother. And this name of brother
we always used in writing to each other. How greatly he
was attached to me may be seen from the following incident.
Once when I had gone to a certain house to assist a soul
in agony, he got to learn that I was in great danger there.
Upon this he at first expressed a terrible distress, and then
immediately said to his wife, that if I should be taken, he
was resolved to watch the roads by which I should be
carried prisoner to London, and take with him a sufficient
number of friends and servants to rescue me by force from
those who had me in custody ; and if he should miss me
on the road, he would accomplish my release one way or
another, even though he should spend his whole fortune
in the venture. Such, then, was his attachment to me at
that time, and this he retained always in the same—nay,
rather in an increased—degree, to the end of his life, as
he showed by the way he spoke of me when pleading for
his life before the public court. At this time, however, as
I said, he was restored to health ; and he and his wife got
together a little domestic church after the pattern of one
in our house, and built a chapel with a sacristy, furnishing
it with costly and beautiful vestments, and obtained a priest
of the Society for their chaplain, who remained with them
to Sir Everard's death.

"What was done by this family was done by others
also. For many of the Catholic gentry coming to our
house, and seeing the arrangements and manner of life,
followed the example themselves, establishing a sort of
congregation in each of their houses, providing handsome
altar furniture, making convenient arrangements for the
residence of priests, and showing especial respect and
reverence to them.

"Among those who came to this determination was a
certain lady resident near Oxford, whose husband was
indeed a Catholic, but overmuch devoted to worldly pursuits. She, however, gave herself to be ruled and directed

by me as far as she could, having such a husband. I often visited them, and was always welcomed by both ; and there I established one of our Fathers, Edward Walpole, whom I mentioned at an early part of this narrative as having left a large patrimony for the sake of following Christ our Lord, in the first year of my residence in England.

"There was another lady also who had a similar wish : she was a relative of my hostess, and she also resided in the county of Oxford. Her husband was a knight of very large property, who hoped to be created a baron, and still hopes for it. This lady came on a visit to our house, and wished to learn the way of meditating, which I taught her ; but as her husband was a heretic it was impossible for her to have a priest in her house, as she greatly wished. She took, however, the resolution of supporting a priest, who should come to her at convenient times. She resolved also to give an hour daily to meditation, and one or two hours daily to spiritual reading, when she had no guests in the house ; also to make a general confession every six months, a practice which was followed also by all those of whom I have just spoken, and by many others whom it is impossible for me to mention individually. On her coming to me every six months for her general confession, I found that she had never omitted her hour of meditation, nor her daily examination of conscience, except on one occasion when her husband insisted on her staying with the guests. Yet she had a large and busy household to superintend, and a continual coming and going of guests.

"It happened on one occasion when I was in this lady's house, and was sitting with her after dinner, the servants having gone down to get their own dinner, that suddenly a guest was shown up who had just arrived. This was an Oxford Doctor of Divinity, a heretic of some note and a persecutor of Catholics ; his name was Dr.

Abbot.[1] He had just before this published a book against
Father Southwell, who had been executed, and Father
Gerard, who had escaped from the Tower, because these
two had defended the doctrine of equivocation, which he
chose to impugn. After this publication the good man
had been made Dean of Winchester, a post which brought
him in a yearly income of eight thousand florins [800*l.*].
This man, then, as I said, was shown up, and entered the
dining-room, dressed in a sort of silk soutane coming down
to his knees, as is the manner of their chief ministers.
We were in appearance sitting at cards, though when the
servants had all left the room we had laid the cards down
to attend to better things. Hearing, however, this gentleman announced, we resumed our game, so that he found
us playing, with a good sum of money on the table.

"I may here mention, that when I played thus with
Catholics, with the view of maintaining among a mixed
company the character in which I appeared, I always
agreed that each one should have his money back afterwards, but should say an *Ave Maria* for each piece that
was returned to him. It was on these terms that I frequently played with my brother Digby and other Catholics,
where it appeared necessary, so that the bystanders thought
we were playing for money, and were in hot earnest over it.

"So also this minister never conceived the slightest
suspicion of me, but after the first courtesies began to talk
at a pretty pace : for this is the only thing those chattering
ministers can do, who possess no solid knowledge, but by
the persuasive words of human wisdom lead souls astray,
and subvert houses, teaching things which are not con-

[1] George Abbot was appointed Dean of Winton in 1599; in 1609 Bishop
of Lichfield and Coventry, from which in about a month he was translated to
London, and thence in 1611 to Canterbury. In July 1621 as he was shooting
at a deer with a crossbow, he shot the keeper, for which King James gave
him a dispensation. In 1627 he was sequestered from his office, and his
metropolitan jurisdiction put into commission, but about a year after he was
restored. He died at Croydon, August 4, 1633, æt. 71.

venient. So he, after much frivolous talk, began to tell us the latest news from London ; how a certain Puritan had thrown himself down from the steeple of a church, having left it in writing that he knew himself to be secure of his eternal salvation. About this writing, however, the learned Doctor said nothing, but I had heard the particulars myself from another quarter.

"'Wretched man !' said I, 'what could induce him thus to destroy body and soul by one and the same act ?'

"' Sir,' said the Doctor, learnedly enough and magisterially, 'we must not judge any man.'

"' True,' I replied, 'it is just possible that as he was falling he repented of his sin, *inter pontem et fontem,* as they say : but this is extremely improbable, since the last act of the man of which we have any means of judging was a mortal sin and deserving of damnation.'

"' But,' said the Doctor, 'we cannot know whether this was such a sin.'

"' Nay,' I replied, 'this is not left to our judgment ; it is God's own verdict, when He forbids us under pain of Hell to kill any one, a prohibition which applies especially to the killing of ourselves, for charity begins from oneself.'

" The good Doctor being here caught, said no more on this point, but turned the subject, and said smiling, 'Gentlemen must not dispute on theological matters.'

"' True,' said I, 'we do not make profession of knowing theology ; but at least we ought to know the law of God, though our profession is to play at cards.'

" The lady with whom I was playing, hearing him speak to me in this way, could scarce keep her countenance, thinking within herself what he would have said if he had known who it was he was answering. The Doctor, however, did not stay much longer. Whether he departed sooner than he at first intended, I know not ; but I know that we much preferred his room to his company."

The lady, in whose house Father Gerard met Dr. Abbot, must have been Agnes Lady Wenman, wife of Sir Richard Wenman, of Thame Park, not far from Oxford. Sir Richard was knighted in 1596 for his conduct at Cadiz, and attained the object of his ambition very long after this was written, for he was made a peer of Ireland in 1628 as Baron and Viscount Wenman. Agnes his wife came of a Catholic family, being the daughter of Sir George Fermor of Easton Neston in Northamptonshire.

CHAPTER XXVI.

LONDON.

1599 TO 1603.

" I MUST now return to London, and relate what happened after John Lilly was taken, and the gentleman imprisoned with whom I rented my London house. This house being now closed to me, I sought out another, but on a different plan. I did not now join in partnership with any one, because I was unwilling to be in the house of one known to be a Catholic. I managed that this new house should be hired by a nephew of Master Roger Lee, whom with his wife I had reconciled to the Catholic Church ;[1] and as he was not known to be a Catholic, the house was entirely free from all suspicion. I had the use of this house for three years, and during that time it was not once searched ; nor even before the Queen's death, though there were many general searches made, and the prisons were choked with Catholics, did they ever come to this house.

" I had a man to keep the house who was a schismatic, but otherwise an honest and upright person. When I was in residence, this man provided me with necessaries ; and when I was away, he managed any business for me according to my written directions. In all appearance he was the servant of the gentleman who owned the house, and so he was esteemed and called by the neighbours ; and since as a schismatic he frequented their churches, they entertained no suspicion of him, nor of the house.

---

[1] Probably Sir Edmund Lenthall of Lachford in Oxfordshire, whose mother was Eleanor Lee. His wife was a Stonor.

"For myself, when I came to town, I always entered the house after dark, and in summer time scarce ever went out while I remained there. But my friends would come to visit me by ones and twos on different days, that no special attention might be drawn to the house from the number of visitors. Nor did they ever bring any servants with them, though some were of very high rank, and usually went about with a large number of attendants. By these means I provided better for them and for myself, and was able to continue longer in this way of life.

"It was from this house, soon after my taking possession of it, that Master Roger Lee and three others went to the noviceship, all of whom are now priests and labourers in the Society. The only one of them who is not now actually labouring is Father Strange, who is at present suffering imprisonment in the Tower of London, where he has had to undergo many grievous tortures, and a long solitary confinement. This solitude, indeed, if we look only to his natural disposition, cannot but be very irksome and oppressive to him; but he is not solitary who has God always present with him, consoling him, and supplying in an eminent degree and full abundance all those comforts which we are wont to go begging for from creatures. This Father Strange used to come to me when I was a prisoner in the Clink. He was a Catholic before I knew him; and seeing that he was a youth of quick parts and good disposition, an only son and heir to a fair property, so that he could well associate with gentlemen, I got him to come often to me, and at length to make the Spiritual Exercises. In the course of these he saw good reason to come to the resolution of following Christ our Lord, and entering the Society. Till he could make full arrangements for this, and sell his property, I got him to reside in the same house with Father Garnet, that the good spirit he had imbibed might not evaporate, but be rather increased. He remained with Father Garnet nearly two years before he

was able to disentangle himself entirely from his worldly
goods : at length cutting the last ties which bound his
bark to the English shore, he passed across the channel
a free man.

"Before he started, however, he brought me a friend
and companion of his who is now Father Hart.[1] He also
is an only son, and his father (a rich man) is, I think, still
alive. I did not give him the Exercises, but I met him
from time to time (for I was free now), and instead of the
Exercises I taught him the method of daily meditation.
I gave him also some pious books to read, among others
Father Jerome Platus ; and it was from this last that he
acquired the spirit of religion and of the Society. He is
now a very useful labourer in England, and well suited to
converse and deal with gentlemen, to whose society he
was accustomed before he left the world.

"The third was the present Father Thomas Smith, who
for these last four years has resided at St. Omers. He
was a Master of Arts of Oxford ; and I found him engaged
as tutor to the young Baron, the son of my hostess : so
that I had many good opportunities of conversing freely
with him. But as he was a schismatic, that is, though a
Catholic by conviction, yet lingering in heresy from infirmity of will, I found it impossible to move him, or even
stir him from his present state of mind. Such people, in
fact, who can truly say with the Prophet, ' My belly
cleaveth to the ground,' are far more difficult to gain than
full heretics, as we find by daily experience. He was
often present at my private exhortations, and also at my

---

[1] Father Walpole in a letter to Father Persons dated the 29th of November,
1590, says, "Hart is come to me, one sent from Father Southwell to be
admitted Coadjutor. If Father Provincial should make difficulty here, the
Province being charged, I pray you write your advice, for he is a very fit man,
of forty years, long time companion to priests, lastly to Mr. Gerard, great
virtue, no impediment." *Father Walpole's Letters,* edited by Dr. Jessopp.
The date is enough to show that the Hart who, as Father Walpole shows,
wished to be a lay-brother is not the same person as Father William Hart, of
whom Father Gerard speaks.

public sermons, but he slept a heavy and lethargic slumber, so that one might easily recognize the power of the strong man armed keeping his house in peace. However, a stronger than he came upon him, and despoiled him, and bound him, and took away his armour in which he trusted. And this stronger One who overcame him was no other than the Child Who was born and given to us. For on the night of our Lord's Nativity, while the whole family were celebrating the feast, he alone of all remained in bed; but he could not sleep, and began to feel an overpowering shame, seeing that even the three boys whom he taught had risen and were engaged in praising God, thus teaching their master, not by words, but by deeds. Roused, therefore, interiorly by the cradle-cries of the Divine Infant, he began to think with himself how much time he had hitherto lost, and how the very boys and the unlearned were entering into God's Kingdom before him. So, trembling and eager to lose no more time, he rose at once, came to the chapel door and knocked, and asked to speak to me. As I was engaged, I sent him a message, asking him to wait till the morning, when I should be at his service. But he would not listen, and sent back word that he must speak with me at once. I therefore bade him have a little patience, and when I had finished Matins, I came out to him, dressed in my alb as I was. When he saw me he threw himself at my feet, and said, with the tears streaming down his cheeks, 'Oh, Father, I beseech you for the love of God to hear my confession.'

 "I wondered at the strangeness of the thing, and bade him be of good heart—that I would hear him at a proper time, but that he must first prepare himself well for it.

 "'Oh, Father,' he cried, 'I have put it off too long already! Do not bid me delay any more.'

 "'It is well,' I replied, 'that you feel the necessity of instant diligence. But this is not delaying, to take a fair and moderate time for preparation. Nay, the confession and absolution would not be good, if preparation and examination are omitted, when they might easily have been made.'

" ' Well, but,' urged he, ' I may die before the time of confession.'

" ' Then I will answer for you before God,' I said : ' do you in the meanwhile conceive in your heart a true sorrow for having offended our good Lord.'

" Upon this he yielded, and retired still weeping ; and after one or two days' diligent examination of conscience, he made his confession, and being reconciled, celebrated with us the conclusion of the feast, the beginning of which he had lost.

" These three, then, of whom I have spoken, crossed over into Belgium with Master Lee, and from thence passing on to Rome, made their noviceship at Saint Andrew's, all except Father Hart. He was admitted rather later, but was sent into England earlier than the others on some business, and is a very useful labourer there.

" When I was in London, I did not allow every one to come to my house whose desire to converse with me I was willing to gratify ; but I would sometimes, especially after dark in winter time, go myself to their houses. On one occasion I was asked by a certain lady to her house to hear the confession of a young nobleman attached to the Court, who was a dear friend of her husband's. Her husband was also a Catholic and well known to me : though quite a young man, he had been one of the principal captains in the Irish War. And the young nobleman just mentioned was a baron, and son to an Irish earl, and at this present writing he has himself succeeded to the earldom on his father's death. This young baron, then, wished to make his confession to me. As I had not known him before, I put a few questions to him, according to my wont, beforehand. I asked him, therefore, if he

x

was prepared at once. He answered that he was. I then asked how often in the year he was accustomed to go to the sacraments. 'Twice or thrice in the year,' he said.

"'It would be better,' said I, 'to come more frequently, and then less preparation would be necessary. As it is, I should advise you to take a few days for the exact and diligent examination of your conscience, according to the method that I will show you : then you will come with greater fruit, and with greater satisfaction to yourself and to me. And for the future I would recommend a more frequent use of the holy sacraments.' And I brought some reasons for my advice.

"He listened to me very patiently, and when I had finished, he replied, 'I will do in future what you recommend, and I would willingly follow your counsel at present, if it were possible ; it is, however, impossible to put off my present confession.'

"'Why is it impossible ? ' I asked.

"'Because,' he replied, 'to-morrow I shall be in circumstances of danger, and I desire to prepare myself by confession to-day.'

"'What danger is this,' I asked again, 'to which you will be exposed ?'

"'There is a gentleman at Court,' he said, 'who has grievously insulted me, so that I was compelled, in defence of my honour, to challenge him to single combat ; and we meet to-morrow at an appointed spot at some distance from town.'

"'My lord,' I exclaimed, 'to approach the sacrament in such a frame of mind, is not to prepare yourself for danger, nor to cleanse your soul (though I doubt not that it was with a good intention you proposed it), but rather to sully your soul more than ever, to affront God still further, and render Him still more your enemy. For to come to confession with a determination of taking vengeance is to put an obstacle to the grace of the sacrament ;

and moreover this particular action on which you are
resolved is not only a sin, but is visited with excommunication. I urge you, therefore, to give up this intention;
you will be able to preserve your honour by some other
way. Nay, the honour you think to preserve by this, is
not real honour, but merely the estimation of bad men
founded on bad principles; men who exalt their own
worldly ideas above the law and honour of God.'

"'It is impossible to withdraw now,' he said, 'for the
thing is known to many, and has been taken even to the
Queen, who has expressly forbidden us to pursue the
matter any further.'

"'Well, then,' said I, 'you have the best possible
reason for laying aside the quarrel, namely, obedience to
the Queen's behest. Moreover, you must remember that
you are known for the intimate friend of the Earl of Essex,
and that if you overcome your adversary, the Queen (if it
be only to spite the Earl) will certainly visit you with
some heavy punishment for having disregarded her commands; but if you should kill him, unquestionably she
will take your life. On the other hand, if you should be
vanquished, what becomes of the honour you wish to
defend? And if you should be slain in that state of soul
in which you go to the fight, you go straight to eternal
fire and everlasting shame : for while you are defending
your body from your adversary's sword, you forget to
parry the mortal thrust that the devil is aiming at your
soul.'

"But spite of all I could say, the fear of the world,
which is fatally powerful with men of this rank, prevailed,
and his reply was, 'I implore you, Father, to pray for me,
and to hear my confession, if you possibly can.'

"'Certainly I cannot hear you,' I said, 'for that honour
which you worship is not necessary to you, in the sense in
which it is to those who are obliged to take their part in
a war. Besides, you are the challenger, and you took this

unlawful course when it was possible for you to follow some other method of vindicating yourself, and so whatever necessity there is for pursuing the matter has been created by yourself. But this is what I will do: I will give you from my reliquary a particle of the Holy Cross, enclosed with an Agnus Dei, and you shall wear it upon you. Perhaps God may have mercy on you for the sake of this, and afford you time for penance. Understand, however, I do not give it you in order to encourage you in your bad purpose, but that you may wear it with all reverence and respect, so that should you come into danger (which certainly I do not desire) God may be moved to preserve your life, in the consideration of the good will you have of honouring His Cross.'

"He took my gift very thankfully and reverentially, and had it sewed inside his shirt over his heart; for it was arranged they should fight in their shirts without cuirass. It happened, God so allowing it, that his adversary made a lunge at his heart and pierced his shirt, but did not touch his skin. He on his side wounded and prostrated his enemy, then gave him his life and came off victorious. He then came to me in high spirits, and told me how he had been preserved by the power of the Holy Cross; then he thanked me very earnestly, and promised to be more on his guard in future. The Queen soon after took a fancy to this young nobleman, and kept him close to her at Court for a time. But tiring soon of this sort of life, at his father's death he married the widow of the Earl of Essex. She was a heretic when he married her, but he soon made her a Catholic; and they both live now as Catholics in Ireland, as I hear."

Richard de Burgh, commonly called Richard of Kinsale from his conduct at that place, Baron of Dunkellin, succeeded his father as fourth Earl of Clanricarde, May 20, 1601. He was subsequently made Earl of St. Albans, and died November 12, 1635. He married Frances, daughter and heiress of Sir Francis Walsingham, widow of Robert second Earl of Essex. Thus Walsingham's only child became a Catholic.

"That knight, moreover, who introduced this young baron to me, followed my counsel at that time, and after devoting several days to a diligent examination of conscience, made a general confession of his whole life, with a view of reforming it for the future. A little later he was desirous of returning to the Irish wars, but as I was in doubt whether this was lawful in conscience, he promised me to resign his appointment and return to England, if the priests there, to whom I referred him as living on the spot, and therefore having a closer knowledge of the circumstances, decided that it was unlawful. Soon after his arrival in Ireland, in a certain fight, while he was bravely mounting a wall and animating his men to follow, he was struck dead by a musket ball. He had, however, before the fight carefully written me a letter and sent it off, informing me that he had consulted the priests in the country, and had received this answer, that it was lawful to fight against the Catholic party, because it was not clear to all why they had taken up arms.

"After his death, a remarkable incident occurred which I will relate. His wife, pious soul, who never had the least idea of her husband's death, about that time heard every night some one knocking at her chamber door, and that so loudly as to wake her. Her maids heard it too, but on opening the door there was no one to be seen. She therefore got a priest to stay with her and her maids till the usual time of the knocking; and when the same noise and knocking at the door were heard, the priest himself went to the door, but found no one. This knocking went on till such time as news of her husband's death reached her: as if it had been a warning from his angel to pray for his soul."

It does not seem rash to assume that the knight

here mentioned was Sir Henry Bagenal,[1] who was born at Carlingford in Ireland, August 3, 1556. He was Marshal of Queen Elizabeth's armies in Ireland for many years. He married Eleanor, third daughter of Sir John Savage of Rock Savage, Knight. Sir Henry Bagenal was killed at Blackwater in Ireland, August 14, 1598, in an attack upon that fort or pass. His widow afterwards married Sir Sackville Trevor, fourth son of Sir John Trevor of Trevorllyn, Knight. We have the following mention of his death in Chamberlain's *Letters:* "August 30, 1598. We have had a great blow in Ireland; Sir Henry Bagenal the Marshal, went with 3,500 foot and 300 horse to relieve Blackwater fort, distressed by Tyrone; the enemy between 8,000 and 10,000 strong attacked him and he was slain with 16 captains and over 700 soldiers."

"While I was in London," Father Gerard continues, "the opportunity often presented itself of visiting men of rank, confirming them in the faith, directing them, and also of converting some; for every one tried to bring the members of his family and his friends to me. One asked me to mount on horseback and ride to meet a friend of his, whom he would throw in my way at a particular spot two miles out of London. This was a man of wealth and influence, and decidedly the principal man of all the county where he lived. He was of the rank next below that of baron[2] (for he was not an earl nor a baron), and was wholly given up to vanities. I met him, and he, being told who I was (for he was anxious to speak with a priest), saluted me kindly; but at the same time was unwilling to recognize me. I put on the character of a Catholic who wished that all men were Catholics, and said that I had heard that he was a good friend to Catholics, but not to himself, because

---

[1] Collins' *Peerage of England*, Supplement to the fifth edition, p. 126.
[2] Probably of one of the higher grades of knighthood, as a Knight Banneret. The dignity of Baronet did not exist before 1611.

he was not a Catholic ; and so we fell upon the question whether this was necessary for salvation, and this I proved in such manner that he did not deny it. But I saw that the greatest difficulty lay in withdrawing his will from the pleasures of the world, and therefore I directed my attack against that quarter, and by God's aid I overthrew the walls, and laid open a way for the entry of good and sound counsels into his heart ; insomuch that he who had up to that time conversed with me as with some man of rank, a friend of his friend, at last said, 'You shall certainly be my confessor.' Then we appointed a time and place where this business might be attended to without inconvenience or hurry ; and after a few days he came to my friend's house near London, and there he abode until after fit preparation he made his confession. Thenceforth he became one of my principal benefactors : for every year, until I left England, he gave me a thousand florins [100*l.*], besides horses, and other occasional necessaries.

"The same person also brought to me his brother-in-law, who was son and brother to an earl, and himself heir to the earldom. I met him also riding on horseback, and at exactly the same spot, and before we separated God touched his heart too, and gave him the grace of conversion. He was fully satisfied on all points relating both to faith and morals, and a few days after I received him into the Church, and I have great confidence that he will, please God, become one of its chief supports. I administered the sacraments to these and others like them in my own house, and on that account I kept it from public notice, that it might not be thought a Catholic house. I thus secured an asylum in London, where the peril of priests, and myself in particular, is ever greatest and most pressing ; and men of rank and influence were able to be there without fear of any sudden and unexpected visitation, and so come to visit me with greater confidence. I learned by experience that this care of mine was very pleasing to them, and profitable by the security gained both for them and myself.

"Having held this house for three years, I let it to a Catholic friend, and took another house nearer the principal street in London, called the Strand. Since most of my friends lived in that street, they were thus able to visit me more easily, and I them. After my removal I discovered how entirely free from suspicion was the house which I had left, and in which I had dwelt for three years; for the servant who kept my house, sent for a gardener with whom he had been acquainted while living in the other house (for the garden of the new house needed to be put in order), and the gardener remarked to him, ' Some Papists have come to live in your old house,' as though they who had previously dwelt there had been good Protestants.

"This new house was very suitable and convenient, and had private entrances on both sides, and I had contrived in it some most excellent hiding-places; and there I should long have remained, free from all peril or even suspicion, if some friends of mine, while I was absent from London, had not availed themselves of the house rather rashly.[1] It remained, however, in the same state up to the time of the great and terrible disturbance of the Powder Plot, as I shall hereafter shortly mention.

"Meantime my friends brought me another who was heir to a barony, and is himself now a peer, and by God's grace I persuaded him to take on his shoulders the yoke of the law of Christ and of the Catholic faith, and made him a member of the Church. Another whom I had previously known in the world, and had seen to be wholly devoted to every kind of vanity, fell sick. He had

---

[1] This is evidently the "house in the fields behind St. Clement's Inn," as Guy Fawkes calls it—"behind St. Clement's," as it appears in Winter's confession—where the oath of secrecy was taken by the conspirators before the Powder Plot.

abounded with riches and pleasures, and passed his days in jollity, destined, however, to fall thence in a moment, had not God patiently waited and in a suitable time led him to penance. He then was lying sick of a grievous illness, but yet had not begun to think of death. I heard that he was sick, and obtained an entry into his chamber at eleven o'clock at night, after the departure of his friends. He recognized me, and was pleased at my visit. I explained why I had come, and warned him to think seriously of the state of his soul, and, instead of a Judge, render God a Friend and most loving Father, however much he might have wasted all his substance. So, then, weakness of body opened the ears of his heart, and in an acceptable time God heard us, and in the day of salvation helped us; insomuch that he offered himself as at once ready to make his confession. I, however, said that I would return on the following night, and advised him meantime to procure that there should be read to him by a friend, whom I named, Father Lewis of Grenada's *Explanation of the Commandments :* that after each Commandment he should occupy some little time in reflection, and call to mind how, and how often, he had offended against that commandment ; that then he should make an act of sorrow regarding each, and so go to the next. He promised that he would do so, and I promised that I would return on the following night. This I did, and heard his confession ; I gave him all the assistance I could, for the time had been short, especially for a sick man, to prepare such a confession, but he dared no longer defer it, although he still seemed tolerably strong. I advised him to use the utmost care in discharging all his debts, which were great, through the extravagant expenditure in which he had indulged : I also exhorted him to redeem his sins by alms. He did both by the will he made the following day, and bequeathed a large sum for pious uses, which as I heard was honestly paid.

"I also bade him prepare for the Holy Communion and Extreme Unction against the following night, and to have some pious book read to him meantime. He not only did what I advised, but exhorted all that came to visit him on the following day to repent at once of their former life, and not defer their amendment, as he had done : 'Do not,' he said, 'look for the mercy which I have found, for this is to be presumptuous and to irritate God ; for I have deserved Hell a thousand times on this account.' And much more to the same effect did he speak, with so much earnestness and freedom, that all marvelled at so sudden a change. They asked him to hide the cross which he had hanging from his neck (for I had lent him my own cross full of relics for him to kiss, and exercise acts of reverence and love) ; but he answered, ' Hide it ! Nay, I would not hide it, even if the most bitter heretics were here. Too long have I refrained from profession of the Catholic faith, and now, if God gave me life, I would publicly profess myself a Catholic :' so that all marvelled and were much edified and moved at his words. He spoke thus to all the peers and great men that visited him. His conversion thus became publicly known, and many of the courtiers afterwards spoke of it. On the third night of my visiting him according to my promise, he again confessed with great expressions of sorrow, and begged for the sacrament of Extreme Unction, and when he received it, himself arranged for me more conveniently to reach the different parts of his body, just as though he had been a Catholic many years. Seeing him in such good dispositions, I asked whether he did not put all his trust in the merits of Christ and in the mercy of God. 'Surely !' said he ; 'did I not do so, and did not that mercy give me salvation, I should have been condemned to the pit of Hell: in myself I find no ground of hope, but rather of trembling. But I feel great hope in the mercy and goodness of God, Who has so long waited for me, and now has called me when I deserved—aye, and thought of—anything but this !' Then he took my hand and said, 'Father, I cannot express how much I am indebted to you, for you were sent by God to give me this happiness.' I found, moreover, that he had no temptation against faith, but most firmly believed and confessed every point, and I saw most clearly that God had poured into his soul the habits of many virtues. Then I erected an altar in his chamber with the ornaments which I had brought, and I said mass, while he assisted with great devotion and comfort. I afterwards gave him the Viaticum, which he received with the utmost reverence. When I had finished everything, I gave him some advice that would be useful should he fall into his agony before my return, and I left him full of consolation. Now, see the providence of God : but a few hours after my departure, as he was persevering in petitions for mercy, and in acts of thanksgiving for the mercy he had received, he rendered up his soul to God. But before his death, he asked the bystanders whether certain purple and red robes could be applied to the use of the altar, which he had received from the King when he was created a Knight of the Order of the Bath. The investiture of this Order takes place only at the coronation of the King, and the knights enjoy precedence before all other knights except those of the most Noble Order of the Garter, almost all of whom are earls or other peers. He, however, was a Knight of the Bath, and he wished that the robes with which he had been invested at the Coronation should be devoted to the use of the altar ; for he said that he had derived great comfort from seeing my vestments, which were merely light and portable, but yet handsome, of red silk embroidered with silver lace. So after his death they gave me his suit of the peculiar robes of that Order, and out of them I made sets of vestments of two colours, one of which the College of St. Omers still possesses. Thus is the pious desire of the deceased fulfilled, in whose conversion I could not fail to see God's great goodness and providence."

A careful examination of the list of the Knights of the Bath created at the coronation of James I., given by Nichols in his *Royal Progresses*, has established a strong probability that the knight whose death is here recorded by Father Gerard was Sir William Browne of Walcot, who died in 1603, the very year of James' accession.

CHAPTER XXVII.

SIR OLIVER MANNERS.

"ABOUT the same time I received into the Church a lady, the wife of a certain knight; who is at the present day a very good and useful friend of our Fathers. Her husband was at this time a heretic, but his brother had been brought by me, through the Spiritual Exercises, to despise the world and follow the counsels of Christ: he introduced me to his sister, and after one or two interviews she embraced the Catholic faith, although she was well assured that she would incur great losses as soon as it should become known to her husband, as in truth it came to pass. For he first tried caresses, then threats, and left no means unemployed to shake her resolution, insomuch that for a long time she had nothing to expect or hope but to be separated from her husband, and stripped of all the goods of this world, that so in patience she might possess her soul. When her husband was on her account deprived of the public employment which he held, she bore it with great fortitude, and remained ever constant and even in mind: at length by her virtue and her patience she rendered her husband a friend to Catholics, and afterwards himself a Catholic. He was reconciled by the ministry of Father Walpole, to whom I had recommended her on my leaving England.

"There were many other conversions, which I cannot mention separately, for I have already carried to too great length the narrative of these events, which are truly very insignificant if they are compared with the actions of others. But one case I cannot pass over, which gave me especial pleasure for the sake of the person concerned ; for I do not know that any one was ever more dear to me.

"Sir Everard Digby, of whom I have spoken above, had a friend for whom he felt a peculiar affection ; he had often recommended him to me, and was anxious to give me an opportunity of making his acquaintance and gaining him over, if it possibly might be : but because he held an office in the Court, requiring daily attendance about the King's person, so that he could not be absent for long together, our desire was long delayed.

"At last Sir Everard met his friend, while we were both together in London ; and he took an opportunity of asking him to come at a certain time to his chamber, to play at cards, for these are the books gentlemen in London study both night and day. He promised to come, and on his arrival he did not find a party at play, but only us two sitting and conversing very seriously ; so Sir Everard asked him to sit down a little, until the rest should arrive. Then in an interval of silence Sir Everard said, 'We two were engaged in a very serious conversation, in fact concerning religion. You know,' he said, addressing the visitor, 'that I am friendly to Catholics, and to the Catholic faith ; I was nevertheless disputing with this gentleman, who is a friend of mine, against the Catholic faith, in order to see what defence he could make ; for he is an earnest Catholic, as I do not hesitate to tell you.' Then turning to me he begged me not to be vexed that he betrayed me to a stranger. 'And I must say,' he continued, 'he so well defended the Catholic faith that I could not answer him, and I am glad that you have come to help me.'

"The visitor was young and confident, and trusting in his own great abilities, expected to carry everything before him, so good was his cause, and so lightly did he esteem me, as he afterwards confessed. So he began to

allege many objections to the arguments before used. I
waited with patience until he ceased speaking, and then
answered in few words. He urged his points, and so we
argued one against the other for a short hour's space.
Afterwards I began to explain my view more fully, and to
confirm it with texts of Holy Scripture and passages from
the Fathers, and with such reasons as came to my mind.
And I felt, as I often did, God supplying me words as I spoke
on His behalf in great might, not for the sake of me that
spoke, nor for any desert of mine, but just as He gives milk
to a mother when she has an infant who needs to be fed
with milk. My young friend was of a docile nature, and
could no way bear to speak against the truth when he saw
it, so that he listened in silence, and God was meantime
speaking to his heart with a voice far more powerful and
efficacious. God, too, gave him ears to hear, so that the
word fell not upon stony ground, nor among thorns, but
into good soil, yea, very good, that yielded by God's grace
a hundredfold in its season. So before he left he was fully
resolved to become a Catholic, and took with him a book
to assist him in preparing for a good confession, which he
made before a week had passed. And from that time it
was not enough for him to walk in the ordinary path of
God's commandments, but God prepared him for higher
things ; and whatever counsels I gave him he received
with eagerness, and retained not only in a faithful memory,
but in a most ready will. He began to use the daily
examination of conscience, and even learned the method of
meditation, and made a meditation every day. He was
forced to rise very early to do this before he went to the
King, which in summer was at break of day, for the King
went hunting every day, and he, by duty of his office, was
necessarily present at the royal breakfast. He would moreover so with his whole soul devour pious books, that he
always had one in his pocket ; and in the King's Court
and in the Presence Chamber, while courtiers and ladies

were standing around, you might see him turn himself to a window, and there read a chapter of Thomas à Kempis' *Imitation of Christ*, a book with which he was most intimate ; and after he had read it, you might see him turn in body but not in mind towards the others, for there he would stand rapt in thought, while the rest perhaps were supposing that he was admiring the beauty of some lady, or thinking over the means to climb to great honours. In truth, he had no need to take particular pains about this, for in the first place he was son and brother to an Earl, and moreover the place and office which he filled were very honourable, giving him the ear of the King every day. His wit could not fail to distinguish favourable opportunities for gaining his requests, and in fact the King had given him an office which he afterwards sold, but which, had he kept it, would have brought him in more than ten thousand florins a year [1,000*l.*]. In short, such was his position that he would undoubtedly have soon risen to great honours ; for he made himself acceptable to all, and was not a little beloved, insomuch that after he had left the Court and given up all hope of worldly honour, I heard it said by some persons of the greatest eminence and experience in the ways of the Court, that they had never in forty years' space known any one so highly valued and beloved in every quarter.

"But, what is far more important, he was beloved in the Court of the King of Kings, and inspired to desire and seek after greater and more abiding blessings. So he conceived the wish of trying the Spiritual Exercises, in the course of which he determined to desert the Court, and devote himself to those pursuits which would render him most pleasing to God and most profitable to his neighbour : so with as little delay as possible he made such a disposition of his goods as would enable him freely to make his escape from England. He then, to the surprise of all, asked and obtained the King's leave to go to Italy, where he still resides, and he is so well known to our Fathers that there is no need to write anything more concerning him ; but this I can say, that wherever I have known him to have been, he has left men filled with great esteem for him, and expectation of yet greater things.

"Besides Sir Everard Digby, he had another friend, a man of much influence, and heir to a large estate, and of great talents, but wholly devoted to the world. He brought this friend to me, and by my agency caused him to become a Catholic. I knew also two young ladies of rank, who were so deeply attached to him that I doubt not they would have preferred him to the greatest lord in England. One was attached to the Court, and had an honourable post about the Queen's person ; the other, who dwelt in the country, was of a noble Catholic family. He himself introduced the first to me, and by my ministry rendered her a Catholic. He then begged her to set her love on a higher object, on God, to Whom the chief love of all was due, and he added, that he had resolved never to love any woman in this world except with the love of charity, and that he would never enter into wedlock. The second he persuaded to become a nun : she is still in religion, and making good progress. I feel confident that he has been chosen and reserved to be the instrument of bringing many souls to follow the counsels of Christ by word and example, and to help ours in many respects."

In some few of the narratives of conversions given by Father Gerard at this portion of his missionary life, it is tantalizing to find that the personal details mentioned by him are insufficient to enable us always to determine who the personages were of whom he speaks. But in many cases we have sufficient data ; and here we can identify Sir Everard Digby's friend as Sir Oliver Manners,[1] fourth son of John fourth Earl of Rutland. His three elder brothers Roger,

[1] Sir Oliver was first cousin once removed of Grace Manners, wife of Sir Francis Fortescue of Salden.

Y

Francis, and George, were successively Earls, and all died childless; the title would therefore have devolved on the fourth son if he had survived.

Sir Oliver Manners was knighted at Belvoir Castle on the 22nd of April 1603, by King James I. on his coming from Scotland. He was Clerk of the Council;[1] to which office, entailing as Father Gerard says "daily attendance about the King's person," he was appointed by warrant dated December 30, 1603. His intimacy with Sir Everard Digby is mentioned by William Ellis and Michael Rapier, Sir Everard's servants, in their examinations[2] after the Gunpowder Plot, November 21 and 22, 1605. It must have been in the spring of that year that he "asked and obtained the King's leave to go to Italy," for we have a "license for Sir Oliver Manners to remain beyond seas for three years after the expiration of his former licence,"[3] dated May 13 and 16, 1608. At the expiration of this term, Edward Lord Vaux of Harrowden wrote[4] to the Earl of Salisbury from Milan, October 26, 1611, that Sir Oliver Manners, who was ill of a fever, entreated favour for prolonging his absence beyond his licence, being unable to return from illness, and because his brother the Earl of Rutland had not sent him any money. There are two letters[5] from Sir Oliver himself to Salisbury, one dated Milan, July 8, 1609, in which he regrets that his illness prevents his return home, but the physicians forbid his using any exertion, even that of writing: the other, dated Florence, May 17, 1610, complaining that his brother the Earl detains his estates, in spite of an Order of the Council to the contrary, although he remains abroad by licence, in company with Lord Vaux and others who are licensed.

---

[1] P.R.O., *Ind. Warrant Book*, p. 15.
[2] *Ibid.*, *Gunpowder Plot Book*, nn. 108, 111.
[3] *Ibid.*, *Docquet.*
[4] *Ibid.*, *Domestic, James I.*, vol. lxvi. n. 96.
[5] *Ibid.*, vol. xlvii. n. 20; vol. liv. n. 51.

Sir Oliver Manners wrote the following letter[1] in Italian to Father Aquaviva, General of the Society, from Turin, April 17, 1611, shortly before his eldest brother's death. "I cannot tell you what comfort I received from the letters of your Paternity. The troubles I then had will tell it better than I can, for when I was seriously ill, my brother the Earl sent to say that I was to expect no more help from England, as the King had entrusted my houses and estates to him, and would not permit him to send me a penny. Precisely at that moment the letters of your Paternity reached me, and seemed to me sent by our Lord to make me touch with my hand how His Divine Majesty never abandons those who hope in Him and suffer for His love; and as at that time I had a great desire of suffering more and more, if so it should please our Lord, so my strength returned to me far more quickly than I could have expected, and thus I assured myself that it was the Divine will that I should reach my intended goal, there to do something for His service, *sive per vitam, sive per mortem.* And so I undertook my journey, and have already reached Turin. To-morrow I start for Lyons. In England I cannot expect anything better than that which has befallen the Baron my companion [Lord Vaux], who is in prison by the King's express orders, and expects to lose all he has; for his mother is already condemned to the punishment called *præmunire,* that is, the loss of all temporalities and perpetual imprisonment, for refusing the oath of allegiance as they call it. The grace I ask from God is so to bear myself that I may always show myself grateful for the many favours of your Paternity, as becomes a disciple of the Society, and for this intention with all humility to ask to be armed with your blessing, and I beg to be a partaker of the holy sacrifices and prayers of you Paternity and of all the Society. In conclusion with all reverence I kiss your hand."

[1] Stonyhurst MSS., *Angl. A.* vol. vi.

In the Secret Archives[1] of the Vatican there is a note
in Italian written about this time which says, "The Earl of
Rutland, brother of Sir Oliver Manners, who was over there
[probably at Rome] with the Baron [Vaux], has fallen
into apoplexy, and being without hope of life, has declared
his brother Sir Francis heir to his estates, making no
mention of Sir Oliver, of whose arrival at Paris there has
been notice, and he is expected in England to be made the
Baron's companion" in prison.

Father Gerard was at this time at Louvain, and wrote
from that place a letter[2] to Father General Aquaviva,
dated August 17, 1611. "Now at length our friend Oliver
has passed over from Paris to England, for the Treasurer
is gone, his and all good men's enemy: [Robert Cecil,
Earl of Salisbury, died May 24, 1612] and others are
about to succeed him, who, as we hope, entertain for Oliver
an ancient and particular affection. Besides, his eldest
brother is dead [Roger, fifth Earl of Rutland, died
June 26, 1612], and the second brother [Francis, sixth
Earl] left inheritor of all the honours and wealth,
so that a manifold occasion is offered to our friend
of helping himself in temporal affairs, and others to
some extent in spiritual and greater goods. Summoned by his family he has left in haste, humbly
asking your Paternity's benediction; in the efficacy of
which he disregards all that heretical fury or perverse
malice can invent against him. The King is going this
summer to his brother the new Earl's castle, to remain
there awhile for hunting. Perhaps Oliver will take that
occasion of presenting himself to the King, who liked
him when he was in his service before he entered the
service of God, and whom he has never offended in
anything, except in choosing to be an abject in the

[1] *Nunciatura Angliæ*, inter Miscell., kindly communicated by the Rev.
Father Stevenson, S.J.
[2] Stonyhurst MSS., *Angl. A.*, vol. iii. n. 111.

house of God, rather than to dwell in the tabernacles of men."

Father Gerard's expression in this letter, that Sir Oliver could help others "to some extent in spiritual and greater goods" refers to a fact that has never been published, that Sir Oliver Manners was ordained priest by Cardinal Bellarmine[1] in Rome on the 5th of April, 1611. He was therefore not ordained when Father Gerard wrote his Narrative; but clearly this was what was in his mind when he wrote that men were filled not only with great esteem for him, but with "expectations of yet greater things." It thus becomes extremely probable that in the letter Father Gerard wrote to Father Persons from Brussels on the 15th of July, 1606, under the title of "his brother" Father Gerard meant Sir Oliver Manners. "A journeyman" in the mouths of Catholics meant a Jesuit, and "a workman" was a priest, and Father Gerard ingeniously expresses his wish that Sir Oliver had passed through the noviciate, and his estimate of his fitness for a priest's work in the words "unless my brother had served his apprenticeship and were made a journeyman, for of his skill and workmanship in framing the best wedding garment there is great and general hope conceived;" and in this passage Father Gerard expresses his preference for Sir Oliver if he were a priest over all others, including even Father Roger Lee. However Sir Oliver did not "serve his apprenticeship" or become a Jesuit, though he was ordained priest after Father Gerard's letter.

The death of Sir Oliver Manners is mentioned by Chamberlain in a letter[2] written to Carleton, dated Sep-

---

[1] The testimonials signed by the Cardinal, dated April 12, 1611, are in the Archives of the English College at Rome. They state that the Cardinal conferred the tonsure, minor orders and sacred orders on five successive days from the 2nd to the 5th of April "Domino Oliverio Manoreo Anglo." Similar testimonials in the same Archives show that the Cardinal ordained George Mallett in 1612, and Toby Mathews and George Gage in 1614.

[2] P.R.O., *Domestic, James I.*, vol. lxxiv. n. 56.

tember 9, 1613.   But it would appear that this was a false
report of his death, for at the end of 1618 Cardinal
Bellarmine wrote[1] to Father Gerard about him as if he
had just been informed of his death.   "The memory of
that excellent Mr. Oliver, whose acquaintance I made very
late, has brought me no little sadness, or rather grief, not
on his account, who is translated from this world to the
joys of Paradise, but for the sake of many whom without
doubt he would have converted to a good life if Divine
Providence had permitted him to live any longer.   But the
good pleasure of God must ever be fulfilled, and the self
same, in order that it may be fulfilled, must ever be
pleasing to us under all circumstances."

[1] Stonyhurst MSS., *Angl. A.*, vol. viii. n. 107.

CHAPTER XXVIII.

QUIET BEFORE THE STORM.

"THE conversions which took place in the country were not few, and some were cases of heads of families; but I have already gone to great length, and I will here recount one only, the beginning and end of which I saw to be good.

"There was a lady, a kinswoman of my hostess, whose husband had now many years been a Catholic, yet neither her husband, nor any of her friends, nor my hostess herself, who loved her as a sister, could ever lead her to become a Catholic. She did not object to listen to Catholics, even to priests, and was fond of earnest argument with them; but she would believe no one but herself, and indeed her talents were greater than I have often met with in a woman. My hostess often mourned over this lady, and grieved that no remedy could be found; she wished that I should once see her. She spoke highly in praise of her talents and amiable disposition, and of her life and behaviour in all respects, with the one solitary exception of her being an obstinate heretic. I asked my hostess therefore to invite her to pay us a visit, although she lived in a distant county. She came according to the invitation, and we took care that she should find me showing myself in public, and dressed as though I had been a guest just arrived from London. On the two first days we did but little, for we knew that we should have plenty of time afterwards, and I wished to remove all timidity from her; for though she had been accustomed to meet priests at that house, yet they had kept mostly to their chambers. But as soon as I judged her to be convinced that I was a Catholic but not a priest, I began slowly to turn my conversation with her often upon religion. At first I spoke little, but to such purpose that she could not answer me; and so I left her, not urging her, but rather leaving her with a desire to hear more. At length after a few days I judged her thoroughly prepared, and I arranged that my hostess should begin to talk seriously upon these topics, and that when she saw me enter into the conversation and carry it on, she should leave us in company with one or two of the lady's daughters, for she had brought three with her. This having been done, we began the combat with, as it seemed to her, various success, for one or two hours; and then she listened to me as I spoke without interruption for two or three hours more. She spoke little in answer, and did not like on the spot to acknowledge herself vanquished, but she thanked me heartily, and went away quite red and flushed in the face. She was truly moved, or rather changed interiorly, and straightway she ran to my hostess and said, 'Oh, cousin, what have you done?'

"'What have I done?' replied the other.

"'Oh, who is it,' she rejoined, 'that you introduced me to? Is he such a one as you represented to me? At any rate he is—' and she spoke in much higher terms of my learning and language than I deserved, and she added that she could not resist what I had urged, nor answer it.

"On the following day God confirmed what He had wrought in her, and she surrendered at discretion, and accepted a book to help her to prepare for confession. Meantime with the mother's consent and assistance, I instructed her three daughters, and when they had learned the catechism, I heard their confessions. The mother, however, during the time of her preparation, began to be filled with trouble and sorrow, not on account of leaving her heresy, but through fear of confession. I, on the contrary, encouraged her to persevere, and adduced arguments against her timidity, but I could not rid her of it, and so seeing that she was ready as far as examination was concerned, but nevertheless put the matter off from day to day, and begged a little more time to prepare, I would not consent. I told her that this came from the enemy, who grieved to leave his habitation, and at length she saw and acknowledged this. For as soon as out of obedience she had made her confession, she felt relieved of a great burden and filled with consolation ; and she told me that now she was glad not to have delayed longer.

"I have often found this, that some souls experience great trouble when they first make confession on being reconciled to the Church of God. Some persons even fall sick and faint, so as to be forced to cease speaking for a time and sit down, until they have recovered a little and are able to continue ; and this has happened even when at their first coming they were in sound health, and ready to confess. And then when they recommenced, they again fell ill, and this happened two or three times in the course of their first confession. But when the confession was finished they not only felt no sickness, but having received absolution they went away full of joy and consolation. Some in fact have remarked to me that did men but know what consolation is gained in confession, they would refuse to be deprived of so great a happiness.

"Among these was to be reckoned this lady, who came forth from confession full of consolation, and gave most hearty thanks to her cousin, for that by her means she had been admitted to share in so great a happiness. So great was God's mercy towards her, that thenceforth she gave herself wholly up to devotion. On her return home she devoted herself to making handsome vestments, and whenever she was able she procured the company of priests. And not content with this, she was anxious to

return wholly to our house, and to dwell with us, in order
to have more frequent access to the sacraments, and the
opportunity of hearing the public and private exhortations
that we had every Sunday and festival day.   She stayed
with us about two years, and all that time she gave herself
up to devotion and to the constant reading of pious books.
She was clearly led to this course of life by the special
mercy and providence of God; for at the end of the
period I have mentioned, although she seemed stout and
strong, she was suddenly attacked with disease, by which
within a few days she was so weakened, that no skill of
the physicians could restore her strength.   She was warned
to prepare for the life to come, and she repeated a good
and careful confession of her whole life.

"At length finding herself in her last agony, she wished
to write a letter to her brother, who was a heretic, and
almost the greatest enemy the Catholics had in the county
where he dwelt.   To him then she wished to send a letter,
written by her daughter's hand but subscribed with her
own, to the following effect :—That he knew that she had
long been a strenuous upholder of this new religion, so
that he might be the more convinced that she would not
have changed it without good grounds, and that she had
certain and unanswerable authorities for the faith which
she had adopted : wherefore she protested to him that
ever since the time when she embraced the faith, she had
lived in peace of conscience, and that never before that
time had she enjoyed true internal consolation : finally
she begged him to have a care for his soul, and proceeded
thus ; 'I, your sister, now at the point of death, by these
my last words, beg and beseech you to embrace the
Catholic and ancient faith; and I protest that there is
no other in which you can be saved.'   These were her
sentiments when almost come into her last agony; from
which I perceived that she was wholly converted from
heresy, and full of charity towards her neighbour ; so

having asked her a few questions, and found that she
was not troubled with any temptations of presumption or
of despair, I gave her as much help as I could in forming
and uttering acts of the opposite virtues. After which,
when she was on the point of death, I offered her a picture
of the Passion of Christ, and she embraced and kissed it
with the greatest affection. I put also a blessed medal
into her hands, and reminded her to invoke the Name of
Jesus in her heart at least, in order to gain the indulgences,
although she could not speak. I then asked her to give
some sign to show that she did thus from her heart,
whereupon she caught hold of the medal and kissed it,
repeating this action several times. Observing she made
answer to me my signs, I bade her conceive a great sorrow
for having ever offended God, Who was so good in Himself,
and had shown so great mercy to her, and to give a sign
of it by raising her hand; she did so with great earnestness: then to conceive sorrow that she had ever been in
heresy, and had resisted God and the Church, of which
also she gave a sign: then to conceive the wish that all
heretics might be converted, and that she willingly offered
her life for their conversion, and she again made the signal
with great earnestness, and also took my hand within her
own, which were already chill, and held it firmly, repeating
the signs that she was pleased with the suggestions I
made to her. And I continued up to her last gasp,
encouraging her, and exhorting her to praise God in her
heart, to desire that all creatures should praise Him, and
to offer her life for this end. And she gave me answer
to everything, now raising, now lowering her hand, just
as I asked her to do in assent to what I suggested. All
the by-standers, who were numerous, and a priest also who
was among them, were in great admiration, and declared
that they never witnessed such a death as this. For she
continued, as I have said, responding to my suggestions
up to the very last breath, raising her hand slightly when

she could no longer raise it much. In these interior acts she gave up her soul, without any trouble of mind or convulsion of body, but like one going off to sleep, she went to rest in peace.

"Her youngest daughter had already died holily in our house before her mother. The second daughter married a rich man, and brought him to me from a considerable distance to be made a Catholic. The eldest still lives in the same house, to be espoused not to man but to God, for she has a vocation to the religious state. In the meantime she lives there religiously, and devotes herself to the service of religious, as the lady of the house always did, and does still.

"It is now high time that I bring this narrative to a close, for I have far exceeded the limits which I first proposed to myself; what remains therefore I will state briefly.

"I gave the Spiritual Exercises in this house to many others, as well to those who formed part of the family as to others; and in each case the fruit which I hoped for was produced. There were two persons who made only the Exercises of the first week, with the view of leading a good and holy life. One of these, now the father of a family, practises many acts of charity, and is no small friend of ours. The other came to me, unasked and unexpected, to make the Exercises, and when I asked him whence he got this idea and intention (for he was a very young man, the grandson of an earl, and the heir of a large property), he replied, 'I read in a book put forth against the Society by one of its enemies, that by means of these Exercises you have induced many to embrace a religious life, and have robbed them of their property. Among other names mine was mentioned as that of one who had made the Exercises under you, and it was said that though you did not succeed in making me a religious, yet you wheedled me out of a large sum of money. Now I know,' he continued, 'that my wife is much devoted to you, because you made her a Catholic ; but I know too, that neither from her nor from me have you ever received a penny. Since therefore they have done you so great a wrong, I have come to make good what they have falsely stated.'"

The book here quoted was evidently Watson's *Decachordon of ten Quodlibetical Questions*, which was "newly imprinted in 1602." And the sentence quoted is clearly, " He also gave the Exercise to the eldest son of Master Walter Hastings." The Earl, whose grandson this young man was, must therefore have been Francis Hastings, second Earl of Huntingdon. The name of the young man is mentioned in connection with Father Gerard's in Cecil's list,[1] so often quoted, of "the Jesuits that lurk in England." " John Gerard, with Mrs. Vaux and young Mr. Hastings." This "young Mr. Hastings" afterwards became Sir Henry Hastings, of Kirby, and then of Braunston, Knight, "who, like the rest of his kindred, was firmly attached to the royal cause during the civil wars, and paid 2072*l.* to the usurping party for redeeming his estates."[2] As his mother was Joyce or Jocosa Roper, sister of the first Lord Teynham, Henry Hastings was first cousin to Elizabeth Vaux, Father Gerard's hostess.

"So he made the Exercises, and with no slight profit ; and he afterwards sent me word, begging me to provide him a priest who could join in society publicly, and without suspicion. I therefore provided one, and was about to send him, when suddenly all things were upset for a time, and all good hindered by the Powder Plot, as it is called. And if proof were wanting that I knew nothing of this affair, this alone would be sufficient, that at that very time I had sent several from England across the sea into these parts. One was a lady, who was going to be a nun

---

[1] *Troubles*, 1st series, p. 191.
[2] *The Huntingdon Peerage*, by Henry Nugent Bell, London,, 1821, p. 61.

in the Benedictine Convent at Brussels, whither I had
sent two others not long before, who are now in high
authority there. Another had been an heretical minister,
whom I had brought to the faith and instructed. He
was the last that I received into the Church before these
disturbances. When these persons with certain others
were on the point of crossing the Channel, orders were
sent to allow no ships to leave; they were consequently
all taken and thrown into prison, from which they were
released two years ago. He who had been a minister
is at present studying in the Roman College; and the
lady of whom I spoke is now professed in the convent
whither she was going when she was taken. Only
one other minister, besides the one just mentioned, did
I convert in England, and he is now a priest and is
working in that vineyard. I also sent over many youths
to the seminaries while I was in this last residence
of mine, who will, by God's help, give their fruit in due
season.

"But if we have received good things from God's
hands, why should we not also bear with evil things?—if
those things can be truly called evil which are sent from
Him, and therefore sent that He may draw good from
them, for those who receive them well, and humbly recognize and adore His providence, both when He gives and
when He takes away. He had indeed given me many
and great consolations in this residence; interior consolations chiefly, from conversions and from the signal
progress in virtue of many souls; but exterior consolations
also were not wanting. For in external matters everything
was well and abundantly supplied me. I had several
excellent horses for my missionary journeys, and all that
I could wish for to carry on the work I had in hand.
Then, in the house itself, the arrangements were made in
the best way both for our health and our convenience.
And for companion I had Father Strange, who is now

in the Tower,[1] (for Sir Everard Digby had obtained Father Percy[2] from the Superior,) and another priest who resided a long time with us. We had moreover good store of useful books, which were kept in a library without any concealment, because they had the appearance of belonging to the young baron, and of having been left him by his uncle [Henry Vaux], who was a very learned and studious nobleman, and was well known for his piety. He had in fact resigned the right and title of the barony to his younger brother [George], the father of the present lord, in order that he might more entirely and securely devote himself to God and his studies. If he had lived a little longer, he would assuredly have been a member of our Society, for on his death-bed this was the only thing that caused him regret, viz., that he could not then be admitted into the Society, a thing he desired most earnestly.

"Our vestments and altar furniture were both plentiful and costly. We had two sets for each colour which the Church uses; one for ordinary use, the other for feast days: some of these latter were embroidered with gold and pearls, and figured by well-skilled hands. We had six massive silver candlesticks on the altar, besides those at the sides for the elevation: the cruets were of silver also, as were the basin for the lavabo, the bell, and the thurible. There were moreover lamps hanging from silver chains, and a silver crucifix on the altar. For greater festivals however I had a crucifix of gold, a foot in height, on the top of which was represented a pelican, while on the right arm of the cross was an eagle with expanded wings carrying on its back its young ones, who were also

---

[1] Qui nunc in rure est.—MS. An evident mistake of the copyist for "in turre," as is clear from a former notice of Father Strange, *supra*, p. 350.

[2] Cecil's list gives "Mr. Percie with Mr. Fittes in Essex." *Troubles*, 1st series, p. 191. "Fittes" must mean "Fitch," which family was closely connected with the Wisemans. If he was there at all, Father Percy must have been there before he became Father Gerard's companion at Harrowden.

attempting to fly; on the left arm a phœnix expiring
in flames that it might leave an offspring after it; and
at the foot was a hen with her chickens, gathering them
under her wings. All this was made of wrought gold by
a celebrated artist.

"I had there also a costly ornament representing the
Holy Name of Jesus, which my hostess had given me the
first Christmas after I came to live in her house. The
Name was formed of pins of solid gold, and the glory
surrounding it had two pins in one ray and three in the
next alternately. The whole was about twice the size of
a sheet of this paper, and contained two hundred and
forty of these gold pins, each pin having a large pearl
attached :—not indeed perfectly shaped pearls, for in that
case the value would have been something fabulous, yet
as it was, the whole ornament, pins and pearls and all,
was worth about a thousand florins [100*l.*]. There was
also at the bottom of it a sort of cypher wrought in gold
and gems by the artist, something in the shape of a
capital letter, expressing the donor's name, and in the
middle of the cypher was a heart, and from this heart
there issued a cross of diamonds. This ornament then
was given me by the devout widow on New Year's Day,
in honour of the most Holy Name of Jesus, commemorated
on that feast. All these ornaments are still kept there
in trust for the Society; and in the meantime serve for
the use of that domestic church and the residence of our
fathers. But I who was not sufficiently grateful to God
for these benefits which I have mentioned and many
others, was compelled to leave them to others who could
use them better and to greater advantage."

CHAPTER XXIX.

THE STORM.

1605.

"Since it was my chief friends who were involved in that disaster of the Powder Plot, the Council on this account believed me to be privy to it, and from the first sought for me with great persistence and severity. They sent certain magistrates to search our house most exactly, with orders, if they found me not, to stay in the house till recalled, to post guards all round the house every night, and to have men on the watch both day and night at a distance of three miles from the house on every side, who were to apprehend all whom they did not know and bring them before the said magistrates. All this was done to the letter. But immediately the news reached us of such a plot having been discovered, and we learnt that certain of our friends had been killed and others taken, expecting that in such a season we too should have something to suffer, we had made all snug before they came, so that they found nothing. They continued searching however for many days, till at last my hostess discovered to the justice in chief command one of the hiding-places in which a few books had been stowed away, thinking that he would then desist from searching any further under the impression that if a priest had been in the house he would have been hidden there, yet they continued in the house for full nine days; and I meanwhile remained shut up in a hiding-hole where I could sit but not stand upright. This time however I did not

z

suffer from hunger, for every night food was brought to
me secretly : nay, after four or five days, when the rigour
of the search was somewhat relaxed, my friends even took
me out at night and warmed me at a fire; for it was
wintry weather, just before Christmas-tide.   And when
nine days had passed, the searching party withdrew,
believing it impossible I could be there so long without
being discovered.

"In the meantime they had taken a priest who,
knowing nothing of the watch set about the place, was
coming to our house for safety.   This good priest (by
name Thomas Laithwaite,[1] who is now of our Society,
and is labouring in England) had left us a few days
before at my request, when we heard of the Plot, in
order to communicate with Father Garnet, and obtain from
him for me instructions how to act in the present crisis.
Even on his way thither he was taken, but escaped again
for that time in the following manner.   His captors took
him to an inn, intending to bring him up for examination
and committal the next day.   On entering the inn, he
took off his cloak and sword and laid them on a bench ;
then on pretence of looking after his horse and getting
him taken to water, he went to the stable, and as there
was a stream near the house, he bade the boy lead the
horse thither at once, and himself went along also.   When
they had come to the stream and the horse was drinking,
'Go,' said he to the lad, 'get ready the hay, and the
straw for his bed, and I will bring him back when he
has drunk.'   The boy returned to the stable without
further thought, and he mounting his horse spurred him
into the stream, and swam him to the opposite bank.
Those in the inn, seeing his cloak and sword still lying
there, had for some time no suspicion of his stratagem ;

[1] Father Thomas Laithwaite died in England, June 10, 1655, in his
seventy-eighth year, forty-nine years after his admission into the Society,
having spent thirty on the English Mission. *Summ. Def. Vide infr.* p. 404.

but hearing from the stable-boy what had happened, they
saw they had been outwitted, and immediately set off in
pursuit. They were however too late, for the fugitive,
knowing the way well, got to the house of a Catholic
before night, and lay hid there for a few days. Then,
finding that he could not get to Father Garnet, and
thinking all danger had passed in our direction, he tried
to return to me. But while avoiding Charybdis he fell
into the clutches of Scylla; for, as I said above, he was
taken on his way to our house, and dragged to London.
They were not able, however, to prove him a priest, and
his brother was allowed to buy him his freedom for a
sum of money.

"Two other priests who were resident with me in that
house (one of whom, as I said before, was Father Strange)
at the beginning of their troubles wished to go to Father
Garnet and remain with him. Both of them however
were taken prisoners on their way; one was thrown into
Bridewell, and was afterwards banished together with other
priests; while Father Strange, the other, was sent to the
Tower, where he suffered much, as has been before
mentioned.

"The history of this Plot, its causes and consequences,
is but too well known; since it has been written by both
friends and enemies, though perhaps by neither exactly
as it ought to be. I myself when I came from England
to Rome, was ordered to put in writing an account of
the whole affair, and did so as well as I could. There
is no need therefore to repeat here, what I wrote at
length on that occasion — in what state England then
was—how the persecution not only was not relaxed on
the accession of the King [James I.], but was even em-
bittered, and carried on more grievously than ever. All
the Catholics therefore expected, and some knew for
certain, that new laws would be made against them in
Parliament, more severe and cruel than the former ones;

that not only would nothing be relaxed of the tyranny of the Queen, but that the yoke which they had so long borne with weary necks would be made yet heavier to bear. Hereupon some of the younger and more impatient sort, seeing that they were scourged, not now with whips only but with scorpions—that no human hope was left them except from such aid as they could give themselves, since peace was now concluded between His Catholic Majesty and the King of England, from which peace the Catholics were excluded (though it was they who had a right to peace and not the wicked)—these persons, I say, seeing this, and forgetting at last that patience in which we ought to possess our souls, and not enduring any longer to see sacred things trodden under foot, and the faithful robbed of their goods and loaded with innumerable evils, to the daily lamentable ruin of weak souls, determined to raise the people of God from this disastrous state, and to wage war in strictest secrecy against the enemies of their own souls and bodies and of the Catholic cause. I say, in secrecy, because it must be acknowledged that any open opposition was no longer possible, since the Catholics were broken in strength and ground down to the earth, and all their arms had been taken from them. Thus it was that these persons I speak of, wishing to deliver themselves and others from this terrible slavery of soul and body, devised this plot, which they thought the only possible way of accomplishing what they wished, viz., by taking off at a single blow all the chief enemies of the Catholic cause.

"On all these points I have written at full in the treatise I mentioned. I have also detailed there the way in which they had determined to proceed, and how one of them [1] disclosed the matter in confession to one of our Fathers when it was already ripe for execution, who refused to hear him any further unless he was allowed

---

[1] This was Catesby, the prime mover of the whole plot.

to inform his Superior; and how the Superior [Father
Garnet], upon hearing so bloody a scheme, at once commanded the Father to deter and prevent his penitent as
much as he could from prosecuting it, and immediately
wrote to the Pope, entreating His Holiness to forbid the
Catholics to take any measures of external violence.
I have also there set down how the Superior himself
and Father Oldcorne were at last taken at [Henlip] the
residence of the latter, after remaining pent up for twelve
days in a hiding-hole :—how with them were also taken
two serving-men, or as I have heard since and fully
believe, two lay-brothers of our Society, both of whom
suffered martyrdom. One of these, Rodolph [Ashley] [1]
by name, suffered with Father Oldcorne, whose companion and attendant he had been, and whose feet he
kissed as the Father was ascending the ladder to his
execution, giving him thanks aloud for the charity and
benevolence he had experienced from him, and praising
God for having allowed him to die in the company of
so holy a priest.

"The other was Little John [Nicholas Owen], who
for nearly twenty years had been Father Garnet's companion, and of whom I have made frequent mention in
the course of this Narrative. He was well known to the
persecutors as the chief deviser and maker of hiding-
places all over England, and consequently as one who
could discover more priests, and do more harm to
Catholics, if he could be brought to make disclosures,
than any other man. They therefore tortured him so
long and so cruelly, that at last he died [2] under their

---

[1] See *Troubles*, First Series, p. 162.

[2] After thus wringing his life from him by torture, his gaolers gave out
that he had committed suicide in prison, to escape further question : thus
adding calumny to murder. And this statement is found in most of the
larger histories of England. The holy brother was never brought into any
court, nor allowed the least chance of communication with any friends ;
nor could anything be learnt of him after his capture, but what his gaolers
chose to tell. That he was tortured barbarously they acknowledged, by

hands ; but they were never able to shake the constancy
of his soul.

"I have related also in that treatise how Fathers
Garnet and Oldcorne were brought up to London, and
frequently examined, especially Father Garnet ; how both
of them were tortured, but Father Oldcorne [1] most : how
this latter was then taken back to Worcester, and there,
though nothing but his priesthood was proved against
him, condemned and executed by hanging and quartering,
and so died a martyr : how Father Garnet was brought to
trial in London, and gave so clear and eloquent defence
of himself, that all were struck with admiration ; but after
a time was so interrupted and brow-beaten by Cecil and
others, that the gentle Father could not proceed with his
defence as he had begun : [2] and how when brought to the
place of execution, by the firmness and modesty of his
whole demeanour, and by the heroic calmness with which
he received or rather embraced his death, he touched the
hard hearts of his cruel enemies, and rendered them well-
affected towards him.

"All these details, which I have here barely enumer-
ated, in my other narrative I have described at full. I
will however add here something on the way in which
the straw was obtained, on which appeared the miraculous
likeness of Father Garnet ; for I was afterwards present
at the death-bed of him who found the straw, or rather to
whom God granted it. This person [John Wilkinson] then
narrated to me a little before his death, that on the morn-

saying that he committed suicide to escape their cruelty ; that he never
revealed anything was also acknowledged. It must be remembered that
those who were killed in prison were always given out by the authorities
as suicides. But who can believe that a man who would suffer the extremity of torture rather than offend God by revealing what would injure
his neighbour, would not also suffer the same extremity rather than offend
God by self-murder? The Day of Judgment will refute this calumny as
well as others.

[1] He was hung up by the hands, in the way Father Gerard has described
of himself, for five hours at a time, and that for five successive days.

[2] James himself said that "the Jesuit had not had fair play."

ing of the holy martyr's execution he had felt himself moved
by an unusual fervour, and by a desire of being present
at his martyrdom, mainly with the view of obtaining some
portion of his relics. He had therefore, he said, pushed
forward close to where the executioner was hacking his
body in pieces, but durst not touch anything for fear of
the officers standing round; just then, the executioner
having severed the venerable head from the body threw
it into a basket full of straw, upon which an ear of straw
leapt out into his hand, or so close to it that he could
remove it without attracting any notice. This ear of
straw he found was stained with blood, so that he kept
it with great reverence and joy; and he protested to me
that for some days he found himself more inclined to
spiritual things and to follow the counsels of Christ than
he had ever been before; so that he felt no peace till he
gave up all he had, and made arrangements for coming
hither across the water, to make his studies for the
priesthood. He had also a strong desire of entering
the Society; and in these pious sentiments he continued
to his death, which took place at St. Omers, and in which
he gave such edification to all about him, that no one
there remembers a holier death than his.

"I will also add here a further testimony regarding
an incident of Father Oldcorne's martyrdom. I mentioned in that other narrative of mine, that I had had
information by letter from England, that this holy martyr's
intestines, being thrown into the fire according to sentence,
burned for sixteen days, exactly the number of years
during which he had kindled in that country the fire of
Divine love and maintained it by his word and example.
Now quite lately I had a conversation on this subject with
a pious priest, who at present goes by the name of Father
North at St. Omers. He tells me that he was himself
a prisoner at Worcester at the time, and that he heard
then from many persons, not only that the fire lasted

all that time notwithstanding a great deal of rain that fell, but that it broke out into high flames, and that multitudes went to see it, who on their return acknowledged the truth of the report: so that at last, on the sixteenth or seventeenth day they were obliged to extinguish the fire, or at least cover it up by heaping earth upon it. This same Father also declared that he subsequently saw in the courtyard of the house where these two Fathers were taken the form of a crown traced out by grass that had grown there. He said that this grass was different both in kind and colour from any other about; that it grew taller also, and traced clearly out the shape of an imperial crown. He added moreover that the beasts that got into the court-yard through the broken gates (for the house from the time of the capture had been neglected and abandoned), browsed there for many months, yet never during the whole time touched this crown or trod upon it. He looked on it as a symbol of the innocence of these Fathers and of their eternal reward."

FATHER GARNET'S STRAW.

NOTE TO CHAPTER XXIX.

FATHER GARNET'S STRAW.

1. A FULLER account of Father Garnet's straw is given by Father Gerard in his history of the Powder Plot.[1] "The first sign," he there says, "by which it pleased God to show the merit and glory of this His martyr was concerning his relics, which were eagerly sought for by many Catholics at the very time of his martyrdom. Amongst which there was one young man [John Wilkinson] who stood by the block where the martyr's body was cut up, with great desire at least to get some drop of his holy blood. And whilst he had these thoughts, not daring to take where he desired for fear of being espied, it fortuned that the hangman having cut off the martyr's head and showed it to the people (as the custom is), he cast it into a basket standing there of purpose, full of straw, to hold the head and quarters when they were divided. Out of this basket did leap a straw or ear void of corn in strange manner into the hand of this young man, which he beholding and seeing some blood on it, kept it with great care, and no little joy that he had obtained his desire. He carried it away safely and delivered it unto a Catholic gentlewoman of his acquaintance [Mrs. Griffin], who kept it in a reliquary with great devotion; and after three or four days [two or three months *interlined in orig. MS.*], a devout Catholic gentleman coming thither, she showed him the bloody straw, which he was also glad to see and reverence; but beholding the same more curiously than the others had done, he saw a perfect face, as if it had been painted, upon one of the husks of the empty ear, and showed the same unto the company, which they did plainly behold, and with no small wonder, but. with much greater joy did acknowledge the mighty hand of God, Who can and doth often use the meanest creatures to set forth His glory, and is able both out of stones and straws to raise a sufficient defence for His faithful servants.

"They put up the straw again with great admiration, and

[1] *Condition of Catholics,* p. 301.

kept it now with much more reverence and devotion than before. This was quickly published to many of the chiefest Catholics about London, who much desiring to see this wonder, it was carried unto divers, who are all witnesses of this truth. At length it came to the Council's ear, and some of them desiring much to see it, it was granted, being now in the keeping of a great person,[1] but with promise to have it safely restored ; so that some of them did see it, and did much admire it, affirming that it must needs be more than natural. Others after desired to see it and to seize upon it, because now the fame did grow so great of this image of Father Garnet drawn by the hand of God, whose image and memory they sought to deface in all they could, that they feared the evidence of the miracle would plead against their proceedings and prove him innocent whom they had punished as guilty. Therefore the Bishop of Canterbury [Archbishop Richard Bancroft] sought to have the miraculous straw into his hands, but it was denied, and none would acknowledge where it was to be found. He learned out the party to whom the keeping of it was first committed, and sent for her husband, who was a known Catholic and a virtuous man. He examined him strictly how it came to pass, and where the straw was. The Catholic affirmed the truth of the thing and described it unto him in words ; but said it was not now in his keeping, and he knew not where to find it. And when they could get no other answer of him, they committed him to prison ; but afterwards, having sundry and great friends in the Court, he got out upon bonds to appear again at certain days' warning.

" In the meantime it happened that two were miraculously cured by application of the same straw. One was a gentlewoman in great peril of her life by danger of childbirth, who, when she had sustained long and painful travail and could not be delivered of her burthen, and now was out of hope of life, unless she might obtain some help from God, some of her friends made earnest means to get this holy straw to bring unto her; which

[1] Father More says that this was the Spanish Ambassador, which is in accordance with Griffin's deposition. He gives an attestation of the Baron de Hobocque, dated in 1625, attesting that he had seen the straw in 1606, when he was in London as Ambassador of the Archdukes of the Low Countries. *Hist. Prov. Angl.* lib. vii. n. 35.

being obtained, and the straw brought and applied with great reverence, presently she received help, and was delivered by the mighty hand of God and merits of the martyr, whom no midwife's skill or endeavour could help before.

"Another was the gentlewoman herself who first had this miraculous relic delivered her to keep. For she being very much subject to sickness, and sometimes in such extremity therewith that you would not think she could be able to live an hour, it happened that in one of her extremest fits, when she could find no medicine or means that could bring her any ease, she earnestly desired a special friend to make suit for the straw to be returned unto her for a small time, which was granted ; and as soon as it came (she receiving it with great devotion and reverence) she presently found ease, and within half an hour was so perfectly well that she rose from her bed, and went to entertain some strangers that then were in the house, and *erat una ex discumbentibus*—['was one of them that were at table.' St. John xii. 2].

"This sudden and strange cure of hers being spoken of by divers Catholics, it came out to be known unto the Council, who sent again for the husband of the gentlewoman, and took this new occasion to commit him the second time to prison.

"The Council afterwards understanding that this miraculous picture in the straw had been shown to divers painters in London, they sent for the painters and willed them to make the like portrait to that which they had seen in a like empty ear of corn ; but they all answered that it was not possible for them to do it, neither could the draught of that face, in so little a room and so loose a groundwork as that empty ear, be otherwise drawn than by supernatural power. And this testimony they gave of it that had both skill to judge and no will to favour the Catholic cause (being in opinion heretics), but only convinced in their understanding by the evidence of the miracle."

2. The Archbishop of Canterbury [Bancroft] to the Lord Chief Justice [Sir John Popham] on the apprehension of Barret [Barnes] and the miracle of Garnet's straw : from the original letter in the Archives of the See of Westminster, vol. viii. p. 41.

" My Lord, I gave a warrant to Mr. Skidmore for the apprehending of one Barret, who went up and down with a miracle of Garnet's head supposed to be upon a straw that was on the hurdle whereupon he was drawn to his execution. This warrant was signed with my Lord Chancellor's hand, my Lord Treasurer's, my Lord of London and mine. Upon the serving of the warrant, the said Barret drew his rapier and hath hurt Skidmore, and is likewise thrust through the thigh by him. This Barret is at a barber's shop in Fleet street not far from the Temple gate. I heartily pray your lordship to send for the stay of him that he may be forthcoming. He is a notable villain. And so I commit your lordship to God. At Lambeth, this 25th day of November 1606.

Your lordship's most assured,

R. CANT.

" To-morrow I will acquaint you with some other particulars."

Addressed " To the Right Honourable the Lord Chief Justice of the King's Bench, one of his Majesty's Most Honourable Privy Council."

Endorsed [1] " The dispersers, Griffin's wife, Mrs. Anne Vaux, sent to her by a gentleman, Mrs. Gage of Bentley."

3. Robert Barnes' examination, from a contemporary copy in the same authority, p. 43.

" The examination of Robert Barnes of Harleton in the County of Cambridge gent., taken by the Lord Archbishop of Canterbury the 27th of November 1606.

" He saith that about the 13th of November, being Thursday, he went to Hugh Griffin's, a tailor, to see if his, this examinate's, gown were made : that until that very time he had never heard of the wheat ear whereupon a visage is supposed to be seen : that Griffin's wife was the first who then told him of it : that she said there was a straw besmeared with Garnet's blood at his execution which had upon it the form of a face : that it was a very strange thing, but was not then at home with her : that she promised him when he came again, to show it him : that accordingly, he going unto her two days after, viz. upon the Saturday, she showed it

[1] This letter has another endorsement, which is not easily decipherable.

him : that he, this examinate, looking upon it through the crystal, first saw a white thing : that she bade him look wistly upon it, and that then he imagined he saw two eyes closed, then a face pale, as he thought : after, a short chin : then a forehead somewhat high : then a perfect face : that he, being of the age of 56, and having endured 10 years' imprisonment, hath a dim sight : that he saw the said face through the crystal and his spectacles by candlelight : that he espied the face, as is before mentioned, within the time that a man would go 40 steps : that after he had discerned the face, he saw (as he thought) two locks of hair standing upright in the midst of the top of the forehead : that having so seen it, he only said to Mrs. Griffin that it was a strange and wonderful sight, and that he hath not told any of it but one or two in Poules [St. Paul's] whose names he remembereth not, and that he told them he made no great account of it : that he maketh no great account of it, because it may be drawn by the art of some painter : that the colour of the cheeks differed from the colour of the eyebrows, and that the parts of the face were distinguished from one another, as it were, with the draught of some hair or of some very small thing, and that the beard was somewhat reddish : that he saw not Garnet for the space of 20 years past, before he came through Cheapside upon the hurdle : that his beard was then whitish, but had been in colour betwixt yellow and red.

" Being demanded why he hath not since that time laboured to satisfy himself whether the said face were made by art or by some extraordinary means, he saith that his business hath been such, as he hath had no time to think of it.

" Being demanded why he did not ask Mrs. Griffin whether it were a face indeed made by art or otherwise, he saith that he made so small account of it, as he asked her no questions about it.

" Thirdly, being demanded how his words concerning the small account he made of it, can agree with his former speeches, where he said it was a very strange and wonderful thing, he answereth that though it were made with art, it is strange and wonderful in his opinion to have so perfect a face made in so little a room."

Endorsed " The copy of the Examination of Robert Barnes taken before the Lord Archbishop of Canterbury 27° Novem. 1606."

4. Francis Bowen's examination. *Ibid.* p. 47.

" The examination of Francis Bowen of London gent., but useth limning,[1] taken by the Lord Archbishop of Canterbury on the 27th of November 1606.

" He saith that betwixt three weeks and a fortnight since one Anser servant to Sir William Wiseman[2] of Essex told this examinate that he had seen an ear of corn with a face upon it, and said that if he, this examinate, would, he could bring him where he might see it: that accordingly he brought this examinate to a house in Clerkenwell where Mrs. Anne Vaux was, and one Mr. Dolman who hath a knight to his brother:[3] that when Anser and this examinate came into the house, the said Dolman and Mrs. Anne Vaux were looking upon the ear, being in a crystal: that upon the said Anser's motion they let him, this examinate, see it: that Mr. Dolman bade this examinate look whether he could espie the face: that he espied it in the while that the *Ave Maria* may be repeated: that upon his espying of it, he perceived it to be a perfect face: that the proportion of the face was in the blade that lay upon the husk of a corn, the corn being out, or rather, the blood made the proportion of the face: that upon the top of his forehead stood up certain hairs: that the forehead was something high, and had as it were two wrinkles overthwart it: that there was then a little stroke went down resembling a nose: the mouth was not well discerned because the hair of the upper lip did hang over it: the beard seemed to be somewhat long and bloody: that the compass of the face seemed to be, either the extremity of the husk, or else some little brown blackish small strokes which he conceived to be of blood congealed of that colour: that the hair above the forehead seemed to be likewise little streaks of blood, and so were the two wrinkles, the two little

---

[1] That is to say that, " though a gentleman, he practises painting."

[2] We thus learn that Father Gerard's friend was knighted early in James' reign. Sir William Wiseman published a book in 1619 called "The Christian Knight."

[3] That is, "whose brother is a knight."

strokes for the eyebrows, the stroke that was made down for the nose, two small streaks resembling the eyes, and the hairs of the beard were like the hairs on the top of the forehead, saving that they were (as is aforesaid) somewhat more of the colour of blood : that there was no more to be seen but the head, as neither the arms, shoulders nor neck : that the face was much like to this in the margent,[1] saving that it was drawn in a better proportion : that all the rest of the face, saving the said streaks, was the husk itself : that he verily thinketh the face upon the ear which he saw in the glass, might have been made as skilfully or more skilfully by a cunning workman : that he verily believeth if the said straw came first into a dishonest man's hand, the face upon the ear might have been counterfeited : that he first heard of the said face about a week before he saw it, but remembereth not by whom : that before he saw it and since he hath heard many Catholics talk of it, and some of them to affirm that the face was like to Garnet's : that one Mr. Martin who taught the children upon the virginals that played in the Blackfriars did ask this examinate whether it were not like Garnet's face."

Endorsed "The copy of the examination of Francis Bowen, taken before the Lord Archbishop of Canterbury 27° Nov. 1606."

5. Hugh Griffin's first examination, from a contemporary copy in the Archives of the Old Chapter.

"The confession of Hugh Griffin, of St. Clement's without Temple Bar, tailor :—taken by the Lord Archbishop of Canterbury, November 27, 1606. He saith that the same day that Garnet was executed [May 3, 1606], one John Wilks [*sic*], a silkman, being come out of his prenticeship two years since, and living now amongst his friends in Yorkshire, brought to this examinate's house a straw with an ear upon it, which he said was one of the straws whereupon Garnet was laid when he was executed ; that the straw and ear were bloody ; that this examinate and his wife desired to have the straw ; that he promised they should have it at his going into the country ; that they advised with the said Wilks to have the straw put into a crystal for the better preserving of it ; that within three or four days or a week (as he remembereth) the

---

[1] There is no face given in the margin of the copy.

straw was set in crystal, according to the former resolution; that
about nine weeks since [about the 25th of September] and not
before, he, this examinate, looking earnestly through the crystal
upon the said straw, with his wife, and one Thomas (who once
served, as he thinketh, the Lady Beeston, wife to Sir Hugh
Beeston) they all together at once discovered a thing like a face
upon the ear of the said straw; that this examinate did first say
to the other two (as he thinketh), 'Do you not discern a thing
upon the ear like a face?' and they answered that they did;
that thereupon he then (as he thinketh) opened the crystal, and
then, upon their earnest looking upon it, they imagined they saw
a face; that this examinate thereupon said to the rest, 'This may
chance to proceed from our fancies,' and therefore desired them
to make no words of it until it were better decided; that he kept
it in his house about a fortnight, and in the meantime looked
upon it forty times (as he thinketh) and sometimes half an hour
or an hour together, until he saw the visage so perfectly as he is
sure he could not be deceived; that the face is so perfectly
apparent, being once found, viz. the forehead, the eyes, the
cheek, the nose, the mouth, the beard, and the neck, as he
supposeth no man living is able to draw the like thing upon the
like subject; that the said Wilks, when he left the straw in the
crystal with this examinate, did not (as he thinketh) ever imagine
that there was any face upon it; that he doth not remember that
any but himself and his wife did see the said face during the
said fortnight, or that himself did acquaint any with it; that
peradventure his wife might tell somebody of it, but whom he
knoweth not, that after the said fortnight ended, when he was
assured as aforesaid, he showed it to Lord William Howard;[1]
that Dr. Taylor being present (as he remembereth) desired to
have had it, to have been showed to the Ambassador of Spain; that
the Lord William kept the said straw, and showed it to such as
he thought fit; that about ten days after, this examinate received
it again from the said Lord William; that he thereupon delivered
it unto Dr. Taylor, in the hope of some good reward to be given
unto him; that he delivered it as he did never expect to have
it again, except it were to borrow it, with the Ambassador's

---

[1] Lord William Howard of Naworth, third son of Thomas fourth Duke of
Norfolk, half-brother of Philip Earl of Arundel.

liking, to show it to some of his friends that would desire to see
it; that his lordship kept it some two or three days; that he,
this examinate, received it again and showed it to some, but he
doth not remember to whom; that he delivered it back again to
Dr. Taylor within a day or two after he had received it from the
Lord William; that Dr. Taylor told him how the Lord Ambassador made great account of it, had sent it to be seen by the
Ambassador of Venice, and that he was very loth to part with it;
that he delivered the said straw to Dr. Taylor, as aforesaid;
that the Lord William first had it for about five days before he,
this examinate, gave it to Dr. Taylor as aforesaid; that this
examinate did show it to Mrs. Anne Vaux, when he had it from
the Lord William and before he returned it back again to
Dr. Taylor after he had borrowed it; that this examinate lent
it at that time to the said Mrs. Anne Vaux; that she had it with
her a day and a half or two days; that he supposeth she showed
it unto divers; that this examinate was much troubled before he
could get it again from Mrs. Anne Vaux; that if any affirm that
there is any light or beams about the said face, he affirmeth that
which is not true; that for aught this examinate knoweth, the
said face is no more like Garnet's face than any other man's that
hath a beard; that he imagineth, the face being so little, no man
is able to say it is like Garnet; that this examinate never did see
Mr. Garnet but when he was brought to the Tower; that he
remembereth that Mr. Garnet was a well-set man, and had a big
face, according to his proportion; that though the face seem but
little at the first view, yet upon diligent looking upon it, it
seemeth still to increase in perfectness and to be bigger, but
that when it is perfectly discerned with the eye, it continueth in
one and the same bigness; that he verily thinketh, except one
be told in which husk the face is, he will very hardly find it; that
all the said perfect visage, to be seen as is aforesaid, is contained
in the length and breadth of the husk of one corn. He also
saith upon occasion of further speech that the crystal wherein the
straw is set was his own before, and that he gave it to the said
Wilks that the straw might be put into it, and took order with
him that the crystal should be set in gold or silver and gilt; that
it is about the breadth of a shilling, but made in the form of a

AA

heart; that it is about a quarter of an inch thick; that the straw is nipped off, and the whole ear lieth round in it."

6. Hugh Griffin's second examination, from the Archives of Westminster, vol. viii. p. 51.

"The second examination of Hugh Griffin of St. Clement's without Temple Bar, tailor, taken by the Lord Archbishop of Canterbury 27° Novemb. 1606.

"He saith that within 8 or 10 days of Garnet's death the ear wherein the face is seen was put in crystal, which must fall out to be about the eleventh or twelfth of May : that about Midsummer John Wilks went into Yorkshire, returned a little before Michaelmas, and went back again into Yorkshire about a week after Michaelmas : that about 8 or 10 weeks since, he first discerned the face in the said ear : that from about the 11th or 12th of May he had the said crystal and ear in his house, before he espied the said visage till about the 18th of September, which was 19 weeks : that all this time of 19 weeks he never looked upon the said crystal : that before the said 19 weeks ended, he had no time to look upon it : that when he first looked upon it about 10 weeks since, he saw a glimmering of a face.

"He saith that when the crystal with the ear was first brought unto him by Wilks, he looked upon it, but did not then espy any visage : that he looked a good while earnestly upon it about 10 weeks since, before he saw the glimmering of a face. And being demanded why he viewed the same longer and more earnestly at this time than he did when it was first brought unto him in the said crystal, he answereth, because he had not leisure when it first was brought unto him, so to view it.

"Being demanded how it came to pass that he never looked upon it for the space of the said 19 weeks, but when his wife and one Thomas were present, he answereth that then he was best at leisure.

"That he thinketh it was never seen, after it was brought unto him first in crystal, until about the 10 weeks before mentioned."

Endorsed "Copy of the second examination of Hugh Griffin, 27° Nov. 1606."

7. Hugh Griffin's third examination : *ibid.* p. 55.

" The examination of Hugh Griffith [*sic*] taken by the Lord Archbishop of Canterbury 3° December [*sic*] 1606.

" He saith that it was a month or 5 weeks after Michaelmas when he saw John Wilkinson [*sic*] last : that he so thinketh because he used the said John his advice in letting a house of Mr. Preston's to the Count Arundell about the first wee[k] as he thinketh after Michaelmas : that the said John h[as] a brother dwelling at the upper end of Cheapside : that [about] 8 days since the said John's mother sent a letter to th[is examinate] signifying unto him that she heard her son wa[s gone] beyond seas, and desiring of him, this examinate, that if he [were] not gone, he would stay him : that it was not John his said brother who brought the said letter but one out of the country : that he knew not of his going beyond seas, if he be gone, nor did ever advise him thereunto.

" Being demanded where the said Thomas is to be found, whom he mentioned in his first examination, he desireth to be foreborne therein, for that being a Catholic he would not bring him into trouble : that he did not see the said Thomas since about 10 days past, as he remembereth.

" Being demanded unto how many he had lent the crystal with the straw, besides the Lord William, and Mrs. Anne Vaux, he desireth to be foreborne, for that he had received blame for that he hath done already : that it might be that the said John did see the face in the crystal, having lain for the most part seven weeks at this examinate's house at his last being at London.

" Being demanded unto whom he imparted the effect of his confession before the Lord Archbishop of Canterbury at his first examination, he desireth to be foreborne the answering of it ; only he saith that he thinketh he told the Lord Chief Justice's man somewhat of it.

" He further saith that he mistook something in his first examination which now he amendeth, saying that John Wilkinson bringing the straw from Garnet's execution, this examinate willed his wife that it might be put into something, for else it would moulde[r] away : that thereupon the same day the said John and this examinate's wife did put it into a little vase of crystal, which his wife had ready made, and that for aught he knoweth it was so laid up and not seen for 19 weeks after : that he knoweth not whether he lent the glass with the straw unto the said John Wilkinson or unto this said Thomas."

Endorsed "Copy of . . . examination . . . December."

8. Thomas Laithwaite's examination : *ibid.* p. 59.

"The second[1] examination of Thomas Laithwaite, servant to the Lady Katharine Gray, taken by the Lord Archbishop of Canterbury 3° December 1606.

"He saith that Hugh Griffith did not send for him upon the Friday morning after he had been first examined before the Lord Archbishop of Canterbury, which was the Tuesday before, viz. on the 27th of November : that no person man or woman came unto him in Hugh Griffith's name for his, this examinate's, repair unto him : that nobody was present when the said Hugh Griffith told him what he had confessed : that what he told him was in Griffith's shop : that he received the crystal with the straw from Griffith about Sunday was a fortnight : that he received it upon one day and brought it back to Griffith the day following : that whilst he had it, he showed it to Sir Hugh Beeston[2] and one Mr. Fortescue : that he re-delivered the said crystal with the straw to Griffith in his chamber, nobody being present : that he never borrowed nor had the said straw from Griffith but once as

---

[1] The copy of the first examination does not seem to have been preserved. Father Gerard has said, *supra*, p. 387, that they could not prove Thomas Laithwaite to be a priest, and in these examinations there is nothing to show that he was suspected of being one. It is noteworthy that Hugh Griffin is asked "where the said Thomas is to be found," at the very time when he was in Archbishop Bancroft's custody. Father Gerard adds that "his brother was allowed to buy his freedom." This would seem to be a confusion with a former imprisonment, for Thomas Laithwaite was one of the 47 priests who were banished in 1606. He had been arrested on his landing at Plymouth in 1604 and condemned to death for his priesthood at the Lammas Assizes at Exeter, and he was then the means of converting his brother Edward, who had come to see him in prison in the hope of reclaiming him to Protestantism. There were five of the family in the Society, three priests who were known by the name of Kensington, Father Thomas whose *alias* was Scott, and the eldest who was a lay-brother (More, *Hist. Prov.* lib. ix. n. 1).

[2] Sir Hugh Beeston, son of Sir George Beeston, who distinguished himself against the Armada and died in September 1601, married Margaret, daughter of Laurence Downes of Worthe, and widow of Philip Worthe of Tydrington.

aforesaid : that the Lady Katharine Gray had seen the said straw, but by whose means he knoweth not ; but afterwards he said, he knoweth not whether ever she saw it or no, nor whether he hath ever hear[d] her acknowledge that she saw it : that he will not tell anything that may bring others in trouble, though it cost him his life.

"He further saith that he knoweth Dr. Taylor and was with him at the Embassador's house of Spain on Friday or Saturday last : that he had no business with him but only was there to see his wife : that he had been acquainted with Dr. Taylor since the beginning of summer : that he never saw the said crystal with the straw either in the Lord Embassador's or in Dr. Taylor's house."

Endorsed "Copy of Thomas Laithwaite's second examination 3° Decem. 1606."

9. The account given by John Wilkinson, when dying at St. Omers, translated from Father More's *Historia Provinciæ Anglicanæ*, lib. vii., n. 35.

"I, John Wilkinson, stricken by a grievous malady, and my life being despaired of by the physicians, that I may acquit myself of an obligation by which I am bounden to God and His saints, will now declare how I found the ear of corn on which the likeness of blessed Father Garnet is to be seen.

"The day previous to Father Garnet's execution, I was taken with a vehement desire of beholding his death, and of carrying away something of his relics. I was filled with an assurance of satisfying my desire so great that I did not doubt but that I should see something whereby God would testify to the innocence of His holy servant. When this thought kept continually recurring to me I endeavoured to drive it from my mind, lest by expecting a miracle where there was no need of one, I might tempt God and offend Him. On the following day very early I betook myself to the place of execution and took up a position as near the scaffold as possible, remaining in the same spot until Garnet came. So great, however, was the concourse of horsemen on the arrival of the Father, and such a crowd of people pressed round that I could not keep my position, nor hear distinctly what was said. I remarked nevertheless many things which caused me no slight consolation. In the first place, the careful arrangement of his shirt that it might not be raised by the wind, which gave me a great idea of his modesty and purity. Again when the ladder was removed, his hands placed over his breast in the form of a cross, although they dropped somewhat, yet retained the same form of the cross over his heart until he expired. This furnished me with greater reason for wonder, as if it had been a sign sent from Heaven, for whilst dying he had prayed that God would not allow the Cross of his Lord to be torn from his heart. I also perceived that when his head was cut off and held up for the view of the spectators, that his countenance was the same and retained the same colour as in life; and at the same time I remarked that I did not hear any one cry out ' Long live the King!' as is the custom on such an occasion. This was a proof to me that even then the people were convinced of his innocence. After his body had been cut up into four parts and together with the head thrown into a basket and placed in a cart, as the crowd by degrees retired I advanced into the space between the scaffold and the cart, still with the same eager desire of carrying off some of his relics. Whilst I was looking round, this ear of corn, concerning which there is now so much talk, somehow or other came into my hands. Straw was thrown from the scaffold into the basket containing the head and members, but whether this ear came from the scaffold or the basket I cannot say, I am certain however that it did not touch the ground. I handed over this ear the same day to Mrs. Griffin, and she placed it in a crystal case, which being rather small caused the ear to be bent round. A few days afterwards in my presence she showed it to one of our acquaintance a very good man. When he had looked at it with much attention he said, ' I do not see anything except a man's face.' Astonished at this remark, we ran to the case and both of us beheld the face which we had not remarked before. Others also being summoned perceived it at the same time. And this is the most true account of the ear which I found, as God knows, and I considered that for His glory I was bound to narrate it."

10. Father Richard Blount, in a letter dated November 8, 1606, says, "A Catholic person in London having kept, since the execution of Mr. Garnet, a straw that was embued in his blood, now these days past being viewed again by the party and others, they espy in the ear of the straw a perfect face of a man dead, his eyes, nose, beard, and neck so lively representing Mr. Garnet as not only in my eyes but in the eyes of others which knew him, it doth lively represent him. This hath been seen by Catholics and Protestants of the best sort and divers others who much admire it &c. This you may boldly report, for besides ourselves a thousand others are witnesses of it."

And in another letter dated March, 1607, "It cannot be a thing natural or artificial. The sprinkling of blood hath made so plain a face, so well proportioned, so lively shadowed, as no art in such a manner is able to counterfeit the like." Stonyhurst MSS., Father Grene's *Collectan. M.*

11. Father Henry More, whose history was published in 1660, says that the straw was kept in the English College of the Society at Liége. The last mention we have met of it is by the Abbé Feller, in the article "Garnett" in his *Dictionnaire Historique,* which was published at Liége in 1797, and therefore after the suppression of the Society. His words are, "L'épi est aujourd-hui entre les mains d'un de mes amis, qui le conserve soigneusement." These words are omitted in the later editions of the Dictionary.

CHAPTER XXX.

ESCAPE.

1606.

" I WILL now add a few words about myself before closing this narrative. I have stated in the other treatise of which I spoke, that a proclamation was issued against three Jesuit Fathers, of whom I was one ; and, though the most unworthy, I was named first in the proclamation, whereas I was the subject of one, and far inferior in all respects to the other. All this, however, I solemnly protest was utterly groundless ; for I knew absolutely nothing of the Plot from any one whatsoever, not even under the seal of confession, as the other two did ; nor had I the slightest notion that any such scheme was entertained by any Catholic gentleman, until by public rumour news was brought us of its discovery, as it was to all others dwelling in that part of the country.

"When I saw by that long search of nine days that I was sought after and aimed at in particular, I wrote a public letter, as if to some friend, in which by many arguments, and by protestations beyond all cavil, I maintained my entire innocence of the charges brought against me. Of this letter I caused many copies to be taken, and to be dropped about the London streets very early in the morning. These were found and read by many persons, and a copy was shown to the King by one of the Lords of Council, who was no enemy either of mine or of my cause. The King, as I heard, was personally satisfied by this. Afterwards, however, when information was given

them of Father Garnet's hiding-place, and they conceived
hopes of catching him, and of turning the whole charge
on the Society, they thought it necessary to publish the
names of some of ours as the principal contrivers of the
Plot. So they put my name down, as well as those of
the other two Fathers, of whom they had heard from a
certain servant of Master Catesby. This man, however,
before his death, repenting of this injury he had done
them, confessed that he had been induced to say what
he did of them against his conscience, by the fear of death
on the one hand, and by the hope of pardon, and by the
persuasions and suggestions of Secretary Cecil on the
other. And it is possible that some persons at that time
had a real suspicion that I was privy to the thing, because
they knew that many of the gentlemen who had been
taken were friends of mine, and were in the habit of
visiting me at my London house. This, indeed, was
acknowledged by one of them in his examination, though
at the same time he affirmed that I knew nothing of their
scheme. Nor did they ever get a single word against me
from any of their examinations. Sir Everard Digby, indeed, who was known to be most intimate with me, and
for that reason was most strictly examined about me,
publicly protested in open court that he never dare mention a syllable of it to me, because I should never have
permitted him to go on with it. When I had heard of
all this, and besides, had learnt several particulars concerning Father Garnet, which proved that any knowledge
he had was under seal of confession, and imparted to him
by the only priest of the Society who knew of it, and that
also only in confession ; it seemed to me that I was sufficiently cleared of the charge, and in order to bring this
fact into notice, I prepared three letters to three Lords
of the Council, a little before the death of the condemned
conspirators, in which I showed more at full that I was
completely ignorant of the whole matter, and pointed out

how they might satisfy themselves of the same while those gentlemen were yet alive. Whether they did so or not, I do not know: but this much I know, that in the whole process of Father Garnet's trial, in which after the receipt of these letters they tried their utmost to defame the whole Society, and in particular to charge this Plot on the English Mission, they never once mentioned me. They spoke indeed of three Fathers as guilty, but they named those two who had heard of it in confession, and Father Oldcorne, not as privy to the Plot beforehand, but as an accomplice *post factum.*

"Nevertheless I took the greatest precaution to remain hidden; and I lay at a place in London known to no one. So by the protection of God I continued safe, and if it had seemed good, I could have remained so still longer. I did not therefore leave England to avoid being taken, but as in that great disturbance it was no time for labouring, but rather for keeping quiet, I took a favourable opportunity that presented itself of passing over into these parts, and reposing a little, that after so long a period of distracting work in all kinds of company, I might open my mouth and draw my breath,[1] and recover strength for future labours. Why, even at that very time when I was keeping so close, and when nearly all my friends were either in prison, or so upset that they could scarcely help themselves, much less me, though I had lost the house I had in London, through the fault of one who disclosed it, as I have said, and though strict watch was kept everywhere, and danger beset one on all sides; yet, before I had settled to leave England, I managed to hire another house in London very fit for my purpose, perhaps more so than the former. I managed also to furnish it with everything necessary, and made some good hiding-places in it; and there I remained in safety the whole of Lent before my departure. Besides this house I also hired another,

[1] Ut aperirem os meum et attraherem spiritum.—*MS.* Psal. cxviii. 131.

finer and larger than this, which I intended should be in common between Father Antony Hoskins and me. This house after my departure was used by the Superior of the mission for a considerable time.

"The first of these last-mentioned houses I brought into some little danger, about the end of Lent, in order to rescue one of our Fathers from imminent danger. The thing happened in this wise. The good Father, by name Thomas Everett, had gone to a gentleman's house in London, where there were some false brethren, or else some talkative ones; for the fact reached the ears of the Council. And as he is something of my height, and has black hair, Cecil thought it was I of whom notice was given him, and said to a private friend of his, 'Now we shall have him,' meaning me. However, he had neither the one nor the other. For I, learning that the Father had gone to this place, where he could not possibly remain hidden, asked my friend, in whose house I had myself been concealed before I had procured and furnished my new abode, to fetch him and keep him close in his house for a time, which he did. Here he remained while the house he had just left was undergoing a strict search. Now it so happened that, after a few days, a search was also made in the very place to which he had been brought, on account of some books of Father Garnet's which had been seen, and which this gentleman used to keep for him. After rifling the place well and finding no one, for Father Everett had betaken himself to a hiding-place, they carried off the master and mistress of the house, and threw them into prison. Now when I heard this, and knew there was no Catholic left in the house, fearing lest the Father should either perish with hunger, or come forth and be taken, I sent persons from my own house, to whom I described the position of his hiding-place. They went thither, and called to him, and knocked at the place, for him to open it: he, however, would neither open nor answer, though they said that I had sent them for him. For, as he did not know their voices, he was afraid that this was a trick of the searchers, who sometimes pretend to depart, and then after a time return, and, assuming a friendly tone, go about the rooms, asking any who are hidden to come out, for that the searchers are all gone. The good Father suspected that this was the case now, and therefore made no answer. My messengers remained a long time trying to reassure him, and at last were obliged to return, but so late that they fell into the hands of the watch. They were detained in custody that night, and got off with some difficulty the next day. One of them, however, was recognized as having formerly lived with a Catholic, and was therefore believed to be a Catholic himself, and as it was now known where he lived (namely, in the house I had hired), this brought that house into suspicion, though it had been ostensibly hired by a schismatic, who was under no suspicion at all. The consequence was that some four days later the chief magistrate of London, who is called the mayor, came with a *posse* of constables to search the house.

"In the meantime, hearing that Father Thomas would not answer, and knowing well that he was there, to prevent his perishing from starvation, I sent another party with the man who had made the hiding-place and knew how to open it. The place was thus opened and the good Father rescued from his perilous position. They brought him to my house, and there he remained. I myself, however, before he arrived, had gone to a friend's house, a very secure place, with the purpose of staying there a little, as I had some fears that the apprehension of my servants a day or two back might bring the searchers to my house. My fears were well founded: for on Holy Thursday, while Father Everett was saying mass, and had just finished the offertory, there was a great tumult and noise at the garden gate; and the mayor used such violence, and made such quick work of it, as to have entered the garden, and the house, and to be now actually mounting the stairs, just as the Father, all vested as he was and with all the altar-furniture bundled up, had entered his hiding-place. So near a matter was it, that the mayor and his company smelt the smoke of the extinguished candles, so that they made sure a priest had been there, and were the more eager in their search. But of the three hiding-places in the house they did not find one. So they departed, taking with them those men whom they found in the house, and who acknowledged themselves to be Catholics, and the schismatic also who passed for the householder. After this, having again released Father Everett from his hiding-hole and advised him to leave London, I determined not to use that house again for some time. And seeing that the times were such as called us rather to remain quiet, than to gird ourselves for work, I took the first opportunity of crossing the sea and coming into these parts.

"I recommended my friends to different Fathers, asking them to have special care of them during my absence. As for my hostess [Mrs. Vaux], she was brought to London after that long search for me, and strictly examined about me by the Lords of the Council; but she answered to everything so discreetly as to escape all blame. At last they produced a letter of hers to a certain relative, asking for the release of Father Strange and another, of whom I spoke before. This relative of hers was the chief man in the county in which they had been taken, and she thought she could by her intercession with him prevail for their release. But the treacherous man, who had often enough, as far as words went, offered to serve her in any way, proved the truth of our Lord's prophecy, 'A man's enemies shall be those of his own household,' for he immediately sent up her letter to the Council. They showed her, therefore, her own letter, and said to her, 'You see now that you are entirely at the King's mercy for life or death; so if you consent to tell us where Father Gerard is, you shall have your life.'

" 'I do not know where he is,' she answered, 'and if I did know, I would not tell you.'

" Then rose one of the lords, who had been a former friend of hers, to accompany her to the door, out of courtesy, and on the way said to her persuasively, 'Have pity on yourself and on your children, and say what is required of you, for otherwise you must certainly die.'

" To which she answered with a loud voice, 'Then, my lord, I will die.'

" This was said when the door had been opened, so that her servants who were waiting for her heard what she said, and all burst into weeping. But the Council only said this to terrify her, for they did not commit her to prison, but sent her to the house of a certain gentleman in the city, and after being held here in custody for a time she was released, but on condition of remaining in London. And one of the principal Lords of the Council acknowledged to a friend that he had nothing against her, except that she was a stout Papist, going ahead of others, and, as it were, a leader in evil.

" Immediately she was released from custody, knowing that I was then in London, quite forgetful of herself, she set about taking care of me, and provided all the furniture and other things necessary for my new house. Moreover, she sent me letters daily, recounting everything that occurred; and when she knew that I wished to cross the sea for a time, she bid me not spare expense, so that I secured a safe passage, for that she would pay everything, though it should cost five thousand florins, and in fact she sent me at once a thousand florins for my journey. I left her in the care of Father Percy, who had already as my companion lived a long time at her house. There he still remains, and does much good. I went straight to

Rome, and being sent back thence to these parts, was fixed at Louvain. What happened to me there may be read, together with the labours of others, in the Annual Letters.

"I have received two signal benefits on the 3rd of May, through the intercession, as I think, of Father Garnet, who went to Heaven on that day. The first was as follows. When I had come to the port where, according to agreement, I was to embark with certain high personages in order to pass unchallenged out of England, they, out of fear, excused themselves from performing their promise. And in this mind they continued till within an hour of the time for embarking. Now just at that time Father Garnet's martyrdom was consummated at London, and he being received into Heaven remembered me upon earth; for the minds of those lords were so changed, that the ambassador himself came to fetch me, and with his own hands helped to dress me in his livery, so that I might be taken for one of his attendants, and so pass free. All went well, and I do not doubt that I owed it to Father Garnet's prayers.

"The other and greater benefit is that three years later, on the same 3rd of May, I was admitted into the body of the Society by the four vows, though most unworthy. This I look upon as the greatest and most signal favour I have ever received, and it seems to me that God wished to show me that I owed this also to the prayers of Father Garnet, from an exact similarity in the circumstance of time between my profession and his martyrdom. For the day originally fixed for both had been the first day of May, the feast of the Holy Apostles SS. Philip and James, and in both cases unforeseen delays postponed the event till the 3rd of May.

"God grant that I may truly love and worthily carry the Cross of Christ, that so I may walk worthy of the vocation whereto I am called. This one thing I have asked of our Lord, and this will I continue to ask, that I may dwell in the house of God all my days, until I prove myself grateful for so great a favour, and though hitherto unfruitful, yet by the fertility of the olive tree in which I have been grafted, I may at length begin to bear some fruit !

"Praise be to God, to the Most Blessed Virgin, to Blessed Father Ignatius, and to my Angel Guardian. Amen."

CHAPTER XXXI.

THE GUNPOWDER PLOT.

HERE the autobiography of Father Gerard ends. He survived his escape from England thirty-one years, but before we proceed to examine such materials as remain to us for tracing his life during that time, we must give insertion to some notes from various sources on the concluding portion of the story he has told us, which narrative we have purposely left uninterrupted, as far as possible. And first respecting the Gunpowder Plot.

As well in his autobiography, as in the Narrative of the Powder Plot written by him, Father Gerard makes mention of three letters sent by him to three Lords of the Privy Council. Who one of these Lords was we do not know, but we take from the Record Office[1] the letter addressed to the Duke of Lenox, enclosing letters to the Earl of Salisbury and Sir Everard Digby.

"Right Honourable,—Seeing all laws, both divine and human, do license the innocent to plead for himself, and the same laws do strictly require and highly commend an open ear in any of authority to give audience and equal trial to a plaintiff in such a case, my hope is that your Grace will excuse this my boldness in offering up by your hands my humble . petition for trial of my innocence touching the late most impious treason, whereof I am wrongfully accused, by some lost companions, I assure me, who, to save themselves from deserved punishment, will not stick to accuse any innocent of any crime wherein

---

[1] P.R.O., *Domestic, James I.*, vol. xviii. n. 35.

BB

their bare word may pass for proof. There is none so innocent but may be wrongfully accused, sith innocency itself in our Lord and Master was accused and condemned as an enemy to the State and no friend to Cæsar. The servant must not look to be more free from wrongs than his Master was. But happy is that man by whom the truth is tried in judgment and innocency cleared.

"I durst not presume, being branded with the odious name of traitor, to offer my petition to my Sovereign (to whom, as God is witness, I wish long life and all happiness as to my own soul). But if by your Grace's means (of whose piety and worthy disposition I have heard so much good) the humble suit of a distressed suppliant (prostrate at his Majesty's feet) may be offered up, I hope it shall be found not unfit for your Grace to offer, and most fit and reasonable for so wise and righteous a Prince to grant.

"My humble petition is only this. That, whereas I have protested before God and the world, I was not privy to that horrible Plot of destroying the King's Majesty and his posterity, &c., by powder (wherewith I am now so publicly taxed in the proclamation), that full trial may be made, whether I be guilty therein or not. And if so it be proved, that then all shame and pain may light upon me ; but if the truth appear on the contrary side, that then I may be cleared from this so grievous an infamation and punishment not deserved. Two kinds of proofs may be made in this cause, which I humbly beseech your Grace, for God's cause, may be performed. One is, that all the principal conspirators (with whom I am said to have practised the foresaid Plot of Powder against the Parliament House) may be asked at their death, as they will answer at the dreadful tribunal unto which they are going, whether ever they did impart the matter to me, or I practise the same with them in the least degree, or whether they can but say of their knowledge that I did know of it. And I know it will then appear that no one of them will accuse me, if it be not apparent they do it in hope of life, but do give signs that they die in the fear of God and hope of their salvation.

"And as by this trial it will appear (in this time most fit for saying truth) that there is not sufficient witness against me, so I humbly desire also trial may be made by examining a witness, who can, if he will, fully clear me, and I hope he will not deny me that right, especially being[1] . . . the place of right and justice himself. Sir Everard Digby can testify for me, how ignorant I was of any such matter but two days before that unnatural parricide should have been practised. I have, for full trial thereof, enclosed a letter unto him, which I humbly beseech may be delivered before your Grace and the other two lords, whose favour and equity I have likewise humbly entreated by these letters unto them. All which I am bold to direct unto your Grace's hands, presuming upon your gracious furtherance, not having other means, in this my distressed case, to have them severally delivered. God of His goodness will reward, I hope, in full measure, this your Grace's favour and pity showed to an innocent wrongly accused, who would rather suffer any death than not to be found ever faithful to God and his Sovereign.

"JOHN GERARD.

"This 23rd of January."

Addressed—"To the Right Honourable the Duke of Lenox, these deliver."

Endorsed in Cecil's hand—"Gerard the Jesuit to the Duke of Lenox."

"Right Honourable,—Although I can expect no other from one in your place, but that you should permit the course of justice to proceed against any that are proved guilty of treason to his Majesty and the State, especially in so foul and unnatural a treason as was lately discovered,

---

[1] Here the paper is torn, and three or four words are consequently illegible.

yet I cannot but hope where there is so much wisdom, and so vigilant a care for the preservation of this State, your lordship will also be pleased to hear, and forward to make trial, who may be wrongfully accused, knowing right well that it is as necessary in any Government to protect the innocent as to punish the offenders.

"What proof there is of my accusation I know not, and therefore cannot answer it. But this I know : that none can truly produce the least proof that ever I was made privy to that treason of which I am accused, and much less a practiser with the principal conspirators in the same, as I am denounced to be. Therefore, sith I know not my accusers, God I hope will be judge between them and me, to Whom I refer my cause, and in Whom my trust is, and ever shall be, that He will right me.

"In the meantime my humble request is, that your lordship, who have been so often seen to be pitiful towards any in distress, and a potent helper to those who were oppressed (a special ornament in so eminent a person, and much commended and rewarded by God Himself), will show your accustomed commiseration in my case, and afford me therein such audience as may be sufficient to make trial of my innocency. Wherein your lordship shall imitate the just proceeding of the highest Lord, from Whom both yourself, and all that govern, have all your power. For God Himself, although He know all things before He call us to account, yet, to give us the form of just proceeding, is said in Holy Scripture to be ever careful in hearing what the accused can say for himself before He proceeds to give sentence. So we read that God said to Abraham, '*Clamor Sodomorum, &c., multiplicatus est, &c., descendam et videbo utrum clamorem qui venit ad me opere compleverint, an non est ita, ut sciam.*' So again in the Gospel when He heard a complaint against His steward, He would not proceed against him without full audience, but called him and said, '*Quid hæc audio de te?*

redde rationem villicationis tuæ.' These most high and worthy examples I trust your lordship will follow in my case, as you have been known to do with others. And then I doubt not but that shall appear true which I have most sincerely protested before God and the world.

"My humble petition therefore is, that a witness may be asked his knowledge who is well able to clear me if he will, and I hope he will not be so unjust in this time of his own danger as to conceal so needful a proof being so demanded of him. Sir Everard Digby doth well know how far I was from knowledge of any such matter but two days before the treason was known to all men. I have therefore written a letter unto him, to require his testimony of that which passed between him and me at that time. Wherein, if I may have your lordship's further-ance to have just trial made of the truth whilst yet he liveth, I shall ever esteem myself most deeply bound to pray for your lordship's happiness both in this world and in the next. In which hope I will rest, your lordship's prone and humble suppliant, never to be proved false to King and country,

"JOHN GERARD.

"This 23rd of January."

Addressed—"To the Right Honourable the Earl of Salisbury, Principal Secretary to his Majesty, these."

Endorsed in Cecil's hand—"Gerard the Jesuit to my son."

"Sir Everard Digby,—I presume so much of your sincerity both to God and man, that I cannot fear you will be loth to utter your knowledge for the clearing of one that is innocent from a most unjust accusation, im-porting both loss of life to him that is accused, and of his good name also, which he much more esteemeth.

"So it is that upon some false information (given, as I suppose, by some base fellows, desirous to save their lives by the loss of their honesty) there is come forth a proclamation against my Superior, and one other of the Society, and myself, as against three notorious practisers with divers of the principal conspirators in this late most odious treason of destroying the King's Majesty and all in the Parliament House with powder. And myself am put in the first place, as the first or chiefest offender therein.

"Now God I call to witness, Who must be my Judge, that I did never know of it before the rumour of the country brought it to the place where I was, after the treason was publicly discovered. And if this protestation be not sincerely true, without any equivocation, and the words thereof so understood by me, as they sound to others, I neither desire nor expect any favour at God's hand when I shall stand before His tribunal. But because this protestation doth only clear me in their opinion who are so persuaded of my conscience that they think I would not condemn my soul to save my body (which I hope by God's grace shall never be my mind): therefore, to give more full proof of my innocency to those also who may doubt the truth of my words, I take witness to yourself whether you, upon your certain knowledge, cannot clear me. I wrote a letter before Christmas which I hoped would be sufficient to have cleared me ; wherein, beside a most serious protestation (such as no honest man can use if he were guilty, as for my part my conscience doth persuade me), I alleged some other reasons which did make it more than probable, in my opinion, that I was neither to be charged with this late treason, nor chargeable with former dealing in State matters. But I did of purpose forbear this proof (which now I allege), although I did assure myself it would clear me from all just suspicion of being privy to that last and greatest treason ; and I did forbear to set it down, in regard I would not take knowledge of any personal acquaintance with you, especially at your own house, not knowing how far you were to be touched for your life, and therefore would not add unto your danger. But now that it appears by your confession and trial in the country that you stand at the King's mercy for greater matters than your acquaintance with a priest, I hope you will not be loth I should publish that which cannot hurt you, and may help myself in a matter of such importance. And as I know you could never like to stoop to so base and unworthy a humour as to flatter or dissemble with any man, so much less can I fear that now (being in the case you are in) you can ever think it fit to dissemble with God, or not to utter your every knowledge, being required as from Him, and in the behalf of truth. Therefore I desire you will bear witness of the truth which followeth (if it be true that I affirm of my demand to you, growing upon my ignorance in the matter then in hand) as you expect truth and mercy at God's hand hereafter.

"First, I desire you to bear witness whether, coming to your house upon All Souls' Day last, before dinner, with intention and hope to celebrate there, and finding all things hid out of the way and many of your household gone, you did not perceive me to be astonished at it, as a thing much contrary to my expectation. Whereupon I asked you what was become of them. And when you told me you had sent them into Warwickshire, and your hounds also, and yourself were going presently after, about a hunting match which you had made, though I seemed satisfied for the present because a stranger was there with you, yet whether I did not soon after (when I had compared many particulars together which seemed strange unto me) draw you into a chamber apart, and there urge you to tell me what was the reason both of that sudden alteration in your house and of divers other things which I had observed before, but did not until then reflect upon them so much, as, for example, the number of horses that you had not long before in your stable, the sums of money which I had been told you had made of your stock and grounds, which (said I) in one of your judgment and provident care of your estate, are not likely to be done without some great cause, and seemed to think you had something in hand for the Catholic cause. Your answer was, 'No, there was nothing in hand that you knew of, or could tell me of.' And when I replied that I had some fear of it by those signs, considering you would not hurt your estate so much in likelihood without some cause equivalent (for I knew very well you meant to pay the statute, and so stood not in fear of losing your stock), and therefore willed you to look well that you followed counsel in your proceedings, or else you might hurt both yourself and the cause, your answer was (which I have remembered often since), 'That you respected the Catholic cause much more than your own commodity, as it should well appear whensoever you undertook anything.' I asked you once again whether, then, there were anything to be done, and whether you expected any help by foreign power, whereunto you answered, holding up the end of your finger, that you would not adventure so much in hope thereof. Then I said, 'I pray God you follow counsel in your doings. If there be any matter in hand, doth Mr. Walley [Father Garnet] know of it?' You answered, 'In truth, I think he doth not.' Then I said further, 'In truth, Sir Everard Digby, if there should be anything in hand, and that you retire yourself and company into Warwickshire, as into a place of most safety, I should think you did not perform the part of a friend to some of your neighbours not far off, and persons that, as you know, deserve every respect, and to whom you have professed much friendship, that they are left behind, and have not any warning to make so much provision for their own safety as were needful in such a time, but to defend themselves from rogues.' Your answer was (as I will be sworn), 'I warrant you it shall not need.' And so you gave me assurance that, if there had been anything needful for them or me to know, you would assuredly have told me. So I rested satisfied and parted from you, and after that I never saw you nor any of the conspirators. These were my questions unto you. And thus clear I was from the knowledge of that Plot against the Parliament House, whereof, notwithstanding, I am accused and proclaimed to be a practiser with the principal conspirators. But I refer me to God and your conscience, who are able to clear me, and I challenge the conscience of any one that certainly expecteth death, and desireth to die in the fear of God and with hope of his salvation, to accuse me of it if he can. God, of His mercy, grant unto us all grace to see and do His will, and to live and die His servants, for they only are and shall be happy for ever.

"Your companion in tribulation, though not in the cause,

"JOHN GERARD."

Postscript.—"I hope you will also witness with me that you have ever seen me much averted from such violent courses, and hopeful rather of help by favour than by force. And, indeed, if I had not now been satisfied by your assurance that there was nothing in hand, it should presently have appeared how much I had misliked any forcible attempts, the counsel of Christ and the commandment of our superiors requiring the contrary, and that in patience we should possess our souls."

Addressed—"To Sir Everard Digby, prisoner in the Tower."

Endorsed in Cecil's hand—"Gerard the priest to Sir Everard Digby."

From Father Bartoli[1] we take a letter written from Rome, twenty-five years after the Powder Plot, addressed

[1] *Inghilterra*, lib. vi. cap. 6, p. 513.

by Father Gerard to Dr. Smith, Bishop of Chalcedon, and Vicar Apostolic of England. The translation from Bartoli's Italian version is a very old one; the date of the letter is September 1, 1630.

"My Lord,—Not long since I received information that a manuscript dissertation, with the title of *Brevis Inquisitio, &c.*, had been circulated in your parts; in the course of which it is pretended that a certain person continues to glory, to the present day, that by working under ground in the mine of Mr. Catesby and other conspirators, by excavating and carrying out the soil with his own hands, he has often found his shirt wet through and dripping with sweat as copiously as if it had been dragged through a river; and that this person is no other than myself, according to the opinion expressed in the letter. I despised such an idle tale as undeserving of an answer, knowing it, as most others must know it, to be not only most false, but, moreover, most remote from probability. I only begged of a good priest, who was setting out for England, to make known to your lordship what I had heard concerning such a deed laid to my charge, so contrary to all truth and justice; and that I hoped you would not give credit to it, but rather on hearing it mentioned by any one, would show the falsehood as it is. But in the meantime, while the priest is yet on his journey, I have learned from good authority that the book has been printed and published, curtailed indeed of that story, which is, however, circulated in manuscript through the hands of many, with every circumstance and embellishment; whence has arisen the general opinion that I am the person there spoken of, the testimony of a priest being alleged, who says that he has heard me boast of it. Truly I cannot sufficiently express my astonishment on perceiving that there can be found a Catholic, and if a priest so much the worse, who has so shameless a conscience

as to dare assert what he must necessarily know to be
false, and injurious to one who never did him any harm
or injury whatever. This I can affirm of myself with
respect to every priest in England, to many of whom I
have often afforded assistance, but, to my knowledge, have
never offended one. Your lordship, moreover, must be
aware how very improbable it is that I should boast of
a crime so false, so horrible. Now, with all due reverence,
I call God to witness that I had no more knowledge of
the conspiracy than a new-born infant might have; that
I never heard any one mention it; that I had not even
a suspicion of the provision of gunpowder for the mine,
excepting only when the Plot was detected, made public,
and known to every one, and when the conspirators appeared openly in arms in the county of Warwick; then
only did I hear of it for the first time, by a message
brought to the place where I resided; and this place
was so ill provided that of itself it proved I could have
no knowledge of the conspiracy, either from the expressions of others or from my own suspicions; there being
in that place neither men nor arms sufficient to defend
us from the marauders, who on every occasion of similar
commotions issue forth and unite in bodies for plunder.
Neither did this happen for want of sufficient means to
furnish and reinforce the house with men and arms, but
solely because we had no suspicion of a commotion, much
less any knowledge of a conspiracy. Besides this, the
accomplices in the Plot were subjected to the most
rigorous examination, and questioned concerning me;
and although some of them under the torture named one
or others of those who were privy to the conspiracy, nevertheless all constantly denied it of me. Sir Everard Digby,
who, of all the others, for many reasons, was most suspected of having possibly revealed the secret to me, protested in open court and declared that he had often been
instigated to say I knew something of the Plot, but that

he had always answered in the negative, alleging the reason why he had never dared to disclose it to me, because, he said, he feared lest I should dissuade him from it. Therefore the greater part of the Privy Councillors considered my innocence established, it being proved by the concurrent testimony of so many, and by a letter in which I defended and cleared myself from such a groundless suspicion. In that letter, besides the reasons therein produced in proof of my innocence, I protested before Heaven and earth that, so far from being engaged in the conspiracy, I was as ignorant of it as man could be. Being at that time in imminent danger of falling into the hands of the Privy Councillors, who with the most refined diligence sent in every direction in quest of me, I had thoughts of surrendering myself up to every torment imaginable, and what is more to be regarded, to the terrible and disgraceful charge of perjury, if having me in their power they could convict me, by legal proof, of being privy to the conspiracy. There was a time when, under Elizabeth, they held me prisoner for something more than three years, during which period, many times and in as many ways as they chose, did they examine me, to discover in general if I had ever meddled in affairs of State. I challenged them to produce in proof a single character in my hand, a single word, or anything else sufficient to show it, and then to punish me when convicted with the most cruel death that could be inflicted. There never was brought forward the smallest trace or shadow of a proof. How much more improbable is it that I should consent to a Plot so inhuman, I who, from the natural disposition of my soul, independently of supernatural motives, hold in abhorrence everything that has the smallest appearance of cruelty. This I can affirm with truth, that from the time I first embraced the profession of life in which I am engaged, down to the present moment, I have never, by God's mercy, desired the grievous harm, much less the death, of any man in the world, although he may have been my most inveterate enemy: how could I then have had any hand or part in the sudden, unexpected, and on that account tremendous death of so many personages of such high quality, for whom I have ever borne the greatest respect. A person was employed to scatter copies of my forementioned letter through various streets of London, and one in particular was delivered to the Earl of Northampton, and by him laid before the King, on whom my reasons so far prevailed to his satisfaction that he would have desisted from the rigorous search made after me, had not Cecil, for his own private ends, rendered him more violent than ever. For being persuaded that some of the conspirators had plotted against his life in particular, and knowing that most of them were my friends, he hoped if he could once lay hold of me, to find out from me how many and who were the conspirators. For this sole reason he never rested until he had again persuaded the King, as a thing evidently known to him and clearly demonstrated, that I was not only an accomplice, but the ringleader in the Plot, and therefore to be the first named in the proclamation; which was so done. Perceiving from this that the persecution was not likely to abate, and that I might be discovered and arrested, I took the advice to withdraw myself for a time, and to 'give place to wrath,' and, after so many years of hard labour in England, with the Apostles 'to come apart into a desert place and rest a little': nor was there any other principal motive of my leaving the kingdom. In fine, this is the simple naked truth; I was totally ignorant of the provision of gunpowder and of the mine; I was and I am as innocent of this and of every other conspiracy as your lordship or any other man living; and this I affirm and swear upon my soul, without any equivocation whatsoever; in such sort, that if the facts do not correspond truly to the meaning of the words, or

if I had any information of the forementioned Plot before
it was made public to the whole world, as I have before
said, I own myself guilty of perjury before God and men ;
and as far as it is true that I had no knowledge of it, so
far and no more do I ask mercy at the throne of God :
and it is very probable that it will not be long before I
must appear at the divine tribunal, considering my age
and the present contagion in the neighbourhood ; for if
it should reach us it is hardly possible I can escape, on
account of the assistance which it is my duty to render
to this Community, whose souls are committed to my
care.[1]   Therefore I am induced to hope that your lordship will not consider me so careless and prodigal of my
eternal salvation, after having spent so many years in no
other employment than that of seeking to know and to
accomplish the will of God, and of teaching the same to
others, as to be now willing to burthen my conscience
and risk the salvation of my soul by a protestation so
solemn and spontaneous, if my conscience were not pure,
my cause evident, and my words true in all sincerity.
Now, as I doubt not that God, the Supreme Judge, Who
sees and knows all things, will pass sentence on my cause
according to its merits, so I hope that your lordship, now
knowing me to be innocent, will not wish me to appear
guilty, by permitting to stand against me without con-
tradiction an accusation so false and of such enormous
infamy.   Since this accusation derives its greatest force
from the authority of your lordship, who, it is publicly
said, gives credit and support to it, I beseech you, by that
love which you have for charity and justice, to oppose the
falsity of the calumny by the truth of this my justification
With respect to the priest, whoever he may be, by whose
false allegation your lordship appears to have been deceived, I desire with all my heart he may meet with true
repentance before he dies, so that we may all live together
and love God in a blessed eternity."

[1] He was then Confessor in the English College at Rome.

Next, we find, in Father Henry More's *History of the English Province S.J.*,[1] a letter from Father Thomas Fitzherbert, Rector of the English College at Rome, of which house Father Gerard was then Confessor. It is not necessary for us to translate it from his Latin version, as it exists in English amongst the Stonyhurst MSS.[2] It is dated some months later than the foregoing letter of Father Gerard, and was sent by Mutius Vitelleschi, General of the Society, to the Bishop of Chalcedon, by the hands of Fathers Henry Floyd and Thomas Babthorpe, who were at the same time bearers of a second letter from Father Gerard to Bishop Smith, extracts from which we subjoin, translated from Bartoli.[3]

"Right Rev. and my honourable good Lord,—Having understood that one of our Society hath been of late traduced, *tacito nomine*, in a printed book as to have bragged that he had sweat in working in the Powder Plot, and that your lordship have named him, and as it seemeth, dost believe him to be Father John Gerard, I think myself obliged to represent to your lordship's consideration some things concerning him, and that matter, as well in respect of the common bond of our religion and his great merits, as also for that he is at this present under my charge (albeit I acknowledge myself unworthy to have such a subject), and lastly for the knowledge I have had many years of his innocency in that point ever since that slanderous calumny was first raised by the heretics against him, at which time I myself and many other of his friends and kinsmen did very diligently and curiously inform ourselves of the truth thereof, and found that he was fully cleared of it even by the public and solemn testimony of the delinquents themselves, namely, of Sir Everard Digby (with whom he was known to be most familiar and confident), who publicly protested at his arraignment that he

---

[1] Lib. vii. n. 44, p. 339.
[2] *Angl. A.* vol. iv. n. 92. [3] *Inghilterra*, pp. 510, 512.

did never acquaint him with their design, being assured
that he would not like of it, but dissuade him from it;
and of this I can show good testimony by letters from
London written hither at the same time, bearing date the
29th of January, in the year 1606. Therefore, to the end
that your lordship may the better believe it, I have thought
good to show the same to some very credible persons, who
are shortly to depart from hence, and do mean to present
themselves to your lordship, of whom you may (if it please
you) understand the truth of it. Besides that for your
better satisfaction, I have also by our right reverend Father
General's express order and commission, commanded him
in their presence upon obedience (which commandment
we hold by our Rule and Institute to bind, under pain
of mortal sin) to declare the truth whether he had any
knowledge of that Powder Plot or no, and he hath in
their presence protested upon his salvation, that he had
never any knowledge of it, either by Sir Everard Digby,
or any other, until it was discovered, and that he came to
know it by common fame; besides that [he] alleged many
pregnant proofs of his innocency therein, which I omit to
write, because he himself doth represent them to your
lordship by a letter of his own; and of this also the witnesses aforesaid may inform your lordship if you be not
otherways satisfied. In the meantime, I have only thought
it my part to give this my testimony of his solemn protestation and oath, and withal to send to your lordship
the enclosed copies of two clauses of letters from England
and Flanders touching this matter, not doubting but that
your lordship's charity will move you to admit the same
as sufficient to clear him of that calumny, seeing there was
never any proof produced against him, nor yet any ground
of that slander but the malicious conceit and suspicion of
heretics, by reason of his acquaintance with some of the
delinquents, in which case a solemn protestation and oath,
as he hath freely and voluntarily made, may suffice both

in conscience and law for a canonical purgation to clear him from all suspicion as well of that fact as of all collusion or double dealing in this his protestation, especially seeing that he hath always been not only *integerrimæ famæ*, but also of singular estimation in England for his many years' most zealous and fruitful labours there, and his constant suffering of imprisonment and torments for the Catholic faith. Besides that, he hath been ever since a worthily esteemed and principal member of our Society, and given sufficient proof of a most religious and sincere conscience, to the edification of us all. This being considered, I cannot but hope that your lordship will rest satisfied of his innocency in this point, and out of your charity procure also to satisfy others who may have, by any speech of your lordship's, conceived worse of him than he hath deserved ; for so your lordship shall provide as well for the reparation of his fame as for the discharge of your own conscience, being bound both by justice and charity to restitution in this case, as I make no doubt but that your lordship would judge if it were another man's case ; yea, and exact also of others if the like wrong had been done either to yourself, or to any kinsman, dear friend, or subject of yours, all which he is to me ; and, therefore, I am the bolder, I will not say to expect this at your lordship's hands (because it doth not become me), but humbly to crave it of you as a thing which I shall take for a favour, no less to myself than to the Society ; and so this to no other end, I humbly take my leave, wishing to your lordship all true felicity, this 15th of March, 1631.

"Your lordship's humble servant,

"THOMAS FITZHERBERT."

"Ex literis P. Ægidii Schondonchii Seminarii Audomarensis Rectoris 1 Martii 1606 :

"'Dum has scribo accepi literas recentissime datas a viro claro quibus significavit Dominum Everardum Dig-

CC

bæum, dum a Judicibus pronuntiaretur in eum mortis sententia, coram eisdem protestatum esse nullum penitus in Anglia Jesuitam hujus rei fuisse conscium, Nam, inquit, familiaris Patri Gerardo si quis alius, neque unquam ausus fui indicare tantillum, veritus ne conaretur frangere nostros conatus. Itaque sancte asseruit se id solo ex puro Catholicæ ac Romanæ Ecclesiæ zelo neque ullo alio humano respectu suscepisse.'

"Out of the letter of Father Michael Walpole written to Father Persons, the 29th of January, 1606:

"'Touching Gerard's letter which I have seen, I can only say this much, that it seemeth to me to be so effectual, as nothing can be more, so that I am fully persuaded that the King's Majesty himself and the whole Council remain satisfied of him [in] their own hearts, and his Majesty is reported for certain to have declared so much in words upon the sight of his letter.'

"In the end, after his name, he writeth as followeth:

"'This letter is confirmed since by Sir Everard Digby's speech at his arraignment, in which he cleared all Jesuits and priests (to his knowledge) upon his salvation. And in particular, that though he was particularly acquainted with Gerard, yet he never durst mention this matter, being fully assured that he would be wholly against it, to which my Lord of Salisbury replied, affirming the contrary, and that he knew him to be guilty.'"

The first extract of the letter enclosed from Father Gerard runs thus:

"It is known to all how those of my blood have loved and served King James. My father knew it to his cost, for he was twice imprisoned for attempting to set free the glorious Queen Mary, the King's mother, and to secure the succession to her children: which intent of his own was so clear to the Ministers of State, that besides imprisonment, to purchase his life of them cost him some thousands of crowns, especially the first time when there were but three accused and he one of them, and of the other two, one lost his life. Of all which King James was mindful when he came from Scotland to be crowned King of England, and my brother at York offered him his service and that of all his house. 'I am particularly bound,' said he, 'to love your blood, on account of the persecution that you have borne for me,' and of that his love he there gave him the first pledge by making him a knight."[1]

The remaining extract concludes our series of exculpatory letters:

"I send your lordship a copy of the three letters that I wrote to three Councillors of State, that you may see in them how I trusted to my innocence, when I offered to put it to the proof in the two ways which I there proposed to them. Further than this, though the conspirators had been put to death, and I saw that the course proposed by me to the Councillors was not accepted, while the matter was fresh, and I yet in London, I requested of our Fathers that I might present myself in person to the Council of State, which I would have done had they but given me leave ; and if the Council would have proceeded against me, not on the score of religion, but for the conspiracy only, which alone was in question, and for which, if they had found me guilty of it, they might have done to me their very worst. This request I can swear that I made and renewed several times to our Fathers, and there are some yet alive who can bear witness to it ; but it did not seem good to them to consent to it."

The matter does not seem to have rested here, unless there is some mistake in a date, for Dr. Lingard[2] quotes

[1] Bartoli, *Inghilterra*, lib. vi. c. 6, p. 510.
[2] *History of England*, ed. 1849, vol. vii. p. 549.

from a MS. copy,[1] dated April 17, 1631, an affidavit made
by Anthony Smith, a secular priest, before the Bishop of
Chalcedon, "that in his hearing, Gerard had said in the
Novitiate at Liége, that he worked in the mine with the
lay conspirators till his clothes were as wet with perspira-
tion as if they had been dipped in water; and that the
general condemnation of the Plot was chiefly owing to
its bad success, as had often happened to the attempts
of unfortunate generals in war." It would seem as if this
were the original accusation, in answer to which the letter
given above was written and that its date should be 1632.
This would be the date if, though written in Rome, it was
in Old Style. Of the attack on Father Gerard, Dr. Lingard
says, "For my own part, upon having read what he wrote
in his own vindication, I cannot doubt his innocence, and
suspect that Smith unintentionally attributed to him what
he had heard him say of some other person."[2]

[1] There are copies in the archives of the See of Westminster. The date of
the following is later than that quoted by Dr. Lingard.
"*Copia.* Ego infrascriptus testor me audivisse P. Joannem Gerardum
Societatis Jesu, dum Superior esset in Novitiatu Anglicano Leodii, jactantem
quod dum foderet sub domo Parlamentaria Londini una cum aliis in actione
pulveraria ipsius et eorum indusia erant ita madida sudore ac si ex aqua
fuissent extracta. Londini 22 Junii 1631. ANTHONIUS SMITHÆUS.
"Concordat cum originali. Ita testor, G. FARRARUS Nots. Aposts"
Endorsed in the handwriting of the Bishop of Chalcedon "Wet shirt in
Latin."
[2] There is a letter extant from Father Blount, the Provincial, to the
General, dated Feb. 10, 1632, which has been understood to relate to the
accusation against Father Gerard, or to a similar accusation against some
other member of the Society. It must, however, relate to some other matter,
as it says, "Vivit enim adhuc author ipse criminis," and that the alleged
offence took place five years before the entrance into the Society of the Father
in question.

NOTE TO CHAPTER XXXI.

BEFORE we close this subject, we think it desirable to answer in detail two particular accusations that have been brought against Father Gerard's veracity by a modern writer. Canon Tierney says:[1] "To show how very little reliance can be placed on the asseverations of Gerard when employed in his own vindication, it is only right to observe that, referring to this transaction" [the Communion of the conspirators after their oath of secresy] "in his manuscript narrative, he first boldly and very properly asserts, on the authority of Winter's confession, that the priest who administered the Sacrament was not privy to the designs of the conspirators; and then ignorant of Fawkes' declaration which had not been published, and supposing that his name had not transpired, as that of the clergyman who had officiated upon the occasion, he returns at once to the artifice which I have elsewhere noticed, of substituting a third person as the narrator, and solemnly protests on his salvation that he knows not the priest from whom Catesby and his associates received the Communion !"

Dr. Lingard also says simply that the Communion was received by the conspirators "from the hand of the Jesuit missionary Father Gerard,"[2] apparently unconscious that he had ever denied it.

We have little doubt that the house in which the oath of secrecy was taken and holy Communion received, was really Father Gerard's house. The "house in the fields behind St. Clement's Inn," as Fawkes calls it; "behind St. Clement's," as it appears in Winter's confession, seems to be the house described by Father Gerard as that which he occupied up to the time of the Powder Plot, "nearer the principal street in London, called the Strand,"[3] in which street most of his friends lived. But he was not the only priest that lived in that house. At least two other

---

[1] Dodd's *Church History*, ed. Tierney, vol. iv. p. 44, note.
[2] *History of England*, ed. 1849, vol. vii. p. 44.
[3] *Supra*, p. 360.

priests[1] resided habitually with him. One was Father Strange, who was in the Tower when the Autobiography was written ; the other, whose name he does not give, " was thrown into Bridewell, and was afterwards banished, together with other priests." Then there was also Thomas Laithwaite,[2] a priest, who afterwards became a Jesuit, who frequented the house if he did not live there. Father Gerard says, " There I should long have remained, free from all peril or even suspicion, if some friends of mine, while I was absent from London, had not availed themselves of the house rather rashly." What meaning can this have but that Catholics were allowed, in Father Gerard's absence, to come to the house to receive the Sacraments, so freely that it became widely known that it was his house ?

Immediately after binding themselves by oath to secrecy, the minds of the conspirators must have been preoccupied with the thoughts of the tremendous undertaking to which they had just pledged themselves ; and it is very unlikely that mention should be made, in subsequent conversation among them, of the name of the priest, whom they had only seen at the altar, especially as he " was not acquainted with their purpose."[3] The only two conspirators who mention Father Gerard's name are Fawkes and Thomas Winter. Fawkes was a stranger, who had "spent most of his time in the wars of Flanders, which is the cause that he was less known here in England."[4] We have no trace of any personal intercourse between Thomas Winter and Father Gerard. What can have been more natural than that they should have been told to meet at Father Gerard's house, and that those who did not know him by sight should have concluded that it was Father Gerard's Mass that they heard ? It surely is more probable that they should have been mistaken in a name than that Father Gerard should have been guilty of perjury in contradicting, from a place of safety, that which was no accusation against him, but a harmless statement that, in ignorance of the oath taken, he had given Communion to certain Catholics.

[1] *Supra* p. 382.
[2] *Supra* p. 386.
[3] Fawkes' confession, P.R.O., *Gunpowder Plot Book*, n. 54.
[4] *Condition of Catholics*, " Narrative of the Gunpowder Plot," p. 59.

Fawkes' confession was extorted by torture. King James had given orders, "The gentler tortours are to be first usid unto him, *et sic per gradus ad ima tenditur*, and so God speede your goode work."[1] Fawkes was under none of the "gentler tortures" when in a tremulous hand he wrote "Guido" on that declaration. "The prisoner is supposed to have fainted before completing"[2] the signature. Before the words exculpating Father Gerard from all knowledge of the conspirators' purpose, the word *Hucusque* appears in the handwriting of Sir Edward Coke, who has underlined the sentence in red. The ideas of justice of this great lawyer permitted him to publish the mention there made of Father Gerard's name, and to suppress the statement of his innocence. There is also a red line drawn beneath the following words in Thomas Winter's examination: "But Gerard knew not of the provision of the powder, to his knowledge."[3]

The second accusation brought by the same writer,[4] is couched as follows: "Relying upon the fidelity of Gerard, who declares *upon his conscience*, that he has 'set down Father Garnet's words truly and sincerely as they lie in his letter,' Dr. Lingard has printed what is given by that writer, and from it has argued, with Greenway, that Garnet on the 4th of October, the date assigned to it both by Gerard and Greenway, was still ignorant of the nature of the Plot. The truth, however, is, that although the *letter* was written on the *fourth*, the *postscript* was not added until the *twenty-first* of October; that from this postscript the two Jesuit writers have selected a sentence, which they have transferred to the body of the letter; and then, concealing both the existence of the postscript and the date of the 21st, have represented the whole as written and dispatched on the 4th. The motive for this proceeding, especially on the part of Greenway, is obvious. That writer's argument is, that the Parliament had been summoned to meet on the 3rd of October, that Garnet had not heard of the intention to prorogue it to the following month (this, to say the least, is very improbable); that,

---

[1] In the King's own hand. P.R.O., *Gunpowder Plot Book*, n. 17.
[2] *Calendar of State Papers*, by M. E. Green. James I. 1603—10, p. 247.
[3] P.R.O., *Gunpowder Plot Book*, n. 164.
[4] Dodd's *Church History*, by Tierney, vol. iv. p. cii.

for anything he could have known to the contrary, the great blow
had already been struck, at the very time when he was writing;
and, consequently, that, had he been acquainted with the intention of Catesby and his confederates, he would never, at such a
moment, have thought of proceeding, as he says he was about to
proceed, towards London, and thus exposing himself to the
almost inevitable danger of falling into the hands of his enemies.
. . . Now the whole of this reasoning is founded on the assumption that the letter bore only the single date of the 4th.   On the
21st, the supposed danger of a journey to London no longer
existed.   At that period, too, Garnet, instead of proceeding
towards the metropolis, had not only removed in the opposite
direction, from Goathurst, in Buckinghamshire, to Harrowden,
the seat of Lord Vaux, in Northamptonshire, but was also
preparing to withdraw himself still further from the capital, and by
the end of the month, was actually at Coughton, in the neighbourhood of Alcester.   In fact, what was written on the 4th, he had
practically contradicted on the 21st, and to have allowed any part
of the letter, therefore, to carry this later date, would have been
to supply the refutation of the very argument which it was
intended to support.   Hence the expedient to which this writer
has had recourse.   The postscript and its date are carefully
suppressed ; and we are told that, looking at the contents of the
letter, Garnet, when he wrote it, could have known nothing of
the designs of the conspirators : 'Quando scrisse questa
lettera, che fu alli quattro d'Ottobre, non sapeva niente del
disegno di questi gentilhuomini, altro che il sospetto che
prima havea havuto.'[1]   Without stopping to notice the falsehood contained in the concluding words of this sentence, and
without intending to offer an opinion here, as to the principal
question of Garnet's conduct, I may still remark that even the
friends of that Jesuit universally admit him to have received the
details of the plot from Greenway about the 21st; and that this
fact alone may be regarded as supplying another and a sufficient
motive both to the latter and to Gerard, for the suppression of
that date."

This note by Canon Tierney produced its effect on Dr.

[1] Greenway's MS., 51 B.

Lingard, and that historian, in the edition of his work published in 1849, remarks upon the matter as follows.[1] "The object for which this letter was made up in the shape which it thus assumes in Gerard's MS., is plain from the reasoning which both he and Greenway found upon it. They contend that, if Garnet had been privy to the conspiracy, he must have believed on the 4th that the explosion had already taken place on the 3rd, the day on which the Parliament had been summoned to meet; though no reason is assigned why he might not, as well as others, have been aware of the prorogation to the 5th of November, and they add that, under such belief, he would never have resolved to encounter the dangers of making, as he proposed to do, a journey to London, though in fact he made no such journey, but changed his route, and was actually, at the time in which he wrote, on his way to the meeting appointed at Dunchurch. Hence it became necessary to suppress the postscript, because it was irreconcileable with such statements. There was, moreover, this benefit in the suppression, that it kept the reader in ignorance (1) of the real date of the letter, the 21st of October, the very time when it is admitted that Greenway made to Garnet a full disclosure of the Plot; and (2) that Garnet took that opportunity of blotting out a most important passage in the letter written on the 4th, with a promise to forward the same passage later in an epistle apart; two facts which would furnish strong presumptions against the alleged innocence of the Provincial."

One word in passing, in reply to the "two facts which would furnish strong presumptions against" Father Garnet's innocence. 1. Dr. Lingard has forgotten that "the full disclosure of the Plot" was made in confession, and that Father Garnet could make no use of it in any way, until the conjuncture arose when the penitent gave him leave. 2. It is true that a passage, written to Father Persons on the 4th of October, was erased by Father Garnet on the 21st; but what presumption does this furnish? The "promise to forward the same passage later in an epistle apart," could not mean that he would write him word of the Powder Plot when it was safe to do so. Is it likely that

[1] Vol. viii. p. 543.

a conspirator would have written to his friend, with all the chances of a letter being intercepted, that they were proposing to blow up the Houses of Parliament? What would he have gained even had he but risked a phrase as oracular as that of the letter to Lord Mounteagle? Such a supposition assumes that Father Garnet was not only guilty of the Plot, but that he had lost all common sense and ordinary caution; and that he was indebted to the accidental return of his letter to his hands, seventeen days after he had written it, for an opportunity of destroying proof under his own hand that he was guilty.

If this consideration is not conclusive, we have but to refer to the context, as given from the original by Mr. Tierney himself,[1] and our sense of the ridiculous must settle the question. Father Garnet must have been the most erratic of letter-writers, if he could insert a reference to the Gunpowder Treason, or to any other treason, between two such subjects as the choice of Lay-brothers and his own want of money. The letter ends as follows.

" 'I pray you send word how many Coadjutors [Jesuit Lay-brothers] you will have. I have one, a citizen of London, of very good experience, which may benefit us, in buying and selling without taxes. But he is fifty years old: and I think it not amiss to have, at the first, some ancient men for such. Send your will herein.'

"A short but separate paragraph of three lines is here carefully obliterated.

" 'I am in wonderful distress, for want of the ordinary allowance from Joseph [Creswell, the Superior in Spain]. I pray you write for all the arrearages, which, if it may all be gotten, I can spare you some. Thus, with humble remembrance to Claud [Aquaviva, the General], Fabio, Perez, Duras, and the rest, I cease, 4° Octobris.' "

But let us address ourselves to the grave accusation made against Fathers Gerard and Greenway. That Dr. Lingard should have made such a statement at all is owing, first, to the fact that at

[1] Tierney's *Dodd*, vol. iv. p. cv. The original letter is now in the archives of the See of Westminster.

the time when he was preparing the new edition of his History, he had no longer access to the manuscript of Father Gerard, of which he had had the use[1] when originally compiling his work. The reader of Father Gerard's Narrative of the Gunpowder Plot, which appeared in print in 1871, can speedily convince himself of this fact. And, secondly, to a misunderstanding of Canon Tierney's note, for which that writer's expressions are to blame. If it had been true, as Dr. Lingard understood Mr. Tierney to say, that Gerard and Greenway drew the same argument from the date of Father Garnet's letter, their conduct would have been entirely indefensible, and they would have deserved the blame brought against them.

The truth however is, and in this lies an ample defence for both the Jesuit Fathers, that this is not so. Father Gerard quotes Father Garnet's letter only and solely to illustrate the state of the Catholics in England. For this purpose, the date of the letter he was quoting was entirely unimportant. Indeed, he originally quoted the letter without any date; and then he interlined the date of Oct. 4th, but laying no more stress upon it than he had laid on the dates of the other letters of July 24th and August 28th. For the same reason it would not occur to him to note that the passage respecting Ireland was taken from a postscript. It was enough for him that he gave Father Garnet's very words, as he declared "upon his conscience" that he did; and that he had Father Garnet's authority for the account that he was giving of the condition and state of feeling of Catholics. When he turned to the letter for a date, it was natural enough that he should take that which was endorsed upon it by Father Persons, who, having erased the date of the 21st which he had originally written upon it, had substituted the 4th, and "in another corner of the paper also, where it appears most likely to catch the eye, inscribed the same date thus, '4° 8bris.'"[2] As there is no ground for blaming Father Persons for thus endorsing a single date on a letter which continued to bear two, so neither is it reasonable to blame Father Gerard for quoting the letter under one date only. It is clear, therefore, that there is no accusation whatever against Father Gerard, and if Father

[1] Vol. iii. p. 37, note.   [2] Tierney's Dodd, vol. iv. p. cvi.

Greenway had not drawn from the date of the letter the argu-ment regarding Father Garnet, none would ever have been made. It is gravely to be regretted that Mr. Tierney should have said that there was "a sufficient motive both to the latter *and to Gerard* for the suppression of that date." This expression evidently misled Dr. Lingard, and led him erroneously to speak of "the reasoning which both he [Gerard] and Greenway found upon it." Had Dr. Lingard not trusted to Mr. Tierney, but referred to Gerard's Narrative, he would have said of the whole charge that which he has said[1] of the alterations of names in the first part of the letter. Of this his expression is, "Had his object been only to present the public with an account of the persecution to which the English Catholics were at that moment subjected, there would not have been great cause to complain." This *was* his only object,[2] and therefore there was, in Dr. Lingard's judgment, no great cause to complain.

Father Greenway derived his information of the letter from Father Gerard's Narrative, of which he was translator. Whether the argument he has founded on the date of the letter has any and what force is not here under discussion, but it is evident that he propounded it in good faith. The original letter was in existence to confute him. If he had seen it or noticed the postscript and its date, he would never have exposed himself to such a confutation. He was misled, innocently enough, but seriously, by the manner in which the letter appeared in Father Gerard's pages which he was translating.

In a word, the accusation is this. Gerard and Greenway found an argument on the fact that a letter of Garnet's was dated the 4th of October, when they knew that it was in his hands on the 21st. And the answer is this. Gerard may have known, but had no need to notice, the fact of the double date, as he founded no argument whatever upon it: Greenway, who did found an argument on it, had no reason for suspecting the exist-ence of a later date on the letter.

[1] Vol. vii. p. 542.
[2] See *Condition of Catholics*, "Narrative of the Gunpowder Plot," p. 79.

CHAPTER XXXII.

IN ENGLAND.

AND now with regard to the brave Elizabeth Vaux. She continued after Father Gerard's departure to lead the same fervent Catholic life with the fearless zeal she had shown when he was with her. The consequence of course was that other troubles and persecutions followed upon those related by Father Gerard. In a letter[1] dated November 13, 1611, John Chamberlain wrote to Sir Dudley Carleton that certain Jesuits were taken at the house of Lord Vaux's mother. She was imprisoned, and her son, who at the time she was taken was on the Continent with Sir Oliver Manners, on his return to England was imprisoned also. He is mentioned in the *Avvisi d'Inghilterra* of the 21st and 24th of April and the 4th of May, 1612, preserved in the Secret Archives of the Vatican.[2] "The persecution of the Catholics continues as usual. Lord Vaux remains in prison, and is in peril of the penalty called *Præmunire*, which is the loss of his estates and perpetual imprisonment, for being constant in refusing to take the oath of allegiance, as it is called. The mother of the Baron has already incurred this penalty, and has lost all she has. She still remains in prison." Later notes among the same papers add that "a letter of the 9th of June from Brussels says that news has come from England of the condemnation of Lord Vaux. Anthony Tracy, an English gentleman who was the baron's com-

[1] P.R.O., *Domestic, James I.* vol. lxvii. n. 25.
[2] *Nunciatura Angliæ*, inter Miscell.; kindly communicated by the Reverend Father Stevenson, S.J.

panion in Tuscany, confirms this news in a letter of his
to Thomas Fitzherbert, written from Florence on the 24th
of June in these words,—'By letters of the 31st of May
I have news from England that on the previous day Lord
Vaux was condemned to lose every thing and to suffer
perpetual imprisonment for his constancy in refusing the
oath of allegiance, as they call it. The very heretics
lament this cruelty. I have news that for his lordship's
greater dishonour the cause was tried in the King's Bench
[*nella Seggia Reale*], in which Court hitherto no nobleman
has appeared, as their causes belong to the Star Chamber."

A still later notice among the same documents, drawn
up from English letters of the 28th of June, and the 5th
and 6th of July, 1612, says, "The mother of Lord Vaux,
having been a long time in prison without the consolation
of the sacraments, begged the Jesuit Fathers to send her
some Father who was not known, to hear her confession
and give her communion. One of the gravest and holiest
men of that Order came then to London, and accepted
this charge, and on St. John Baptist's day went to the
prison. When he arrived there, they let him enter into
the rooms where the lady was, but when he had entered
the gaoler laid hands on him with such haste that he
had scarcely time to consume the Blessed Sacrament that
he was carrying for her communion. Nothing is known
by the heretics as to her having sent for the Father, so
she has not incurred any fresh penalties on this account.
But the Father has been treated with great rigour, and
is in hopes that he may give his life for our holy faith;
and it appears that our Lord has been pleased to take
this occasion to call him to martyrdom in reward of his
merits and Apostolic labours."

The name of this Father, together with other details
which vary to some extent from those just given, will be
found in a letter written by Father Gerard from Louvain
to Father Aquaviva, the General of the Society, dated the

17th of August, 1612. We translate from the Latin original.[1] "Lord Vaux remains in prison, under condemnation but by no means cast down. He seems with invincible courage to trample on rather than to be deprived of the world, and not so much to have lost as to have contemned its good things. His praise certainly is in the mouths of all men. And his cause is so honourable to him and to the Catholic religion, and so disgraceful to his enemies, that the King seemed to be ready to let his lordship go, and to restore him all his goods, when—God so disposing it and preserving His servant for great things,—some men making a more careful search than usual, found out that the mother of the Baron, who was herself under condemnation and in prison, but who retained all her fervour and devotion, had received a priest into her cell on the very feast of St. John the Baptist. When the officers entered, they found a good Father who had just completed the holy Sacrifice, and was in the act of distributing the most holy Body of Christ to those who were assisting. Mrs. Vaux herself, and two others, had communicated. The priest turned back to the altar and quietly received the remaining Hosts, lest they should fall into sacrilegious hands. The first man who entered the room, seeing the altar well appointed and all of them kneeling before the Blessed Sacrament, was astounded; and forgetting the fierceness with which, under similar circumstances, most people rush upon a priest, only uttered these words: 'Has not your ladyship suffered enough already for this sort of thing?'

"The wonder is of old standing on the part of those who do not understand how blessed is the life that God will give to those who never change their fidelity to Him, and who, fearing God more than the King, even though they have but just escaped death, still wish to bury the dead. So our good Father Cornforth was taken, a very

[1] Stonyhurst MSS., *Angl. A.* vol. iii. n. 111.

holy man, whose life well deserves recording. He was carried off to the pseudo-Prelate of Canterbury [Archbishop Abbot], and as he could not conceal his priesthood on account of the circumstances in which he was taken, so neither would he, for his safety's sake, hide his religious state. So he was sent off to that prison [Newgate] from which they usually take their victims when they want an offering for the god of heresy. Canterbury then went to the King in all haste and fury, and putting fire to the cotton to raise a flame, so inflamed the King's mind against the Baron, that he seems to have diverted him from his inclination to set him free to the very reverse. But notwithstanding all this, as the Baron has those Councillors for him who are most powerful with the King, we all hope that the King will soon be pacified, and that all will end well for our friend, especially if your Paternity and yours will help him with your holy prayers."

However we learn from a letter[1] to Father Persons, written in November 1612, that Father Cornforth soon escaped. "Several Catholic priests have lately escaped out of Newgate; their names are Cornforth, Young, Mayler, Yates *alias* Boulton, Green, Parr, and Cooper. Much search hath been made for them, but none taken. The occasion of their escaping was their hard usage, without compassion or mercy; whereupon they refused to give their words to be true prisoners, but told their keeper that as long as they were used so hardly they would give no such word but would escape if they could, and within a few days after they got away; and as those seven went away, so they might all have gone to the number of twenty, but they refused it, choosing rather to stay. Those that remained in prison have since been cast into the dungeon, with fetters and gyves."

In the Public Record Office we have various papers which add a little to what Father Gerard has here written.

---

[1] Stonyhurst MSS., *Angl. A.*, vol. iii. n. 114; *Records*, vol. ii. p. xiii.

Letters[1] dated February 26 and October 22, 1612, say that Mrs. Vaux, Lord Vaux's mother, was condemned to perpetual imprisonment for refusing to take the oath of allegiance, and that Lord Vaux was transferred to the custody of the Dean of Westminster. The Privy Councillor, who was their friend, was Henry Howard, Earl of Northampton. There are three letters[2] extant from him, dated the 3rd, 12th, and 20th of August, 1612, to Viscount Rochester in behalf of the Vauxes. In the first he says that Lord Vaux's sister [Katherine, wife of Henry Nevill, afterwards Lord Abergavenny] has presented a petition that her brother and mother may, on account of the hot season, be removed from their keeper's house in town to that in the country ; but they being imprisoned for life on a *præmunire*, the matter rests with the King. And this in the third letter he says the Archbishop and Council consented to, if they can still be under charge of their keeper. The second letter thanks Lord Rochester for his intercession in behalf of Lord Vaux and his mother, and adds that they expect but little mercy where the Metropolitan [Archbishop Abbot] is mediator. We have the grant[3] to Lord Vaux of Harrowden of his lands &c. at Harrowden and elsewhere, in the counties of Essex, Bedford, Nottingham, Lincoln, and Cambridge, which were forfeited to the King on his conviction in a *præmunire* for refusing the oath of allegiance. Later on, May 4, 1625, Charles I. granted him a special pardon[4] for " not repairing to the Protestant church and forbearing the same," which is recited to be " a contempt of the King's crown and dignity."

One of Lord Vaux's sisters seems to have trodden in the footsteps of her namesake and aunt, Father Garnet's

[1] P.R.O., *Domestic, James I.*, vol. lxviii. n. 67 ; vol. lxxi. n. 24 ; Chamberlain to Carleton.
[2] *Ibid.* vol. lxx. nn. 25, 46, 55.
[3] *Ibid. Sign. Man.* vol. iii. n. 6.
[4] Rymer's *Fœdera*, t. xviii. f. 44.

DD

friend, Anne Vaux. The Jesuits kept a school at her house, Stanley Grange, in Derbyshire. Archbishop Laud thus endorsed the information[1] sent him,—" Received October 8, 1635. Mr. Lumley's information concerning Stafford and Derby." It said, " The place where the most of the gentlemen's sons do remain is in Derbyshire, four miles off from Derby town, at one Mrs. Anne Vaux's house, called Stanley Grange, sister to the Lord Vaux, where there is the Lord Abergavenny's grandchild, with one Mr. Fossiter's son and divers more, which cometh to the number of ten or eleven."

The proclamation for the apprehension of the three Jesuit Fathers, accused of complicity in the Gunpowder Plot,[2] gives a description of Father Gerard, whom, as we may remember, Father Garnet had called[3] " Long John with the little beard." It runs thus,—" John Gerard, *alias* Brooke, of stature tall, and according thereunto well set; his complexion swart or blackish: his face large; his cheeks sticking out, and somewhat hollow underneath the cheeks; the hair of his head long, if it be not cut off; his beard close, saving little mustachoes, and a little tuft under his lower lip; about forty years old."

With this description we may compare another[4] sent by a man named John Byrde to Sir Robert Cecil some years before, which is to be found among the documents at Hatfield. It is dated August 27, 1601. " Gerard's discovery may the better be, by observing this description of him and his habit. To be of stature tall, high shouldered, especially when his cope is on his back, black

---

[1] P.R.O., *Domestic, Charles I.*, vol. ccxcix. n. 36 ; *Records*, vol. ii. p. 317. The warrant issued in consequence of this information is misplaced in the Calendar of State Papers, *Domestic, Charles I.*, vol. ccxciv. n. 74.

[2] P.R.O., *Proclamation Book*, p. 121.

[3] *Supra*, p. 145.

[4] Hatfield MSS., $\frac{87}{144}$. For this interesting extract we are indebted to the Reverend Augustus Jessopp, D.D.

haired, and of complexion swarth, hawk nosed, high tem-
pled, and for the most part attired costly and defencibly
in buff leather garnished with gold or silver lace, satin
doublet, and velvet hose of all colours with clocks corresponding, and rapiers and daggers gilt or silvered."[1]

To this we may add the description of Father Gerard
given by the ruffian Topcliffe,[2] whose spelling is sufficiently "kewryoos" to be worth retaining. It is dated
1583 in the Calendar of State Papers, but this is evidently
erroneous, as Father John Gerard escaped from the Tower
in 1597. "Jhon Gerrarde ye Jhezew^t preest that escaip
out of the Tower and Richard Blount a Seam^ry preest
of estymacion, and a thirde preest intend to passe ou^r
rather after then wi^th the Lo Imbass at Dov^r Rye or
thirabowtts upon y^t coast. They have provided for a
Culler to passe w^thout suspycion a Seale like a Seale of
the Counsall table to bleare the Eye^s of Seartchers and
officers. Therefore it were not amysse That some order
were left wth my Lorde Trasorr that he gyve order that
the Lres do passe under such a Seale from y^r Lls But
under & wth summe prevey marke upon the lres besides
the seale. Then any passendg^r that carryethe a lre

---

[1] Father Gerard has told us that Father Everard was mistaken for him
because he was "black haired." It is therefore plain that a description given
by Justice Young in a letter of the 26th of April, 1593, is not intended for
Father Gerard : "There is one Standishe, a fair man, fully faced, with whitish
hair and thin, and goeth in a suit of blue satin and a suit of black velvet, and
his rapier hilts silvered. He is a priest, and keepeth in Sussex, and is much
at the Court." On this there is a note in Sir John Puckering's hand, "Doctor
Lewes' man reveals that Bishop of Cassano saith this man is a dangerous
desperate state man." P.R.O., *Domestic, Elizabeth*, vol. ccxliv. n. 144. One
of Father Gerard's names was Standish, but he was not in Sussex. There
were priests of this name. About the date of Justice Young's letter, James
Young, the spy, reported that "he did know of none [about London] except
Standish, who resorteth to one Mrs. Gardiner's, that liveth in Fleet-street.
The man is of a swarthen complexion, and speaketh very fast, and useth a
cork shoe of the left foot, which is somewhat shorter than the right." *Ibid.*
vol. ccxlv. n. 38. Father Tesimond mentions a Thomas Standish, who
suffered long imprisonment. *Troubles*, 1st series, p. 163.
[2] P.R.O., *Domestic, Elizabeth*, vol. clxv. n. 21.

w^thowte suche a prevey m^rk Is fytt to be stayed for a
time Until hee bee knowen.

"Jhon Gerrarde ye Jhezew^t is about 30 years oulde
Of a good stature sumwhat highe^r then Sr Tho Layton
and upright in his paysse and countenance sum what
stayring in his look or Eyes Currilde heire by Nature &
blackyshe & and apt not to have much heire of his bearde.
I thincke his noase sum what wide and turning Upp
Blubarde Lipps turninge outward Especially the over
Lipps most Uppwards towards the Noase Kewryoos in
speetche If he do now contynewe his custome And in
his speetche he flourrethe & smyles much and a falteringe
or Lispinge, or dooblinge of his Tonge in his speeche

"Yor honor^s as you will comāde me

"RIC TOPCLYFFE, *alias* ⌣‿⌣ "

What Sir Thomas Leighton's height may have been
we do not know, but in the copy of this description sent
by Cecil to Anne Lady Markham,[1] a pen has been
passed through the words "Sir Thomas Leighton," and
the word "ordinary" is written in its stead. The proclamation was nearer the truth than Topcliffe as to Father
Gerard's age, for he was then forty-two.

A correspondence between Cecil and Lady Markham
betrays to us an offer made by her "to deliver the person
of Gerard into the hands of the State." Her object was to
obtain the pardon of her husband, Sir Griffin Markham,[2]
who was in banishment for having taken part in Watson's
conspiracy. Gilbert, Earl of Shaftesbury, in a letter[3] to
Cecil, says of "a certain lady of Nottinghamshire, called

[1] P.R.O., *Domestic, James I.*, vol. xviii. n. 19.
[2] Sir Griffin Markham himself "made several discoveries to Sir Thomas
Edmondes, then Ambassador at Brussels, concerning the persons concerned in
the Gunpowder Plot." Birch's *Elizabeth*, vol. i. p. 158, quoting *Historical
View of the negociations between the Courts of England, France, and Brussels,*
pp. 252, 255.
[3] P.R.O., *Domestic, James I.*, vol. xlvii. n. 96.

the Lady Markham," "this more I know, that there is not the like pragmatical-headed lady in this part of England."

Her letters[1] are interesting for the mention of Harry Hurlston, that is Mr. Henry Huddlestone,[2] Father Gerard's convert and fast friend, as also for the account of her two servants who had gone to live with Father Gerard; but still more for the testimony she bears to the general belief entertained by Catholics in Father Gerard's sanctity and to the improbability in the judgment of all who knew him of his being a party to the Plot.

"Right honourable,—Your lordship may think me slack in performing that which I so freely made promise of, but the death of my father hath so much appalled me as I am not fit to do as I would. I did hear Mr. Gerard was taken, which something stayed me. Moreover your lordship hath Mr. Ha. Hurlston in hold, who may direct you the best concerning him of any I know, as also I take it Sir Everard Digby can for Mr. Walley [Father Garnet]; but thus it is I cannot learn where Mrs. Vaux is, neither if I knew durst I visit her. And this is most strange to me: neither of those which were my servants comes to me, which makes me think they remove with Mr. Gerard, or are imprisoned; but I rather think they are shifted out of the way, because their attendance will make their master more acceptable, one of them being an exquisite painter and the other a perfect good embroiderer. The painter is a black man, and taller than the embroiderer, whose hair is yellowish, and was called Christopher Parker by his true name. The painter was called Brian Hunston. I am bold to inform you thus largely of them, because I verily suppose they attend their wandering friend and master, but where, till I either see them or hear some directions I cannot imagine; but I protest to your lordship,

[1] *Ibid.* vol. xvi. n. 18; vol. xviii. n. 4. [2] *Supra*, p. 97.

if I could learn I am resolved he should speak with you, if by any means I could procure it, for I fear this most vile and hateful Plot hath taken deep and dangerous root, because I meet with many that will as easily be persuaded there was no gunpowder laid as that [that] holy good man was an actor in the Plot; and surely the generality did ever so much admire him that they were happy or blessed in hearing him, and their roof sanctified by his appearance in their house. I am to go shortly into the country. If it would please your lordship to give me leave to send a man to my husband I should be much bound to you, for I cannot tell till I hear from him how to determine of those businesses occasioned by my father's death. I humbly beseech you commiserate my affliction and grant me this poor request, if it stand with your liking, and I shall ever pray for your increase of honour and happiness. So I humbly take my leave this 18th of November, 1605.

"Your lordship's most humble to command,

"ANNE MARKHAM."

Endorsed, "The Lady Markham to my lord."

"Right honourable,—Afore I came out of London I sent to know your lordship's pleasure, but mine uncle could not meet with Mr. Levinus, and indeed I did think my credit was so decayed with the Padre that I could not do as I would, employ my best endeavours to perform thereby to express my great desire of your lordship's good opinion. Now I find either necessity of their part or my two servants' credits hath given me so much power as I shall shortly see Mr. Gerard, but for the day or certain time they are too crafty to appoint, but whensoever I will do my best to keep him within my kenning till I hear from your lordship, and then, my credit preserved, which is dearer to me than life, your command shall be as truly obeyed as if your most trusty servant were commanded. I do perceive there are great business in hand, and your lordship is, next to his Majesty, most shot at, but what the project is I dare not be very inquisitive of, because it is not ripe, as by circumstance I perceive ; and I labour to make myself in good estimation with them, which would not be if I covet to know more than they like. This, I protest to God, is only to do service to your lordship. There had been some of them with me ere this, but great occasion hath drawn them to haste into other places, whither I know not. If the watch had continued but two days longer, Mr. Gerard had been pined out at Harrowden. I hear Ric. the butler[1] is close in the Gatehouse, yet your lordship knows that prisons are places of such corruption as money will help letters to their friends to tell what they have been examined of, so they will guess shrewdly how to

---

[1] "Ric. the butler" is one of two of Mrs. Vaux's servants, whose examinations have been preserved at Montacute House, among the papers of Sir Edward Phelips, of which a copy has been deposited in the Public Record Office by the Historical MSS. Commission.

"The examination of Francis Swetnam, servant to Mrs. Elizabeth Vaux, and served her in the bakehouse, taken the third of December, 1605. Saith that he hath been a recusant these two years, but will now come to the Church, for that he had rather adventure his own soul than loosen his five children, but cannot give any reason why he should adventure his soul by coming to Church. Saith that he was taken in his mistress' house and brought up with her to London, but denieth that he was ever at any mass, or that he knoweth any priest, and cannot deliver any other material thing to be set down. The mark of Francis O Swetnam, Jul. Cæsar, Rogr. Wilbraham, E. Phelipps, Jo. Croke, George More, Walter Cope, Fr. Bacon, John Doddridge" (f. 25).

"The examination of Richard Richardson, butler to Mrs. Vaux. He saith he hath served his mistress about six years, and hath not come to Church since he was eleven years old. Saith that since Midsummer last Catesby was at Harwardds [Harrowden] only one time, which was about St. Luke's day ; and that Sir Everard Digby was there only twice, the former about the 6th of August and the latter about St. Luke's day ; and that Francis Tresham was not there this twelvemonth ; Mr. Rookwood these three years ; and that Winter, Grant, Percy, Morgan, were never there during his service. And for matter of faith or revealing of priests or masses, he desireth to be spared, because it concerneth his soul. Richard Richardson, Jul. Cæsar, Rogr. Wilbraham, Jo. Croke, John Doddridge, Walter Cope, George More, Fr. Bacon." *Endorsed*—"6° December 1605" (f. 32).

shift. I have none that I do trust about me with my resolution to do my best endeavour to preserve your lordship, therefore I am enforced to be brief. I beseech you pardon it in me that writes in fear, but if it please your honour to send your note or directions to mine Uncle Harvey, I will expect till that he send them, and ever pray God to protect you from these most dangerous conspirators. For the true trial of my devotion in that prayer I will most sincerely labour your preservation, so I humbly take my leave this 3rd of January.

"Your lordship's at command,

"ANNE MARKHAM."

"To the Right Honourable my very good lord the Earl of Salisbury, haste this." *Endorsed*, "3rd January, 1605[6]. Lady Markham to my lord."

The following is Cecil's answer.[1]

"Madam,—Although I do confess my great mislike of the daily resort and residence of the priests and especially of the Jesuits, whose end can be no other than of pernicious consequence to this estate, yet, being in hope that warnings would make them retire from further tempting of law, I have used no extraordinary concern for their apprehension, being, I confess, full of tenderness in matters of blood. But having now discovered by many confessions of the late conspirators that some of these Jesuits have passed so far as to be persuaders and actors in this barbarous conspiracy, which excludeth almost all offices of humanity from men that have softer hearts, I have thought good to take your offer for his Majesty's service, to deliver the person of Gerard (who is one of those) into the hands of the State. For which purpose, although your letter doth not well express what you would have done, whereby

[1] P.R.O., *Domestic, James I.*, vol. xviii. n. 19.

both the service may be effected and your name covered ;
yet I have procured a warrant, here inclosed, which will be
sufficient to authorize and command any man to whom
you shall direct it, which I have left to your own choice to
put in, because I know not who they are which dwell
thereabouts in whom you dare repose trust. And unless
you have the warrant presently and in the instant to
execute, I know the inconvenience of the protraction. You
shall therefore do very well to observe how the warrant is
made, and thereby shall you perceive that the party to
whomsoever it is directed is authorized sufficiently, and
will receive the warrant from any body's hands whom you
shall send ; so as if you will choose any of your own
to carry it to any such gentleman as you shall like, that
third party need not say he comes from you, but from
some other, and yet he may bring the gentleman that
you shall name upon the back of the warrant to execute
all things according to your direction. Lastly, madam, I
say this unto you, that either your religion is very foul, or
you will make no difficulty to discover such a pernicious
creature, as differs so far from the rest of the Society (as I
am persuaded) ; wherein I will add thus much further, that
you shall be an instrument of reflecting his Majesty's good
opinion to your husband, and confirm the conceit I have of
you, that you would not trouble yourself and me in this
kind unless you meant sincerely. And so I commit you to
God. From the Court at Whitehall, this 15th of January,
1605[6].

> " Your ladyship's loving friend,
>
> " SALISBURY.

" There are only three of your Churchmen in this
wicked predicament, Gerard, Father Walley, and Father
Greenway, so it is indifferent to the State which of these
be come by. This letter is sent according to your direction
to Mr. Stringer, who shall receive it from the next post to

him, and the packet to the post is signed by the post-master's hand, and not by mine, who knoweth not the contents nor anything of you, and yet his hand will make the less suspicion. I desire you to keep safe both this mine own letter and the warrant, because I may have both delivered again hereafter, if there be no cause continuing to use them hereafter, and I will do the like with your letter, which I reserve for you."

Endorsed,—" To the Lady Markham."

To Cecil's precaution in requiring Lady Markham to return his letter to him we owe our knowledge of it ; and to his neglecting to " do the like " with her letters we are indebted for them. Lady Markham has spread in vain before Cecil's eyes the bait of a project aimed specially at himself, next to the King. He has measured his correspondent accurately, but he has thought it possible that through her he might secure Father Gerard or one of the other fathers. He can however hardly have been ignorant that Lady Markham was quoted by Watson in the *Dechachordon*[1] as the authority for a malicious libel on Father Gerard, which would make him very wary of her for ever after. " They will make all the secular priests leap at a crust ere long; for so said that good holy father John Gerard of late to the Lady Markham in Nottinghamshire, who told it shortly after to Master Atkinson."

Lady Markham was wrong in saying that " if the watch had continued two days longer, Mr. Gerard had been pined out at Harrowden." He has himself told us[2] that the search lasted nine days, but that he was in no danger of suffering from hunger. The search must have been immediately after the discovery of the Plot, for it is mentioned

[1] P. 83. There is a similar libel at p. 14, of "another surmized holy father of their society, in whose mouth a man would think butter could not melt," and in the margin there is the name "John Gerard."
[2] *Supra*, p. 386.

in a letter[1] dated the 10th of November, 1605. "Mr. Baptista came to Lady Vaux's to find Jarrett [Gerard, not Garnet, as in Mr. Green's Calendar] Superior of the English Jesuits." Some news of Father Gerard's hiding reached Father Garnet in prison, for in a letter[2] addressed by Fr. Oldcorne to the Council, dated March 25, 1606, in which he relates what had passed in the Tower between Father Garnet and himself, but in a way that could not be hurtful to any one, the following passage occurs. "Also Mr. Garnet told me that while he was in the Gatehouse he received a note written in orange (but he told me not from whom) whereby he understood that Father Tesimond was gone over sea, and that Father Gerard would presently follow him after he had recovered a little more strength : 'whereby,' said Garnet, 'I gather he hath been lately in some secret place, as we were ; but by this I hope he hath recovered his strength, and is also passed over the sea.'"

From the book of an enemy we gather the name of one who gave shelter to Father Gerard when he was obliged to leave Mrs. Vaux's house. Wadsworth, who was for many years an active pursuivant employed against Catholics, wrote a vile book called "The English Spanish Pilgrim," which was published in 1629. In it[3] he says that Father Gerard was sheltered by "Doctor Taylor, Doctor of the Law," and, if we so rightly understand a badly worded sentence, "interpreter to the Spanish Ambassador." Wadsworth says, "Mr. Henry Taylor . . . took St. Omers in his way to visit his mother there living, where then Father Blount being resident, the Provincial of the English Jesuits, and she remembering him of the services that her late husband, Dr. Taylor,[4] Doctor of the

---

[1] P.R.O., *Domestic, James I.*, vol. xvi. n. 44. George Southaick to Levinus Munck.

[2] *Ibid. Gunpowder Plot Book*, n. 214.

[3] P. 25.

[4] Probably this is the Dr. Taylor who is mentioned in Hugh Griffin's deposition, *supra*, p. 400.

Law, had done for their Society, in protecting in his
chamber that Jesuit Father Gerat, a complotter of the
Gunpowder Treason, and then interpreter to the Spanish
Ambassador in England, in consideration whereof the
Provincial Blount gave him a letter of favour to Gondomar,
the then Ambassador in England . . . which Count
Gondomar . . . having read . . . made choice of him for
his Secretary, and now since the death of his master, he is
retainer to his Catholic Majesty."

CHAPTER XXXIII.

ACROSS THE CHANNEL.

1606 TO 1609.

FATHER GERARD has told us that he crossed the Channel on the 3rd of May, 1606, the very day on which Father Garnet was martyred in St. Paul's Churchyard. The "certain high personages" in whose suite he says he passed over, were the Ambassadors of Spain and Flanders.[1] Who they were, and what was said on Father Gerard's arrival in Belgium we learn from a letter[2] from Father Baldwin then at Brussels to Father Persons at Rome, dated May 20, 1606. The deciphering is in a contemporary hand. "Since my last, five days ago, arrived at —5 (St. Omers) 469 (Father Gerard), where also is one [Richard Fulwood] whom 456 (H. Garnet) was wont to use in all his chief business of passage, receiving and retaining all things. I take it he be 229 (Jesuit) also. They are yet 267 (secret), and so it is requisite for a time, especially in that the 194 225 (Marquis Ambassador) brought them, and by his dexterous and courteous manner had great care of them. The Marquis of St. Germain came hither two days ago, and both he and Don Blasco de Arragon came as well informed of our English matters as I could wish. They have made relation accordingly to the Nuncio, and this morning to me, who have been with them for a long while. They praise the courage and constancy of Catholics marvellously, and have an apprehension of the daily increase

[1] Bartoli, *Inghilterra*, p. 586.   [2] Stonyhurst MSS., *Angl. A.* vol. vi.

of them; also that the better sort in England are inclined Catholicly and such in profession. They speak much of the zeal of the Lady of Shrewsbury and of the indignation of the King, who hearing of the manner of Father Old-corne's death and requesting all Catholics to pray for him and say *De profundis*, there were found so many to say that aloud as they were esteemed a great part of the number, and so many by signs and voices to have given show of Catholic profession as all were amazed. Thus they report; and also that Father Garnet was to be executed the day which they came away, in Paul's Churchyard, although another writing from St. Omers says that it was deferred the day following, for that the day first appointed was May Day, and Father Garnet, being advertised of his death, should answer, 'What then, will you make a May-game of me?' Howsoever, it is held for certain that he is dead, and that Marquis told the Nuncio that therefore he departed the sooner, as unwilling to be present at such a tragedy. . . . I think Father Gerard may live in these countries after that Mr. Owen is delivered (of whom the Archduke mindeth to have great care), yet he who is said to have had correspondence with him, one Philips [Phelippes][1] the decipherer, is now committed to the Tower. And it were very necessary one of ours remain in Paris, for which place Father Keynes may serve for a time, at least in that he is a man not noted, and hath the French tongue, as having lived there. Father Schon-

---

[1] This Phelippes is the man by whom Mary Queen of Scots was done to death. He could not have expected much favour on the accession of her son to the Crown of England, yet he had the effrontery in a petition to the King in 1622, after saying "that he had been forced, since his Majesty's coming to this Crown, to part with a pension had for deciphering, towards satisfaction of a debt owing to the last Queen, which she was in mind to have pardoned," to put in a claim to James' favour "for his feat of deciphering, by the which England was sometime preserved to him and sometime his Majesty to England when he knew not of it." *Cotton MSS.*, Julius, C. iii. f. 297. Phelippes' arrest in consequence of his correspondence with Hugh Owen is given in Poulet's *Letter-books*, p. 116.

donch [Rector of St. Omers] is of my opinion, and Father Gerard will do well in his place [at St. Omers] after some month or two, if things alter not much ; for he can hardly be in any other place in regard of his indisposition, if it be as I have heard. I shall soon know more thereof. Father Lee were good in England in my opinion, for the consolation of many of ours, and Father Gerard's friends, all which I remit to your consideration."

Father Gerard must have remained six weeks at St. Omers, recovering from the illness caused by all he had passed through. On the 3rd of July, 1606, Father Baldwin wrote[1] again from Brussels to Father Persons. " I have not as yet received from England from any of our Fathers ; only John Powell, the interpreter of the Spanish .Ambassador, relateth what passed at the execution of Father Garnet, upon the 13th May *stylo novo* and the 3rd *stylo vetere*. He hath given exceeding satisfaction to all sorts, and much confounded our enemies of the one sort and other. He was drawn according to the usual manner to Paul's Churchyard upon a hurdle and straw; his arms were not bound, neither when he was executed. Such concourse of people as hath not been seen. . . . The Spanish Ambassador would not remain in London that day ; he hath got his shirt, and some of his blood is sent to Spain, which I have seen here, also his apparel is gotten, as I hear. Here now is Richard Fulwood, who telleth me that Father Gerard is very sick at St. Omers ; that said you would have him come to Rome. I fear me that journey will kill him."

Father Gerard rallied quickly from his sickness at St. Omers, for in less than a fortnight after this he wrote from Brussels to Father Persons, under the pseudonym of Francis Harrison. The letter is so characteristic of the man that, though long, we give it in full from the original at Stonyhurst.[2]

[1] Stonyhurst MSS., *Angl. A.* vol. vi.   [2] *Ibid.*

" July 15, 1606.

" JESUS . MARIA.

" Pax C^{ti.}

" My dear and respected Father,—I have received your letters of the — last, wherein you show your fatherly care and undeserved love unto me, as were sufficient to bind unto you any grateful heart, although he were not tied with former obligations. But I am so much and so many ways bound unto you before by favours of the highest kind, that these do only tie me unto you with new knots, though I was before so wholly yours and so firmly tied, that sincerely I had rather not to be than to be untied. I beseech you, sir, that you will be pleased to present my humble duty unto Father General, in whose favour through your good word do procure me that place which I can no ways deserve, yet this I hope you may promise for me, that I will now begin to do my best endeavours, that I may be framed in all things as is fit for a child of that most holy family whereof he hath the care, that both by my voice and hands he may acknowledge me for his child, the better to deserve the blessing of so great and good a Father. I would now acknowledge my duty by letters, but that I am ashamed of my Latin, and loth to trouble with so rude lines, unless there were further occasion or that you thought it needful. But I hope to come and do my duty in person so soon that it will not be necessary to signify it by letters. I will stay as you appoint until I have your letters for coming forward, and in the meantime will not be solicitous one whit, having no desire in the world whereof I would not most willingly leave the whole care unto you, and indeed desiring to have no other desires but yours so far as I may be able to discern them, after that I have expressed my reasons as I know you would have me to do, and after that you know me better and my many great wants, which, that they may be more exactly known

unto you, makes me so desirous to be with you for some
time, howsoever it may please you to dispose of me
afterwards.

"And if the chief cause why you think it best for me
to stay a while in these parts be for that you would have
me secret as yet, and especially not to be seen with you
there [in Rome] whilst the appellants are negociating their
uncharitable accusations of their brethren, then I suppose
you will think I may be fully as secret there as here, if I
be first wary in my coming into the town, and then be
your prisoner for some time (which I most desire), and
then go to St. Andrew's [the Noviciate of the Society on
the Quirinal], without visiting any holy places and being
seen in the town until you think it convenient. And
because, in my second and third letters, I expressed my
earnest desire of this private course at my first coming,
I suppose I shall hear from you in your next letter or
the next but one, that you think best I come forward,
unless you wish my stay for some other reasons than the
desire of my being secret.

"I grant I might perform my desire of some time of
recollection either in Louvain or in the new house [the
proposed English Noviciate] if it go forwards, under Father
Talbot [the Master of Novices]; but I have many reasons
why I desire to be with you for some time, which I think
you would allow of if you know them. And I would be
glad also if it might be to begin in St. Andrew's, to draw
there some lively water out of the chiefest fountain, and
this rather in the winter than to come the next spring,
because I much fear my health if I be there in the heats.
But after I have been there for some time, for so long a time
as you shall think it convenient that I stay in that school, I
shall be Father Talbot's Minister here, or to have some office
of action under him, if my health do require any exercise
of body. I hear there is one prepared for Minister that
is very fit, but I could have care of the Church, and then

EE

perhaps shall get some stuff to furnish it from some friends
of mine in England ; or I could have care of the garden,
for I am excellent at that (if you will permit me to praise
myself) for that was much of my recreation in England,
and I hope my brother [probably Sir Oliver Manners]
will witness with me that he hath seen a good many
plants of my setting, and tasted the fruit of some of them.
But indeed, dear Father, if it may stand with your liking,
I would be very glad to see you and be with you for
some days before I settle anywhere, how private soever
my abode there be, either at the first or for the whole
time of my stay, as yourself shall see it best.

"As for the settling of any with my friends, I have
done it before my departure, leaving my old companion
and dear friend Father Percy in the place where I was,
who is so much esteemed and desired by them, as none
can be likely to be more profitable. Most of my other
special friends I commended partly to Father Anthony
[Hoskins] and partly to him, both which are most grateful
[pleasing] to all my friends and acquaintance, and indeed
I know not any two there that, in my simple opinion,
better deserve it. As concerning Father Roger Lee's
going into England, if you please that I write justly that
I think, there be divers reasons for which I think it, at this
time, very inconvenient. First, in that he is so profitable
where he is [Minister at St. Omers], that it will not be easy
to find another [who] will do so much good in that place ;
and, in one word to express my opinion, for aught I see,
the most good of the house, both for external discipline
and for progress in spirit, dependeth upon his care and
effectual industry, wherein I should think it more needful
to provide him more helpers of like desires and practical
endeavours, who would conspire with him and have talents
to effect, both with the good Rector [Father Schondonch]
and with the scholars, that which they should together find
to be most expedient. The Fathers which be there do

very well, but are not of like apprehensions and proceedings, and I suppose if yourself did see all particulars, you
would think Father Roger to be a strong helper to the
good of that house, and that it would flourish much if it
had some others of his like. I know not where to name
one upon the sudden, unless it be Father Henry Flud
[Floyd], whose zeal and practical proceedings I think
would be very profitable for that house, if he may be
spared ; and truly in my opinion, upon the good of that
house dependeth much the good and quiet of the other
Colleges, besides much edification to many, both friends
and enemies, unto whom this is a continual spectacle.

"But besides this reason (which alone I take to be
sufficient) I wish Father Roger's stay for the good he may
hereafter do in England, which I do hope will be great,
and therefore great pity it should now be lost before the
fruit of so likely a tree can come to ripeness. For, sir,
yourself can better judge that none can be much profitable
in England until he have gotten acquaintance there, and
until his acquaintance by their trial of him have gotten
a great opinion and estimation of him, which then they
will spread from one to another, and every one will bring
his friend, who upon hearing will be desirous to try, but
after trial will say unto the friend that brought him, *Jam
non propter sermonem tuum credimus sed ipsi*, &c. By this
means one shall have, after some continuance, more
acquaintances and devoted friends than he can satisfy,
and more business in that kind than he can turn his hands
unto ; but this is supposing he may at the first go up and
down to get this acquaintance, and to be so known unto
many ; and until he have means so to do, if he have never
so good talents, yet he shall not do so much good as a
meaner person that is better acquainted. Now in this
time I do verily think, if the laws be put in execution,
there will be no means at all to get acquaintance, but the
best acquainted shall have difficulty to help his known

friends, and to be helped by them with safe places of abode as [I have declared at] large in my last letters, and they must lie much still and private and do [good part of] their [work by means of le]tters. Therefore, although I know Father Roger would be much esteemed of my special friends as any that could be sent (unless my brother[1] had served his apprenticeship and were made a journeyman, for of his skill and workmanship in framing the best wedding garment there is great and general hope conceived) yet, things staying as they do in England, and Father Roger so well acquainted now with the place as himself (which truly I think would be hard to find) my friends also being already furnished in England: these reasons move me to think it neither needful nor best that Father Roger go thither as yet; which yet in a more quiet time I shall be bold to beg for, if I see the College where he is so furnished that without great loss it might want him. I find Father Roger desirous of England if it were thought best, but wholly desirous to do that which you yourself do think most convenient; but when I urge him to speak his very thoughts whether he do think the College would be at want, he cannot deny but that the College hath need rather of more than less help, and surely I think if it were another's case of whom he might with humility acknowledge how profitable he is, I do think he would absolutely do his best to hinder it, as I do.

"For the answer to your questions, though in my last long letters I did in part answer to most of them before I received yours, yet now I will briefly again set down my opinion to the several points, Father Baldwin having written of them in his last, I being at St. Omers; but now I am come to him, being advised by the physician there to go to the Spa for the drying up of my rheum, which here I shall take further counsel of, how far it is needful,

---

[1] Sir Oliver Manners was ordained in April 1611, as we have said (*supra*, p. 373), about five years from the date of this letter.

and whether the great rains have not made the waters of less force. I am here private, and more private than I could be at St. Omers whilst the banished priests [1] are passing by. I think I shall hear within two or three posts your further pleasure; if not, I will return [to St. Omers] and then begin to talk with the youths there, or do any service I can as you appointed in your last. In the meantime, with many humble thanks for your many undeserved favours, I rest this 15th of July [1606].

"Your Reverence's son and servant wholly to command,

"FR. HARRISON."

Addressed—*Al molto Rev. in Christo Padre, il Padre Roberto Parsonio, Rettore del Collegio delli Inglesi, Roma.*

It was probably very soon indeed after this that Father Gerard received directions from Father Persons to go to Rome, for the order must have come so soon that in his autobiography he puts it that "he went straight to Rome." We learn from Father More[2] that he was sent thence to Tivoli for a while, for rest of mind and body. Father Persons was staying there for his health, as we learn from a letter[3] of his dated the 8th of October, 1606; and, as a further pleasure for Father Gerard, Brother John Lilly, who had twice risked everything to set him free, was at Tivoli with Father Persons.

We have a letter,[4] dated "this Simon and Jude's day, 1606," from Father Andrew Whyte, afterwards the Apostle of Maryland, addressed "To his especial good friend Mr. Garret give these at Rome." This Father Whyte was one of the banished priests, and he would therefore

---

[1] Bishop Challoner gives a list of 47 priests from different prisons who were sent this year, 1606, into perpetual banishment. *Missionary Priests*, vol. ii. p. 29.

[2] *Hist. Prov.* lib. vii. n. 43, p. 339.

[3] Stonyhurst MSS., Father Grene's *Collectan. P.* f. 437.

[4] *Ibid. Angl. A.* vol. iii. n. 70.

know for certain that at the time he wrote his letter at the
end of October Father Gerard had gone towards Rome.
He wrote to ask him to speak to Father Persons to get
Richard Green received into the Society, who had been
sent to College by Father Gerard, and had been imprisoned
"about the time of this late commotion." Green "was
received very kindly by Father Walley [Garnet] and
provided for very charitably in a manner as one of the
Society, with a promise that the year following he should
be received without fail;" but now, as "few or none of
Father Walley's writings or determinations were found,
and Richard Fulwood gone which should have given
particular testimony," Father Whyte begs that "he may
either be sent to the Novitiates of other countries with
the licence of the General, or else may have a promise to
be the next that is received at Louvain."

On the feast of St. Thomas of Canterbury in the same
year, December 29, 1606, Father Gerard had not yet
returned from Tivoli to Rome, for on that day Father
Persons wrote[1] from Rome to "Customer," that is the
archpriest, in the words already quoted respecting his
innocence of the Gunpowder Plot. "The man you name,
to wit Ger., passed this way some months gone, but made
little or no abode lest offence might be taken thereat.
Only I can say that during the few days which he remained, he gave great edification for his behaviour and
sundry great testimonies of his rare virtue, but most of
all of his innocency concerning that crime whereof he was
imputed in the proclamation, about which himself procured that his General should officially examine, in presence of divers witnesses, commanding him *in virtute
sanctæ obedientiæ* to utter the truth therein to his Superior,
whereupon he swore and protested that he was wholly
innocent therein, which the rest of his behaviour doth
easily make probable. I shall cause him to be advertised

[1] Stonyhurst MSS., Father Grene's *Collectan. P.* f. 449, 477.

by the first commodity of the note you write about his friend."

Early probably in 1607 Father Gerard left Tivoli for Rome, where he was appointed English Penitentiary[1] at St. Peter's. The confessionals of that Basilica, like those of the Holy House at Loretto, were served by a College of Jesuit Fathers, and both Churches required confessors of every nationality. There was thus an English Father employed at each of these sanctuaries ; but unfortunately our records are very fragmentary, and of the Penitentiaries we have little information beyond that which has been left us by Father Christopher Grene, who at the distance of nearly a century succeeded Father Gerard as English Penitentiary at St. Peter's. How long Father Gerard was there we are left to gather from other sources, and there is little to rely upon except the date that we attribute to his autobiography and the signs of its having been written in Belgium. Of the latter there cannot be any doubt when we notice that towards its conclusion the writer says, " I went straight to Rome, and being sent back thence to these parts, was fixed at Louvain." At Louvain therefore it was written, and the time, as we have seen, was later than John Lilly's departure to England in June 1609, and of course later than his own solemn Profession of the four vows, which was on the 3rd of May 1609.

His Profession, nearly twenty-one years after his admission into the Society, may have been at Rome just before leaving or at Louvain just after arriving. We are in possession of the confidential report which was made to Father General respecting him, previous to his Profession. By a singular chance the paper in which it is contained is the only one of similar reports that has come to our hands. The Latin original, from which we trans-

---

[1] Stonyhurst MSS., Father Southwell's *Catalogus primorum patrum*, p. 32. Archives of the English College at Rome, *Scritture*, vol. xxx. ; 1632.

late, is amongst the Stonyhurst manuscripts.[1] Father
Gerard's name is the ninth on the paper. " Father John
Gerard, English, forty-five years old, nineteen in the
Society [that is, reckoning from the time when he took
his scholastic vows, at the end of his two years' novice-
ship], twenty-one on the English mission. He studied at
Rome in the English College controversy and cases of
conscience for four years [including, it is to be supposed,
his period of study at Rheims]. He was admitted [to his
scholastic vows] in England, where he made his noviceship. He is a very spiritual man ; he is endowed with an
admirable power of gaining souls ; he has also more than
a middling talent for preaching ; and he is held to be not
unfit for government. If these talents can supply the
defect of learning, taking also into account all that he
has suffered for the Catholic faith, then he is proposed
for the four vows. It would be a consolation both to
himself and to the many Catholics of note by whom he
is held in high esteem. But if not, then he is proposed
for profession of the three vows."

Both Father Bartoli and Father More remark that
Father Gerard was admitted to the solemn vows of a
Professed Father by a special favour, as his learning,
owing to the short course of study through which he had
passed, fell short of that which the Society requires as
a condition of Profession. Father Bartoli says[2] that this
" most rare but most just privilege " was conferred on
him, " as virtue, in which he exceeded the standard, supplied for the studies in which he fell short of it."

His first employment as a Professed Father of the
Society was to be *Socius* or Companion of Father Thomas
Talbot, who was Rector and Master of Novices in the
English Novitiate house at Louvain. It was of this house
that he spoke in his letter to Father Persons on his arrival
in Belgium in July 1606, expressing his " desire of some

[1] *Angl. A.* vol. vi.   [2] *Inghilterra*, p. 586.

time of recollection," which he said he granted he could do "in the new house, if it go forwards, under Father Talbot," though he acknowledged his preference for the old novitiate at St. Andrew's on the Quirinal, which he calls "the chiefest fountain." In the same letter he says that he should "be glad to be Father Talbot's minister here," after he had spent some time at St. Andrew's; and it is probable that he was appointed to the very office he thus named when he was made Socius to the Master of Novices at Louvain, after two years of residence at Rome in the College of the Penitentiaries of St. Peter's.

CHAPTER XXXIV.

LOUVAIN AND LIEGE.

1609 TO 1622.

ST. JOHN'S at Louvain, the first Novitiate of the English
Province, was the foundation of Doña Luisa de Carvajal,
the devout Spanish lady, whose life was devoted, in
virtue of a remarkable vocation, to the encouragement of
the suffering Catholics in England. By her will, dated
the 22nd of December 1604, she left 12,000 ducats for
the establishment of an English Jesuit Novitiate, and
though she did not die till ten years later,—that is, on
the 2nd of January 1614,—and though the money she
gave was all she had in the world,[1] she would have the
good work begin at once without waiting for her death.
The will,[2] of which she was thus herself the executrix,
is an admirable specimen of true Spanish devotion and
humility. After commending her soul to God by the
intercession of our Blessed Lady, she proceeds—"For the
love of God I humbly pray the Superiors of the Society
of Jesus and the Præpositus of the Professed House [at
Valladolid], as a favour, to grant me some little place
in their church where my body may be buried, in consideration of the devotion I have ever entertained for
their holy Religious Order; to which Order, in the manner
that I have thought would be most to the glory of God,
I offer with the greatest affection a gift which, though

---

[1] *The Life of Luisa de Carvajal*, by Lady Georgiana Fullerton, London,
1873, p. 137.
[2] Father More, *Hist. Prov.* lib. vii. cap. 3, p. 291.

but small, is all that I have. And if a burial place be
refused me in that church, my executors will obtain for
me a resting place in some other church of the Society;[1]
and if they are unable to obtain this, let me be buried
in some monastery in which, for the love of God, they
may be willing to give burial to a poor person like myself,
and let my funeral be conducted in accordance with this
my poverty. As executors I name Father Richard Walpole, the Vice-Prefect of the English Mission, and the
Confessor of the English College in this city, or their
successors. After them (and I have named them first
from respect to their priestly dignity) I name the Countess
de la Miranda, Doña Maria de Zuniga, Doña Maria Gasca,
Don Francis de Contreras, Señor Melchior de Molina,
and Don Luis de Carrillo y Toledo, Count of Caracena.
First of all I declare that many years ago when I was
with my uncle, I made a vow to God to dedicate all my
property to the glory and greatest service of God. Then
His Divine Majesty gave me large desires and a vehement
attraction to devote myself above all things to the preservation and advancement of the English Fathers of the
Society of Jesus, who sustain that kingdom like strong
columns, defend it from an otherwise inevitable ruin, and
supply efficacious means of salvation for thousands and
thousands of souls. Wherefore I offer all my goods to
the most holy Virgin our Lady. I place them under her
protection, and I name and leave her universal heir of all
my property. And I give possession of it henceforward
to that most glorious Virgin, and in her name and place
to Father Robert Persons, or failing him, to the Father
who shall succeed him as Superior of the Mission, but
with this condition and obligation, that such goods shall

---

[1] When this saintly noble lady died, "the Fathers of the Society of Jesus
at Louvain declared that her remains belonged by right to the Novitiate she
had founded, and wrote very soon and very pressingly to the Spanish Ambassador on the subject," but by the King's command she was buried in the
Convent of the Incarnation at Madrid. *Life*, p. 285.

be applied to the founding of a Novitiate of English religious of the Society of Jesus, in whatever kingdom or part of the world shall seem to Father Persons to be to the greater glory of God ; but in case that England shall be brought back to the faith and obedience of the Roman Church, my will is that the said revenue be transferred into that kingdom, for the foundation of a Novitiate there, unless it should seem better to Father Persons, for reasons concerning the Catholic religion, to leave the Novitiate outside that kingdom.

"If the foundation of the Novitiate is delayed on account of the insufficiency of the sum in question, it is to be put out to interest, which said interest will be allowed to accumulate until it suffices for the purpose in view. If in the mean time, however, some pressing need in connection with the mission and conversion of England should occur, part of that interest may be employed for that end, provided that the ultimate object is never lost sight of. All the poor furniture of my house, its images and its books, I leave to the English Novitiate. I wish the holy crucifix I have, which belonged to my uncle, to be placed in the said Novitiate with particular veneration, as well as the particle of the wood of the true Cross which I carry about me, and for that purpose it will be put into a cross or little reliquary of gold, the same that the Emperor Henry III. carried about with him, which was given to me by the Marquis of Almaçan, Don Francis Hurtado de Mendoza."

Doña Luisa then makes a provision for her friend Sister Ines of the Assumption, and begs her brother to understand that "if she does not remember him in the disposal of her fortune, it is from no want of love for him, but from a strict obligation of conscience which leaves her no option on the subject, and that if he acquiesces and takes pleasure in the fact that our Lord has chosen her to be only His, he will share in the reward, and find that spiritual blessings are not to be less esteemed than temporal ones." And lastly, she "asks her heirs, with the permission of the Superior whom she humbly and earnestly asks to grant it, that an image of our Lady with her Divine Son in her arms may be placed above the principal altar in the future Novitiate, and a devout mass with music celebrated there on each of her feasts."

Time was not lost in carrying out the intentions of this pious benefactress.[1] In 1606 Father Persons rented a large house in Louvain, and in it established the first Novitiate of the English Province of the Society of Jesus. The house belonged to the Commandery of St. Nicholas of the Knights of Malta, and was obtained by them in the middle of the fourteenth century from the Duke of Brabant, in exchange for Kisselstein, a fortress to which the Knights Hospitallers had succeeded on the suppression of the Templars. The Commandery took possession about the year 1330 of the house and chapel which were built in 1140. The Church was built in 1457, and from the Patron Saint of the Order of Malta it was called St. John's, though it was dedicated to St. Gregory the Apostle of England and other saints.

St. John's at Louvain was in a magnificent position on Mont César. Some portion of the house still remains, though the Church was entirely swept away in 1799. The hill on which it stood, took its name from the neighbouring Château César,[2] the Castle which, dating from the beginning of the eleventh century, when it was built by Lambert I., Count of Louvain, took its imperial title from Charles V., who restored it in 1511. In it Edward III. of England and his Queen Philippa of Hainault spent the winter of 1338, and Albert and Isabella the Archdukes visited it in 1617 on their return from their annual pil-

[1] Father More, *Hist. Prov.* lib. viii. n. 8, p. 355.

[2] For our information respecting Louvain we have drawn largely on the fine work *Louvain Monumental*, by M. Van Even, archivist of the town.

grimage to Our Lady of Montaigu. Charles V. came to live there first in 1504, when Adrien Flourens of Utrecht, then professor of Theology in the University of Louvain, afterwards Pope Adrian VI., was his tutor.

The Church of the Knights of St. John on Mont César was a large one, and is the most prominent object in the foreground of the print of Louvain engraved by Juste Lipse in 1605.[1] It had a large nave, lighted by eight windows, and over the western door was a lofty tower, surmounted by a wooden spire. It was almost at the northernmost point within the walls of the town, on the left hand after entering the Porte de Malines, and this tower was visible half a league from Malines, as that of St. Rombaut can be seen half a league from Louvain. In the Church there was a wooden statue of St. John the Evangelist weeping at the foot of the Cross, called *St. Jean le pleureur* or *St. Jan de Gryzer*, which was held in great veneration, and to it women brought crying children on pilgrimage. A trace of the forgotten dedication to St. Gregory was to be found in a children's fair which on the feast of that Saint was held on the grass before the Church doors. The house was close to the ramparts, and Father More who lived there with Father Gerard, could hardly help noting that from the high ground where it stood there was a grand view of the whole city. Below was a walled garden, and on the slope of the hill there were pleasant walks among the vines which were ranged in terraces; and the whole, though within the protection of the walls of a town, was as quiet and calm as befitted a house of prayer.

The Novitiate commenced at St. John's in February

---

[1] *Lovanium,* Antverpiæ *ex officina Plantiniana,* 1610, 4o. ed. 2a. It has not been thought necessary to give a list of names corresponding with the numbers and letters on the print. It will be enough to say that 11 is the Porte de Malines, 12 the Château César, and 13 St. John's. The buildings adjoining the church on the reader's left, with two arches extending across the road, are still in existence.

OLD LOUVAIN

1607 with six priests, two scholastics and five lay-brothers as Novices under Father Thomas Talbot as their Novice Master. The first Novice of the new house was Father Thomas Garnet, the nephew of the martyred Provincial, who was himself martyred at Tyburn on the 23rd of June, 1608. He had been consequently but a few months in the midst of the exercises of the Noviceship, but he had been admitted into the Society by his uncle on the 29th of September, 1604,[1] and his virtue had been exercised amid the severer trials of the Tower of London. His vows were made at Louvain on the 2nd of July, 1607, and he was again in prison in England before the year was out. A miraculous cure granted at his intercession is related by Father John Gerard in the letter, written from Louvain on the 17th of August, 1612, a long extract from which concerning Mrs. Vaux has already been given.[2]

In 1614, St. John's, in addition to its novices, received Jesuit scholastics who were students in philosophy and theology. A house in the garden was then fitted up for the Novitiate, and Father Henry Bedingfeld, better known by the name of Silisdon, was installed at St. John's as Rector of the new house of studies. This arrangement did not last long, for at the end of this year the Novitiate was transferred to Liége and Father Gerard was made Rector and Master of Novices. In 1622 the Novitiate was once more transferred, and it then settled down at Watten where it remained up to the time of the expulsion of the Society from France in October, 1762, and for the short time that remained before the suppression, the Novitiate with the school of little boys which had been opened at Watten, was known as the *Petit Collége* at Bruges. When the Novitiate was removed from Liége to Watten, the former house, of which Father Gerard may be regarded as the founder, became the Theologate; and St. John's at Louvain which had done the English Fathers of the

---

[1] *Records*, vol ii. p. 479.   [2] *Supra*, p. 447.

Society such friendly service, was let by the Knights of Malta to the Irish Dominicans from 1626 to 1650. The College of Liége continued to be the house of studies of the English Province from the year 1622 to the suppression of the Society. In accordance with the terms of the Brief of suppression the fathers were permitted by the Prince Bishop of Liége to continue to live there together, a secular priest being in the first instance appointed their Superior: and thither the ancient College of St. Omers, which had been for nine years known as the *Grand Collége* at Bruges, was transferred. Finally Liége was left for Stonyhurst in consequence of the perils of the French Revolution, in 1792, and in both places, before the restoration of the Society, the College was known as "the Academy" and its community as "the gentlemen of the Academy." The Scholasticate, which as we have seen began at St. John's Louvain under Father Henry Silisdon in 1614, and was removed to Liége in 1622, was re-established at the Seminary, under the wing of Stonyhurst College in 1830, and in 1848 the theological studies found their present home in St. Beuno's College near St. Asaph. The Novitiate, Luisa de Carvajal's especial care, began on the re-commencement of the Society in England in 1803, at Hodder Place near Stonyhurst, whence it was removed in 1854 to Beaumont Lodge near Windsor, and again, in 1861 to Manresa House, Roehampton. Hodder Place became a school for little boys in preparation for Stonyhurst College, as Watten was to St. Omers, and the Petit Collége to the Grand Collége at Bruges. Those who are interested in the existing houses cannot fail to be interested also in the men and places that gave them their beginning.

The establishment of the house at Liége, from which men of the last generation came to England, was the work of Father John Gerard. "He built it from the foundations in a beautiful form by alms collected from all quarters," says

Father Nathaniel Southwell.[1] No less than thirty letters
have come down to us written by Father Gerard in the
year 1614, addressed to the Prefect of the English Mission,
Father Thomas Owen, Rector of the English College at
Rome. They treat chiefly of the purchase of the new
house at Liége and of the transfer of the Novitiate to that
city. Some extracts relating to Father Gerard himself
will be found interesting. Of these letters some are signed
John Nelson, and others John Tomson. In the later years
of his life he seems to have been known chiefly by the
name of Tomson, though the last name by which he was
disguised was Thomas Roberts. At various times in his
life he was called by the names of Starkie, Standish,
Tanfield, Staunton, Lee, Brooke, Harrison, Nelson, Tomson,
and Roberts.

The choice of Liége as a residence seems to have been
mainly owing to the disquiet caused to the Catholics in
the Low Countries by the remonstrances of the English
Government. We have some specimens of it in the following extracts, in which we find Father Gerard true to the
natural fearlessness of his character. "Concerning[2] my
wariness in avoiding the eyes of spies, I have been all this
year [1614] more sparing in that kind than divers friends
here did think needful, although some one or two did
think it dangerous to go any journey, as doubting I might
be killed by the way; but this was but according to their
accustomed fears with which I have been long acquainted.
But indeed, Father, I am so far from desire to go many
journeys, that it is a pain to me to think of going any
whither: and the reason why I never went to any of those
places your Reverence mentioneth in this year past (but
only the last Lent to Mechlin for Mr. Rouse) was not that
I thought it dangerous (being known so well to live here
public that it cannot be unknown to any spies), nor for

[1] Stonyhurst MSS., *Catalogus primorum patrum*, p. 32.
[2] Stonyhurst MSS., *Angl. A.* vol. iv. n. 5.

FF

that I wanted leave, for I had the other Provincial's particular and willing grant, without my own asking, to go to any place of these countries ; but it was because I had rather be at home, and in the town of Louvain itself I go not abroad half so much as I think were needful for the contentment of others.   I was not at the Teresians, where the Mother of the house (to whom I gave the Exercise four years ago) and Father Scott's[1] sister do much desire my often coming, any more than once since the last Lent.   At the Monastery of St. Monica's, my cousin Shirley hath requested my coming thither for these three or four months, to bestow one afternoon upon her and some younger nuns whom she hath charge of, that they may all together ask me what spiritual questions they may like best, and I have never yet found a fit time for it. The gentlemen in the town[2] I doubt I visit not once in a quarter of a year, and I have some reason to think that either they think me careless of them, or afraid to be seen abroad, as though my case were very dangerous, which would also make them or any other that should come to town more fearful to come into my company, and consequently hinder the little good that I might do with them. But I hope I shall be as wary as your Reverence wisheth, and if this course go forwards of being Rector without the name of Rector, there will be less inconvenience, whosoever see me seeing me still as a private man."   In this he alludes to a plan of his own, that Father Blackfan should have the title of Rector, although he was himself appointed to the Rectorship of the Novitiate.

[1] This is Father Thomas Laithwaite.   More, *Hist. Prov.* lib. ix. n. 1, p. 391 ; *supra*, p. 386.

[2] In 1617 Sir Thomas Leeds was Prefect and Sir Ralph Babthorpe Secretary of the Congregation of the Blessed Virgin at Louvain.   Stonyhurst MSS., *Angl. A.* vol. iv. n. 47.   A considerable number of Catholic families had settled in Louvain, and in 1614 they were disturbed by a summons to appear in England under pain of losing their possessions.   On a remonstrance being made by the Spanish Ambassador, King James disclaimed the summons, on which the magistrates of Louvain expelled the pursuivant from the town. More, *Hist. Prov.* lib. ix. n. 10, p. 406.

The next letter[1] is dated April 6, 1614. "I have yours of the 15th of March, and see in that, as in all of yours, your fatherly care of me, which by the grace of God I will labour to deserve. I am well satisfied with Father General's order, and shall endeavour to get this building finished for the Novitiate [in the garden at St. John's] as soon as I can, and then will settle to my book as much as my health and letters will permit. . . . Having writ thus far, I was called to go to Brussels with Father Rector (by Father Blacfan's and Father Percy his advice) to speak with the Duke's[2] Secretary, who telling Father Percy the last week that the Agent [of King James] did solicit against me, and that he could not well answer him unless he delivered him some reasons in writing for my innocency, this writing was promised him by Father Percy; but I being loth to have any such writing sent, as thinking it the likeliest means to raise a new persecution against me, though for the Secretary's satisfaction we drew and delivered him a brief note of four or five effectual proofs, yet both to the Secretary first, and afterwards to the Nuncio, I told this day that if any such writing were sent, it would do me great harm, for Canterbury [Archbishop Abbot], having such a writing, would doubtless show it at the Council table, and then those lords who do know me to be innocent and wish me well, will be as it were forced to speak against me, lest they should seem to favour me, and so the King should be more incensed. The Nuncio did promise Father Rector and me that he would deal seriously both with the Secretary and the Prince himself in the cause."

Writing[3] under the date of April 18, 1614, he shows that he thinks that too much importance had been given to the Agent's interference. "I think your Reverence

[1] Stonyhurst MSS., *Angl. A.* vol. iv. n. 6.
[2] The Archduke Albert, Governor of Flanders.
[3] Stonyhurst MSS., *Angl. A.* vol. iv. n. 7.

was made to believe by letters sent about Easter, that there was some new troubles against me here, out of England, and consequently that there was need of such information to the Nuncio and Father Provincial as had been given. But when I heard of it, I said it was nothing but Trumbol his own device, in hope to work upon the weakness of the Prince; and so now it proves, for on my going to the Secretary himself with our Father Rector, as I wrote from Brussels, and giving him a paper of some few points for my innocency, with the request he would not deliver it but show it if he would to the Agent, the Secretary answered he would advertise me if it were needful; but since the note was showed unto Trumbol, and he showed to be satisfied with it, and afterwards meeting the Secretary told him that he took it to be only matter of religion, but that being now made matter of State, he, being a servant employed in matter of State, could not but seek to concur with them that employed him,—as it were granting that himself was satisfied, and yielding a reason why he had moved the matter. And this being understood both by the Prince and the Nuncio, they were very glad of it. . . . I write this from Mechlin, whither Sir William [Stanley] was desirous to have me come for his comfort now and after the death and funeral of his lady."

But such a man as Father Gerard was not likely to be left in peace in those intriguing times. In the August following, Father Silisdon writes thus to Father Owen.[1] "Even now I have advice that his Majesty of England hath made two complaints to the Prince, and that the first is against Father Gerard's being in his dominions." The consequence was that a transfer to another territory became desirable, and Father Gerard set his heart on migrating with his novices into the capital of the Prince Bishop of Liége. His reasons for the preference he details in a letter[2]

---

[1] Stonyhurst MSS., *Angl. A.* vol. iv. n. 17. [2] *Ibid.* n. 22.

from that city, written under the signature of John Nelson, September 19, 1614. "There be many causes to be alleged why here, rather than in any place; as, the commodity of dealing with our English in the summer, the opportunity of keeping our Novices unknown, the excellent seat, far beyond Louvain, and that bestowed upon us, the present helps sent for this beginning, with great likelihood of much more, the great favour which is to be expected from this Prince and his family, and is to be strengthened by my two cousins Sir William and Mr. Morton, and Sir William hath written to him that he doth much joy in his cousin who is there to be Rector."

The two cousins of whom Father Gerard here speaks were two very powerful friends. The one was Sir William Stanley, who showed himself a kind friend to Father Gerard and his charge by negotiating the purchase money —at least that portion of it which had to be paid down —probably (as Father Gerard speaks of the "seat being bestowed upon us") regarding it as a gift. Whatever else was requisite for the purchase was provided by Brother William Browne,[1] who though grandson, brother and uncle of Viscounts Montague,—his grandfather was Queen Mary's Ambassador to the Holy See—was himself content to spend his life in the humble duties of a Jesuit lay-brother.

The "Mr. Morton" was Sir George Talbot of Grafton, afterwards ninth Earl of Shrewsbury. He was a scholar of some repute,[2] and an intimate friend of Maximilian, Duke of Bavaria. As Ferdinand, the Prince-bishop of Liége, was Maximilian's brother, it was no little help to

---

[1] F. More, *Hist. Prov.* lib. ix. n. 11, p. 406.

[2] "Sir Basil Brooke telleth that our German friend is very well at his house and in protection of the King, that Canterbury has used him very kindly, and entreated him, as one whose scholarship is famous, to make use of his library [as] it shall please him." Father Silisdon to Father Owen, August 25, 1614. Endorsed by Father Owen, "Sir George Talbot well entertained by K. and Cant." Stonyhurst MSS., *Angl. A.* vol iv. n. 17.

Father Gerard to be on cousinly terms with George Talbot.
Duke Maximilian became a generous benefactor to the
new house at Liége. In 1618 he sent Father Gerard,
through Sir George Talbot, 5,000 florins for the noviceship.[1] In a letter dated the 25th of January, 1620, the
Duke writes to Father Gerard, who had promised to pray
that he might have a son,—"I bound myself once by
vow to your blessed Ignatius, that if he would obtain
this favour for me, I would give my son the name of
Ignatius, and would build and endow a College of the
Society wherever Father General might judge it most
useful. What if God should purpose thus to provide for
you ?"[2] In July of the same year he wrote, "We have
sent you a contribution of 1,300 German florins by Father
Mayer for a tabernacle for the Blessed Sacrament, and
for a niche for an image of the Blessed Virgin." Even
after Father Gerard's departure from the house, Duke
Maximilian's liberality to it did not fail. Father Henry
Bedingfeld *alias* Silisdon, Father Gerard's successor as
Master of Novices, removed the Novitiate from Liége to
Watten[3] in 1624, and not long after, the Duke settled a
permanent endowment upon the English College of Liége,[4]
when the scholastics were brought from St. John's at
Louvain to the house that Father Gerard had established ten years before.

That house, which Father Gerard called "the excellent
seat far beyond Louvain," was like that of Louvain in

[1] Father More, *Hist. Prov.* lib. ix. n. 15, p. 414.

[2] *Ibid.* pp. 415, 424. Maximilian had two sons by his second wife, Mary
Anne of Austria, when he was over 60 years of age, and the eldest he named
Ignatius.

[3] The Priory of Watten, with its revenue of 3,000 florins of Brabant, was
transferred to the Society in 1611 by James Blase, O.S.F., Bishop of St.Omers.
The proposal had been approved by the King of Spain in 1604 and by Pope
Paul V. in 1607, but the jealousy of the English felt by the Archduke Albert
delayed the establishment of an English Novitiate there till after his death
in 1622. More, *Hist. Prov.* lib. vii. nn. 5—7 ; pp. 294—298, 416.

[4] A note to a manuscript Catalogue of 1625 tells us that the College had
funds for the support of 44 inmates.

OLD LIÉGE

this respect, that it was situated close to the ramparts
on high ground commanding a fine view of the city. It
was situated [1] on Mont S. Martin, close to the Citadel, and
it had ten acres of ground attached to it, which were laid
out in terraces up to the city walls. St. John's was only
a rented house, but that at Liége was purchased. Its
price was less than " 200*l.* in present money and the rent
of 30*l.* with which the house and grounds are already
charged, which then we may redeem by little and little,
as we get friends to buy it out."[2] As the rentcharge
could be redeemed at fifteen years purchase, the whole
price was thus under 650*l.*

Here Father Gerard was Rector and Master of Novices
for eight years.[3] His Socius or "Compagnion," as he
calls him, was Father Henry More, subsequently the Historian of the Province, who thus fulfilled under Father
Gerard those duties in the Noviceship that Father Gerard
had performed at Louvain under Father Talbot. When
discussing, before his appointment, those fathers who
were fitted for that office, after mentioning others, Father
Gerard says,[4] "Father Nicholson is far short of either of
them for my turn, for he is no good Latinist, I think
little better than myself, though he be much better
scholar ; neither hath he any other language but Spanish,
of which I shall have small use. Father Henry More
hath French well, Dutch prettily, and Italian sufficiently,
besides Spanish very well, and Latin as I could wish
him."

---

[1] The English College may be distinguished, in the accompanying view of
ancient Liége, as the large building, the tower of which (surmounted by a
short spire and a ball), comes out of a quadrangle, at the right hand corner of
which, and below the front, are long flights of steps. The city wall, descending
from the citadel, will be seen to be not far behind the building. Three sides
of the square of buildings still exist, and are used for military stores, but it is
said that they are doomed to speedy destruction.

[2] Stonyhurst MSS., *Angl. A.* vol. iv. n. 23.

[3] Father Nathaniel Southwell, *Catalogus primorum patrum,* p. 32.

[4] Stonyhurst MSS., *Angl. A.* vol. iv. n. 20.

As to his first Novices, there were twelve, which made what he styled "a pretty beginning;" but his Community soon increased in numbers, for in 1617 Father More[1] says there were 45 in the College at Liége, of whom 30 were Novices.   Of the first twelve he said[2] that they were "the two that expect at Liége, the two that are come from Rome, and four out of Spain, with Mr. Lewkner and Mr. Whitmore, besides Grafton, when he comes, and a tailor now servant in this house, who by all judgments here is as fit to be received, as Brother Silvester, the young tailor now in the Noviceship, is fit to be dismissed."

Of the "two that expect at Liége," a previous letter[3] had said, "Here be Mr. Mansel and Mr. Owen Shelley, by the names of Mr. Griffin and Mr. Tichborne; both expect, the first with some lothness to stay long, the second is wholly resigned.   The first is a pious man, and to those that know his fashion will be profitable for some uses in the Society, but the second will be practical and fit for any thing, and in truth I think he will do very well."   This Father Owen Shelley was afterwards Rector of the College of Liége, and his career justified Father Gerard's judgment of his character.

Amongst the "four which are come out of Spain" were two that must have constantly served to remind their Rector at Liége of the Gunpowder Plot, as the remonstrances of King James' Agent had managed to do at Louvain.   "One of them," he says,[4] "is akin to Father Garnet, and of his name, though we call him Gilford, as he was called at St. Omers.   [The other is] William Ellis,[5] but we call him John Williams, for he was page to Sir Edward Digby, and taken with him,

---

[1] *Hist. Prov.* p. 424.

[2] Stonyhurst MSS., *Angl. A.* vol. iv. n. 29.

[3] *Ibid.* n. 23.

[4] *Ibid.* n. 29.

[5] Examination of William Ellis, servant to Sir Everard Digby, taken November 21, 1605.   P.R.O., *Gunpowder Plot Book*, n. 108.

though he might have escaped, for his master offered him horse and money to shift for himself, but the youth said he would live and die with him; and so, being taken, was condemned at Stafford, and should have been executed. He was offered to have his life if he would go to their church, which he refused. In the end they saved him and some others. He never [yielded] in the least point. He hath good friends near Sir Everard Digby's whom I know, and he is heir to 80*l.* a year, if his father do him right."

At the close of this short notice of Father Gerard's Rectorship it will be but right to record an unfavourable judgment passed upon him, as it will help us to form a true appreciation of his character. It is the only instance that has come down to us of blame on the part of one of his own brothers in Religion. "I see a general fear in all ours, those of best judgment, of the success of Father Nelson's government, and unless he hath a companion that may moderate him, his zeal will, I fear, carry him too far; and I fear it so much the more because I see him loth to have anybody with him who is likely to propose anything to him contrary to his own zealous desires." This is in a confidential letter[1] from Father Silisdon to Father Owen, dated October 31, 1614, so that as it was written before the transfer to Liége, it was a misgiving lest he should be indiscreet as a Rector, rather than a judgment on his actual conduct as a Superior. As he was left in office for eight years, and as, after that, he was placed in another position of great responsibility for four years more, we may be sure that the misgiving was not verified by the event.

Father Gerard's eight years of Rectorship at Liége were between 1614 and 1622. At the end of that time he was removed from Liége to Rome because his Superiors

---

[1] Stonyhurst MSS., *Angl. A.* vol. iv. n. 31.

wished him no longer to give an active support to a new Institute of Religious women in the rise of which he had taken much interest. Their foundress was Mary Ward, a very remarkable person, whose life is now in process of publication,[1] so that in this place it will be enough to refer to the forthcoming work for the interesting details of her biography and for the vicissitudes of the Institute founded by her. The Convent of her nuns at Liége was opened in 1616, while Father Gerard was Rector of the English Jesuit College, and the first house occupied by them must have been very close to the College on Mont S. Martin. In 1618 they removed to a good house on the height of Pierreuse, like their former house not far from the Citadel, in the possession of which, in 1642, they were succeeded by the English Canonesses of the Holy Sepulchre.[2]

One letter remains in existence which was written by Mary Ward to "Rev. Father Tomson *alias* Jhon Garet [John Gerard]." It is dated in the year 1619, and relates to a time when she was making a retreat under Father Gerard's direction. It is an interesting letter, but as it will appear in Mary Ward's life, with the narrative of the circumstances that called it forth, it is omitted here.

It has been said that it was to withdraw Father Gerard entirely from all connection with Mary Ward and her Institute that he was called to Rome. By the help of a money transaction in which he was concerned with them and the mention in the same affair of his successor as Rector, we are able to approximate to the date of his departure from Liége. Among the St. Omers'

---

[1] In the *Month* Mary Ward's life is being published under the title of "A Yorkshire Lady." It is announced that these chapters will be republished in a separate form.

[2] This Convent was transferred in 1665 to the house called the Maison des Coquins or Hôpital de St. Christophe in the faubourg d'Avroy. At the French Revolution the Canonesses of the Holy Sepulchre were obliged to leave Liége, and they settled at New Hall, near Chelmsford, in Essex, in 1799.

papers at Brussels there is one which says that there was a
mortgage of 3,000 florins on some houses belonging to the
Society at Liége made by Father John Gerard, as security
for money raised by Mary Ward. Father Blount, the
Vice Provincial, at once transferred the houses to Thomas
Sackville, who was jointly responsible with the Nuns
for the debt, and this deed is dated April 26, 1621 ; and
four days afterwards Father Gerard declared the houses to
be their property. By a deed dated March 10, 1622,
Thomas Sackville conveyed the houses to Dame Barbara
Babthorpe the Superioress, and as this deed mentions
Father Henry Silisdon as then Rector, we see that by that
date[1] Father Gerard had ceased to be Rector, and probably had already left Liége for Rome.

But Father Gerard carried his sympathy for Mary
Ward and her Institute with him, as some letters[2] of his
witness which are preserved in the Convent of the
"English Ladies" of the Institute of the Blessed Virgin
Mary at Nymphenburg in Bavaria. One of them is addressed to a nephew of his old friend Father Roger Lee,
Henry Lee, who was a secular priest, acting as Chaplain
to Mary Ward and her "Company" at Munich. In it he
says with St. Raphael that God particularly tries those
whom He especially loves ; and then adds, "This I have
always seen to be their case, and though I have kept
silence to them, as it was needful I should, and must still
continue to do so, yet I have pleaded their cause where
only I can avail them, that is with Him Who is best able
to help them, and Who will not despise the humble and
earnest prayers, though of His unworthy servants. To

[1] This accords with the *Florus Anglo-Bavaricus*, p. 11, and corrects Dr.
Oliver's statement that Father Silisdon succeeded Father Gerard as Rector
and Master of Novices in 1620 and transferred the Novitiate to Watten in
1622. The error arose from a misunderstanding of Father More, *Hist. Prov.*
p. 416. The transfer to Watten took place in 1624. *Vide supr.* p. 486.

[2] These letters have been copied by the kind permission of Madame Mary
Paur, the General Superioress of the Institute.

Him I have, and do, and will continue to offer my poor
and instant petitions many times every day, and no day
but they have a chief part in my masses, and many times
the whole when I have not other obligations. Other helps
I cannot afford, either in spiritual or corporal assistance,
my hands being tied. Thus much for my opinion of their
patience and my good wishes to their persons, not to be
altered but by their altering from God's service, which I
am confident never will be." This letter is dated from
Ghent, or "Gant" as the English called it then, where
he wrote it on the 8th of March 1627. Father Gerard
when he wrote this letter was looking forward to the
confirmation of their Institute, though not "in this Pope's
time;" and he tells them to be "very wary not to speak of
any great differences which have been between them and
our English Fathers, for besides that charity requires it,
with most hath been but mistakings, and such things as we
read to have happened among the saints." This was
written in the absence of the Superior but by his leave;
and there are details respecting Father Gerard's position
at Ghent which will be useful to us in our next chapter.

There is another letter from him written after he had
again returned to Rome, dated the 13th of August 1628,
and addressed "To the Reverend Mother Mrs. Winifred
Campion, Vice-rectrice of their College in Monachium, at
Monachium" [Munich]. In this letter he speaks of Mary
Ward as at Rome; for after asking some questions of the
number of their novices and scholars, he says, "These
things if you mention in any letter to Mother Superior
here, it will be as much as I can wish, and with less trouble
to yourself. I hope those grand crosses which God did
permit to be raised against you by those complaining
letters which were written against you, will by God's providence be allayed, Who will be sure to turn all such things
to the good of His servants, *dans nivem sicut lanam*, and
make it keep warm the roots of corn and to bring forth a

greater harvest in due season." Father Gerard mentions among those "who be of my acquaintance my very good daughter Mrs. Francis[1] Brooksbie and Mrs. Bedingfeld, which two are indeed very dear to me in our Lord Jesus, and I hope they will be very profitable in your company." And he bids his correspondent "remember my service to the Reverend Mr. Dr. Ansloe," their chaplain, whom he had mentioned in the former letter also.

Besides these, in the Convent at Nymphenburg there is a very long letter which exists in German only, without a signature, dated the 6th of October 1629, written in like terms of warm friendship. This letter has no passages of historical interest. It is endorsed in German, "We have the strongest reasons to believe that this letter was written in the English language by Father John Tomson (Gerard). It has been translated into German—is to be kept in secret and not shown to many."

[1] The feminine form Frances is modern.

CHAPTER XXXV.

GHENT AND ROME.

1623 TO 1637.

DURING his residence at Liége, amongst Father Gerard's correspondents were two Venerable Servants of God, Robert Cardinal Bellarmine, and Father Luis de la Puente, better known by the Latinized form of his name, de Ponte. As by a man's friends we can obtain an insight into his character, we have thought it desirable to give the few letters to Father Gerard from these two holy men that have come down to us. Cardinal Bellarmine's autograph[1] is preserved at Stonyhurst. We translate the letter from the original Latin.

" Very Reverend and beloved Father in Christ,—I have received your Reverence's letter dated from Liége the 23rd of November with the little presents inclosed in it, an English knife, a little case (either bone or ivory, I do not know which), and three small toothpicks. I do not know whether these were sent me for use, or as having some special meaning. Whichever it be, they are welcome as a proof of friendship and brotherhood.

" The memory of that excellent Mr. Oliver [Sir Oliver Manners, whom he had ordained seven years before], has brought me no little sadness or rather grief, not on his account who is translated from this world to the joys of Paradise, but for the sake of many whom without doubt he would have converted to a good life if Divine Provi-

[1] Stonyhurst MSS., *Angl. A.* vol. iii. n. 107.

dence had permitted him to live a while longer. But the good pleasure of God must ever be fulfilled, and the self-same, in order that it may be fulfilled, must ever be pleasing to us under all circumstances.

"I was pleased to read what your Reverence relates in your letter of your journeys, of your office of Master of Novices, of the building which you have bought at Liége, of the visitation of his Serene Highness Ferdinand, the Prince Bishop of Liége, and of the promise that the Priory [of Watten], on its next vacancy, shall be applied to the College. If my assistance in carrying this out can be of any use to you with the Pope, it shall not be wanting.

"Of Dr. Singleton I have heard much, and have defended him to the best of my power as long as I could, but the party opposed to him has prevailed. Nor do I see how I can help him at so great a distance, and especially as I should be suspected because I am a Jesuit. The devil is envious of the harmony between the English at Douay and the Fathers of the Society, for which the good Cardinal Allen cared so much ; but all means must be tried to re-establish a true and sincere friendship and agreement in teaching ; otherwise a kingdom divided against itself shall be brought to desolation. For many reasons I say freely that nothing can be done by me in his behalf ; first, as I was just saying, because I should be under suspicion, being a Jesuit. Then, because I am an old man of seven-and-seventy years of age, and I daily expect the dissolution of my tabernacle. Thirdly, because I cannot think of any way by which I could help him. The common manner of helping men of this sort is to give them ecclesiastical benefices ; but here in Rome the multitude of those who aspire to and seek after such benefits is so great that their number is almost infinite. Nor are they only Italians, but Spaniards also, Frenchmen, Germans, who look for nothing but benefices at Rome. I myself, who was thought to have some influence with the Pope, have laboured for more than ten years for a Spaniard, an excellent man and a great friend of mine, to obtain for him a good benefice falling vacant in his own country. I could say the same of Flemish and German friends of mine. What then would be the case with English people, in whose country there are no ecclesiastical benefices for Catholics? But, since these temporal things are nothing when compared to eternal benefices, our friend Dr. Singleton must not be cast down if our Lord treats him now, as of old He treated His Apostles, who He willed should enter into the Kingdom of Heaven through many tribulations. But I must not be too lengthy, for I know that both he and your Reverence stand in no need of my exhortations. I know that your Reverence will have hard work to read my bad writing, but Father Coffin[1] would have it that I should write to you with my own hand.

"With this I bid your Reverence farewell. Commend me to the prayers of Dr. Singleton, and of all your College; but your Reverence's self especially, for our old friendship and brotherhood, must diligently commend me to the Lord our God. From Rome on Christmas-day, December 25 1618.[2]

"Your Reverence's brother and servant in Christ,

"ROBERT CARD. BELLARMINE.

"To the Very Reverend Father John Tomson, S.J.,

"Rector of the College of the English Novices at Liége."

The two letters which have come down to us, addressed to Father Gerard by the Venerable Father Luis de la Puente, were written as his residence at Liége was drawing

---

[1] Father Edward Coffin was Confessor of the English College for nearly twenty years, in which office he was succeeded by Father Gerard.

[2] Dr. Oliver has misread this date 1611, which was before Father Gerard went to Liége and at which time Sir Oliver Manners was in Italy. Cardinal Bellarmine was born October 4, 1542, so that he was in his seventy-seventh year in 1618–9.

to a close. We translate from Father Christopher Grene's transcript[1] from the originals.

"I.H.S.

"P.C.

"When I received your Reverence's letters I was unable to answer them at once for I was suffering from extreme weakness, which usually afflicts me every year all through the winter. Blessed be our great God, from Whose Providence come health and sickness, life and death, and whatever prosperity and adversity there is in the world. The height of felicity in this life is to be superior to all these things, seeking only God's good pleasure in all things, for life in His will, and health, honour, happiness, spiritual progress, and all sanctity consist in the fulfilment of the will of God: and so every day I would that at every breath I could say, *Fiat in me, de me, et per me, et circa me, sanctissima et dulcissima voluntas Tua, in omnibus et per omnia, nunc et semper ac in æternum. Amen.* 'May Thy most holy and most sweet will be done in me, concerning me, and by me and around me, in all things and by all things, now and always and for ever. Amen.' God always pours His spirit of prayer into those who so submit their will to His; wherefore the Psalmist says, 'Be subject unto the Lord, and pray to Him,' for when any one with prompt obedience and entire resignation humbly submits himself to God, God Himself, Who does the will of those that fear Him, in a certain way is made subject to him, so that He does whatever He is asked, God becoming subject to the voice of a man—not of any man soever, but of the man who obeys God. A wonderful power of prayer and of obedience! Let us pray, dear Father, that we may be perfectly obedient, and let us obey, that we may be able to pray, and to speak worthily with God.

[1] Stonyhurst MSS., Father Grene's *Collectan. P.* vol. ii. p. 532.

GG

"It will wonderfully help both one and the other to meditate profoundly on these two things; to wit, Who God is in Himself and what He is towards us, and then what we are of ourselves and what towards God. For whilst I think of God, His Trinity and Unity, most beautiful, most wise, most holy, most full of love for me, immense and everywhere present, the fountain of all good things that are in me and beyond me, from Whom I myself depend, and all that is mine, and everything that I use and enjoy, how can I do otherwise than love Him with all my strength? How shall I not praise Him and thank Him constantly? How shall I not give my whole self to His service? And these affections become the more ardent as I ponder that I have nothing of myself, that I am nothing, and that I and all that is mine would be reduced to nothing unless I were preserved by Him. Now whilst, within this immensity of God, I consider what I have been and what I am towards Him, I am horrified and tremble as I ponder on my malice, my ingratitude, my slothfulness. Hence arise feelings of hatred of self, of humiliation and self-denial, and various acts and exercises of penançe, which not only nourish humility by which a man through a truthful knowledge of himself becomes vile to himself, but they also arouse a most ardent charity by which he loves his Supreme Benefactor, Who has conferred and still confers so many and such great benefits on one who is ungrateful and unworthy. Thus the mind is elevated to perfect contemplation and union with God Himself, and, as it were forgetful of itself, is immersed in Him, or rather God hides it in the concealment of His countenance from all disturbance of men.

"Here is a short epitome of my mystical theology, which I have put out at rather greater length in my book; but why should I teach these things to a doctor of others and my own master? Surely I have become foolish, but your letters compelled me. Would that you would help me by your prayers, that what I write in my letters I may perform in deed. Forgive my humble and poor style, for I know not any more elegant; but I am sure that you do not care for words, but for the sense that is in the words. I value very highly the cross which you have sent me, and I will always bear it with me. I hope, by the intercession of the Blessed Virgin, who appeared in that tree,[1] and who confers such benefits on those who are there and those who visit her, that I may be a partaker of those benefits, for though I am absent in the body I am present in spirit. I humbly commend myself to the holy sacrifices of your Reverence.

"Your Reverence's unworthy servant in Christ,

"+ LUDOVICUS DE PONTE. +

"Valladolid, March 23, 1621."

Postscript.—"By God's help I have finished a great work. Its title is *Expositio Moralis in Canticum Canticorum,* and it contains exhortations on all the mysteries and virtues of the Christian religion. It is divided into two volumes, and each volume into five books. The arrangement is new and singular, but not without foundation in the Sacred Text. The matter is grave in itself, and very copious, taken out of Holy Scripture and the holy Fathers. The style is humble, but clear and chaste, and not out of harmony with matter that is spiritual and sacred, and therefore elevated. It is printed at Paris, and will soon reach Germany and Belgium. Would that

---

[1] An allusion, no doubt, to one of the Belgian sanctuaries of our Blessed Lady, perhaps that at Montaigu. Or it may refer to the wood of the tree in which was found the image of our Lady of Foy, a village in the Province of Namur. Father Gerard sent from Rome an attestation dated July 16, 1633, to testify that he had had three images made of this wood, that he left one at Liége, took one to Ghent, which he gave to the English Benedictinesses there, and gave the third to Anne Countess of Arundel, who, it seems, gave it to the Novitiate at Watten. This paper is in the Archives de l'Etat at Brussels.

it may be to the glory of God, the edification of the Church, and of use to one's neighbour."

The other letter from the same Father was written in reply to one from Father Gerard announcing that he was about to leave Belgium.

" I.H.S.

" P.C.

" May the Almighty and most pitiful Lord accompany you in the journey that you are beginning, for with such a Guide and Companion you will be everywhere safe and cheerful, and making true progress. Let Him ever dwell in your memory, understanding, and will, for His most sweet providence especially protects those who make their journeys in obedience to Superiors, as Jacob did, who at his father's bidding journeyed through the desert of Mesopotamia, where he heard the voice of the Lord which said to him, 'I will be thy Keeper, whithersoever thou goest.' Trusting to this hope, and protected by this guardianship, you will happily fulfil what you are beginning.

" I commend myself to your Reverence's sacrifices and prayers, for my weakness oppresses me much ; but may the Will of God be done in me and about me in all things, to Whom concerning all things be glory for ever.   Amen.

" + Ludovicus de la Puente +

" Valladolid, Feb. 2, 1622."

With such saintly suggestions from his friend Father Gerard left Liége, and it is probable that he saw Father de la Puente soon after he received this letter, for he was sent to Spain first, and then to Rome, which place he reached on the 15th of January, 1623.[1]   His stay in

---

[1] Stonyhurst MSS., Father Grene's *Miscell. de Coll. Angl.* p. 19, quoting " Baines his diary."

Rome was not long, and we may assume that his explanations respecting the aid given by him to the English
Virgins was satisfactory to his Superiors for he was sent
back to Belgium. The charge now entrusted to him was
similar to that which he had fulfilled for the past eight
years. In accordance with the Institute of St. Ignatius,
the Society is accustomed to send its young priests, after
the conclusion of their studies and before taking their
last vows, to pass a year in retirement with the religious
exercises and duties of the Noviceship. This year is
called the Third Probation, the Tertianship, or the third
year. As this is the close of the long course of probation
to which the members of the Society are subjected, as
those who enter it are all priests, as they have been in
the Society at least ten years and often sixteen or seventeen, it will be understood that the choice of a Father for
the responsible position of Superior and Instructor of the
Fathers who pass through their Tertianship, is a mark of
the highest esteem and confidence. This is one of the
few offices in the Society to which none but a Professed
Father can be appointed ; and it is laid down in the
Constitutions that it is desirable that the Father chosen
should have been a Superior, as for instance a Provincial
whose term of office is concluded. From the appointment
of Father John Gerard to be Instructor of the Fathers in
their Third Probation in the English House at Ghent, we
may draw our own conclusion as to the position held
by him amongst the English Jesuits of his time. This
office he held for four years, that is to say from 1623 to
1627.

The house of the Society in Ghent in which the
English Fathers received their final preparation for the
labours and perils of the English Mission was the foundation of Father John Gerard's old benefactress Anne,
Countess of Arundel : yet her biographer says that her
good deed in making that foundation was so secretly

done that Father Gerard himself did not know who the foundress was for whom his prayers were said.

After describing the bountifulness to others of this admirable lady, the widow of the martyred Philip, Earl of Arundel, the author of her life[1] who was himself her chaplain and a Jesuit, thus records her bounty to the Society. "Besides her keeping ever some one of them in her house for the space of more than forty years, and the relieving in sundry occasions divers other particular persons of them, she gave every year a very large alms to their community here in England, and continued it to her dying day. And to the end they might not want that or a better means of support after her decease, she sent at several times 2,500*l.* beyond seas, there to be put in bank and increased till her death, and then the profit employed for their use and maintenance here. And, notwithstanding all that money came after [a] few years by casuality to be lost, yet was she not discouraged thereat, but afterwards buying a house in the city of Gant in Flanders, where those of them who had ended their studies might make their third probation and better prepare themselves to labour in God's vineyard according to their Institute, she furnished it with all things necessary for their use, maintained it during her life, and left competent means for the perpetual maintenance thereof, with order that whenever it shall please God to convert England again to the Catholic Faith, that house should be transported and placed in the city of Carlisle; to the end that not only those of that city and her tenants thereabouts but all the whole country adjoining might receive spiritual assistance by the preaching, teaching, and other pious labours and endeavours of those Religious persons whom she intended should be maintained therein."

The charity and devotion of Lady Arundel was imi-

---

[1] *The Lives of Philip Howard, Earl of Arundel, and of Anne Dacres, his wife,* pp. 218—220.

tated by her household, and her biographer says[1] that Mr. Robert Spiller, her steward for many years, "was noted to be very forward even both in relieving the poor, and farthering many deeds of charity, especially in helping the Society on all occasions. To the which he not only gave a yearly considerable alms, but both in his life and at his death was very liberal towards them, leaving a good part of his wealth for the increase and advancement of the means of that house which was erected by the Countess at Gant."

The good Countess derived an immense consolation from her foundation at Ghent, and that through the instrumentality of Father Gerard, when he was Rector there. Her son Thomas Howard, Earl of Arundel and Surrey, who had been carefully brought up by her in the Catholic religion, "partly through fear, partly through desire of favour with the King," by whom he had been restored to his father's honours, "accommodated himself to the times much more than he ought to have done, to the incredible grief of his good mother." The consequence of this was that his two sons were brought up Protestants. The reconciliation to the Church of the eldest of these her grandsons is the only fact with which we are acquainted connected with the four years of Father Gerard's stay in Ghent. It is thus related in the book[2] from which we have been quoting.

"James Lord Maltravers, the Earl's eldest son and heir, [was] a comely gentleman of rare wit and extraordinary expectation, who died at Gant in Flanders in July 1624, being about eighteen years of age. This young nobleman coming out of Italy together with the Countess his mother, and his brother Henry, who succeeded him in title and birthright, being now in France, ready to come for England where they had sent most of their retinue, upon I know not what motive, they directed their journey towards

[1] *Ibid.* p. 241.   [2] *Ibid.* p. 232.

Holland with intention to have kissed the hands of the
Lady Elizabeth, sister to his Majesty, and taking the city
of Gant in their way, there he sickened of the small pox
and died.   But before his death [he] was so fortunate as to
be visited by Father John Gerard, a priest of the Society,
who together with others lived there in the house which
his grandmother a little before had erected, though neither
he nor any of his company, nor perhaps any one of those
who then lived in that house knew it was set up and maintained by her, so secret was it kept.   By that Father he
was in fine reconciled to the Holy Church, having never
been a Catholic before, nor known to be so much as the
least affected that way ; because the man who by his
father's appointment taught and tutored him both in
England and Italy was not only an heretic but also a
minister.   At the hands of the said Father he received all
the holy Sacraments necessary for a due preparation to
death, which he received with so good a disposition that he
left no small hopes of his going to a better life.   When his
grandmother had notice of his conversion and death,
instead of lamenting the loss, as parents are wont to do in
such cases, she gave God many thanks, rejoicing that he
had made so good an end.   And when considering that if
he either came into England, or died in Holland or any
other city almost of Flanders, France and Italy, he either
could not at all, or not so conveniently, have had the like
means of dying well as he had at Gant, she not only
admired the providence of God therein, but took it as
a special favour from Him, and as a sign He was well
pleased with the work she then had there begun, and
thereby was not a little animated to the finishing thereof,
acknowledging moreover that thereby she was already
abundantly rewarded for all that she had done.   For had
it been put to her choice, what she would have asked
in this world in lieu of her reward, there was nothing
which she would have demanded sooner than the conver-

sion of some of her children, that being the thing which next after her own salvation she used most frequently to beg at the hand of Almighty God."

In a letter which the Countess wrote to her grandson Lord Maltravers before his conversion, and kept by her to be delivered to him after her death, she spoke of her foundation at Ghent. "She desired him if· he lived to see Catholic times in this kingdom, that he would favour and further the house she had set up at Gant (though not naming it) for the Society, and that he would leave the like order to his children and posterity, hoping that God would bless both him and them the more for it, and grant that she might have the more joy of them in heaven with an eternal happiness."

The letter to Henry Lee, Mary Ward's chaplain at Munich, quoted in the preceding chapter, was written by Father Gerard under the name of John Tomson in the year in which he left Ghent for Rome. It is dated "Gant, this 8th of March 1627," and it tells us that the Rector of the Tertian House at Ghent was Father Edward Bedingfeld *alias* Silisdon, the brother of his own successor as Rector and Master of Novices. "You will all have a good friend," he writes of Mary Ward's nuns and their chaplain, "in Mr. Doctor Atsloe. He is a great friend of Father Henry Silisdon, who is Rector at Watten and is my friend also, and writes to us both often. I think he knoweth Father Edward Silisdon,[1] Father Henry his brother, who is Superior of this house,[2] for he writes to me ever by the name of Rector of our house; whereas the Instructor of the Tertian Fathers is only Superior

---

[1] This Rectorship of Father Edward Silisdon was unknown to Dr. Oliver, who gives a list of the Rectors of Ghent from which this name is omitted.

[2] In 1625 Father John Norton *alias* Knatchbull was Rector, as we learn from a Provincial Catalogue of that date. A note attached to this Catalogue says that the Tertianship at Ghent had funds to maintain 15 in Community, though there were then but 7 in the house, none of whom were in their tertianship.

over them, but not of the rest of the family, as it is in a complete Noviceship, such as ours was at Liége." Of Mary Ward herself he writes, "I pray you tell your best friend and mine I do of purpose forbear to write to her, but much desire to see her here, which she may very well do, her brother [Father George Ward, S.J.] being here. But as for the Exercise for which she hath leave [that is, that Father Gerard might give her a retreat], I doubt it will not prove best. Pardon my scribbling, for my right hand with much writing shakes much."

From 1627 to 1637, the last ten years of his life, Father Gerard was confessor to the English College at Rome. As we have one fact to mark the period of his life at Ghent, so also we have one to commemorate this its last stage in Rome. He was the means of the conversion of Francis Slingsby,[1] who subsequently entered the Society and soon after his ordination to the priesthood died in the odour of sanctity at Naples on the 6th of December, 1642. After his death a collection of papers relating to him was made, which was in Rome in Father Grene's time, but has since the suppression of the Society found its way to the Burgundian Library[2] at Brussels. In this collection we find the correspondence of Father John Gerard with his Benjamin, the spiritual child of his old age, and these letters show that his activity and zeal continued to the last. It is very touching to read the mutual expressions of warm affection that passed between these two holy souls. Two long letters written by Father Gerard to Francis Slingsby are signed "Thomas Roberts,"

---

[1] He was the eldest son of Sir Francis Slingsby of Kilmore near Cork, and of Elizabeth Cuffe his wife. He was converted at Rome in September 1633, entered the College there as a Convictor February 6, 1639, was ordained priest June 30, 1641, entered the Society Sept. 30 in the same year, and died early in the second year of his noviceship. *Records*, vol. vi. p. 348. Father Gerard, however, was dead before Francis Slingsby came to the College.

[2] MSS. 3824-5, nn. 18, 19.

and are dated the 2nd of March and the 16th of May, 1637, the latter but two months before his death. The "shaking hand," as he himself calls it, is the only sign of weakness they show. He was then, it seems, writing a book on "friendship," and had sent another book to Flanders for publication.

A few extracts from these letters will fitly close our narrative. They were addressed to Francis Slingsby, under the name of Lewis Newman,[1] at Dublin, where for a time, a little later, Slingsby was sent as a prisoner to the Castle for his religion. The first of Father Gerard's two letters says, "I was much joyed at the good of your worthy mother and sister, [that is, at their having just become Catholics,] whom I will now more often and more earnestly commend to God *ut desideria, de ipsius inspiratione concepta, nulla possint tentatione mutari.* I have sent by Mr. Ford [probably Father James Ford, S.J.] (who this day parted from hence to you) small but holy tokens to those your ·two kinswomen, whom now I must respect and love, as if they were to me in like degree as they are to you. To your mother a tooth of St. Gaudentia, Virgin and Martyr, and we will use so to write of her by that name, which she hath now cause to take and to be *vere gaudens,* being now *filia·Dei et hæres regni cælestis,* and going daily forward to take possession of it. May she therefore not say with the kingly prophet *Lætata sum?* To your sister I have sent a relic of St. Xaverius, for I doubt not but she will be ever devout unto him, and he ready to protect and help her, she being born to God upon his day. I have sent also a poor token to yourself and one to Mr. Nugent [Father Robert Nugent, S.J.]. We all do pray for you, and your poorest friend will not fail to do it in that manner and measure as if all his friends were united in one. I beseech you, tell your two kinswomen that I will offer for

---

[1] His *alias* at the English College at Rome was Percy. *Records,* vol. vi. p. 348.

them at these holy places, that being the best service I can do them. All happiness rest with you."

The other letter, dated May 16, 1637, was written to induce Francis Slingsby not to be deterred by temporal considerations from going at once to the Novitiate. "Yours of the 10th of February found me in the Spiritual Exercise, in which I had received from the goodness of God more comfort than I deserved. But indeed the reading of yours was a great increase unto them, to see the efficacy of His grace, and His bounteous hand so opened to a person so dear unto me, and to whom I much desired no less than the best. I received much comfort to see your so constant perseverance in perfect indifference, and your entire resignation to the Will of God, to be declared unto you by His substitute. And the like contentment it gave to Scævola [Mutius Vitelleschi, the General] himself, when he read the same twice repeated in your letter, which I delivered unto him translated, that he might judge the better of the case you proposed. . . . Scævola is and will be much better pleased with my friend alone, and with the internal riches which he will bring with him, and which cannot be taken from him, and which will be much greater by this act of renunciation, than if, with less measure of interior goods, he brought with him a much greater proportion of exterior riches. Therefore it is his absolute desire (*omnibus auditis et mature consideratis*) that his Joseph do break away from the world, though he leave his cloak behind him. God hath clothes enow for His servants, and He that giveth feathers to the birds of the air and furs to the beasts that live within the earth, will not be wanting to those His chosen servants whom He loveth so dearly and who labour for Him."

We thus know that Father John Gerard's last Retreat was made three or four months before his death, and in the "Spiritual Exercise" that was so familiar to him he received, as he tells his dearest friend, "from the goodness of

God more comfort than he deserved." He died at Rome in the English College on the 27th of July, 1637, at the ripe age of seventy-three.

The last ten years of Father Gerard's life were thus spent as the spiritual father of aspirants to the English Mission, preparing them for its toils and dangers. His manly, earnest, faithful soul was the very stuff of which martyrs are made, and we may well conceive how the presence of the grand old man must have stirred the hearts of those "flores Martyrum," the students of the English College at Rome. When Father Gerard came amongst them in 1627, twenty-nine who had been trained for the priesthood within those walls, had already given their lives for that priesthood on the gibbet and had bled on the scaffold in their native land. The lesson that George Gilbert's pictures round their chapel walls taught the students who were preparing themselves in Rome for the priesthood that in England it was high treason for them to have received, that same lesson they learned from the old man in their midst who had had personal experience of the torture-chamber, and of whom they could say, as good Father Christopher Grene afterwards said of him, *Non ipse martyrio, sed ipsi martyrium defuit.*

INDEX.

HH